Management Accounting (3)

Custom Edition for University of West of Scotland

Compiled by Dr Abeer Hassan

ISBN 13: 9781307021905

McGraw-Hill Custom Publishing

http://create.mheducation.com/uk/

Published by McGraw-Hill Education, 2 Penn Plaza, New York, NY 10121.

ISBN: 9781307021905

Management Accounting (3)

CUSTOM EDITION

Contents

Managerial Accounting, Third Edition; Whitecotton, Libby, Phillips; 2017

1. Introduction to Managerial Accounting 2
2. Decentralized Performance Evaluation 42
3. Measuring and Evaluating Financial Performance 86

Management Accounting, Fifth Edition; Seal, Rohde, Garrison, Noreen; 2014

4. Performance measurement and reporting on segments 122
5. Business process management: towards the lean operation 169

Contemporary Management, Tenth Edition; Jones, George ;2018

6. Ethics and Social Responsibility 212
7. Managing in the Global Environment 246

Credits

1. Introduction to Managerial Accounting: *Chapter 1 from Managerial Accounting, Third Edition by Whitecotton, Libby, Phillips, 2017* 2

2. Decentralized Performance Evaluation: *Chapter 10 from Managerial Accounting, Third Edition by Whitecotton, Libby, Phillips, 2017* 42

3. Measuring and Evaluating Financial Performance: *Chapter 13 from Managerial Accounting, Third Edition by Whitecotton, Libby, Phillips, 2017* 86

4. Performance measurement and reporting on segments: *Chapter 14 from Management Accounting Fifth Edition by Seal, Rohde, Garrison, Noreen, 2014* 122

5. Business process management: towards the lean operation: *Chapter 18 from Management Accounting Fifth Edition by Seal, Rohde, Garrison, Noreen, 2014* 169

6. Ethics and Social Responsibility: *Chapter 4 from Contemporary Management, Tenth Edition by Jones, George, 2018* 212

7. Managing in the Global Environment: *Chapter 6 from Contemporary Management, Tenth Edition by Jones, George, 2018* 246

Managerial Accounting, Third Edition; Whitecotton, Libby, Phillips; 2017

CHAPTER 1

Introduction to Managerial Accounting

At the beginning of each chapter, you'll see a list of learning objectives that identify the key topics you need to master. You can also use the list as an outline for taking notes as you read through the chapter.

YOUR LEARNING OBJECTIVES

LO 1-1 Describe the key differences between financial accounting and managerial accounting.

LO 1-2 Describe how managerial accounting is used in different types of organizations to support the key functions of management.

LO 1-3 Describe the role of ethics in managerial decision making, the Sarbanes-Oxley Act, and sustainability accounting.

LO 1-4 Define and give examples of different types of cost:

Out-of-pocket or opportunity costs
Direct or indirect costs
Variable or fixed costs
Manufacturing or nonmanufacturing costs
Product or period costs
Relevant or irrelevant costs

© Frazer Harrison/Getty Images for Los Angeles Magazine

FOCUS COMPANY: California Pizza Kitchen

www.cpk.com

From Legendary Pizza to a Global Brand

As you start what is probably your second accounting course, you may be wondering why you need to take yet another accounting class. Wasn't one course enough? Which of the following best describes your motivation for learning about managerial accounting?

Top 10 Reasons to Take a Managerial Accounting Course

10. Accounting is truly interesting and exciting.
9. I always wanted to be an accountant when I grow up.
8. My advisor said I had to take it.
7. Accountants get good-paying jobs, even in the worst economy.
6. The accountant is always the hero in action movies.
5. I want to get rich and stay that way.
4. The rich guy always gets the girl in romance movies.
3. I want to start my own business and need to create a business plan.
2. Accounting will fulfill my foreign language requirement. (It's Greek to me.)
1. I'm enrolled in an accounting course???

Whatever your reason for taking this course, it will come in handy at some point in your future. This is true regardless of your intended career path, whether it is to start your own business, work for a large corporation, go into politics, work in health care, become a fashion designer, teach high school, work on a farm, or start a charitable foundation. Accounting is the language of business, and understanding it will help you make better business and personal decisions.

Throughout this book, you will see how managerial accounting is used by managers in real-world companies. Most of these companies sell a product or service that you encounter everyday, like a cup of Starbucks coffee, your iPhone, or the pizza you may have for lunch. Let's begin with a company that put a new spin on pizza with innovative flavors like BBQ chicken and Thai peanut sauce.

California Pizza Kitchen (CPK) was started in 1985 when two disillusioned attorneys, Larry Flax and Rick Rosenfield, decided to ditch their legal pads and open a restaurant in Beverly Hills, California. Their hearth-baked pizzas were an instant hit with an LA crowd seeking delicious and innovative food served in a casual but upscale setting. Since then, CPK has broadened its menu selection and expanded to more than 200 cities and 15 countries around the world. Today, you can enjoy one of CPK's delicious menu items in over 250 full-service restaurants; at CPK/ASAP "quick serve" stations in airports, universities, and sports arenas; or by purchasing a CPK pizza from the freezer of your local supermarket to bake at home.

As you read this chapter, try putting yourself in the shoes of one of the following managers:

- General manager responsible for the day-to-day operations of a CPK restaurant, including staffing, customer service, cost management, and compliance with Food and Drug Administration (FDA) regulations.
- Kitchen manager responsible for preparing delicious food while controlling the cost of ingredients and training the kitchen staff.
- Purchasing manager responsible for buying the freshest ingredients at the lowest possible price, from both local and national suppliers.
- Regional manager responsible for the overall success of 25 CPK restaurants throughout the Pacific Northwest. Your annual performance evaluation is based on sales growth, profitability, and customer satisfaction.
- Senior executive responsible for expanding the CPK brand into new domestic and global markets.

Think about the types of decisions you would have to make in your chosen role and, most of all, the information you would need to make those decisions. Chances are that much of that information would come from the company's managerial accounting system.

ORGANIZATION OF THE CHAPTER

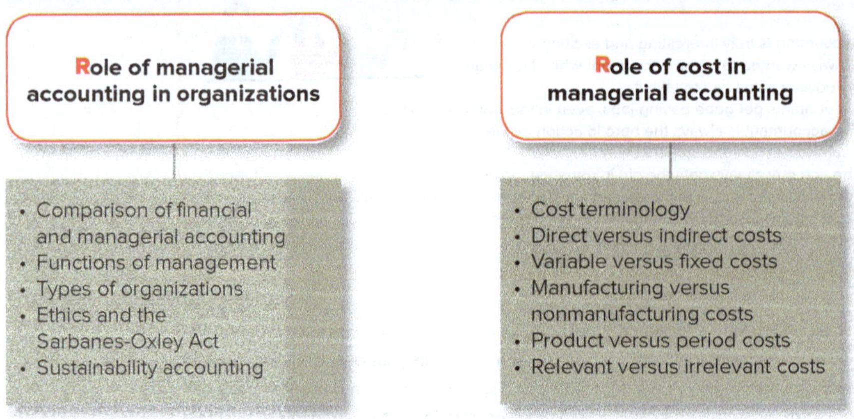

At the start of each chapter, you'll find an organizational graphic that provides a visual framework to show how the chapter concepts fit together.

Role of Managerial Accounting in Organizations

The primary goal of any accounting system is to capture, summarize, and report useful information to users so that they can make informed decisions. The key difference between financial accounting and managerial accounting is the intended user of the information. **Financial accounting** information is aimed at **external users**, or those outside the organization such as investors, creditors, and regulators. **Managerial accounting** information is aimed at **internal users**, or those working inside the organization, such as business owners, managers, and employees.

> **Learning Objective 1-1**
> Describe the key differences between financial accounting and managerial accounting.

COMPARISON OF FINANCIAL AND MANAGERIAL ACCOUNTING

Because the intended users of the information are different, there are several other differences between financial and managerial accounting. Accountants prepare external financial statements according to generally accepted accounting principles (GAAP), which provide external users certain advantages in terms of their comparability and objectivity. However, internal managers often need more detailed information than those financial reports can capture. Managers need information that is timely and relevant to the specific decision at hand. Rather than knowing what happened last year or last quarter, managers need to know what is happening today and be able to predict what will happen tomorrow. See Exhibit 1.1 for a summary of the key differences between financial accounting and managerial accounting.

> **COACH'S TIP**
> Financial accounting is sometimes referred to as **external** reporting while managerial accounting is referred to as **internal** reporting. The difference is whether the intended users are inside or outside the company.

Throughout this text, we will provide you with tips to highlight explanations of selected topics. Please read them carefully.

EXHIBIT 1.1 Differences between Financial and Managerial Accounting

	Financial Accounting	Managerial Accounting

User perspective	Used by external parties, such as investors, creditors, and regulators	Used by internal parties, such as managers and employees
Types of reports	Classified financial statements prepared according to GAAP	Various internal reports, such as budgets, performance evaluations, and cost reports
Nature of information	Objective, reliable, historical	Subjective, relevant, future oriented
Frequency of reporting	Prepared periodically (monthly, quarterly, annually)	Prepared as needed, perhaps day-to-day or even in real time
Level of detail	Information reported for the company as a whole	Information reported at the decision-making level (by product, region, customer, or other business segment)

To illustrate these differences, let's return to California Pizza Kitchen (CPK). Until 2011, CPK was a publicly traded company whose stock was listed on the NASDAQ stock exchange. The Securities and Exchange Commission (SEC) requires all publicly traded companies to file quarterly and annual reports that include an income statement, balance sheet, statement of cash flows, and disclosures about the accounting methods used to prepare the financial statements. These reports are publicly available to anyone with an interest in the company, including government regulators, financial analysts, and investors who are considering buying or selling stock in the company. The year-end financial statements of publicly traded companies must be audited by an independent accounting firm, such as Ernst and Young or KPMG, to determine whether the reports were prepared according to GAAP.

In 2011, CPK was acquired for $470 million by Golden Gate Capital, a private-equity firm that owns other well-known restaurant chains, such as On the Border. Because it is now privately owned, CPK is no longer required to report its financial results to the SEC and the public at large. The last time that CPK released financial results to the public was in April of 2011, shortly before being bought by Golden Gate Capital. Although the external financial statements provide a glimpse into the company's financial performance, they are probably not that relevant to most of CPK's managers and employees who are more concerned about the day to day operations of the business than the corporate financial statements. The results reported in the external financial statements are generally most relevant to the C-suite executives (CEO, CFO, etc.) who are directly responsible for the financial performance of the company and who must answer to the firm's shareholders and board of directors.

The managerial accounting system, in contrast, provides the more detailed information that managers "behind the scenes" need to do their jobs. This internally-oriented information is not publicly available and is generally considered to be proprietary in nature. Even so, we can gain some insight into the internal accounting system by considering statements made by managers in the press releases that often accompany the external financial statements. For example, in their final press release before the buyout, co-CEOs Rick Rosenfield and Larry Flax stated that they would improve future shareholder value by focusing on "menu-optimization," "cost management at both the restaurant and corporate level," "shifting the sales mix to higher margin items," "expanding international locations," and "new product introductions that are in line with health and wellness trends."[1] The managerial accounting systems needs to capture and report information to the managers who are responsible for achieving these more specific objectives.

To better understand how managerial accounting is used, we must consider the various functions that managers perform and what types of information they need to do their jobs.

FUNCTIONS OF MANAGEMENT

Learning Objective 1-2
Describe how managerial accounting is used in different types of organizations to support the key functions of management.

Regardless of the type and size of the organization they manage, all managers perform the same basic functions: Planning, Implementing, and Controlling. These functions are part of a continuous or ongoing cycle, called the Plan-Implement-Control cycle, as illustrated in Exhibit 1.2. Throughout this cycle, managers must make a variety of decisions, and the managerial accounting system must provide information to help them make those decisions.

- **Planning** is the future-oriented part of the management cycle. The first step in planning is to establish goals or objectives, along with the tactics that will be used to achieve those goals. Managers have to make a variety of "who, what, when, where, and how" decisions as they plan. For example: Who is my target customer? What product or service do they need and how much will they pay for it? Where and when will I provide the product and service? What resources will I need? Once managers know the answers to these questions, the next step is to create a **budget** that lays out the plan in monetary or financial terms. The budget helps managers organize their plan and ensure that they have the necessary resources to carry it out.
- **Implementing** means putting the plan into action. During the implementation phase, managers must lead, direct, and motivate others to achieve the objectives set in the

[1]Press Release May 5, 2011: "California Pizza Kitchen Announces Financial Results for the First Quarter of 2011.

EXHIBIT 1.2 Plan-Implement-Control Cycle

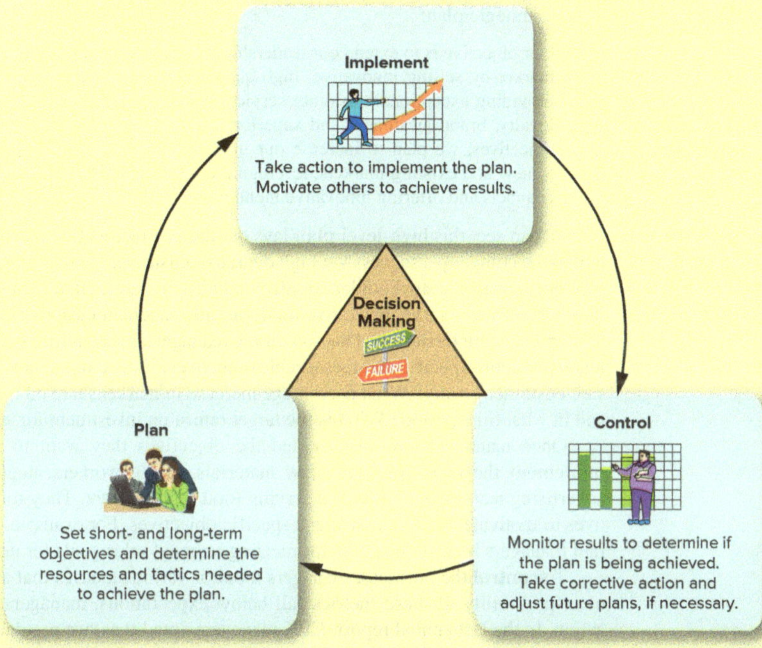

planning stage. The decisions made during the implementation phase are sometimes called operational decisions. For example: Who should I purchase supplies from? When do I need them? How many employees should I hire? How much should I pay them? How do I train them? Again, the managerial accounting system should provide useful information to help managers answer these and other questions.

- **Controlling** is the final step in the management process. During the control phase, managers keep track of how they are doing and whether any actions must be taken to adjust the plan. The managerial accounting system plays a key role in helping managers measure and monitor the company's performance to see whether the planned objectives are being met. If not, managers may need to take corrective action to get back on track.

An easy way to think about the Plan-Implement-Control cycle is in terms of an air traffic control system. Before the flight, the pilot must file a flight **plan** that details when and where the plane will be flying. **Implementing** includes all of the actions the pilot takes to fly the plane. The pilot may fly the plane himself, or delegate it to a copilot. The **control** system includes the cockpit instruments the pilot uses to guide the plane, as well as the monitoring systems used by air traffic control. The goal of these control mechanisms is to make sure the plane does not deviate too far from the flight plan. When that happens, the system should provide a signal that the pilot needs to take corrective action.

To extend this analogy to the business world, managers are like pilots flying a plane and the managerial accounting system is the set of tools that help the pilot get the plane to its destination. The tools can be as simple as a report on a piece of paper, or as sophisticated as an information system that provides real-time data to managers on their handheld devices. These tools must provide timely, relevant, and accurate information to help managers do their jobs.

At California Pizza Kitchen, everyone from the kitchen manager to the CEO needs information to plan, implement, and control within their area of responsibility. Because the kitchen manager will be making very different decisions than the CEO, the managerial accounting system must provide information for both day-to-day operational decisions and long-term strategic decisions.

In its last publicly released annual report, CPK provided the following statement of its overall strategic plan:

> Our objective is to extend our leadership position in the restaurant and premium pizza market by selling innovative, high-quality pizzas . . . and related products and by providing exceptional customer service, thereby building a high degree of customer loyalty, brand awareness and superior returns for our stockholders. To reach these objectives, we plan to increase our market share by expanding our restaurant base in new and existing markets, leveraging our partnerships in nontraditional and retail channels and offering innovative menu items.[2]

As you can see, this high-level **plan** lays out the key factors that managers believe are important to the company's success—a high degree of customer loyalty, increased market share, and superior returns for stockholders. It also includes the tactics that managers will use to achieve these objectives—serve innovative food, provide excellent customer service, and expand into new and existing territories. One role of the managerial accounting system is to translate these goals into more specific and measurable objectives. For example, how will the company measure customer loyalty? What percentage increase in market share do managers want to achieve and in what time period? What is the target return on investment for shareholders?

Once managers have determined the objectives they want to achieve, they begin to **implement** the plan by buying raw materials, hiring workers, negotiating with suppliers, advertising new menu items, and serving food to customers. They might also provide incentives to motivate workers to achieve specific objectives. For example, they might give restaurant managers bonuses or perks for meeting targeted sales goals for new menu items.

To **control** the business, managers monitor various metrics that are relevant to their area of responsibility. If these metrics fall below expectations, managers should take corrective action. In the last annual report, CPK managers noted that "we regularly review the sales mix of our menu items and replace lower selling items in each category with new menu items once or twice per year. Because of our ability to quickly adapt our menu, we believe that we are able to meet our customers' changing tastes and expectations."[3]

As you can see, the managerial functions of planning, implementing, and controlling are interconnected. One function leads to another, and managers use feedback from the process to improve future decision making. Throughout, managers must make a variety of decisions and they need relevant, up-to-date information, including cost estimates, competitor pricing, market demand, and consumer preferences. Much of this information comes from the managerial accounting system.

Before we move on, try the next Self-Study Practice to make sure you understand the major differences between financial and managerial accounting and the key functions of management.

Selling Goods and Services to Customers

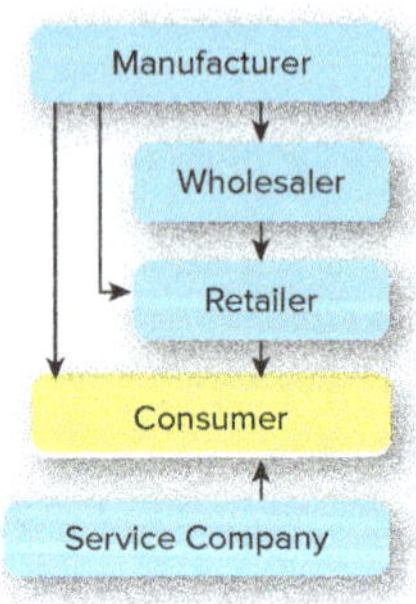

TYPES OF ORGANIZATIONS

Managerial accounting information is used by managers in all types of organizations: large and small, public and private, profit and nonprofit. Traditionally, businesses are classified into one of three categories:

- **Manufacturing firms** purchase raw materials from suppliers and convert them into finished products, such as Apple iPods, Harley Davidson motorcycles, Levi Strauss jeans, and Ford cars and trucks.
- **Merchandising companies** sell the goods that manufacturers produce. Merchandisers that sell exclusively to other businesses are called **wholesalers**. Merchandisers that sell to the general public are called **retailers**. For example, Sam's Club started out

[2]California Pizza Kitchen, Inc., Annual Report for the fiscal year ended January 2, 2011, Form 10-K, United States Securities and Exchange Commission, filed March 17, 2011.

[3]Ibid.

How's it going? Self-Study Practice

1. Which of the following statements best describes the difference between financial accounting and managerial accounting?
   a. Managerial accounting targets external stakeholders while financial accounting targets individuals within the company.
   b. Financial accounting relies more on subjective, future-oriented information than managerial accounting does.
   c. A major focus of managerial accounting is the preparation of the income statement, while a major focus of financial accounting is the preparation of the budget.
   d. Managerial accounting tends to focus on relevant, subjective, and future-oriented information while financial accounting relies primarily on objective, reliable, and historical information.
2. Which of the following statement(s) regarding the key management functions is (are) false? (You may select more than one answer.)
   a. Planning involves setting long-term objectives and the short-term tactics necessary to achieve those objectives.
   b. Implementing involves comparing actual results to planned objectives and making adjustments as necessary.
   c. Controlling includes all of the operational decisions made to implement the plan.
   d. All of the above.

After you have finished, check your answers against the solutions in the margin.

The best way to know whether you are reading the chapter carefully enough is to see how well you do on a short exercise. Therefore, at important points throughout each chapter, you will find an exercise that will reinforce the concepts you have just learned and provide feedback on how well you learned them. We urge you not to skip these practices. When you are finished, check your answers against the solution in the margin.

Solution to Self-Study Practice
1. d
2. b and c are both false.

as a wholesaler and then expanded into the retail market. Other well-known retailers include Walmart, Macy's, Bed Bath & Beyond, and Safeway.

- **Service companies** provide a service to customers or clients. A few well-known service providers are Hilton Hotels, Southwest Airlines, Expedia.com, and Federal Express. Many small businesses provide services to consumers and other businesses, including hair salons, law firms, architects, and home repair specialists.

COACH'S TIP

Do you think CPK is a manufacturing firm, a merchandising firm, or a service firm? Compare your answer to the discussion below.

Increasingly, the lines between manufacturing, merchandising, and service companies are becoming less clear. Many businesses, including California Pizza Kitchen, do not fall neatly into a single category. Some would consider CPK to be a service firm because it serves food to customers. Others would consider it a manufacturing company because it purchases raw materials (ingredients) and converts them into a finished product (a meal). And what about the frozen CPK pizzas that you can buy in your local supermarket? Those products are manufactured by Nestle, which pays CPK a royalty fee (percentage of sales revenue) to use its recipes and brand.

The bottom line is that CPK is not a pure manufacturing or service company. Unlike a traditional manufacturing company, a restaurant does not have a large inventory of work in process or finished goods available for sale. But unlike a traditional service industry that provides **intangible** services, a restaurant produces a tangible product (that you can see, feel, and taste) and sells it directly to the end consumer.

Still, the distinction between these types of businesses is important because, as we will see in later chapters, the focus of managerial accounting is somewhat different in manufacturing firms than in merchandising and service firms. In the past, managerial accountants focused much of their efforts on preparing reports to keep track of the costs of raw materials, labor, and other costs incurred to produce a physical product. Today, nonmanufacturing firms make up an increasingly large proportion of the marketplace. In 2011, the U.S. government estimated that 76 percent of the nation's gross domestic product (GDP) came from nonmanufacturing (service and merchandising) activities.[4] The chart below shows the trend in employment in goods-producing and service-providing industries over the past 40 years. As you can see, the number of employees working in service sector jobs has increased dramatically over the past 40 years, while the number of employees working in manufacturing jobs has remained relatively constant. Today, about 85% of the people employed in America work in nonmanufacturing fields such as health care, education, and retail, and the trend toward service industries is expected to continue.

Growth in Services and Merchandising Jobs

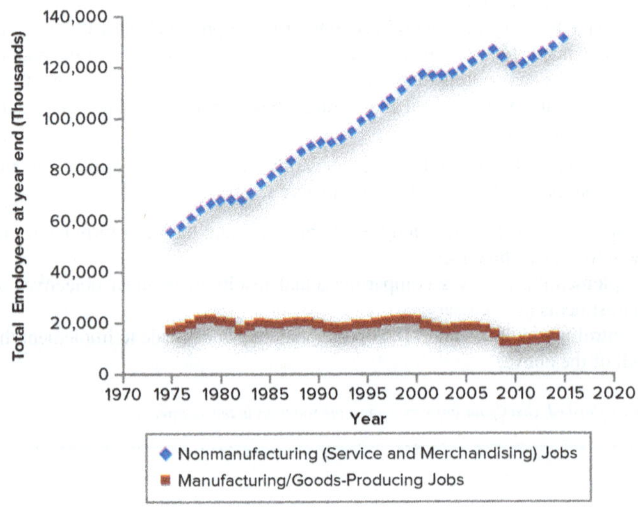

Data from U.S. Department of Labor, Bureau of Labor Statistics, Employment Database. http://www.bls.gov/data/#employment, accessed April 21, 2015.

> **COACH'S TIP**
>
> When you graduate, you are about four times more likely to go to work in a service or merchandising setting than a manufacturing company. Even so, you need to have a basic understanding of how managerial accounting works in manufacturing firms because you will most likely still work with manufacturing firms, perhaps as a buyer or other business partner. To make the manufacturing process more tangible, we will use examples of products that you encounter every day, so that you can more easily visualize how the products are made.

The first few chapters of this textbook illustrate how to use managerial accounting to determine the cost of a physical product such as a pizza, a custom home, or an automobile. Later chapters illustrate how managers in nonmanufacturing firms such as Starbucks Coffee, IKEA, and Cold Stone Creamery use managerial accounting for decision making, planning, controlling, and performance evaluation.

Finally, it is important to note that managerial accounting information is vital to nonprofit organizations, including hospitals, universities, and charitable organizations. Although these organizations do not exist strictly to earn profit for shareholders, their managers still need timely and relevant information to prepare budgets, manage resources, and make strategic and operational decisions.

ETHICS AND THE SARBANES-OXLEY ACT

> **Learning Objective 1-3**
> Describe the role of ethics in managerial decision making, the Sarbanes-Oxley Act, and sustainability accounting.

All managers, regardless of the type of organization they work for, are responsible for creating and maintaining an ethical work environment, including the reporting of accounting information. **Ethics** refers to the standards of conduct for judging right from wrong, honest from dishonest, and fair from unfair. Although some accounting and business problems have clear right or wrong answers, many situations require accountants and managers to weigh the pros and cons of alternatives before making final decisions.

Often, there is no one right answer to ethical dilemmas and hard choices will need to be made. Do not tolerate acts of fraud, such as employees making up false expenses for reimbursement, punching in a time card belonging to a fellow employee who will be late for work,

[4] CIA, *The World Factbook*, https://www.cia.gov/library/publications/the-world-factbook/fields/2012.html.

or copying someone's ideas and claiming them as your own. Also be aware that not all ethical dilemmas are clear-cut. Some situations will require you to weigh one moral principle (e.g., honesty) against another (e.g., loyalty). When faced with an ethical dilemma, you should follow a three-step process:

1. Identify who will be affected by the situation—both those who will appear to benefit (often the manager or employee) and those who will be harmed (other employees, the company's reputation, owners, creditors, and the public in general).
2. Identify and evaluate the alternative courses of action.
3. Choose the alternative that is the most ethical—and that you would be proud to have reported in the news.

Unfortunately, not everyone abides by these general guidelines. For example, the reputation of business managers and accountants was tarnished in the late 1990s and early 2000s due to high-profile scandals at companies like at Enron and WorldCom. In response to these scandals, Congress enacted the **Sarbanes-Oxley (SOX) Act of 2002**. Although SOX was primarily aimed at renewing investor confidence in the external financial reporting system, it has many implications for managers as well.

The Sarbanes-Oxley Act focuses on three factors that affect the accounting reporting environment: opportunity, incentives, and character.

Opportunities for Error and Fraud

SOX attempts to reduce the **opportunity** for error and fraud. A requirement under SOX is that management must conduct a review of the company's internal control system and issue a report that indicates whether the controls are effective at preventing errors and fraud. This requirement places more responsibility on all managers (not just accountants) for the accuracy of the reporting system. For example, marketing managers are now responsible for making sure their staff members submit accurate sales and expense reports. SOX also places additional responsibilities on the boards of directors and external auditors to reduce the opportunity for errors and fraud.

Incentives for Committing Fraud

SOX attempts to counteract the **incentive** to commit fraud by providing much stiffer penalties in terms of monetary fines and jail time. For example, violators must repay any money obtained via fraud and can be assessed additional fines of up to $5 million. Executives cannot avoid these penalties by declaring personal bankruptcy, which explains why a former sales director at Computer Associates will be giving 15 percent of every paycheck he earns for the rest of his life to a fraud restitution fund. SOX also increased the maximum jail sentence for fraudulent reporting to 20 years. Total jail time can add up to even more than that because federal sentencing guidelines allow judges to declare consecutive jail terms for each violation.

Most chapters include Spotlight features focusing on decision making, ethics, and sustainability. These features are designed to illustrate the relevance of accounting in real-world decision making.

SPOTLIGHT ON Ethics

Accounting Scandals

Typically, fear of personal failure and greed drives accounting scandals. Initially, some people may appear to benefit from fraudulent reporting. In the long run, however, fraud harms most individuals and organizations. When it is uncovered, the corporation's stock price drops dramatically. In the case involving MicroStrategy, the stock price dropped 65 percent from $243 to $86 per share in a single day of trading. Creditors are also harmed by fraud. WorldCom's creditors recovered only 42 percent of what they were owed. They lost $36 billion. Innocent employees also are harmed by fraud. At Enron, 5,600 employees lost their jobs, and many lost all of their retirement savings. The auditing firm Arthur Andersen, which once employed 28,000 people, went out of business after becoming entangled in the WorldCom and Enron frauds.

Character of Managers and Employees

Finally, SOX emphasizes the importance of the **character** of managers and employees. Admittedly, it is difficult for a law to make people act appropriately, but SOX introduces new rules that should help employees of good character make the right decision when confronted with ethical dilemmas. For example, audit committees are now required to create tip lines that allow employees to secretly submit concerns they may have about suspicious accounting or auditing practices. SOX also gives federal employees whistle-blower protection to prevent retaliation by those charged with fraud.

Finally, to reinforce good character, public companies must adopt a code of ethics for senior financial officers. Unfortunately, simply adopting a code of ethics does not ensure that managers will act ethically. Most experts agree that ethics must be embedded in the organizational culture and that top managers who lead by example will drive ethical behavior in the organization.

According to a recent Statement on Management Accounting (SMA) released by the Institute of Management Accountants (IMA), companies with strong ethical cultures are rewarded with higher productivity, improved team dynamics, lower risks of fraud, streamlined processes, improved product quality, and higher customer satisfaction. But to achieve these rewards, companies must move beyond simply complying with laws such as SOX and create a culture that embeds ethics throughout the organization.

Before we move on, take a moment to complete the following Self-Study Practice to make sure you can identify factors that influence ethical behavior.

How's it going? Self-Study Practice

Identify whether each of the following actions is most likely to increase (+) or decrease (−) the risk of error or fraud arising from opportunities (O), incentives (I), or an individual's character (C).

	+/−	I/O/C
1. Enron implemented a "rank-and-yank" practice that involved ranking the financial performance of each business unit and then firing managers in the lowest 20 percent.	_____	_____
2. Microsoft Corporation invites anonymous or confidential submission of questionable accounting or auditing matters to msft.buscond@alertline.com.	_____	_____
3. The H. J. Heinz Company's board of directors is one of the strongest boards in the United States, according to Institutional Shareholder Services.	_____	_____

After you have finished, check your answers against the solutions in the margin.

Solution to Self-Study Practice

1. +/I (increased pressure to report stronger financial results)
2. −/C (less likelihood that unethical behavior will go unreported)
3. −/O (strong oversight by directors)

SUSTAINABILITY ACCOUNTING

Managerial accounting has traditionally focused on providing managers with the information they need to make decisions that create economic value or profit for shareholders. In today's changing world, managers are responsible for more than achieving financial results, and are accountable to many groups other than shareholders. Modern managers must balance the priorities and needs of many stakeholders, including employees, customers, suppliers, regulators, and society. **Sustainability accounting** is an emerging area of accounting that is aimed at providing managers with a broader set of information to meet the needs of multiple stakeholders, with the goal of ensuring the company's long-term survival in an uncertain and resource-constrained world.

The simplest definition of sustainability is the ability to last or survive for a long time. When applied to business, **sustainability** is the ability to meet the needs of today without sacrificing the ability of future generations to meet their own needs. To accomplish this goal, we must consider three factors: society, economy, and the environment. These three pillars of sustainability are called the **triple bottom line** and are often represented by **3 Ps: People, Profit, and Planet.**

Accountants can play a key role in helping organizations become more sustainable by measuring and managing triple bottom line performance. While traditional accounting systems focused almost exclusively on economic results (e.g., profit), sustainability accounting expands the focus to measure the impact of business decisions on social issues (people) and the environment (planet). Just as accountants have always measured and managed a firm's economic performance, today's accountants often measure and manage a firm's social impact and environmental performance as well.

The following diagram provides a historical perspective on the relative importance of the three factors that make up the triple bottom line.

COACH'S TIP

Although some people equate sustainability with being environmentally friendly or "green," it is a much broader concept than that. A truly sustainable business strategy is one that simultaneously achieves economic results while creating benefits for society (e.g., reduce poverty, respect human rights, prevent disease) and the environment (e.g., limit climate change, reduce greenhouse gas emissions).

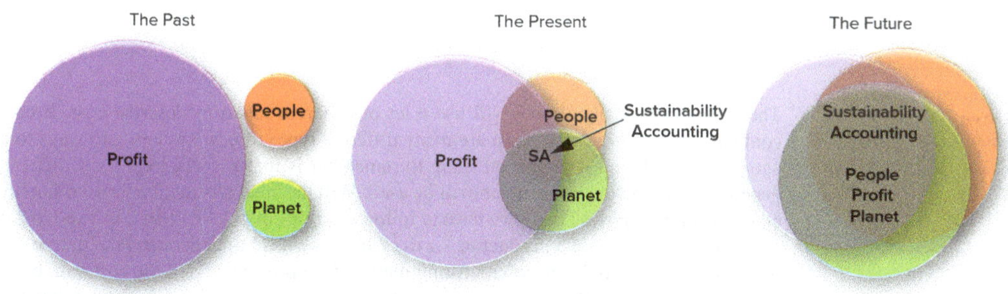

In the past, accounting focused primarily on profitability measures such as net income (revenue – expenses), return on equity, and other measures of economic success. Social and environmental factors were not usually at the forefront of managers' decision making, and in many cases financial results were achieved at the expense of society (people) and the environment (planet).

Today, managers are beginning to recognize that a business strategy focused solely on achieving economic or financial results is not sustainable. In the long-run, a business cannot survive without people (e.g., customers, employees, and suppliers) and natural resources (e.g., water, clean air, and fuel). As a result, modern organizations are building sustainable business practices into their business strategies and including sustainability accounting methods such as the triple bottom line into their performance management systems. For example, most public companies now issue **corporate social responsibility (CSR)** reports that provide sustainability-related information, including measures of social and environmental impact.

While sustainability accounting is an emerging and critically important area in accounting, the reality is that most of today's businesses and managers are still driven *primarily* by economic results. For sustainability initiatives to really take shape and change the way a company does business, it must be linked to the company's overall corporate strategy and embedded in the day to day operations and culture of the company. As that happens, sustainability can become a more integrated part of the business model, and sustainability accounting measures such as the triple bottom line are likely to emerge as a more mainstream part of the reporting process.

Throughout this textbook, we will highlight some of the sustainability initiatives and reporting issues faced by managers in real-world companies and relate these initiatives to other topics in managerial accounting.

Role of Cost in Managerial Accounting

As described earlier in this chapter, the goal of managerial accounting is to provide managers with the information they need to plan, implement, and control within their area of responsibility. Much of the information that managers need to make decisions is based on cost data. For example, a restaurant manager at CPK might need to know how much it costs to prepare a new menu item to decide how much to charge for it. A kitchen manager might need to know the cost of a specific pizza component such as dough or sauce to decide whether to make it in-house or buy it from a supplier. Managers also need cost information to prepare daily, weekly, and monthly operating budgets. These budgets help managers ensure that they have the necessary resources to run the business and to control spending.

Cost information is important for accountants too. They use it to value inventory and determine the profitability of various products, regions, divisions, or other segments of the business. Although accountants and managers should consider things other than cost when making decisions, cost control remains a critical concern for most organizations, particularly in a tough economy or when profit margins are declining due to increased competition. In the next section, we describe alternative ways to categorize costs based on different criteria.

COST TERMINOLOGY

Learning Objective 1-4
Define and give examples of different types of cost.

Throughout this textbook, we will use a lot of different labels to describe cost. It can be confusing at times because there are many different types of cost systems and ways to categorize cost. The most important thing to remember is that we will treat costs differently depending on how the information will be used. Will the cost information be used for financial reporting purposes? If so, we have to follow the rules of GAAP. Will it be used to determine the profitability of a product or service? If so, we need to understand the nature of the product or service to decide what costing method is appropriate. Will the cost data be used for decision making? If so, we need to consider how costs will behave or change depending on what decision alternatives the manager is considering. Will it be used to evaluate the performance of a manager? If so, we need to think about what costs are under the manager's direct control.

In this chapter, we introduce the terminology you will use to categorize or sort cost into different "buckets," including

COACH'S TIP

The key thing to remember is that **different costs terms are used for different purposes.** Thus, a single cost can be classified in more than one way, depending on how the information will be used.

- Direct or Indirect
- Variable or Fixed
- Manufacturing or Nonmanufacturing
- Product or Period
- Relevant or Irrelevant

Each of these classifications will be based on different criteria depending on how the information will be used. In later chapters, you will learn more about how to use this cost information for different managerial purposes, including product costing, cost management, decision making, planning and control, and performance evaluation. For now, you just need to recognize and define the terms.

To make these classifications more concrete, we will use California Pizza Kitchen's actual operating costs as an example. Exhibit 1.3 shows the breakdown of CPK's total operating costs as reported in their last publicly-issued financial report. As you can see, CPK's operating costs are made up of wages and salaries (37%); food, beverages, and supplies (23%); occupancy costs such as rent, utilities, and property taxes (22%); general and administrative expenses (8%); and other miscellaneous expenses (10%). The "other" category includes the costs to open a new restaurant, such as rent during the construction period, hiring and training the initial workforce, buying the food used in training, and marketing costs.

EXHIBIT 1.3 CPK Operating Costs

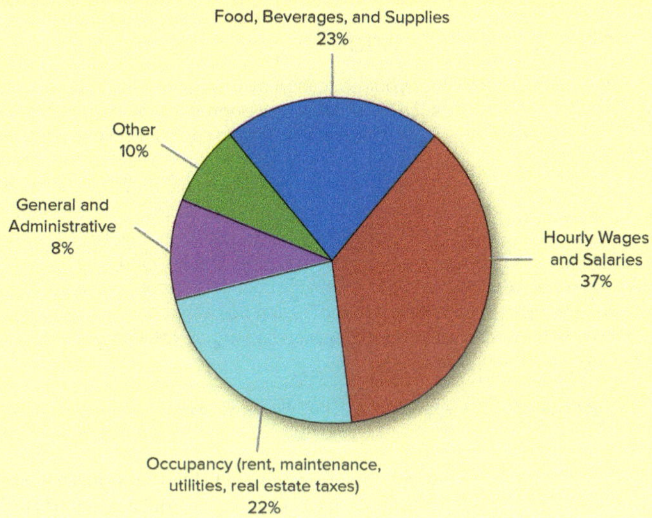

All of the operating costs shown in Exhibit 1.3 are out-of-pocket costs, or costs that CPK pays outright, including food and beverages, labor, and occupancy costs. **Out-of-pocket costs** involve an actual cash payment. In your personal life, these are costs you pay "out of your pocket" for things such as food, clothing, and entertainment.

Unlike an out-of-pocket cost that involves an outlay of cash, an **opportunity cost** is the cost of **not** doing something. In other words, it is the forgone benefit (or lost opportunity) of the path not taken. Anytime you choose to do one thing instead of another because of limited time or money, you incur an opportunity cost. For example, if you are going to school full-time, you are giving up the opportunity to earn money by working full-time. The potential earnings you could be making if you were not in school is an opportunity cost of pursuing your education.

Opportunity costs occur in business any time resources are constrained and managers must choose to do one thing at the expense of another. For example, a manager at CPK might be asked to close the restaurant to host a private event such as a corporate holiday party. By doing so, the company loses the opportunity to sell food and drinks to other customers. The managerial accounting system can help managers identify the opportunity cost based on the amount of profit that would normally be generated on a given night. If that opportunity cost is too high, managers might decide that they will only host private events on certain days or times of the week when business is slow.

DIRECT VERSUS INDIRECT COSTS

When managers use cost information, they typically want to know the cost of something specific. It could be a menu item (e.g., a 16-inch BBQ pizza), a particular ingredient (e.g., pizza dough), an activity (e.g., serving a customer), or a specific part of the business (e.g., a restaurant). We call these specific things *cost objects*. A **cost object** is any item we want to know the cost of. In your own personal life, you might want to know the cost of attending school for a semester, the cost to buy and operate a car, or the cost of a vacation you would like to take over Spring break. Each of these items would be considered a cost object.

SPOTLIGHT ON **Decision Making**

Should You Continue Your Education?

You have obviously made the decision to further your education by taking this class. At some point in the future, you may even think of pursuing an advanced degree, such as an MBA, law degree, or medical degree.

The decision to pursue a degree is a very important one that should consider both the costs and benefits. As you know, the costs of education, including tuition, fees, and books, are very high. You also incur opportunity costs when you forgo working to go to school. These costs must be offset by the future career opportunities (and higher salary) the degree will bring.

If you ever consider getting an MBA, Forbes has an online decision tool that can help you weigh the costs and benefits of the advanced degree.* This tool estimates the five-year gain from an MBA as the difference between the salary and bonuses you would expect to earn in the five years after graduation minus the tuition and potential earnings you would give up while getting your MBA. Because these costs and benefits occur across a number of years, the online tool factors in the time value of money, or the opportunity cost of giving up cash today to earn cash at some point in the future.

This same approach can be applied to almost any decision so long as you can estimate the future costs and benefits of the particular decision you are trying to make.

* http://www.forbes.com/2005/08/16/cz_05mba_business_schools_gain_calulator.html

COACH'S TIP

Whether a cost is direct or indirect depends on whether it is both **possible** and **reasonable** to trace the cost to a cost object. Some minor costs, such as salt, pepper, and olive oil, may not be worth the effort needed to trace them to individual menu items. Costs that *could* be traced but are not worth the effort to trace are also classified as **indirect costs**.

As an example, assume you want to know how much it is costing you to take this accounting course. In that case, the course (managerial accounting) is the cost object. How would you go about determining the cost of this course? You would probably start with the costs that are easily attributed to a specific course, such as the cost of tuition and books. Costs that **can be directly and reasonably traced** to the cost object are called **direct costs**. But there are other costs associated with your education that aren't directly related to one course. Examples include the cost of driving to and from campus, the cost of your computer, and the cost of the supplies you use in class. Even if you could keep track of the cost of gas you need to get to campus, or the cost of the pencils and paper you use in class, it probably isn't worth the effort to do so. Costs that **cannot be traced** to the cost object, or that are **not worth the effort** of tracing, are called **indirect costs**. When classifying a cost as direct or indirect, the question to ask is whether the cost can be directly and conveniently traced to the cost object. If the answer is yes, it is a direct cost. If it is no, it is an indirect cost.

At California Pizza Kitchen, costs can also be classified as direct or indirect. Recall that 23 percent of CPK's operating cost is for food, beverages, and supplies. Can all of these costs be traced to a specific cost object, such as a new menu item that managers are trying to price? The cost of ingredients used to make the menu item would generally be classified as a direct cost, so long as it is worth the effort to trace the cost. However, it may not be worth the effort to try to figure out the exact cost of every ingredient that goes into the menu item. If CPK doesn't see value in tracing these costs to the cost object, they would be classified as indirect costs instead.

Labor costs, which make up 37 percent of CPK's annual operating costs, can also be categorized as either direct or indirect depending on whether they can be directly and conveniently traced to a specific cost object. If the cost object is a menu item or customer, direct labor would include the cost of any employees who are involved in preparing meals or serving customers, such as line cooks, bartenders, waiters, and waitresses. Indirect labor would include the kitchen manager and general restaurant manager because these individuals are generally responsible for supervising other employees rather than preparing and serving meals directly to customers.

What about the 22 percent that CPK spends on occupancy costs such as rent, maintenance, utilities, and property taxes? If we are trying to determine the cost of serving a specific customer (the cost object), costs such as rent and supervision would be considered indirect costs. However, if the manager is trying to determine the cost of operating a specific restaurant (the cost object), occupancy costs such as rent and utilities would be direct costs. CPK calls these costs "direct operating and occupancy costs" because they are associated with a specific restaurant. Costs incurred outside of the restaurant, such as general and administrative expenses and national advertising, would be considered indirect. Remember, whether a cost is considered direct or indirect depends on the cost object we are trying to trace it to. See Exhibit 1.4 for examples of direct and indirect costs in other industries.

EXHIBIT 1.4 Real-World Examples of Direct versus Indirect Costs

	Direct Costs	Cost Object	Indirect Costs
Supercuts Hair Salon	Stylist's time →	 Individual haircut and style	← Styling products, receptionist's service, depreciation on salon equipment
The Gap	Cost of the merchandise, commissions paid to salesperson →	 Pair of blue jeans	← Store supervision, rent, and inventory control
Dell	Cost of the components, wages of workers who assembled the computer, and delivery costs →	 Personal computer	← Production supervision, factory space, and quality control

Top: © Ken Cavanagh/McGraw-Hill Education; Middle: © Stockbyte/SuperStock; Bottom: © Creatas Images/Jupiter Images

VARIABLE VERSUS FIXED COSTS

For internal decision making, managers often want to know how costs will change if something else changes, such as the number of units produced or the number of customers served. **Variable costs** are those that change, in total, in direct proportion to changes in activity levels. In describing its major operating costs, CPK's annual report states that "food, beverage, and paper supplies are variable and increase with sales volume."[5] In other words, as CPK prepares more meals and serves more customers, the total cost of food, beverages, and supplies will also increase.

As you can see from the following graph, although **total** variable costs vary with the number of customers served, the **per-unit** or **average** cost of food, beverages, and supplies will remain the same, regardless of the number of customers served. For example, if the number of customers served doubles, CPK will need to purchase more ingredients, such as pizza dough. But the amount of dough used to make each pizza doesn't change. (Note: for simplicity, this scenario ignores other factors that drive down unit variable costs, such as discounts for buying ingredients in bulk.)

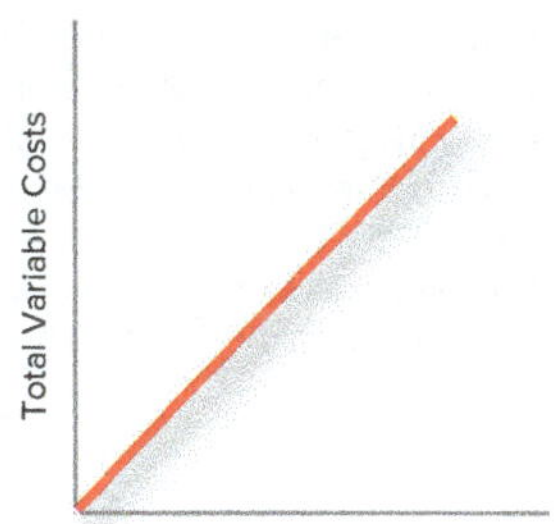

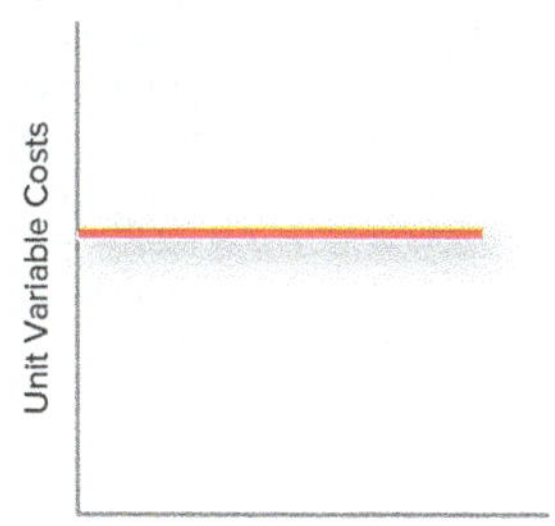

COACH'S TIP

In deciding whether a cost is variable or fixed, be sure to think about whether the **total cost** will change. Looking at average or unit cost will reveal an entirely different pattern, which we examine more closely in Chapter 5.

---

[5] California Pizza Kitchen, Inc., Annual Report for the fiscal year ended January 2, 2011, Form 10-K, United States Securities and Exchange Commission, filed March 17, 2011.

Fixed costs are those that stay the same, in total, regardless of activity level. Examples of fixed costs for CPK include rent, manager salaries, depreciation, and property taxes. When we say that a cost is fixed, that doesn't mean it will never change; it simply means that the total cost won't change simply because we produce more units or serve more customers.

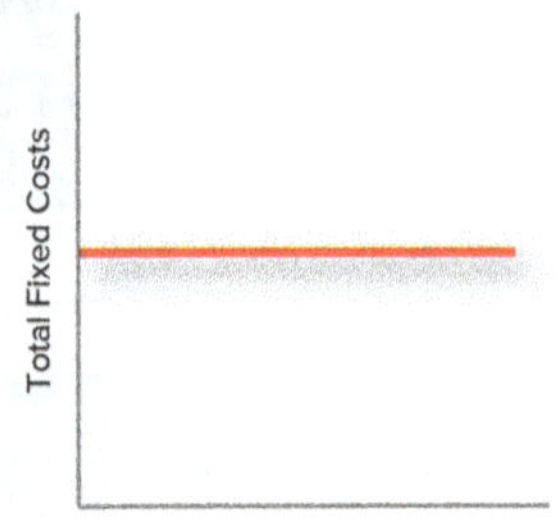

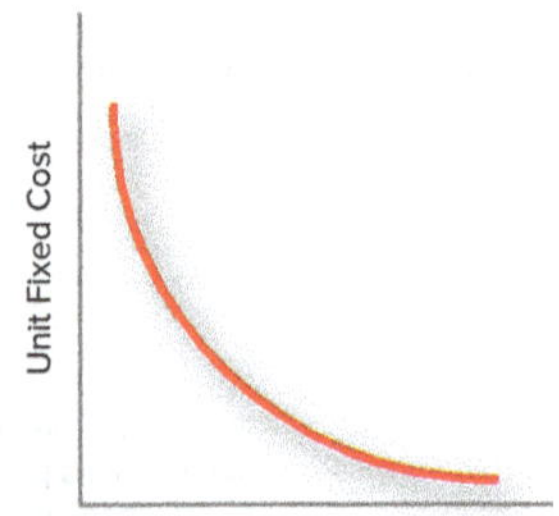

Although **total** fixed costs are constant, **average** or **per-unit** fixed costs vary inversely with the number of units produced or the number of customers served. That is because spreading a constant amount over more units or customers drives down the average cost. For example, if the number of customers served doubles, total rent cost remains the same, but the average cost of rent **per customer** will decrease because we divide the total rent cost by a larger number of customers.

In most real-world businesses, costs do not behave in the perfectly predictable patterns described. For example, CPK's annual report states that "direct operating and occupancy costs generally increase with sales volume, but decline as a percentage of restaurant sales."[6] This tells us that direct operating and occupancy costs are not strictly variable or strictly fixed. Some costs, such as server wages and utilities, will increase with higher levels of sales, while other costs, such as management salaries and property taxes, will be incurred regardless of sales. These so-called *mixed costs* are discussed in more detail in Chapter 5.

SPOTLIGHT ON Decision Making

Predicting Fixed and Variable Costs

Assume you are the treasurer of a student club at your university and you are on the planning committee for the end-of-year social event. The committee is in charge of finding a location; renting tables and chairs; and hiring a DJ, photographer, and caterer for the event. Your responsibility as treasurer is to set the budget for the event and make sure the committee stays within that budget.

Which costs would you expect to vary with the number of people attending? Which costs will be the same regardless of how many people attend the event? Why is it important for you to know the answers to these questions? When planning a social event, the cost of the venue, DJ, and photographer will be incurred regardless of how many people attend the event. The cost of catering (food and drinks), tables, and chairs will vary with the number of people who are expected to attend. You need to understand these relationships to prepare a budget for the event because the total cost will depend on the number of guests.

Managers must answer similar questions when making business decisions. They need to understand which costs will vary with the number of units produced or the number of customers served and which will be incurred regardless of these factors.

[6]California Pizza Kitchen, Inc., Annual Report for the fiscal year ended January 2, 2011, Form 10-K, United States Securities and Exchange Commission, filed March 17, 2011.

MANUFACTURING VERSUS NONMANUFACTURING COSTS

For financial reporting purposes, costs must also be classified based on whether they relate to manufacturing or nonmanufacturing activities. This distinction applies only to companies that make a physical product, such as Dell (computers), Honda (cars and trucks), Harley Davidson (motorcycles), and Maytag (appliances). It does not apply to merchandisers or service companies that do not make a physical product.

Because CPK is not a traditional manufacturing company, let's consider the costs incurred by Nestle to manufacture, distribute, and sell frozen pizzas under the CPK brand. To differentiate between manufacturing and nonmanufacturing costs, we need to consider whether the cost specifically relates to manufacturing or **making** the frozen pizzas, as opposed to marketing, delivering, and selling them.

Manufacturing costs represent all of the costs associated with producing or manufacturing a physical product. They are generally classified into one of three categories:

- **Direct materials** include the major material inputs that can be directly and conveniently traced to each unit of product (the cost object). For a frozen pizza manufacturer, direct materials include the major ingredients (e.g., dough, sauce, cheese, and meat), as well as packaging materials (e.g., plastic and cardboard). Miscellaneous ingredients and materials (e.g., seasonings and glue for the cardboard box) that are not worth tracing to each individual product would be considered indirect materials and included in manufacturing overhead.
- **Direct labor** refers to the "hands on" labor that can be directly and conveniently traced to the product, such as the wages of employees on the pizza production line and in the packaging department. It does not include employees who rarely touch the product as it is being produced, such as supervisors, maintenance workers, and factory engineers. The costs associated with those employees are considered indirect labor and counted as part of manufacturing overhead.
- **Manufacturing overhead** includes all manufacturing costs **other than direct materials and direct labor** incurred to produce a physical product. It includes all of the costs associated with *making* the product that cannot be traced to a specific unit, such as indirect materials, indirect labor, factory rent, factory insurance, and factory utilities. Manufacturing overhead does *not* include costs related to things that happen outside of the factory walls (e.g., marketing, distribution, or sales), only those indirect costs that are related to manufacturing the product.

Taken together, direct materials and direct labor are referred to as **prime costs**. For manual production processes, the direct materials and direct labor often represent the *primary* costs incurred to make a product. As manufacturing has become more automated and labor has shifted from direct labor (i.e., line-worker wages) to indirect labor (i.e., supervisor salaries), manufacturing overhead has become a much more significant percentage of total manufacturing cost.

Prime Cost =
Direct Materials
+
Direct Labor

Direct labor and manufacturing overhead are referred to collectively as **conversion costs**. These are the costs needed to *convert* direct materials into a finished product. For Nestle, conversion costs include all costs incurred to convert raw ingredients into a finished product (pizza).

Conversion Cost =
Direct Labor
+
Manufacturing Overhead

Notice that direct labor is included in both prime costs (direct materials + direct labor) and in conversion costs (direct labor + manufacturing overhead). As such, you cannot add prime costs to conversion costs to determine the total manufacturing cost, because direct labor is included in both components. The sum of the three manufacturing costs (direct materials + direct labor + manufacturing overhead) gives us the total manufacturing cost. Alternatively, you could add prime cost to conversion costs and then subtract the direct labor to prevent it from being counted twice.

Nonmanufacturing costs are the costs associated with running the business and selling the product as opposed to manufacturing the product. They are generally classified into one of two groups:

- **Marketing or selling expenses** are incurred to get the final product to the customer. For Nestle, they would include advertising, sales commissions, and the cost of distributing the frozen pizzas to grocery stores.

- **General and administrative expenses** are associated with running the overall business. They include general management salaries, rent, and utilities for corporate headquarters, and corporate service functions such as the accounting, payroll, and legal departments. Nestle would also place the salaries of those who manage the company's relationship with CPK under this category.

PRODUCT VERSUS PERIOD COSTS

COACH'S TIP

The distinction between period and product costs is a matter of **when** the cost is matched against revenue on the income statement. Period costs are expensed as soon as they are incurred. Product costs are recorded initially as inventory and do not appear on the income statement until the product is sold.

The difference between product costs and period costs determines **how and when** the cost will be matched up against revenue on the income statement. This distinction really has more to do with financial accounting (external reporting) than managerial accounting. However, it is important for manufacturing firms that hold significant amounts of inventory because it determines whether a cost is counted as inventory (an asset on the balance sheet) or as an expense on the income statement. Classifying a cost as product or period can affect the reported profitability of the company's products, customers, and divisions.

For external reporting purposes, GAAP requires that all manufacturing costs be treated as **product costs**, or costs that are assigned to the product as it is being manufactured. Product costs are also called **inventoriable costs** because they are counted as inventory (an asset) until the product is sold. Remember that manufacturing costs include direct materials (e.g., major ingredients and packaging materials), direct labor (e.g., wages of employees who make the pizzas), and manufacturing overhead (e.g., supervisor salaries, miscellaneous ingredients, factory rent, and utilities, etc.). These costs must follow the flow of the product as it is being produced and are initially recorded in one of the following inventory accounts, depending on where the product is in the production process: Raw Materials Inventory, Work in Process Inventory, or Finished Goods Inventory. Once the product is finally sold, product costs are reported as Cost of Goods Sold and matched up against sales revenue on the income statement.

Nonmanufacturing costs are called **period costs** or period expenses because they are expensed during the period incurred. Unlike product costs that flow through several inventory accounts before being reported as Cost of Goods Sold, nonmanufacturing costs are expensed as soon as they are incurred. Examples of nonmanufacturing or period expenses include advertising, sales commissions, distribution expenses, and general and administrative salaries. Refer to Exhibit 1.5 for an illustration of the different treatment of product and period costs under GAAP.

Later chapters demonstrate how to account for the flow of manufacturing costs through the various inventory accounts before being reported as Cost of Goods Sold. For now, you simply need to recognize that manufacturing costs (product costs) will be treated differently than nonmanufacturing costs (period costs) for financial reporting purposes.

RELEVANT VERSUS IRRELEVANT COSTS

For managerial accounting information to be useful for decision making, it must be **relevant** to the specific decision that managers are trying to make. In today's information age, managers have access to a tremendous amount of data, much of which is irrelevant to the decision at hand. In addition, managers sometimes fail to incorporate relevant information into their decisions because it is not easily captured by the accounting system. Determining what information is relevant to managerial decisions is one of the most important skills that you will learn in this course. A **relevant cost** has the potential to influence a decision; an **irrelevant cost** will not influence a decision. For a cost to be relevant, it must occur **in the future** and **differ** between the various alternatives the manager is considering. Costs that differ between decision alternatives are sometimes called incremental or **differential costs**. For example,

EXHIBIT 1.5 Product and Period Cost Flows

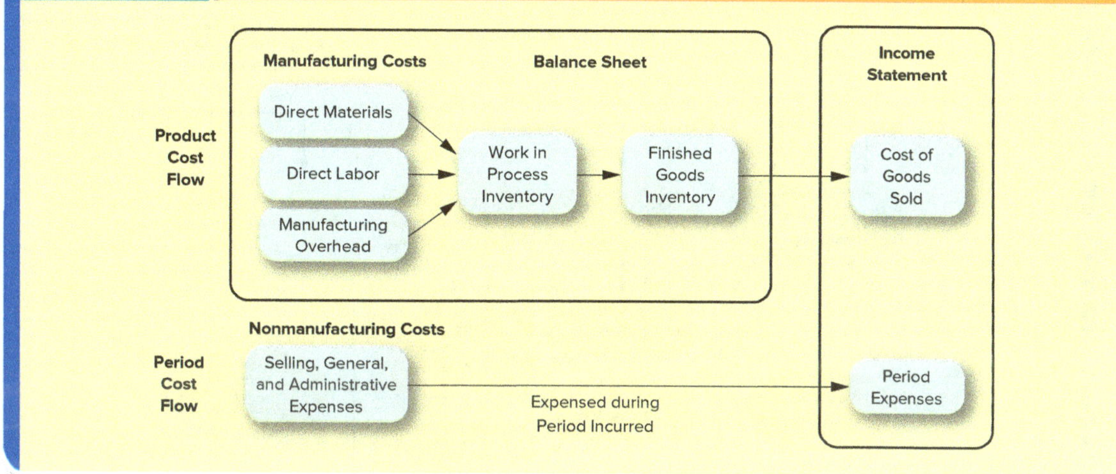

a manager at CPK might be trying to decide whether to make or buy pizza dough, lease or purchase restaurant equipment, or keep or drop an unprofitable menu item. Different costs are relevant and irrelevant for each of these scenarios. For example, the cost of wheat or flour used to make pizza dough is relevant to the decision about whether to make or buy the dough, but is not relevant to the decision about whether to lease or purchase equipment. In addition, if a cost has already been incurred, the amount spent in the past is not relevant to what a manager decides to do in the future. So, if CPK has already purchased enough dough to last the rest of the month, the amount of money spent on the dough is irrelevant to the decision about whether to continue to buy pizza dough or to begin making it. The money has already been spent. Costs that have already been incurred are called **sunk costs**. Although **sunk costs are irrelevant** for decision making, it is often very difficult for managers to ignore what happened in the past and focus only on the future.

Assume, for example, that you are thinking of selling your old car and buying a new one. Is the amount you paid for your old car a relevant cost? The answer is no; it is a sunk cost that will not change regardless of what you do in the future. However, the amount of money you can get for your old car now (its current value) and the cost of the new car are relevant to your decision. Any difference in fuel costs and insurance for the old car versus the new one is also relevant. What about the parking fee you pay each semester? Is that a relevant cost? The answer is no because you will have to pay for parking no matter which car you drive.

Now assume that you are thinking of getting rid of your car altogether and either riding a bike or relying on public transportation. Is the cost of on-campus parking relevant to that decision? In this case, the cost is relevant because it will change depending on whether or not you own a car. In later chapters, we rely heavily on this concept of relevant versus irrelevant costs to analyze a variety of managerial decisions.

Exhibit 1.6 provides a summary of the various ways to categorize or classify costs. Each classification requires you to ask a different question to determine how the information will be used in managerial accounting. We will reference this terminology throughout the book as we consider how managers use cost and other managerial accounting information to make decisions for their organization.

EXHIBIT 1.6 Cost Classification System: Different Costs for Different Purposes

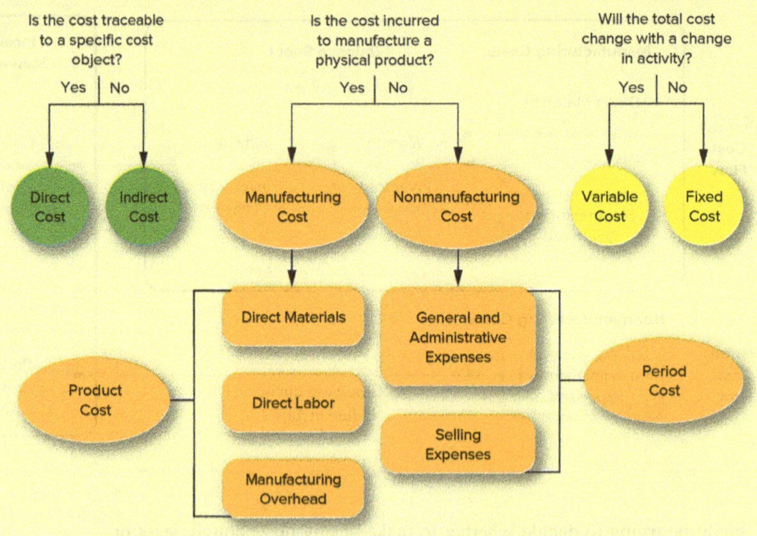

Before continuing, complete the following Self-Study Practice to see how well you understand the cost terminology.

How's it going? Self-Study Practice

Match the appropriate description on the right to the terms on the left.

_____ 1. Product costs
_____ 2. Period costs
_____ 3. Manufacturing costs
_____ 4. Nonmanufacturing costs
_____ 5. Variable costs
_____ 6. Fixed costs
_____ 7. Direct costs
_____ 8. Indirect costs
_____ 9. Out-of-pocket costs
_____ 10. Opportunity cost
_____ 11. Sunk costs

A. Costs that remain the same in total regardless of activity level.
B. Costs that involve an outlay of cash for items such as rent, utilities, and salaries.
C. The benefit that you forgo when you select one alternative over another.
D. Costs that can be directly and conveniently traced to a specific cost object.
E. Costs that have already been incurred and thus are not relevant to future decisions.
F. Costs that are expensed in the period they are incurred.
G. Costs that are incurred while making a physical product, such as direct materials, direct labor, and manufacturing overhead.
H. Costs that cannot be directly or conveniently traced to a specific cost object.
I. Costs that change in total in direct proportion to a change in activity level.
J. Costs that are attached to the product as it is produced and included in inventory until the product is sold.
K. Costs that are not related to producing a product, such as selling and administrative costs.

After you have finished, check your answers against the solutions in the margin.

Solution to Self-Study Practice
1. J 7. D
2. F 8. H
3. G 9. B
4. K 10. C
5. I 11. E
6. A

SUPPLEMENT 1A CAREERS THAT DEPEND ON ACCOUNTING KNOWLEDGE

Accounting knowledge can make the difference in your ability to land a dream job, whether you hope to work in production and operations management, human resources, finance, or marketing, or another field. Exhibit 1S.1 displays nonaccounting jobs that could be available to you at the world's leading companies and explains how accounting knowledge can be vital to these positions.

EXHIBIT 1S.1 Accounting Knowledge Can Benefit All Majors

Production and Operations Management

Production Manager, Nintendo: Figure out how to make a $250 3DS for $100.71.

Outsourcing Specialist, Apple: Coordinate more than 20 suppliers of parts for the next iPad, at the same total cost as legacy iPads.

Human Resources

Compensation Analyst, Google: Develop affordable, attractive global pay programs.

Labor Relations Manager, NBA Players' Union: Assist in salary renegotiations involving the $58 million salary cap and 57% revenue sharing guarantee.

Accounting

Finance

Investment Analyst, Goldman Sachs: Assess value of investing $50 million in Facebook.

Financial Analyst, Target Corporation: Help credit card segment reduce the number of days awaiting collections from customers.

Marketing

Brand Manager, H. J. Heinz Company: Set prices to achieve 5% annual sales growth.

Customer Business Developer, Procter & Gamble: Collaborate with accounting to enhance customer profits and cash flows.

Sources: http://techland.time.com/2011/03/29/the-incredibly-cheap-100-nintendo-3ds; http://blogs.forbes.com/johnray/2011/03/11/isuppli-teardown-of-the-ipad-2-investor-edition/; http://www.isuppli.com/Teardowns/News/Pages/iPad-2-Carries-Bill-of-Materials-of-$326-60-IHS-iSuppli-Teardown-Analysis-Shows.aspx; http://www.nytimes.com/2011/05/25/sports/basketball/players-accuse-nba-of-failing-to-bargain-in-good-faith.html?_r=1&ref=nationallaborrelationsboard.

Photo: © Rubberball/Getty Images

REVIEW THE CHAPTER

DEMONSTRATION CASE

Barnaby's Bicycle Company manufactures high-quality mountain bikes. The company's managerial accountant has come to you for help. She needs to classify and identify each of the following costs before she can calculate the cost to produce each mountain bike.

Classify each of the costs listed in the chart on the following page into three categories based on the following questions:

1. Can this cost be directly and conveniently traced to each bicycle that is manufactured, or is doing so either not possible or not worth the effort?
2. Is this cost related to manufacturing the bicycles? If so, what type of cost is it? Or is it a nonmanufacturing or period expense?
3. Will the total cost vary with the number of bicycles manufactured and sold, or will it remain the same regardless of how many bikes are produced and sold?

The first item in the chart is completed as an example.

	QUESTION 1		QUESTION 2				QUESTION 3	
			PRODUCT COSTS			PERIOD COSTS	COST BEHAVIOR	
	Direct Cost	Indirect Cost	Direct Materials	Direct Labor	Mfg. Overhead	Nonmfg. Expenses	Variable Cost	Fixed Cost
Alloy tubing used to make the bicycle frames	X		X				X	
Hourly wages paid to employees who cut and weld the alloy tubing								
Factory rent								
Bicycle wheels and tires								
Miscellaneous bicycle components								
Insurance on the factory								
Insurance on the president's company car								

Suggested Solution

	QUESTION 1		QUESTION 2				QUESTION 3	
			PRODUCT COSTS			PERIOD COSTS	COST BEHAVIOR	
	Direct Cost	Indirect Cost	Direct Materials	Direct Labor	Mfg. Overhead	Nonmfg. Expenses	Variable Cost	Fixed Cost
Alloy tubing used to make the bicycle frames	X		X				X	
Hourly wages paid to employees who cut and weld the alloy tubing	X			X			X	
Factory rent		X			X			X
Bicycle wheels and tires	X		X				X	
Miscellaneous bicycle components		X			X		X	
Insurance on the factory		X			X			X
Insurance on the president's company car		X				X		X

CHAPTER SUMMARY

LO 1-1 Describe the key differences between financial accounting and managerial accounting. p. 5

- Financial accounting information is used by external stakeholders, such as investors, creditors, and bankers.
- Managerial accounting information is used by managers inside the organization.

- Other differences:
  - Financial accounting information tends to be reliable, objective, and historical in nature.
  - Managerial accounting information tends to be relevant, timely, and future oriented.
  - Financial accounting is reported through the income statement, balance sheet, and cash flow statement.
  - Managerial accounting relies on a variety of reports targeted at specific decisions, including budgets, cost reports, and performance evaluations.
  - Financial accounting reports are prepared on a monthly, quarterly, or annual basis.
  - Managerial accounting reports are prepared as needed.
  - Financial accounting reports are prepared at the company level.
  - Managerial accounting reports are prepared at the divisional or departmental level appropriate to the decision being made.

Describe how managerial accounting is used in different types of organizations to support the key functions of management. p. 6 **LO 1-2**

- Managerial accounting is used in all types of organizations, including manufacturing, merchandising, and service firms.
- Although managerial accounting often focuses on manufacturing firms, it is becoming increasingly important for service companies and merchandisers, which are gaining importance in today's economy. It is also useful for nonprofit organizations such as universities, charities, and hospitals.
- Regardless of the type of organization, all managers perform the same basic functions:
  - Planning, or setting long-term objectives along with the short-term tactics needed to achieve them.
  - Implementing, or putting the plan into action.
  - Controlling, or monitoring actual results against the plan and making any necessary adjustments.

Describe the role of ethics in managerial decision making, the Sarbanes-Oxley Act, and sustainability accounting. p. 10 **LO 1-3**

- Ethics refers to the standards for judging right from wrong, honest from dishonest, and fair from unfair. Managers confront ethical dilemmas that do not have clear-cut answers. They must apply their own personal judgment and values to weigh the pros and cons of alternative courses of action.
- The Sarbanes-Oxley (SOX) Act of 2002 increases managers' responsibility for creating and maintaining an ethical business and reporting environment. It attempts to reduce fraudulent reporting in three key ways:
  - **Opportunity**. SOX requires managers to issue a report that indicates whether the company's internal controls are effective in preventing fraud and inaccurate reporting. The act also places increased responsibility on the Board of Directors, audit committee, and external auditor.
  - **Incentives**. SOX imposes stiffer penalties, including jail time and monetary fines, for those who commit fraud.
  - **Character**. SOX emphasizes the importance of individual character in preventing fraudulent reporting and requires public companies to implement anonymous tip lines, whistle-blower protection, and codes of ethics.
- Sustainability is an emerging field that allows organizations to achieve economic results while fulfilling their obligations to society and protecting the environment for future generations. The triple bottom line measures a company's performance toward its sustainability goals by including measures of economic success (profit), social impact (people), and environmental impact (planet).

Define and give examples of different types of costs. p. 14 **LO 1-4**

- Costs can be classified in a variety of ways, depending on how the information will be used:
  - Out-of-pocket costs require a cash outlay.
  - Opportunity costs are the benefits you give up when you choose one alternative over another.
  - Direct costs can be directly and conveniently traced to a specific cost object.

- Indirect costs either cannot be traced to a specific cost object or are not worth the effort of tracing.
- Variable costs change, in total, in direct proportion to changes in activity.
- Fixed costs remain the same, in total, regardless of activity.
- Manufacturing costs are associated with making a physical product. They can be classified as direct materials, direct labor, or manufacturing overhead.
- Nonmanufacturing costs are associated with selling a product or service or running the overall business.
- GAAP requires manufacturing costs to be treated as product costs and nonmanufacturing costs to be treated as period costs.
- Product costs are assigned to a product as it is being produced; they accumulate in inventory accounts until the product is sold.
- Period costs are reported as expenses as they are incurred.
- Relevant costs are future-oriented costs that differ between decision alternatives.
- Irrelevant costs are those that remain the same regardless of the alternatives and thus will not affect the decision.

KEY TERMS

Budget p. 6
Controlling p. 7
Conversion Costs p. 19
Cost Object p. 15
Differential Costs p. 20
Direct Costs p. 16
Direct Labor p. 19
Direct Materials p. 19
Ethics p. 10
Financial Accounting p. 5
Fixed Costs p. 18
General and Administrative Expenses p. 20
Implementing p. 6
Indirect Costs p. 16
Inventoriable Costs p. 20
Irrelevant Cost p. 20
Managerial Accounting p. 5
Manufacturing Costs p. 19
Manufacturing Firms p. 8
Manufacturing Overhead p. 18
Marketing or Selling Expenses p. 19
Merchandising Companies p. 8
Nonmanufacturing Costs p. 19
Opportunity Cost p. 15
Out-of-Pocket Cost p. 15
Period Costs p. 20
Planning p. 6
Prime Costs p. 19
Product Costs p. 20
Relevant Cost p. 20
Sarbanes-Oxley (SOX) Act of 2002 p. 11
Service Companies p. 9
Sunk Costs p. 21
Sustainability p. 13
Sustainability Accounting p. 12
People, Profit, and Planet p. 13
Triple Bottom Line p. 13
Variable Costs p. 17

PRACTICE MATERIAL

QUESTIONS

1. What is the primary difference between financial accounting and managerial accounting?
2. Explain how the primary difference between financial and managerial accounting results in other differences between the two.
3. Why are traditional, GAAP-based financial statements not necessarily useful to managers and other internal parties?
4. Explain the difference between service companies, merchandising companies, and manufacturing companies.
5. Consider the area within a 3-mile radius of your campus. What service companies, merchandising companies, and manufacturing firms are located within that area?
6. What are the three basic functions of management?
7. How are the three basic management functions interrelated?
8. What are ethics and why is ethical behavior important to managers?
9. What events or factors led to the creation and enactment of the Sarbanes-Oxley Act of 2002?
10. How did the Sarbanes-Oxley Act affect managers' responsibility for creating and maintaining an ethical business and reporting environment?
11. How did the Sarbanes-Oxley Act attempt to reduce fraudulent reporting by addressing opportunity, incentives, and character?

12. According to a recent Statement on Management Accounting (SMA), what are some of the potential benefits of a strong ethical business climate?

13. Why are businesses starting to incorporate sustainability into their business model?

14. What factors does sustainability accounting include that traditional accounting systems do not?

15. Think about your activities over the last week. Identify two exchanges or transactions for which the cost incurred would be measured in dollars and two that were nonmonetary.

16. Think about all of the choices you make on a day-to-day basis: everything from driving versus riding a bike to school or deciding where to have lunch. Pick three decisions you have made today. Identify an out-of-pocket and opportunity cost for each decision.

17. Why is it important for managers to be able to determine the cost of a particular item? Name one decision that a company might make using cost information.

18. Explain the difference between a direct cost and an indirect cost. Take a look at your purse or wallet. Name two direct costs of making your purse or wallet. Name two indirect costs of making it.

19. Explain the difference between fixed and variable costs. Give an example of a cost that varies with the number of miles you drive your car each week and an example of a cost that is fixed regardless of how many miles you drive your car each week.

20. Explain the difference between relevant and irrelevant costs. What are the two criteria used to determine whether a cost is relevant?

21. Suppose you and your friends are planning a trip for spring break. You have narrowed the destination choices to Panama City, Florida, and Galveston Bay, Texas. List two costs that are relevant to this decision and two costs that are irrelevant to this decision.

22. What are prime costs? Why have they decreased in importance over time?

23. What types of costs are included in manufacturing overhead? Other than direct materials and direct labor, what costs would *not* be included in manufacturing overhead?

24. Why can't prime cost and conversion cost be added together to arrive at total manufacturing cost?

25. What is the difference between product and period costs in terms of how and when they are treated in the financial statements (balance sheet and income statement)?

26. Explain why product costs are also called *inventoriable costs* and how those costs move through a company's financial statements.

27. What triggers the movement of product costs from an asset on the balance sheet to an expense on the income statement?

28. If you wanted to know the total amount of period costs for a company, which financial statement(s) would you consult?

29. Suppose a company accountant incorrectly classified advertising costs as a product cost. What impact would this have on the company's financial statements?

MULTIPLE CHOICE

1. The **primary** difference between financial accounting and managerial accounting is that

- **a.** Financial accounting is used by internal parties while managerial accounting is used by external parties.
- **b.** Financial accounting is future oriented while managerial accounting is historical in nature.
- **c.** Financial accounting is used by external parties while managerial accounting is used by internal parties.
- **d.** Financial accounting is prepared as needed (perhaps even daily), but managerial accounting is prepared periodically (monthly, quarterly, annually).

2. Which of the following companies is most likely to be considered a manufacturing company?

- **a.** Burger King.
- **b.** Abercrombie and Fitch.
- **c.** Supercuts.
- **d.** Maytag.

3. Which of the functions of management involves monitoring actual results to see whether the objectives set in the planning stage are being met and, if necessary, taking corrective action to adjust the objectives or implementation of the plan?

- **a.** Implementing.
- **b.** Controlling.
- **c.** Planning.
- **d.** Selling.

4. Suppose you have decided that you would like to purchase a new home in five years. To do this, you will need a down payment of approximately $20,000, which means that you need to save $350 each month for the next five years. This is an example of

- **a.** Directing/Leading.
- **b.** Controlling.
- **c.** Planning/Organizing.
- **d.** Selling.

5. If the number of units produced increases, then

- **a.** Unit variable costs will increase.
- **b.** Unit fixed costs will decrease.

c. Total variable costs will remain the same.
d. Total fixed costs will increase.

Use the following information regarding Garcia Company for questions 6–8.

Factory rent	$5,000
Direct labor	8,000
Indirect materials	1,000
Direct materials used	3,500
Sales commissions	2,500
Factory manager's salary	4,000
Advertising	1,500

6. What is Garcia's total manufacturing cost?
   a. $25,500.
   b. $24,000.
   c. $21,500.
   d. $10,000.
7. What is Garcia's prime cost?
   a. $11,500.
   b. $12,500.
   c. $15,500.
   d. $21,000.
8. What is Garcia's manufacturing overhead?
   a. $24,000.
   b. $12,500.
   c. $14,000.
   d. $10,000.
9. Suppose you are trying to decide whether to sell your accounting book at the end of the semester or keep it as a reference book for future courses. If you decide to keep the book, the money you would have received from selling it is a(n)
   a. Sunk cost.
   b. Opportunity cost.
   c. Out-of-pocket cost.
   d. Indirect cost.
10. Which of the following would *not* be treated as a product cost under GAAP?
   a. Direct materials.
   b. Manufacturing supervisor's salary.
   c. Sales commissions.
   d. All of the above are product costs.

Answers to Multiple-Choice Questions located in back of the text.

MINI-EXERCISES

connect

LO 1-1 **M1-1 Comparing Financial and Managerial Accounting**

Match each of the following characteristics that describe **financial** accounting, **managerial** accounting, **both** financial and managerial accounting, or **neither** financial nor managerial accounting.

____ 1. Is future oriented.
____ 2. Is used primarily by external parties.
____ 3. Is relied on for making decisions.
____ 4. Is historical in nature.
____ 5. Has reports that can be obtained through the company website or requested from the company CFO for publicly traded companies.
____ 6. Is reported in aggregate for the company as a whole.
____ 7. Has reports that may be created daily or even in real time.
____ 8. Is used mostly by managers within the company.
____ 9. Must be accurate to help decision makers.
____ 10. Is always available on the Internet to any interested party.

A. Financial accounting
B. Managerial accounting
C. Both financial and managerial accounting
D. Neither financial nor managerial accounting

LO 1-2 **M1-2 Identifying Management Functions**

You were recently hired as a production manager for Medallion Company. You just received a memo regarding a company meeting being held this week. The memo stated that one topic of discussion will be the basic management functions as they relate to the production department. You are expected to lead this discussion. To prepare for the discussion, briefly list the three basic functions of management and how those functions might relate to your position as production manager.

M1-3 Classifying Sarbanes-Oxley (SOX) Objectives and Requirements

LO 1-3

Match each of the following SOX requirements to the corresponding objective by entering the appropriate letter in the space provided.

____ 1. Establish a tip line for employees to report questionable acts.
____ 2. Increase maximum fines to $5 million.
____ 3. Require management to report on effectiveness of internal controls.
____ 4. Legislate whistle-blower protections.
____ 5. Require external auditors' report on effectiveness of internal controls.

A. Counteract incentives for fraud.
B. Reduce opportunities for error and fraud.
C. Encourage good character.

M1-4 Identifying Ethical Dilemmas

LO 1-3

The following is a short list of scenarios. Write a brief statement about whether you believe the scenario is an ethical dilemma and, if so, who will be harmed by the unethical behavior.

1. You are a tax accounting professional and a client informs you that some of the receipts used in preparing the tax return have been falsified.
2. A friend gives you his accounting homework assignment. You change his name to yours on the top of the paper and turn in the assignment as your work.
3. You are an employee at a local clothing store. Your manager asks you to sell her a few expensive items priced at $1,200 but charge her only $100.

M1-5 Classifying Costs

LO 1-4

Top Shelf Company builds oak bookcases. Determine whether each of the following is a direct material (DM), direct labor (DL), manufacturing overhead (MOH), or a period (P) cost for Top Shelf.

____ 1. Depreciation on factory equipment.
____ 2. Depreciation on delivery trucks.
____ 3. Wood used to build a bookcase.
____ 4. Production supervisor's salary.
____ 5. Glue and screws used in the bookcases.
____ 6. Wages of persons who assemble the bookcases.
____ 7. Cost to run an ad on local radio stations.
____ 8. Rent for the factory.
____ 9. CEO's salary.
____ 10. Wages of person who sands the wood after it is cut.

M1-6 Classifying and Calculating Cost

LO 1-4

Refer to M1-5. Assume that you have the following information about Top Shelf's costs for the most recent month:

Depreciation on factory equipment	$1,800
Depreciation on delivery trucks	800
Wood used to build bookcases	1,500
Production supervisor's salary	2,800
Glue and screws used in the bookcases	250
Wages of persons who assemble the bookcases	2,500
Cost to run an ad on local radio stations	600
Rent for the factory	3,500
CEO's salary	3,000
Wages of person who sands the wood after it is cut	1,600

Determine each of the following costs for Top Shelf.

1. Direct materials used.
2. Direct labor.
3. Manufacturing overhead.
4. Prime cost.
5. Conversion cost.
6. Total manufacturing cost.
7. Total nonmanufacturing (period) cost.

LO 1-4

M1-7 Classifying Costs

You are considering the possibility of pursuing a master's degree after completing your undergraduate degree.

1. List three costs (or benefits) that would be relevant to this decision, including at least one opportunity cost.
2. List two costs that would be irrelevant to this decision.

LO 1-4

M1-8 Classifying Costs

Lighten Up Lamps, Inc., manufactures table lamps and other lighting products. For each of the following costs, use an X to indicate the category of product cost and whether it is a prime cost, conversion cost, or both.

	PRODUCT COSTS				
	Direct Materials	Direct Labor	Mfg. Overhead	Prime Cost	Conversion Cost
Production supervisor salary					
Cost of lamp shades					
Wages of person who assembles lamps					
Factory rent					
Wages of person who paints lamps					
Factory utilities					
Screws used to assemble lamps					

LO 1-4

M1-9 Calculating Missing Amounts

For each of the following independent cases A through D, compute the missing values in the table below.

Case	Direct Materials	Direct Labor	Manufacturing Overhead	Prime Cost	Conversion Cost
A	$900	$1,300	$2,000	$?	$?
B	400	?	1,325	2,650	?
C	?	700	1,500	2,880	?
D	?	750	?	1,600	2,000

LO 1-2

M1-10 Classifying Type of Company

Indicate whether each of the following businesses would most likely be classified as a service company (S), merchandising company (Mer), or manufacturing company (Man).

_____ 1. Merry Maids.

_____ 2. Dell Computer.

_____ 3. Brinks Security.

_____ 4. Kmart.

_____ 5. PetSmart.

____ 6. Ford Motor Company.
____ 7. Bank One.
____ 8. Ralph Lauren.
____ 9. Dillard's.
____ 10. Sam's Club.

M1-11 Identifying Direct and Indirect Costs for a Service Company LO 1-4

Refer to M1-10. Choose one of the companies you classified as a service company. For that company, identify two direct costs and two indirect costs. What is the cost object?

M1-12 Identifying Direct and Indirect Costs for a Merchandising Company LO 1-4

Refer to M1-10. Choose one of the companies you classified as a merchandising company. For that company, identify two direct costs and two indirect costs. What is the cost object?

EXERCISES

connect

E1-1 Making Decisions Using Managerial Accounting LO 1-1

Suppose you are a sales manager for Books on Wheels, Inc., which makes rolling book carts often used by libraries. The company is considering adding a new product aimed at university students. The new product will be a small, collapsible, wheeled tote designed specifically to aid students in transporting textbooks across campus.

Required:

1. List five questions you and the company would need to answer before proceeding with the development and marketing of this new product.
2. For each question identified in requirement 1, identify the information you would need to answer the question as well as the expected source of that information.
3. Identify three serious consequences of either not obtaining the information you need or obtaining inaccurate information.

E1-2 Identifying Management Functions LO 1-2

Refer to E1-1. Suppose that, after a thorough investigation, Books on Wheels decided to go forward with the new product aimed at university students. The product, The Campus Cart, has gone into production, and the first units have already been delivered to campuses across the country.

Required:

Match each of the following steps that took place as Books on Wheels moved through the decision making, production, marketing, and sale of The Campus Cart with the correct phase of the management process.

____	1. Identifying five college campuses to serve as test markets.	A. Planning
____	2. Setting the goal of $1 million in annual sales by the year 2015.	B. Implementing
____	3. Hiring workers for the manufacturing facility.	C. Controlling
____	4. Overseeing the production and shipment of The Campus Cart.	
____	5. Preparing one-, three-, and five-year budgets that detail the necessary resources and costs that will be incurred to meet the projected sales forecasts.	
____	6. Deciding which new markets to expand into based on the first year's sales results.	
____	7. Implementing a bonus system to reward employees for meeting sales and production goals.	
____	8. Deciding to spend more advertising dollars in regions where sales were slower than expected.	

LO 1-3

E1-3 Identify sustainability issues affecting the triple bottom line.

For each of the following sustainability initiatives, indicate whether it will impact social (S), environmental (En), or economic (Ec) factors in the triple bottom line. Include more than one factor as appropriate.

_____ 1. Implementing a health and wellness program to improve employees' health, reduce stress, improve productivity, and reduce employee turn-over.

_____ 2. Ensuring that all future construction projects are LEED certified.

_____ 3. Implementing a just-in-time inventory system to reduce inventory costs and improve product quality.

_____ 4. Providing all employees with glass water bottles to reduce the use of plastic water bottles and the cost of company-sponsored lunches.

_____ 5. Purchasing web conferencing software to give employees the flexibility to work remotely, reduce the number of miles they must commute to work, and save on travel costs for off-site meetings.

_____ 6. Creating a code of conduct for suppliers to establish guidelines on labor wages, working conditions, health and safety.

_____ 7. Expanding into international markets to increase market share.

LO 1-4

E1-4 Classifying Costs

Suppose you have just finished your third year of college and expect to graduate with a bachelor's degree in accounting after completing two more semesters of coursework. The salary for entry-level positions with an accounting degree is approximately $48,000 in your area. Shelton Industries has just offered you a position in its northwest regional office. The position has an annual salary of $40,000 and would not require you to complete your undergraduate degree. If you accept the position, you would have to move to Seattle.

Required:

Identify with an X whether each of the following costs/benefits would be relevant to the decision to accept the offer from Shelton or stay in school. You may have more than one X for each item.

	Relevant Cost or Benefit	Irrelevant Cost or Benefit	Sunk Cost	Opportunity Cost
$40,000 salary from Shelton				
Anticipated $48,000 salary with an accounting degree				
Tuition and books for years 1–3 of college				
Cost to relocate to Seattle				
Tuition and books for remaining two semesters				
$19,000 from your part-time job, which you plan to keep until you graduate				
Cost to rent an apartment in Seattle (assume you are currently living at home with your parents)				
Food and entertainment expenses, which are expected to be the same in Seattle as where you currently live				
Increased promotional opportunities that will come from having a college degree				

CHAPTER 1 Introduction to Managerial Accounting 33

E1-5 Classifying Costs LO 1-4

Seth's Skateboard Company incurs the costs listed in the following table.

Required:

Use an X to categorize each of the following costs. You may have more than one X for each item.

	PRODUCT COSTS			Period Cost	Prime Cost	Conversion Cost
	Direct Materials	Direct Labor	Mfg. Overhead			
Production supervisor salary						
Cost of fiberglass						
Wages of assembly person						
Sales commission						
Cost of high-grade wheels						
Screws						
Factory rent						
Wages of skateboard painter						
Factory utilities						
Utilities for corporate office						

E1-6 Calculating Costs LO 1-4

Cotton White, Inc., makes specialty clothing for chefs. The company reported the following costs for 2015:

Factory rent	$42,000
Company advertising	18,000
Wages paid to seamstresses	75,000
Depreciation on salespersons' vehicles	25,000
Thread	1,000
Utilities for factory	22,000
Cutting room supervisor's salary	30,000
President's salary	75,000
Premium quality cotton material	42,000
Buttons	750
Factory insurance	15,000
Depreciation on sewing machines	6,000
Wages paid to cutters	50,000

Required:

Compute the following for Cotton White:

1. Direct materials.
2. Direct labor.
3. Manufacturing overhead.
4. Total manufacturing cost.
5. Prime cost.
6. Conversion cost.
7. Total period cost.

LO 1-4 **E1-7 Calculating Missing Amounts**

For each of the following independent cases (A through E), compute the missing values in the table:

Case	Prime Cost	Conversion Cost	Direct Materials	Direct Labor	Manufacturing Overhead	Total Manufacturing Cost
A	$?	$?	$2,000	$1,500	$3,500	$?
B	6,600	11,500	2,300	?	7,200	?
C	?	8,000	1,400	3,250	?	9,400
D	?	?	?	2,100	3,100	6,200
E	11,500	20,500	3,800	?	?	?

LO 1-4 **E1-8 Classifying and Calculating Costs**

The following information is available for Wonderway, Inc., for 2015:

Factory rent	$40,000
Company advertising	20,000
Wages paid to laborers	82,000
Depreciation for president's vehicle	8,000
Indirect production labor	1,800
Utilities for factory	36,000
Production supervisor's salary	30,000
President's salary	60,000
Direct materials used	34,500
Sales commissions	7,500
Factory insurance	12,000
Depreciation on factory equipment	26,000

Required:

Calculate each of the following costs for Wonderway:

1. Direct labor.
2. Manufacturing overhead.
3. Prime cost.
4. Conversion cost.
5. Total manufacturing cost.
6. Period expenses.

LO 1-4 **E1-9 Classifying Costs**

Blockett Company makes automobile sunshades and incurs the costs listed in the table below.

Required:

Use an X to categorize each of the following costs. You may have more than one X for each item.

	Period Cost	PRODUCT COSTS Direct Materials	 Direct Labor	 Mfg. Overhead	Prime Cost	Conversion Cost
Company president's salary						
Factory rent						
Cost of reflective material						
Wages of material cutter						
Wages of office receptionist						
Thread and glue						
Depreciation for salesperson's car						
Factory supervisor's salary						
Factory utilities						
Factory insurance						

E1-10 Classifying and Calculating Cost LO 1-4

Noteworthy, Inc., produces and sells small electronic keyboards. Assume that you have the following information about Noteworthy's costs for the most recent month.

Depreciation on factory equipment	$ 800
Depreciation on CEO's company car	100
Speakers used in the keyboard	1,100
Production supervisor's salary	2,800
Glue and screws used in the keyboards	370
Wages of persons who install the speakers	3,000
Cost to run an ad on local radio stations	600
Utilities for the factory	1,200
Personnel manager's salary	2,500
Wages of person who attaches legs to keyboards	1,950

Required:

Determine each of the following for Noteworthy:

1. Total product cost.
2. Prime cost.
3. Manufacturing overhead.
4. Direct labor.
5. Conversion cost.
6. Total variable cost (with number of units produced as the activity).
7. Total fixed cost (with number of units produced as the activity).

E1-11 Identifying Relevant and Irrelevant Costs LO 1-4

Suppose that your brother, Raymond, recently bought a new laptop computer for $800 to use in his land surveying business. After purchasing several add-on components for $400, he realized that they are not compatible with the laptop and, therefore, he cannot use the computer for its intended purpose of mapping land coordinates using GPS satellites. He has also purchased a one-year service agreement and warranty for the add-on components for $75. The computer cannot be returned, but Raymond has found a new laptop costing $1,200 that will work with his GPS mapping components. Raymond is trying to decide what to do now and has asked your advice.

Required:

1. Identify the costs that are relevant to Raymond's decision.
2. Are there any costs that are irrelevant?
3. Suppose that Raymond made the following statement: "I can't get a new computer now. I have to get my money's worth from the old one." Is Raymond's logic correct?

E1-12 Calculating Missing Amounts LO 1-4

For each of the following independent cases (A–E), compute the missing values in the table:

Case	Prime Cost	Conversion Cost	Direct Materials	Direct Labor	Manufacturing Overhead	Total Manufacturing Cost
A	$ 9,400	$ 16,100	$ 4,300	$?	$11,000	$?
B	?	?	12,000	7,300	24,500	43,800
C	55,300	107,500	43,200	?	?	?
D	?	47,350	21,400	13,250	?	68,750
E	?	?	?	15,100	22,900	55,700

E1-13 Explaining Manufacturing Cost Categories LO 1-4

Manufacturing costs can be classified into three categories—direct materials, direct labor, and manufacturing overhead. Over the years, manufacturing companies have changed significantly with advances in technology and the automation of many manufacturing processes.

Required:

Explain how the relative proportion of materials, labor, and overhead is likely to have changed over the last 100 years. Be specific in your discussion of which types of costs have increased and which have decreased.

LO 1-4 **E1-14 Explaining Effects of Cost Misclassification**

LEVEL UP

Donna is a cost accountant for Northwind Corp. She is very efficient and hard-working; however, she occasionally transposes numbers when recording transactions. While working late recently, Donna accidentally recorded $19,000 of advertising cost instead of the correct $91,000. The transaction was correctly recorded in all other respects.

Required:

Explain how Donna's error will affect the following:

1. Manufacturing Costs.
2. Inventory.
3. Cost of Goods Sold.
4. Period Expenses.
5. Net Income.

GROUP A PROBLEMS

connect

LO 1-1 **PA1-1 Comparing Financial and Managerial Accounting**

You have been asked to take part in an upcoming Young Professionals meeting in your area. The program planned for the evening will cover many aspects of today's business world. Specifically, you have been asked to explain why there are two types of accounting—financial and managerial—and why they are both relevant to a company's employees. The program director would like for you to cover differences between the two types of accounting as well as how each type plays a role within today's competitive environment.

You will have 15 minutes for your presentation plus a 15-minute question-and-answer period at the end. Your audience is composed primarily of entry-level managers from all fields (marketing, human resources, production, etc.). Assume that they all have some familiarity with accounting, but few are practicing accountants.

Required:

1. Prepare a detailed outline identifying your topic of discussion.
2. List at least five questions you may be asked during the question-and-answer period. Briefly discuss your answers to these questions.

LO 1-2 **PA1-2 Identifying Management Functions**

Your friend, Suzie Whitson, has designed a new type of outdoor toy that helps children learn basic concepts such as colors, numbers, and shapes. Suzie's product will target two groups: day care centers in warm climates and home school programs. Suzie has come to you for help in getting her idea off the ground. She has never managed a business before and is not sure what functions she will need to perform to make her venture successful.

Required:

Briefly explain to Suzie the three major functions of management. For each function, give three examples of questions that Suzie will need to answer to make her business venture a success.

LO 1-3 **PA1-3 Identifying and Resolving Ethical Dilemmas**

You are one of three partners who own and operate Mary's Maid Service. The company has been operating for seven years. One of the other partners has always prepared the company's annual financial statements. Recently, you proposed that the statements be audited each year because it would benefit the partners and prevent possible disagreements about the division of profits. The partner who prepares the statements proposed that his Uncle Ray, who has a lot of financial experience, do the job for a low cost. Your other partner remained silent.

Required:

1. What position would you take on the proposal? Justify your response.
2. What would you recommend? Give the basis for your recommendation.

PA1-4 Classifying Costs; Calculating Total Costs; Identifying Impact of Misclassification LO 1-4

Assume that Suzie Whitson (PA1-2) has decided to begin production of her outdoor children's toy. Her company is Jiffy Jet and costs for last month follow.

Factory rent	$ 3,200
Company advertising	1,000
Wages paid to assembly workers	30,000
Depreciation for salespersons' vehicles	2,000
Screws	500
Utilities for factory	900
Assembly supervisor's salary	3,500
Sandpaper	150
President's salary	6,000
Plastic tubing	4,200
Paint	250
Sales commissions	1,200
Factory insurance	1,000
Depreciation on cutting machines	2,000
Wages paid to painters	7,500

Required:

1. Identify each of the preceding costs as either a product or a period cost. If the cost is a product cost, decide whether it is for direct materials (DM), direct labor (DL), or manufacturing overhead (MOH).
2. Determine the total cost for each of the following:
   a. Direct materials.
   b. Direct labor.
   c. Manufacturing overhead.
   d. Prime cost.
   e. Conversion cost.
   f. Total product cost.
3. Suppose all period costs were incorrectly identified as product costs. What impact could that have on Jiffy Jet's financial statements? Be specific.

GROUP B PROBLEMS

PB1-1 Comparing Product and Period Costs LO 1-4

You have been asked to take part in an upcoming Young Professionals meeting in your area. The program planned for the evening focuses on today's manufacturing environment. Specifically, you have been asked to explain how manufacturing firms determine how much it costs to make their product and why some costs are initially recorded as inventory while other costs are expensed immediately. The program director would like for you to (1) discuss the rules for determining whether a cost should be treated as a product cost or period cost and (2) explain the types of costs that would be included in each category, how each flows through the accounting system, and the implications of the distinction between product costs and period costs for financial reporting (income statement versus balance sheet).

You will have 15 minutes for your presentation plus a 15-minute question-and-answer period at the end. Your audience is composed primarily of entry-level production personnel although people from other fields (marketing, human resources, production, etc.) will be attending. Assume that they all have some familiarity with accounting but few are practicing accountants.

Required:

1. Prepare a detailed outline identifying your topic of discussion.
2. List at least five questions you may be asked during the question-and-answer period. Briefly discuss your answers to these questions.

LO 1-2 **PB1-2 Identifying Management Functions**

Your friend, Maria Cottonwood, has designed a new type of fire extinguisher that is very small and easy to use. It will target two groups of people: people who have trouble operating heavy, traditional extinguishers (e.g., the elderly or people with disabilities) and people who need to store extinguishers in small spaces such as a vehicle. Maria has come to you for help in getting her idea off the ground. She has never managed a business before and she is not sure what functions she will need to perform to make her venture successful.

Required:

Briefly explain to Maria the three major functions of management. For each function, give three examples of questions that Maria will need to answer to make her business venture a success.

LO 1-3 **PB1-3 Identifying and Resolving Ethical Dilemmas**

When some people think about inventory theft, they imagine a shoplifter running out of a store with goods stuffed inside a jacket or bag. But that's not what the managers at the Famous Footwear store on Chicago's Madison Street were dealing with. Their own employees were the ones stealing the inventory. One scam involved dishonest cashiers who would let their friends take a pair of Skechers without paying for them. To make it look like the shoes had been bought, cashiers would ring up a sale, but instead of charging $50 for shoes, they would charge only $2 for a bottle of shoe polish. When the company's managers saw a drop in gross profit, they decided to put the accounting system to work. In just two years, the company cut its Madison Street inventory losses in half. Here's how a newspaper described the store's improvements:

Retailers Crack Down on Employee Theft
SouthCoast Today, September 10, 2000, Chicago
By Calmetta Coleman, *Wall Street Journal* Staff Writer

. . . Famous Footwear installed a chainwide register-monitoring system to sniff out suspicious transactions, such as unusually large numbers of refunds or voids, or repeated sales of cheap goods.

. . . [B]efore an employee can issue a cash refund, a second worker must be present to see the customer and inspect the merchandise.

. . . [T]he chain has set up a toll-free hotline for employees to use to report suspicions about co-workers.

These improvements in inventory control came as welcome news for investors and creditors of Brown Shoe Company, the company that owns Famous Footwear.

Required:

1. Explain how the register-monitoring system would allow Famous Footwear to cut down on employee theft.
2. Think of and describe at least four different parties that are harmed by the type of inventory theft described in this case.

PB1-4 Classifying Costs, Calculating Total Costs, and Identifying Impact of Classifications

LO 1-4

Assume that Maria Cottonwood (PB1-2) has decided to begin production of her fire extinguisher. Her company is Blaze Be Gone, whose costs for last month follow.

Factory rent	$ 2,000
Company advertising	500
Wages paid to assembly workers	25,000
Depreciation for salespersons' vehicles	1,000
Screws	250
Utilities for factory	800
Production supervisor's salary	4,000
Sandpaper	150
President's salary	6,000
Sheet metal	7,500
Paint	750
Sales commissions	1,700
Factory insurance	2,000
Depreciation on factory machinery	5,000
Wages paid to painters	5,500

Required:

1. Identify each of the preceding costs as either a product or a period cost. If the cost is a product cost, decide whether it is for direct materials (DM), direct labor (DL), or manufacturing overhead (MOH).
2. Determine the total amount for each of the following:
   a. Direct materials.
   b. Direct labor.
   c. Manufacturing overhead.
   d. Prime cost.
   e. Conversion cost.
   f. Total product cost.
3. Explain why the depreciation on the salespersons' vehicles is treated differently than the depreciation on the factory machines. How might this difference impact Maria's financial statements in terms of the balance sheet and income statement?

SKILLS DEVELOPMENT CASES

S1-1 Video Case Assignment: Identifying Manufacturing Costs

LO 1-4

Go to www.YouTube.com and search for **How It's Made**, a television show produced by the Discovery Channel that shows how thousands of products and services are created. Find a product that interests you by browsing through the episode list or using search terms such as *baseball bats* or *stackable potato chips.*

Watch the video and answer the following questions:

- What product did you choose? Briefly describe how the product is made.
- What are the major material inputs into the product? Pick one type of material used to make this product and find out how much it costs. List one decision that managers might make based on the cost of materials.
- Did you observe any direct labor in the video? Did you observe any indirect labor? What is the difference?
- List three examples of manufacturing overhead that you observed in the video. How does manufacturing overhead differ from direct materials and direct labor?
- How much do you think it costs to make a single unit of this product? List two decisions that managers would make based on the cost of the product.
- List two costs the company incurs that are not related to **making** the product. How and why are these costs treated differently than the manufacturing costs identified previously?

LO 1-4 **S1-2 Identifying Changes in Manufacturing Process and Costs Due to Automation**

In recent years, many companies have invested in equipment to automate processes that were once performed manually. A simple example is a drive-through car wash, where robots wash and dry the cars rather than people.

Required:

Think of another company that might upgrade to an automated system and answer the following questions.

1. What physical changes would the conversion to automation cause in the way the company does business?
2. What impact, both positive and negative, might automation have on employee morale?
3. What impact might automation have on the skill level of the company's workforce?
4. How might automation affect the quality of the product and the efficiency of the company's processes?
5. How would you expect automation to affect direct materials, direct labor, and overhead costs? Would you expect any of these costs to increase or decrease?
6. How would you expect automation to affect variable costs and fixed costs? Would you expect either of these costs to increase or decrease?
7. How might automation affect the price consumers pay for the product?
8. How might automation affect the company's bottom line, both immediately and several years in the future?

LO 1-2 **S1-3 Identifying Service, Merchandising, and Manufacturing Firms: Internet Research**

As discussed in the chapter, companies are often classified into one of three categories: service, merchandising, and manufacturing.

Required:

1. Choose one well-known company from each category and explore that company's website. On the website, find a brief company description as well as the most recent published financial statements. Based on the company description, support your categorization of the company as service, merchandising, or manufacturing. If the company falls into more than one of these categories, describe how.
2. Look at the income statement and balance sheet for the company and list any factors that would support your categorization of the company as a service, merchandising, or manufacturing organization.

S1-4 Interviewing Local Manager to Identify Sustainability Initiatives LO 1-3

Required:

Arrange a visit with a local business and interview the manager about the firm's sustainability goals and initiatives. The objective of the interview is to gain an understanding of what the company is currently doing in the area of sustainability and to make recommendations for actions the company could take to improve its triple bottom line. Some potential interview questions are listed below:

1. What does sustainability mean to you and to your business?
2. Have you implemented any sustainability initiatives over the past five years.
3. Have you heard of the triple bottom line? If so, what are you doing to enhance performance in the three key areas? If not, describe the triple bottom line for them and ask what they are doing to to enhance performance in the three key areas.
4. What does your company do to enhance or serve the community in which you operate?
5. Describe how you and your employees are rewarded. Is it through annual raises, bonuses, perks, or promotions? Are these rewards linked to performance? How do you measure performance?
6. Do you think implementing sustainable business practices can help attract and retain better employees or more loyal customers?

CHAPTER 10

Decentralized Performance Evaluation

YOUR LEARNING OBJECTIVES

LO 10-1	List and explain the advantages and disadvantages of decentralization.
LO 10-2	Describe the different types of responsibility centers and explain how managers of each type are evaluated.
LO 10-3	Describe the four dimensions of the balanced scorecard and explain how they are used to evaluate managerial performance.
LO 10-4	Compute and interpret return on investment, investment turnover, and profit margin.
LO 10-5	Compute and interpret residual income.
LO 10-6	Explain how transfer prices are set in decentralized organizations.

© McGraw-Hill Education

FOCUS COMPANY: Apple Inc.

There's an App for That

www.apple.com

Apple Computers Inc. began in 1976 when two guys named Steve started building circuit boards in a garage to sell to fellow computer geeks at the Homebrew Computer Club. Steve Wozniak was the technical wizard who built the computers, while Steve Jobs was an ambitious entrepreneur looking to start his own company. When they got their first big order for 50 computers, their biggest problem was figuring out how to pay for the components when they had little cash and no assets to use as collateral for a loan. But Steve Jobs somehow convinced a local supplier to let them buy the parts on 30-day credit terms. As Steve Wozniak tells it, "Steve is very persuasive. We'd get the parts and then stuff them into the circuit boards, have them soldered, get them back in the garage and test them. And we could turn the whole cycle around in ten days and get paid. It worked really great because we had only one level of management."[1]

When companies are small, the owners can make all of the decisions about how to build, market, distribute, and price their products and services. But as a company grows, takes on outside investors, expands into new regions, introduces new products, and hires employees to manage various parts of the business, it is no longer possible for the owners to be directly involved in every aspect of the company's operations. Instead, owners must delegate responsibility to employees and managers to make decisions on their behalf. The delegation of responsibility and decision-making authority throughout an organization is called *decentralization*.

[1]Stephen Wozniak, "Homebrew and How the Apple Came to Be," n.d., http://www.atariarchives.org/deli/homebrew_and_how_the_apple.php.

Today, Apple Inc. is a multibillion dollar company that designs and markets some of the world's most popular consumer electronics, including the iPhone, iPad, iPod, Mac computers, and revolutionary services such as iTunes and the App store. The company employs more than 50,000 people and has operations around the globe.

As you read this chapter, put yourself in the shoes of a stakeholder at Apple and consider the following questions:

- As an Apple customer, how would you evaluate the company's performance?
- If you were a sales manager in an Apple retail store, how would your boss evaluate your performance?
- If you were a distribution manager responsible for shipping Apple products to Best Buy and Costco, how would your boss evaluate your performance?
- If you were a development engineer responsible for designing a new model of iPhone, how would your boss evaluate your performance?
- If you owned stock in Apple, how would you measure the company's performance?

As you can see, performance can be measured in different ways depending on what and who is being evaluated. Throughout this chapter, we use Apple to illustrate several methods for evaluating managerial performance in a decentralized organization. Although most of the details we use in our examples are hypothetical, they are intended to illustrate the techniques that Apple and other companies use to evaluate the performance of their managers and business units.

ORGANIZATION OF THE CHAPTER

Decentralization of responsibility	Designing a performance evaluation system	Transfer pricing
• Advantages and disadvantages of decentralization • Types of responsibility centers	• Balanced scorecard • Financial performance measures • Limitations of financial performance measures	• Market-price method • Cost-based method • Negotiation

Decentralization of Responsibility

As children, most of us couldn't wait to grow up and do everything our parents told us we were too young to do—drive a car, stay out late, date, or get a job. It didn't take long, though, to realize that all that freedom comes with a great deal of responsibility. With responsibility comes the authority to make decisions for ourselves, to take action on behalf of others, and, ultimately, to be held accountable for our decisions and actions.

In business, employees are given the responsibility and authority to make decisions on behalf of their employer. How do organizations make sure that employees act responsibly or make decisions that are in the organization's best interest? The methods they use are not very different from the ones parents use to monitor and control their children, including setting clear rules and guidelines for conduct, directly observing behavior, and measuring and evaluating the outcome of their decisions. The approach organizations use depends, in part, on how decision-making authority is delegated throughout the organization.

ADVANTAGES AND DISADVANTAGES OF DECENTRALIZATION

Learning Objective 10-1
List and explain the advantages and disadvantages of decentralization.

In a **decentralized organization**, decision-making authority is spread throughout the organization, and lower-level managers are given the authority and responsibility of managing their individual units. In a **centralized organization**, decision-making authority is kept at the very top of the organization. High-level executives make all the strategic and operational decisions and charge lower-level managers with implementing those decisions.

In most organizations, the distinction between centralized and decentralized operations is not an either-or matter but a question of **how much** decision-making authority to delegate. The advantages and disadvantages of decentralization are summarized as follows:

Advantages of Decentralization	Disadvantages of Decentralization
• Recognizes that lower-level managers may have more knowledge about their area of responsibility and can make quicker and more informed decisions. • Fosters the development of managerial expertise. • Allows top management to focus on strategic issues without worrying about the day-to-day details.	• Sometimes results in the duplication of resources when managers in multiple areas perform the same function. • Gives managers the opportunity to make decisions that benefit themselves, but are not necessarily in the best interest of the organization.

The primary advantage of decentralization is that lower-level managers are "closer to the action" and thus have better information about their area of the business. They can make more informed and faster decisions, allowing upper management to focus on strategic issues rather than operational details. Decentralization also allows employees to develop their managerial skills so that they can move into more senior positions within the organization.

On the flip-side, decentralization may result in duplication of resources when people in different parts of the business are performing the same function. To minimize this issue, many companies choose to centralize key support functions that cut across the organization, such as human resources, accounting, information technology, and purchasing.

Another major disadvantage of decentralization is that it gives managers the opportunity to make decisions that are in their own self-interest, but may not be in the best interest of the company and its owners. The performance evaluation system provides a way to monitor and motivate managers to make decisions that are in the best interest of the company. Ideally, the company's incentive and reward system should be designed so that the manager's goals are aligned with the organization's goals and objectives. Unfortunately, that is much easier said than done, and companies find it difficult to achieve in practice.

In the next section, we use Apple to illustrate a variety of methods for measuring and evaluating managerial performance. To do so, we need to understand how Apple is organized and what managers in the various business units are responsible for. Refer to Exhibit 10.1 for an illustration of Apple's organizational structure, based on information provided in the company's 2014 annual report.

EXHIBIT 10.1 Organizational Chart for Apple

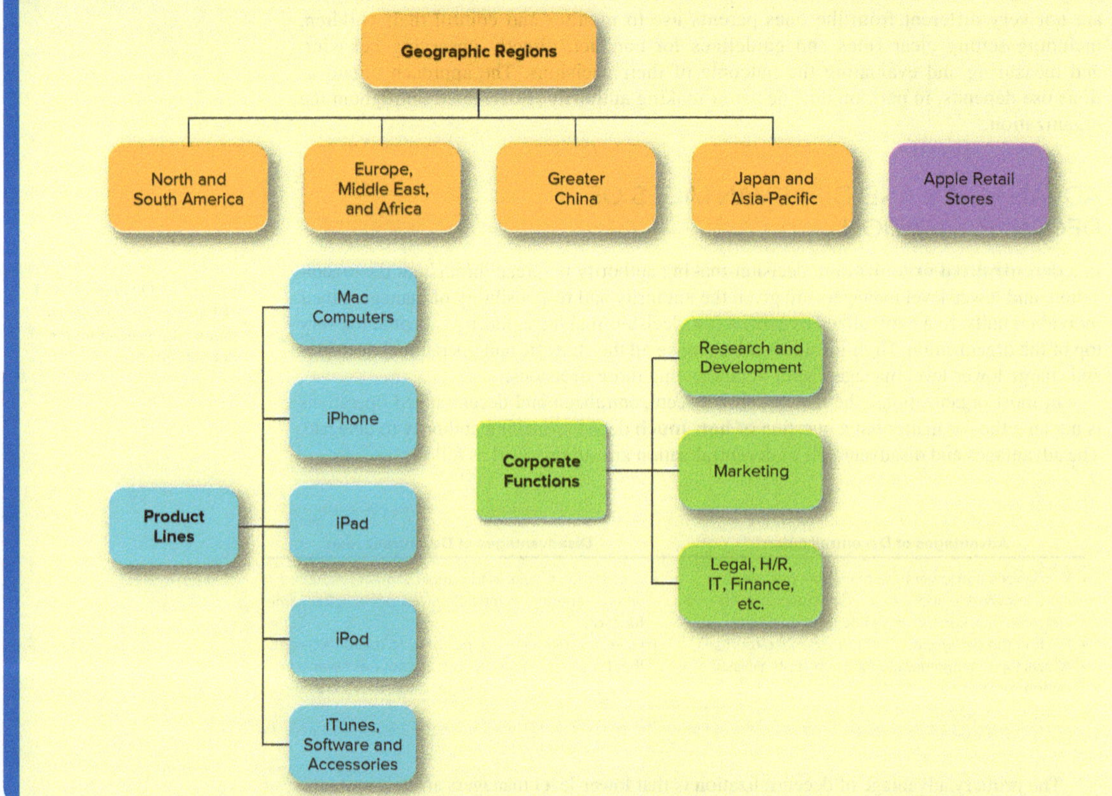

According to its annual report, Apple manages its business primarily on a geographic basis, with operations divided into North/South America, Europe/Middle East/Africa, Greater China, and Japan/Asia-Pacific. Apple retail stores are operated as a separate business unit from these geographic segments. In addition to these geographic divisions, Apple is also organized by major product lines and service offerings. Exhibit 10.2 shows the relative size of Apple's major operating units expressed as a percentage of the company's net sales revenue for 2014.

As you can see, Apple's largest geographic region is North and South America, which made up about 36 percent of total sales revenue in 2014. The iPhone was by far the largest source of revenue, representing 56 percent of 2014 net revenues. In addition to these revenue-generating units, Apple also has many corporate support functions that operate out of Apple's headquarters in Cupertino, California, including research and development, supply chain management, finance, information technology, and human resources.

Like many large corporations, Apple uses a matrix reporting structure, where managerial responsibility cuts across geographic region, product type, and support function. For example, Apple might have a manager who is responsible for supply and demand planning (function) for the iPad (product line) for the northeastern United States (region). This manager would report to and be evaluated by multiple supervisors, including a supply chain supervisor, product supervisor, and regional supervisor.

EXHIBIT 10.2 Revenue Percentages for Apple's Operating Units

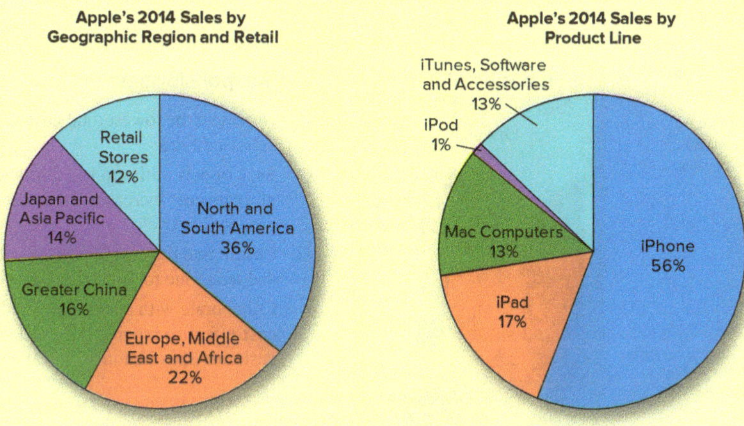

TYPES OF RESPONSIBILITY CENTERS

> **Learning Objective 10-2**
> Describe the different types of responsibility centers and explain how managers in each type are evaluated.

In **responsibility accounting**, managers are given responsibility for a particular part of the business and are then evaluated based on performance in that area. The area of business that managers are responsible for is referred to as a **responsibility center**. As described in the previous section, responsibility centers can be based on geographic regions, product lines, functional characteristics, or some combination of the three.

One of the most important concepts in responsibility accounting is the **controllability principle**, which states that managers should be held responsible only for what they can control. In general, there are four types of responsibility centers that vary according to what the manager can control and, thus, what he/she should be held responsible for:

- The manager of a **cost center** is responsible for controlling **cost.**
- The manager of a **revenue center** is responsible for generating **revenue.**
- The manager of a **profit center** is responsible for generating **profit** (revenue minus cost).
- The manager of an **investment center** is responsible for **profit** (revenue minus cost) and the **investment of assets.**

Next, we provide examples to illustrate how managers in each of these responsibility centers might be evaluated. Although we focus primarily on managers' responsibility for financial performance, it is important to note that managers are responsible for nonfinancial performance as well. We will discuss a mechanism for measuring performance on nonfinancial dimensions in a later section.

Cost Centers

Cost center managers have the authority to incur costs to support their areas of responsibility. All of Apple's corporate support functions would be treated as cost centers, including advertising, human resources, purchasing, supply chain management, information technology, legal services, and accounting. Notice that these cost centers do not generate revenue directly from the customer, although they may have an impact on revenue through other measures, such as customer satisfaction and service quality.

A common example of a cost center manager is a purchasing agent who is responsible for buying materials that will be used to build or repair a product. As an example, consider the following job description for a purchasing manager.

COACH'S TIP

Notice that these job descriptions tell employees what they will be responsible for and how they will be evaluated.

Purchasing Manager (Service and Repair Division)

© Mash/Getty Images

Job Responsibilities:

- Negotiate the lowest total **cost** for parts and subassemblies.
- Seek opportunities to leverage spend and volume to mitigate **cost** increases late in the service phase of the product life cycle.
- Ensure that the cost database contains accurate **cost** and lead time for all active part numbers.
- Collaborate with cross-functional teams to ensure **cost**-effective repair strategies leading to higher customer satisfaction at lowest costs.

As you can see from this job description, cost center managers are evaluated based primarily on their ability to manage or control cost. One of the tools that organizations use to measure the performance of cost center managers is the budgetary planning and control system described in previous chapters. For example, a purchasing manager is responsible for the direct materials price variance, which indicates whether the price paid for materials was more or less than budgeted. But the purchasing manager should not be held responsible for the direct materials quantity or usage variance because he or she has no control over how the materials are actually used in production. In addition to controlling costs, cost center managers should be held responsible for the quality of service provided to other units within the organization.

Revenue Centers

Revenue center managers are responsible for generating revenues for their segment of the business. Companies often give revenue center managers sales targets or quotas and then evaluate and reward them based on whether they meet those targets.

Consider the following job description for a revenue center manager:

Account Manager Online Sales Team

© Fuse/Getty Images

Job Responsibilities:

- The Account Manager is responsible for meeting all **revenue** and unit goals by selling products, systems, and services **within an assigned sales territory.**
- The ideal candidate should possess a track record of **sales success** and proven ability to **exceed all sales goals.**
- The Account Manager will have responsibility for accounts within an assigned territory while acquiring new accounts to meet individual and strategic team goals.

As you can see, revenue center managers are evaluated primarily based on their ability to meet revenue or sales goals. Later in the chapter, we consider other measures for evaluating revenue center managers, including customer satisfaction, customer retention, and customer turnover.

Profit Centers

Profit center managers are responsible for generating profits for their area of the business. Unlike cost center managers who are primarily responsible for cost, and revenue center managers who are primarily responsible for revenue, profit center managers are responsible for both. Consider the following job description for a product manager responsible for the overall profitability of the iPhone.

Product Manager (iPhone)

© Monkey Business Images Ltd/ Getty Images

Job Responsibilities:

- Responsible for driving strategic initiatives related to the success of the iPhone in the Apple Retail Stores.
- Ownership and development of all iPhone metrics including **sales, profitability, and customer experience.**
- Lead all contract negotiations between Apple Retail and carriers.
- Work closely with key internal partners including: Marketing, Finance, Training, Operations, Information Systems, Legal, Fulfillment, and Logistics.

The most common method of evaluating a profit center manager is based on the **segmented income statement,** or an income statement that is broken down by product line, region, or other business segment. This type of income statement was introduced in a previous chapter as a way of evaluating whether a business segment should be continued or discontinued based on its **segment margin.** The segment margin is also useful for evaluating the manager of a profit center because it separates those costs that are within the segment manager's control from those costs that are outside it. **Remember that managers should be held accountable only for the costs and revenues that are within their control.**

Segment margin is calculated as sales revenue less all costs that are directly attributable to a particular business segment, including variable costs and direct fixed costs. A **direct fixed cost** is one that is incurred by the business segment and is therefore within the control of the segment manager. Even though these costs are fixed, or independent of the number of units produced or sold, they are incurred to support that specific business segment and are therefore considered within the segment manger's control. In contrast, **common fixed costs** are typically incurred at a higher level of the organization and are therefore outside of the segment manager's control. In evaluating a profit center manager, we should focus on the segment margin rather than the bottom-line profit margin, which includes costs that are not controllable by the manager.

As you can see, a profit center manager has more responsibility than cost and revenue center managers. Because they are responsible for both revenues and costs, profit center managers often supervise revenue and cost center managers, who have direct responsibility for these key metrics that affect profitability.

Investment Centers

Investment center managers have the authority to make decisions about how and where to invest the company's assets to drive long-term profitability. They have more responsibility than cost center, revenue center, and profit center managers because they are also responsible for investing the company's assets. Consider the following job description for a real estate manager:

Real Estate Manager

© Jill Braaten/McGraw-Hill Education

Job Responsibilities:

- Set and implement strategy for retail real estate, including **identifying new locations,** closing real estate transactions, and managing all real estate negotiations.
- Develop and execute real estate and **capital expenditure plan.**
- Create initial store business model and **pro forma financial statements.**
- Present locations for approval. Negotiate and close real estate deals.
- Partner with internal teams for successful store development. Work with senior executives, store operations, design, development, and analysis teams to create and implement company-wide initiatives.

In addition to being responsible for profitability, investment center managers have to make decisions about how to invest the company's assets. As such, the metrics used to evaluate investment center managers must take into account both profitability and the amount of investment used to generate that profitability. Later in this chapter, we discuss some common measures used to evaluate investment center performance. The next chapter describes several tools that managers can use to make sound capital investment decisions.

For now, complete the following Self-Study Practice to make sure that you understand the differences between the four types of responsibility centers.

How's it going? Self-Study Practice

Which of the following statements about responsibility centers is (are) true? You may select more than one answer.

1. Cost center managers are responsible for generating sales in their area of the business.
2. Revenue center managers are responsible for controlling costs and generating revenue in their area of the business.
3. Profit center managers are responsible for controlling costs and generating revenue but not for investing assets.
4. Investment center managers are responsible for investing assets but not for controlling costs or generating revenue.
5. None of these statements is true.

After you have finished, check your answers against the solution in the margin.

Solution to Self-Study Practice
The only true statement is 3.

Designing a Performance Evaluation System

A major advantage of decentralization is that it allows top-level managers to focus on the strategic objectives of the business, while lower-level managers are given authority to make decisions about how to run their particular part of the business. The goal of a performance evaluation system is to ensure that managers make decisions that are consistent with the company's strategic objectives as opposed to other factors, such as their own self-interest.

The performance evaluation system should reflect the company's business strategy. For example, a company such as Apple that competes on the basis of innovation and product differentiation is likely to have a very different strategy than a company that sells commodity-type products in a well-established industry. In a recent annual report, Apple stated its business strategy as follows:

> *"The Company's business strategy leverages its unique ability to . . . provide its customers products and solutions with innovative design, superior ease-of-use and seamless integration. The Company believes a high-quality buying experience with knowledgeable salespersons who can convey the value of the Company's products and services greatly enhances its ability to attract and retain customers. Therefore, the Company's strategy also includes building and expanding its own retail and online stores and its third-party distribution network to effectively reach more customers and provide them with a high-quality sales and post-sales support experience. The Company believes continual investment in research and development ("R&D"), marketing and advertising is critical to the development and sale of innovative products and technologies."* (Apple, 2014 Form 10K)

Apple's performance evaluation system should reflect this business strategy and include measures that provide feedback to managers about how they are contributing to the company's success. In other words, it should help managers understand how the decisions they make on a daily basis will help the company achieve its strategic objectives. This is important because not all employees will see the immediate effect of their actions on the company's financial results. For example, a manager in a retail store can see the relationship between his efforts (customer service) and financial results (sales revenue), but a manager who works in research and development may not see the results of his efforts for years. The next section discusses the balanced scorecard, a performance measurement system designed to align managers' goals with the organization's strategic vision, regardless of the manager's position within the company. The balanced scorecard is designed to focus managers' attention on a broad set of performance metrics that are linked to the company's strategy.

BALANCED SCORECARD

Learning Objective 10-3
Describe the four dimensions of the balanced scorecard and explain how they are used to evaluate managerial performance.

The **balanced scorecard** is a comprehensive performance measurement system that translates an organization's strategic vision into a set of operational performance metrics. The balanced scorecard measures performance along several dimensions and includes measures that reflect past performance (called *lagging indicators*) as well as future performance (called *leading indicators*).

The basic idea of the balanced scorecard is that organizations must excel along the following dimensions to achieve the company's strategic vision:

- Financial perspective.
- Customer perspective.
- Internal business processes perspective.
- Learning and growth perspective.

Exhibit 10.3 illustrates these dimensions.

EXHIBIT 10.3 The Four Dimensions of the Balanced Scorecard

Each perspective of the balanced scorecard should include specific objectives and measures that tell managers what they need to do to contribute to the company's overall success. The measures provide feedback to managers about how they are performing and what they need to improve upon.

For the balanced scorecard to be effective, the objectives and measures included in each category should be linked so that performance on one dimension of the scorecard will eventually lead to performance in another area. For example, the learning and growth perspective typically contains leading indicators, or measures that predict *future* performance. These leading indicators should result in improved business processes and customer satisfaction, which will ultimately contribute to financial performance. As an example, consider the simplified balanced scorecard linkages for Apple shown in Exhibit 10.4.

Notice that each dimension of the balanced scorecard includes objectives (goals) and specific measures (metrics) that are used to assess whether the objectives are being met. In this hypothetical example, Apple's objectives are stated fairly generically. In reality, the balanced scorecard would include specific goals or targets for each metric that indicate whether managers are on track to achieve the stated objectives.

Apple's objective for learning and growth is to foster an environment of creativity and innovation by hiring the most passionate and talented employees and investing heavily in research and development. Some specific metrics that Apple could use to measure success on this dimension include the dollars spent on research and development (R&D), the number of new patent applications, and employee satisfaction, which could be measured by the employee turnover rate. Although most of this data is proprietary and housed in Apple's internal accounting system, the total amount of money spent on research and development is reported in Apple's external financial statements, and summarized as follows:

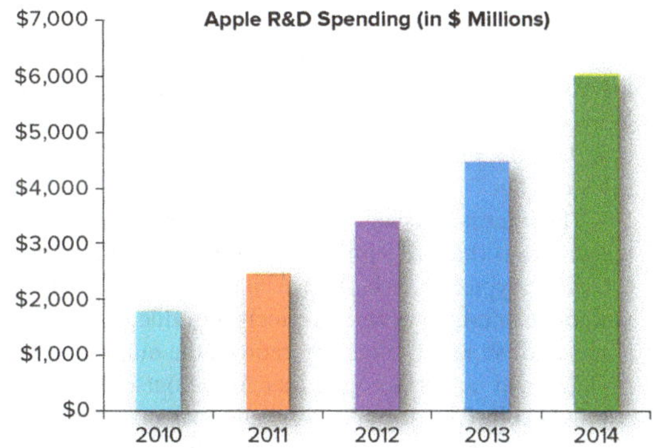

EXHIBIT 10.4 Applying the Balanced Scorecard to Apple Inc.

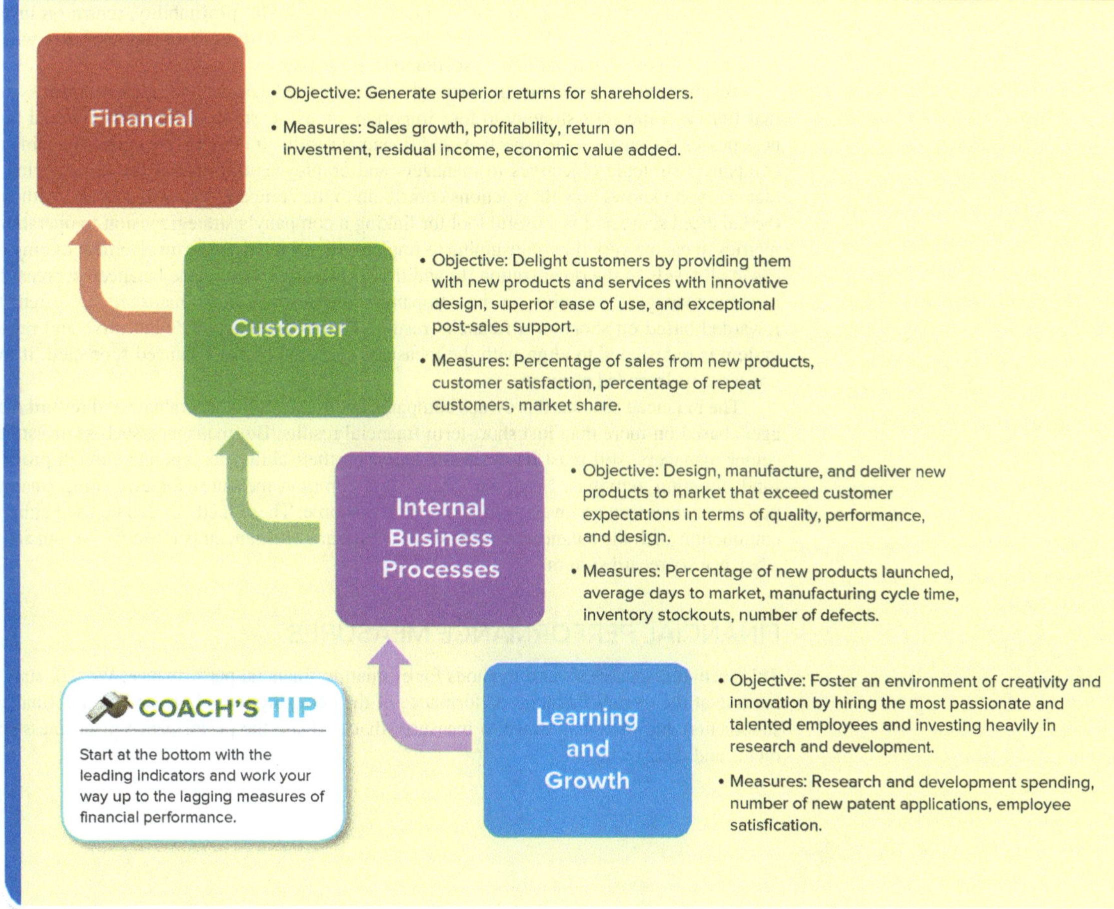

Although GAAP requires companies to expense research and development costs during the period incurred, the benefits of R&D may not show up in the financial statements for years. But if the R&D efforts are successful, they should eventually translate into increased financial performance through other metrics, such as the number of new patents awarded; the number of new products introduced; customer satisfaction; and, eventually, sales revenue.

The internal business processes perspective of the balanced scorecard focuses on all of the activities that are required to get products from the idea stage into the hands of customers. Some typical metrics that Apple might use to measure performance on this dimension include the number of new products introduced, the number of days from product launch to store shelf, supplier reliability ratings, the number of inventory stock-outs, and the number of defects. It is worth noting that Apple outsources most of its manufacturing activities to companies in China. For a company that manufactures its own products, metrics such as average manufacturing cost and manufacturing cycle time would also be included in the internal business processes perspective of the balanced scorecard.

The customer perspective provides the link between internal business processes and financial results. Potential metrics include percentage of sales from new products, customer satisfaction, percentage of repeat customers, and market share. Performance on these metrics should translate directly into financial performance.

> **COACH'S TIP**
>
> Giving employees an ownership interest in the company (e.g., stock or stock options) is another mechanism for aligning the goals of employees and owners.

Apple's financial objective is to generate superior returns for its shareholders, including Apple employees who own a sizeable portion of the company's stock. Some common metrics used to measure financial performance include sales growth, profitability, return on investment, residual income, and economic value added. Some of these financial measures will be discussed in more detail in the next section of this chapter.

To summarize, the balanced scorecard is an integrated performance measurement system that links a company's strategy to four important areas: learning and growth, internal business processes, customer perspective, and financial results. It is useful for communicating the company's strategic objectives to managers and employees throughout the organization so that everyone knows how their actions contribute to the company's overall success. Although the balanced scorecard is a useful tool for linking a company's strategic vision to operational metrics, it can be very time-consuming to implement and requires the involvement of employees at all levels of the organization. In addition, while the intent of the balanced scorecard is to focus managers' attention on the company's long-term strategy, managers are often still rewarded based on short-term financial results. Unless the company's incentive and reward system is redesigned to align with the measures captured by the balanced scorecard, it may not serve its intended purpose.

The balanced scorecard provides companies with the ability to evaluate and reward managers based on more than just short-term financial results. But managers, such as investment center managers, still must be evaluated based on their ability to generate enough profit to fund investing activities. Next, we discuss two common measures for evaluating financial performance, return on investment and residual income. These methods can be used either in conjunction with the balanced scorecard (as a measure of financial perspective) or outside of a balance scorecard system.

FINANCIAL PERFORMANCE MEASURES

This section discusses several methods for evaluating financial performance. We will start by looking at the overall financial performance of the company (based on the external financial statements) and then drill down to measures that evaluate the performance of business segments and their managers.

SPOTLIGHT ON Sustainability

Sustainability and the Balanced Scorecard

There is an old saying in business that "you can't manage what you can't measure." The flip side to this statement is that "what gets measured is what gets managed." These statements are still true today and are relevant for managers as they integrate sustainability practices into their business strategy. Without measuring sustainability performance, managers are essentially flying blind and have no way of knowing whether they are achieving their sustainability goals and what they need to do to improve.

The balanced scorecard provides a useful tool for organizations to incorporate sustainability goals and metrics into the performance evaluation system. The goal of the balanced scorecard is to include a broad set of financial and nonfinancial performance indicators that are linked to the company's long-term strategy. This approach aligns well with sustainability, which requires a long-term view that focuses managers' attention on more than just economic or financial results. While traditional accounting methods are effective for measuring economic or financial results, the balanced scorecard can be expanded to include measures that capture the environmental and societal aspects of the triple bottom line.

There are three ways that organizations can use the balanced scorecard to integrate sustainability metrics into the performance evaluation system:

1. Add one or more categories to the existing scorecard to capture sustainability goals and measures. For example, a company might add a fifth category to capture all sustainability measures. Alternatively, they could add two categories, one for environmental and another for societal metrics.
2. Create a separate sustainability balanced scorecard (SBSC) that focuses exclusively on sustainability goals and metrics. The scorecard could still include the traditional balanced scorecard categories, but it could also be expanded to include other categories such as society or community.
3. Integrate sustainability objectives and measures into the existing categories of the balanced scorecard. For example, environmental measures often align well with internal business processes, while social measures align well with the customer perspective (for customer-focused initiatives) or the learning and growth perspective (for employee-focused initiatives). Some companies also add a fifth category to capture community or social initiatives that don't fall into one of the other categories.

Although the first approach is simplest and the second signals the importance of sustainability to internal and external stakeholders, most experts agree that the best approach is to integrate sustainability measurements into the existing performance evaluation system. This is particularly important for companies that view sustainability as an integral part of their daily operations and core business strategy, as opposed to an add-on or afterthought.

Refer to Problems PA10-6 and PB10-6 for a demonstration of how the sustainability measures identified by the Global Reporting Initiative (GRI) and other sources could be incorporated into the balanced scorecard.

Return on Investment

Learning Objective 10-4
Compute and interpret return on investment, investment turnover, and profit margin.

One of the most common ways to measure financial performance is **return on investment (ROI)**. In general, ROI is computed by dividing some measure of profitability, such as net operating income, by some measure of investment, such as average invested assets. There are many variations of ROI, including return on assets (ROA), return on capital employed (ROCE), and return on equity (ROE). The difference is the value used to measure investment in the denominator of the ROI formula. For our examples, we will use the most commonly accepted definition of ROI, which calculates the return on average invested assets, as follows:

$$\text{Return on Investment (ROI)} = \frac{\text{Net Operating Income}}{\text{Average Invested Assets}}$$

A company's overall ROI can be computed from information provided in its external financial statements. Consider the following information summarizing Apple's financial results for fiscal years 2013 and 2014:

APPLE INC.
Consolidated Income Statements
(in millions)

	For the Year Ended September 27, 2014	For the Year Ended September 28, 2013
Net sales	$182,795	$170,910
Cost of sales	112,258	106,606
Gross margin	70,537	64,304
Operating expenses:		
Research and development	6,041	4,475
Selling, general, and administrative	11,993	10,830
Total operating expenses	18,034	15,305
Net operating income	52,503	48,999
Other income and expense	980	1,156
Income before provision for income taxes	53,483	50,155
Provision for income taxes	13,973	13,118
Net income	$ 39,510	$ 37,037

APPLE INC.
Consolidated Balance Sheets
(in millions)

	September 27, 2014	September 28, 2013
ASSETS:		
Total current assets	$ 68,531	$ 73,286
Long-term marketable securities	130,162	106,215
Property, plant, and equipment, net	20,624	16,597
Goodwill	4,616	1,577
Acquired intangible assets, net	4,142	4,179
Other assets	3,764	5,146
Total assets	$231,839	$207,000
LIABILITIES AND SHAREHOLDERS' EQUITY:		
Total liabilities	120,292	83,451
Total shareholders' equity	111,547	123,549
Total liabilities and shareholders' equity	$231,839	$207,000

The numerator in the ROI calculation is net operating income. This is a line item on the income statement that represents net income from normal operating activities, before "other" income, interest, and taxes. Apple's net operating income for fiscal year 2014 was $52,503 million (or $52.5 billion).

The denominator in the ROI calculation is average invested assets. Because ROI is computed over a period of time, such as a quarter or year, we need to average the value of invested assets at the beginning and end of that period. We would compute Apple's **average** investment in assets (in millions) for fiscal year 2014 as follows:

$$\text{Average Invested Assets} = \frac{\text{Beginning Total Assets} + \text{Ending Total Assets}}{2}$$

$$\text{Average Invested Assets} = \frac{\$207{,}000 + \$231{,}839}{2} = \$219{,}420$$

Based on these numbers, Apple's ROI for 2014 would be:

$$\text{Return on Investment} = \frac{\text{Net Operating Income}}{\text{Average Invested Assets}} = \frac{\$52{,}503}{\$219{,}420} = 23.9\%$$

Apple's ROI of 23.9 percent was among the best in its industry during 2014. As a point of comparison, Microsoft's ROI for fiscal year 2014 was 17.6 percent, while Samsung's ROI for the same period was 11.3 percent. At a company-wide level, this financial metric suggests that Apple was providing a high level of return for its shareholders. But we need a bit more detail to evaluate the individual managers who contributed to this overall measure of performance.

Return on investment can also be used to evaluate the performance of investment center managers, who are responsible for profitability and investing in assets for a particular segment of the business. The data needed to evaluate investment center managers is captured by the company's internal accounting system, but is not publicly available. To demonstrate how ROI can be used to evaluate investment center managers in a decentralized organization, consider the following hypothetical data for two Apple divisions: Apple retail store and Apple online store.

	Retail Store	Online Store
Sales revenue	$ 3,000,000	$ 6,000,000
Less: Operating expenses	(2,880,000)	(5,400,000)
Net operating income	$ 120,000	$ 600,000
Average invested assets	$ 2,000,000	$ 2,000,000
Return on investment	$\frac{\$120{,}000}{\$2{,}000{,}000} = 6\%$	$\frac{\$600{,}000}{\$2{,}000{,}000} = 30\%$

Notice that both divisions have the same level of investment ($2,000,000 in average invested assets). Yet the Apple retail division had an ROI of 6 percent, compared to 30 percent for the online Apple store. To gain a better understanding of the factors contributing to ROI, it is useful to break it into two separate components: **investment turnover** and **profit margin**.

$$\text{Return on Investment (ROI)} = \text{Investment Turnover} \times \text{Profit Margin}$$

$$\frac{\text{Net Operating Income}}{\text{Average Invested Assets}} = \frac{\text{Sales Revenue}}{\text{Average Invested Assets}} \times \frac{\text{Net Operating Income}}{\text{Sales Revenue}}$$

Developed by executives at DuPont in the early 1900s, this method is often referred to as the **DuPont method**. **Investment turnover** is the ratio of sales revenue to average invested assets. **Profit margin** is the ratio of net operating income to sales revenue. Notice that sales revenue is included in both ratios and when cancelled out, leaves you with the original ROI formula used here. Essentially, the DuPont formula shows that, to increase ROI, managers must either generate more sales revenue from their asset base (increase investment turnover), or increase their profit margin by reducing costs without affecting revenue.

Applying the DuPont method to Apple's two hypothetical divisions provides the following results:

	Retail Store	Online Store
Sales revenue	$3,000,000	$6,000,000
Less: Operating expenses	(2,880,000)	(5,400,000)
Net operating income	$ 120,000	$ 600,000
Investment Turnover		
Sales Revenue / Average Invested Assets	$\frac{\$3{,}000{,}000}{\$2{,}000{,}000} = 1.5$	$\frac{\$6{,}000{,}000}{\$2{,}000{,}000} = 3.0$
Profit Margin		
Net Operating Income / Sales Revenue	$\frac{\$120{,}000}{\$3{,}000{,}000} = 0.04$	$\frac{\$600{,}000}{\$6{,}000{,}000} = 0.10$
Return on Investment	1.5 × 4% = 6%	3 × 10% = 30%

COACH'S TIP

The online store generates $3.00 in sales revenue for every $1.00 of invested assets while the retail store only generates $1.50 in sales for each $1.00 of investment.

The online store reports 10 percent of every sales dollar as operating income, while the Apple retail store has a profit margin of only 4 percent.

The combined effect is a much higher return on investment for the online store than the retail store.

The relationship between investment turnover, profit margin, and return on investment is shown graphically in Exhibit 10.5.

This analysis shows that two factors are driving the difference in ROI for Apple's two segments. The first factor is the amount of sales revenue generated per dollar invested in assets. The investment turnover ratio indicates how efficiently the company uses assets to generate sales revenue. Apple's retail division generates sales equal to 1.5 times its investment base; Apple's online store generates twice that amount—3 times its investment base—from the same level of investment.

EXHIBIT 10.5 Investment Turnover, Profit Margin, and Return on Investment

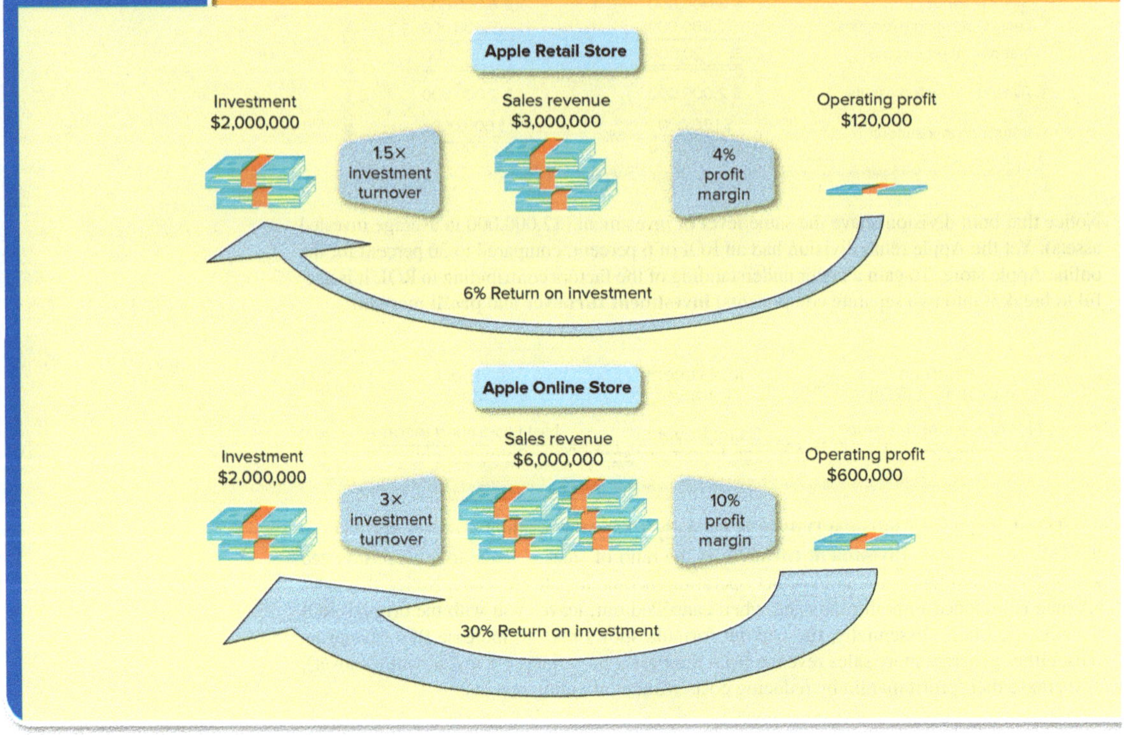

The second factor that drives the difference in ROI is profit margin. The profit margin shows how much of a segment's sales revenue remains as operating income after operating costs have been deducted. Apple's online store generates $0.10 in operating profit for every dollar of sales; Apple's retail division generates only $0.04 for every dollar of sales. This difference in profit margin is rooted in the different cost structures of the two segments. Apple's brick and mortar stores tend to have relatively high fixed costs (for rental space, utilities, and other overhead costs) compared to the online store. In sum, Apple's online store generates more sales revenue from the same level of investment **and** keeps a higher percentage of that sales revenue as operating income. The end result is that the ROI for Apple's online store (30%) is much higher than that for Apple's retail division (6%).

Next, we will discuss an alternative method of evaluating financial performance, residual income. First, to make sure you understand how to calculate ROI, profit margin, and investment turnover, complete the following Self-Study Practice.

How's it going? — Self-Study Practice

Consider the following sample data for Apple's North and South America region:

Sales revenue	$1,000,000
Operating expenses	900,000
Net operating income	100,000
Average invested assets	400,000

1. Compute the region's ROI, profit margin, and investment turnover.
2. Show how the ROI is related to profit margin and investment turnover.

After you have finished, check your answers against the solution in the margin.

Solution to Self-Study Practice

1. ROI = $100,000 ÷ $400,000 = 25%
   Profit margin = $100,000 ÷ $1,000,000 = 10%
   Investment turnover = $1,000,000 ÷ 400,000 = 2.5
2. ROI = Profit Margin × Investment Turnover
   = 10% × 2.5 = 25%

Residual Income

Learning Objective 10-5
Compute and interpret residual income.

An alternative measure for evaluating financial performance involves making a comparison between net operating income and the minimum acceptable profit based on the **required rate of return**. The required rate of return is also called the **hurdle rate**. Managers set the hurdle rate to reflect the lowest possible return they are willing to accept on a given investment. The hurdle rate will depend on a number of factors, including the risk of the investment, the cost of financing it, and the return that could be earned in other investments (e.g., opportunity cost).

Residual income is the amount of net operating income earned over and above the minimum amount needed to meet the required rate of return. It's computed as follows:

Residual Income = Net Operating Income − Minimum Acceptable Profit

Residual Income = Net Operating Income − (Average Invested Assets × Hurdle Rate)

A positive residual income means that the investment generated more than the minimum acceptable operating profit. A negative residual income means that the investment did not meet the minimum acceptable profit based on the required rate of return, or hurdle rate.

To continue our previous example, assume that Apple's hurdle rate is 10 percent. In our previous example, both divisions had an average investment in assets of $2,000,000. Thus, the minimum acceptable profit would be $200,000 ($2,000,000 × 10%). Comparing each division's net operating income to this minimum requirement results in the following residual income analysis:

COACH'S TIP

The **hurdle rate** is the minimum acceptable rate of return on investment. It is also called the *required rate of return.*

	Retail Store	Online Store
Net operating income	$ 120,000	$ 600,000
Less: Minimum acceptable profit ($2,000,000 × 10% hurdle rate)	(200,000)	(200,000)
Residual income	$ (80,000)	$ 400,000

Notice that the Apple retail store has a negative residual income of $80,000. A negative residual income occurs because the division's net operating income ($120,000) is less than the minimum required income of $200,000. The online store's residual income is $400,000. This is "extra" profit, over and above the minimum requirement of $200,000.

Residual income can also be computed by comparing each division's ROI to the hurdle rate and then multiplying by the average investment in assets, as follows:

	Retail Store	Online Store
Return on investment	6%	30%
Less: Hurdle rate	(10%)	(10%)
Residual return	(4%)	20%
Average invested assets	× $2,000,000	× $2,000,000
Residual income	$ (80,000)	$ 400,000

The retail store's ROI of 6% is less than the 10% hurdle rate. Multiplying the 4% shortfall in ROI by average invested assets of $2,000,000 results in a negative residual income of $80,000. The online store's ROI was 30%, or 20% more than the required rate of return, resulting in residual income of $400,000 (20% × $2,000,000).

Before you continue, complete the following Self-Study Practice to make sure you understand how to calculate residual income and its relationship to ROI.

How's it going? Self-Study Practice

Consider the following hypothetical data for Apple's North and South America region:

Net operating income	$100,000
Average invested assets	$400,000
Return on investment	25%

1. Using a hurdle rate of 10 percent, compute the division's residual income.
2. Explain how residual income is related to the 25 percent ROI.

After you have finished, check your answers against the solution in the margin.

Solution to Self-Study Practice

1. Residual Income = Net Operating Income − (Average Invested Assets × Hurdle Rate)
$100,000 − ($400,000 × 10%) = $60,000 Residual Income
2. The 25 percent ROI is higher than the 10 percent hurdle rate: Excess of 15% × $400,000 Average Invested Assets = $60,000 Residual Income.

Return on Investment versus Residual Income

Although ROI and residual income are directly related, ROI suffers from one major disadvantage that residual income does not. ROI can sometimes cause managers to reject an investment because it would lower the division's ROI, even though the investment might benefit the company as a whole.

To illustrate, assume that the manager of Apple's online store has an opportunity to develop a new technology that would require an up-front investment of $1,000,000. The technology would save the company $150,000 a year in operating costs. Thus, the project's expected ROI is 15 percent ($150,000 ÷ $1,000,000). Recall from previous examples that the online store has an ROI of 30 percent, and Apple's minimum required rate of return (hurdle rate) is 10 percent. Will the manager of the online store want to invest in the project? The answer to this question depends on whether the manager is evaluated based on ROI or residual income. The proposed project would generate a positive residual income because its expected return (15%) is more than the required 10 percent hurdle rate. However, the project would have a negative impact on the division's ROI because the 15 percent return is less than the current ROI of 30 percent. If the manager invests in this project, the division's ROI will drop from 30 percent to 25 percent, as shown in the following table:

	Status Quo (without project)	Effect of Proposed Project	If Project Is Accepted
Return on Investment Analysis			
Net operating income	$600,000	150,000	$750,000
Average invested assets	÷ $2,000,000	÷ $1,000,000	÷ $3,000,000
Return on investment	30%	15%	25%
Residual Income Analysis			
Net operating income	$600,000	$150,000	$750,000
Less: Minimum acceptable profit (10% of average invested assets)	(200,000)	(100,000)	(300,000)
Residual income	$400,000	$ 50,000	$450,000

COACH'S TIP

Notice that the project would have a negative effect on the online store's ROI because its rate of return is less than the current ROI of 30 percent.

The project would generate a positive residual income, however, because its return is higher than the company's required rate of return of 10 percent.

This example shows how a performance evaluation system can create **goal incongruence**, or a conflict of interest between what is best for the manager and what is best for the organization and its owners. A manager who is evaluated and rewarded based on ROI may not be willing to invest in a project that is in the best interest of the company if doing so will have a negative impact on the manager's own performance evaluation. The residual income method helps to align the manager's goals with the organization's objective of earning a minimum ROI of 10 percent. Regardless of the division's current ROI, its residual income will increase as long as the manager invests only in projects that exceed the company's minimum required return.

Economic Value Added

Economic value added (EVA™) is a metric developed by Stern, Stewart and Co. to measure the economic wealth that is created when a company's after-tax net operating income exceeds its **cost of capital**. From a simple calculation perspective, EVA is very similar to the residual income computation. However, EVA makes a number of important adjustments, which are summarized as follows:

- Measures profitability based on **after-tax net operating income** rather than pretax net operating income. Many managerial decisions have important tax ramifications and so performance should be measured on an after-tax basis.
- Uses the **cost of capital** as the hurdle rate. Conceptually, the cost of capital represents the after-tax cost of financing the company's operations through some combination of debt and equity. The cost of capital is described in more detail in the next chapter.
- Uses **total capital employed** as the measure of investment rather than average invested assets. The reason is that accounting rules (GAAP) only allow certain types of investments to be capitalized or treated as assets. Using total capital employed allows companies like Apple to capitalize other important investments, such as research and development, brand equity, and a highly trained or creative workforce (human capital).

EVA provides a measure of whether the company is generating sufficient after-tax income to cover the cost of capital. While the detailed calculations of EVA are beyond the scope of this textbook, you should understand how it relates to residual income and what it tells managers about the company's financial performance. If EVA is positive, the company is creating economic wealth by generating profits in excess of its cost of capital. If EVA is negative, the company is not generating enough after-tax profit to cover its cost of capital, which reduces the company's overall economic value.

LIMITATIONS OF FINANCIAL PERFORMANCE MEASURES

In this section, we discussed several measures that can be used to measure financial performance, including return on investment (ROI), residual income, and economic value added (EVA). While each method provides a different view of the company's financial performance, it is important to note that they are all lagging measures of performance. In other words, they tell you how a particular part of the business did in the past, but not necessarily how it will do in the future. As previously discussed, a performance evaluation system should be designed to focus manager's attention on more than just the bottom line. If managers are evaluated and rewarded based entirely on financial results, they may not make decisions that are in the best interest of the organization in the long-run.

As we have seen, performance evaluation systems that encourage alignment between managers' goals and the organization's goals create an environment in which managers are more likely to make decisions that are consistent with the organization's objectives rather than their own self-interest. A performance evaluation system can also impact managers' willingness to cooperate with other divisions to achieve the larger company's objectives, as we will see in the next section on transfer pricing.

Transfer Pricing

Learning Objective 10-6
Explain how transfer prices are set in decentralized organizations.

The final issue we consider in this chapter is how decentralized organizations deal with the transfer or sale of goods and services between divisions. A **transfer price** is the amount that one division charges when it sells goods or services to another division of the same company. Transfers happen quite often in today's business environment because many large corporations are composed of several relatively independent business units that are owned by the same parent company. Business transactions between units or divisions of the same company are called **related-party transactions**.

Perhaps the easiest way to think about transfer prices is in terms of the deal you would get if you bought something from a relative. Maybe you want to buy a car from your brother-in-law, a meal at your cousin's restaurant, or a cut and style at your sister's hair salon. How much would you expect to pay for a product or service when buying from a relative? Exhibit 10.6 illustrates the range of potential transfer prices for this type of related-party transaction.

At a minimum, you should be willing to pay for any variable costs that your relative incurs. For example, if your brother, an auto mechanic, agrees to repair your car, you should at least be willing to pay for the parts. The minimum transfer price is called the *floor*.

EXHIBIT 10.6 Range of Potential Transfer Prices

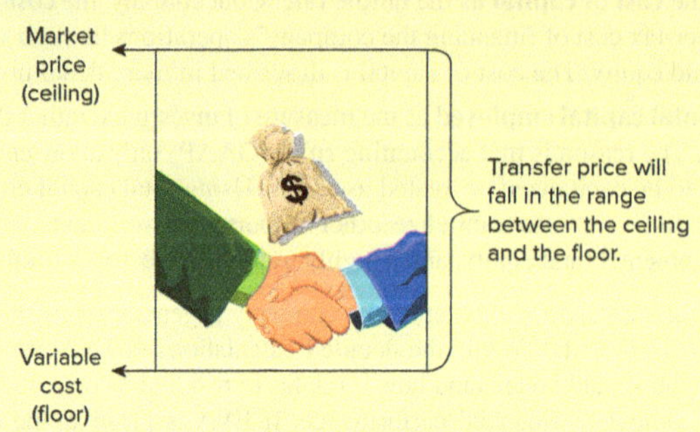

COACH'S TIP
In transfer pricing, the seller would like to charge the full market price, while the buyer would prefer to pay only variable costs. Managers often negotiate to a "fair" price somewhere in between.

The maximum amount you should be willing to pay (the *ceiling)* is the going market rate for the product or service. In other words, you should not have to pay more for the product or service than you would if you bought it elsewhere or for the amount that a complete stranger would pay.

The same rules apply to transfer prices in decentralized organizations. The only difference is that the managers of decentralized business units are not necessarily friendly relatives. As in the famous line from the film *The Godfather,* "It's not personal; it's just business."

If business managers are evaluated based on their ability to control costs and/or generate revenue, their goals may be diametrically opposed, even if they do work in the same company. Although the transfer price does not really matter from the overall company's perspective,[2] it can make a big difference to each individual manager's performance evaluation.

Consider the following estimated cost and price information for the Apple iPad Air 2. According to iSupply, a company that breaks down popular consumer products to determine their component cost, the total bill of materials (BOM) or component cost of an iPad Air 2 (16 GB) without cellular is about $270. When estimated assembly costs of $5 are added in, it brings the total manufacturing cost to $275 per unit. This is the cost of the device itself, excluding shipping, marketing, general and administrative, and research and development expenses. For this example, we assume that the retail price of the Apple iPad Air 2 is $499 and that the wholesale price, or price paid by retailers such as Best Buy and Walmart, is $399. These costs and prices are summarized as follows:

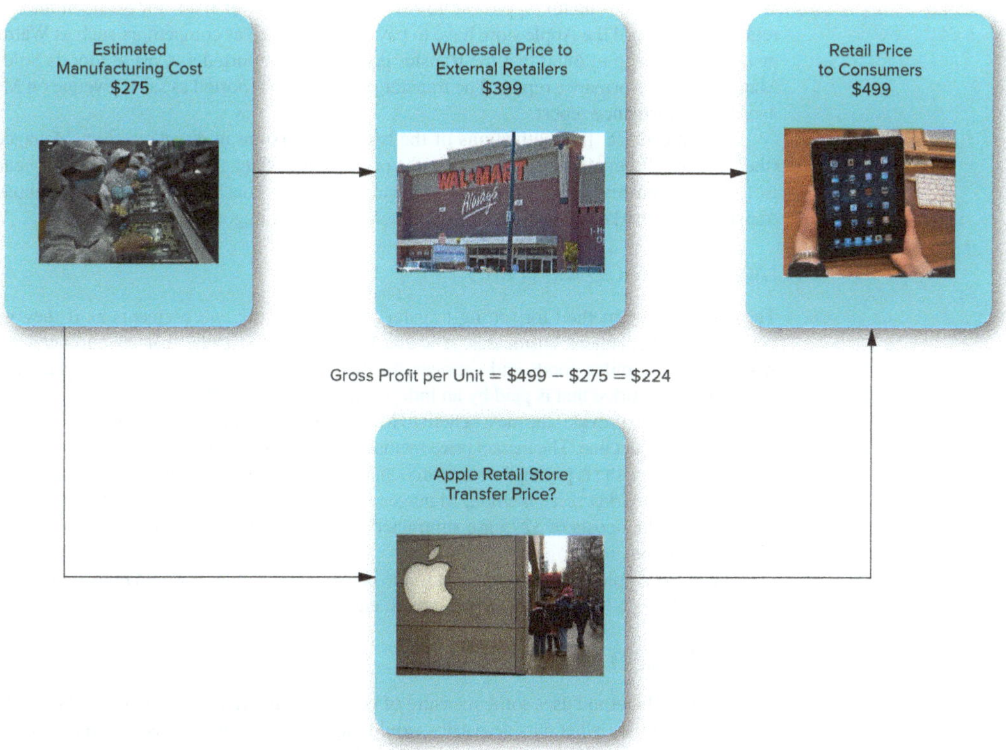

Left: © STR/AFP/GettyImages; Middle: © John Flournoy/McGraw-Hill Education; Right: © Mark Dierker/McGraw-Hill Education; Bottom: © Christopher Kerrigan/McGraw-Hill Education

[2] Transfer prices **can** have a major impact on multinational companies due to variations in tax rates from one country to the next. The tax implications of transfer prices are extremely complex and must be considered as part of the tax planning process.

The difference between the retail price of $499 and the manufacturing cost of $275 is gross profit per unit of $224. Remember that gross profit excludes nonmanufacturing expenses, such as shipping, marketing, general and administrative, and research and development expenses.

If the device is sold through an outside party like Walmart, the gross profit of $224 will be shared between Apple and Walmart. If Walmart pays the wholesale price of $399, Apple's share of the gross profit is $124 per unit ($399 wholesale price − $275 manufacturing cost). If Walmart sells the device to consumers for $499, its share of the gross profit would be $100 per unit ($499 retail price − $399 wholesale cost).

But what if the device is sold through an Apple store? If it bypasses the "middleman," Apple can keep the entire $224 in gross profit. The internal transfer price will simply determine how the revenues and costs are split between the buying and selling divisions and their managers.

To illustrate how transfer pricing affects managers in decentralized organizations, consider the following managers of two hypothetical Apple responsibility centers:

> Manager A: Responsible for the profitability of an Apple retail store. Evaluated and rewarded based on net operating income (sales revenue − operating costs). A major component of operating costs is the cost of merchandise sold.
>
> Manager B: Responsible for selling iPads to Apple stores and other retailers, such as Best Buy and Walmart. Evaluated and rewarded based on the total sales revenue earned within a territory, including sales to the Apple store operated by Manager A.

What transfer price should Apple use to record the purchase of iPads for resale at an Apple retail store? Should the Apple store have to pay the same price as competitors such as Walmart or Best Buy? Keep in mind that the transfer price will be reported as Cost of Goods Sold on Manager A's performance report. The transfer price will be reported as sales revenue on Manager B's performance report.

As you can see, the motivations of the two managers are in direct conflict. Manager A (the buyer) will benefit from a low transfer price, while Manager B (the seller) will benefit from a high transfer price. Apple can take one of three approaches to determine the internal transfer price: market-price method, cost-based method, or negotiation.

MARKET-PRICE METHOD

The market-price method for setting transfer prices treats the two segments as if they were completely independent businesses. The market price is the price that an unrelated party would pay for similar goods and services. In this example, the relevant market price is the $399 wholesale price that is paid by an independent retailer like Walmart.

This scenario provides the most benefit to Manager B (the seller) because it maximizes the revenue for his product line. The market price method does little to benefit the Apple retail store manager because he or she is paying the same amount that competitors are paying for the same product.

Under the market price method, Manager A would report sales revenue of $399 per unit. When the product costs of $275 are subtracted, it leaves $124 per unit in gross profit for the iPad product line.

When the Apple store sells the unit to the consumer for $499, it would report gross profit of $100 ($499 − $399), the same gross profit earned by external retailers.

COST-BASED METHOD

The cost-based method uses some measure of cost to set the transfer price. Instead of looking to the market to see what outside parties would pay for the product or service, the cost-based method looks internally to determine how much it costs to produce the product or provide the service. The transfer price could be based on variable cost, full cost, or cost plus some percentage mark-up.

In this example, the minimum transfer price is the variable cost of the device ($275). Remember that this does not include selling, marketing, administrative overhead, or research and development costs. The buyer would also be expected to pay any additional variable selling costs such as shipping expenses.

This minimum transfer price provides the most benefit to the buyer (Manager A) because it results in the lowest cost and highest gross profit for Manager A. The Apple store would report gross profit of \$224 per unit (\$499 − \$275). The seller would report sales revenue of \$275, just enough to cover the cost of the device itself, leaving zero gross profit.

Many companies have a cost-plus transfer pricing policy. For example, Apple could have a policy that dictates that all internal transfers will be recorded at cost plus 25 percent. If so, the transfer price would be set at 125 percent of the \$275 device cost, or approximately \$344 (\$275 × 125%). Manager B would report sales revenue of \$344 and gross profit of \$69 (\$344 − \$275). When the product is sold to the end user, the Apple store manager would report gross profit of \$155 (\$499 − \$344).

Notice that, in all of these scenarios, the total gross profit reported by the two divisions is \$224 per unit. The transfer price just determines how this profit is split between the two divisions. This is only important if the managers of the divisions are evaluated based on their ability to control cost, generate revenue, or create profit. If they are evaluated based on other measures, such as customer satisfaction or total firm value (e.g., economic value added), the internal transfer price is less critical.

NEGOTIATION

A final option is to let division managers negotiate transfer prices. In this method, the negotiated price should fall somewhere between the minimum transfer price (floor), or variable cost (\$275), and the ceiling, or wholesale price to the retailer (\$399). As in any negotiation, the price will depend on the relative power of the buyer and seller, their negotiation skills, and how much inside information each party has about the other division's cost, capacity, and demand.

In this particular example, the manager of the Apple retail store probably does not have a lot of power to negotiate because it is a "captive customer." The store only sells Apple products, which means the manager is not able to negotiate based on the price of competing products. As such, the negotiated transfer price is probably going to be very close to the wholesale market price of \$399.

Another issue that affects negotiation is the capacity of the selling division. If the selling division has excess capacity (extra units available for sale), the sales manager is more likely to accept a lower transfer price, because some revenue is better than no revenue. However, if the selling division has limited capacity (more demand than supply), the manager will be not be willing to sell for much below the market price.

Because the parent company (Apple) earns more profit when its products are sold through Apple stores (online or retail) rather than through a third party, the company must carefully design its performance evaluation system to encourage managers to work together to achieve company goals.

To make sure you understand the different ways to set transfer prices in decentralized organizations, complete the following Self-Study Practice.

How's it going? Self-Study Practice

Kraft Foods owns both Tombstone Pizza and Kraft Cheese. Assume that Tombstone Pizza (the buyer) has approached Kraft Cheese (the seller) to ask for a special deal on the cheese used to produce Tombstone's frozen pizza.

Which of the following statements is true?

1. The minimum price the seller should accept is the variable cost of producing and selling the cheese.
2. The maximum price the buyer should pay is the market price.
3. Both statements above are true.
4. None of these statements is true.

After you have finished, check your answers against the solution in the margin.

Solution to Self-Study Practice
Statements 1, 2, and 3 are true.

REVIEW THE CHAPTER

DEMONSTRATION CASE

Consider the following data for two divisions of Peter Piper Pizza:

	Northwest Region	Southwest Region
Average invested assets	$ 6,000,000	$ 6,000,000
Sales revenue	$ 18,000,000	$ 9,000,000
Less: Operating expenses	(17,460,000)	(8,100,000)
Net operating income	$ 540,000	$ 900,000

Required:

1. Compute the investment turnover, profit margin, return on investment, and residual income for each division. Assume a 10 percent hurdle rate.
2. Explain the relationship between each division's residual income and its return on investment.
3. The manager of the Southwest Region has the opportunity to invest an additional $2,000,000 in a project expected to generate additional operating income of $220,000 per year. Calculate Southwest's new return on investment and residual income if the manager accepts the project.
4. Would Southwest's manager, who is evaluated based on the region's ROI, want to invest in the project? What if the manager were evaluated based on residual income? Why or why not?

Suggested Solution

1.

	Northwest Region	Southwest Region
Investment Turnover $= \frac{\text{Sales Revenue}}{\text{Average Invested Assets}}$	$\frac{\$18{,}000{,}000}{\$6{,}000{,}000} = 3$	$\frac{\$9{,}000{,}000}{\$6{,}000{,}000} = 1.50$
Profit Margin $= \frac{\text{Net Operating Income}}{\text{Sales Revenue}}$	$\frac{\$540{,}000}{\$18{,}000{,}000} = 3\%$	$\frac{\$900{,}000}{\$9{,}000{,}000} = 10\%$
Return on Investment $= \frac{\text{Net Operating Income}}{\text{Average Invested Assets}}$	$\frac{\$540{,}000}{\$6{,}000{,}000} = 9\%$	$\frac{\$900{,}000}{\$6{,}000{,}000} = 15\%$
Net operating income	$ 540,000	$ 900,000
Minimum acceptable profit (10% × average invested assets)	(600,000)	(600,000)
Residual income	$ (60,000)	$ 300,000

2. The Northwest Region has a negative residual income because its return on investment, which is 9 percent, is less than the 10 percent hurdle rate [1 percent of $6,000,000 = $(60,000)].
   The Southwest Region has a positive residual income because its return on investment, which is 15 percent, is higher than the 10 percent hurdle rate (5 percent of $6,000,000 = $300,000).

3.

	Southwest Region (before project)	Proposed Project	Southwest Region (if project is accepted)
Return on Investment Analysis			
$\frac{\text{Net Operating Income}}{\text{Average Invested Assets}}$ = Return on Investment	$\frac{\$900{,}000}{\$6{,}000{,}000} = 15\%$	$\frac{\$220{,}000}{\$2{,}000{,}000} = 11\%$	$\frac{\$1{,}120{,}000}{\$8{,}000{,}000} = 14\%$
Residual Income Analysis			
Net operating income	$ 900,000	$ 220,000	$1,120,000
Minimum acceptable profit (10% of average invested assets)	(600,000)	(200,000)	(800,000)
Residual income	$ 300,000	$ 20,000	$ 320,000

4. If the manager's evaluation is based on return on investment (ROI), Southwest's regional manager probably would **not** want to invest in the project because it would lower the division's ROI. The project's expected ROI of 11 percent is less than the division's current ROI of 15 percent. Thus, investing the extra $2,000,000 would lower the region's ROI to 14 percent.

   However, if the manager's evaluation is based on the region's residual income, the manager **would** want to invest in the project because it would increase the region's residual income. Residual income will increase as long as the project's return (11 percent) is higher than the minimum required rate of return (10 percent).

CHAPTER SUMMARY

List and explain the advantages and disadvantages of decentralization. p. 423 LO 10-1

- Decentralization means delegating decision-making authority to managers at all levels of the organization.
- The advantages of decentralization include the ability to make decisions more quickly based on local information, the development of managerial expertise, and the increased opportunity for upper management to focus on strategic issues.
- The disadvantages of decentralization include the potential for duplicating resources and for making suboptimal decisions (those that are not made in the best interests of the organization as a whole).

Describe the different types of responsibility centers and explain how managers in each type are evaluated. p. 425 LO 10-2

- **Cost center:** Managers are responsible for controlling costs within their area of responsibility, such as distribution, advertising, accounting, or human resources. Cost center managers are evaluated based on their ability to control costs while providing the necessary support to the organization.
- **Revenue center:** Managers are responsible for generating sales revenue within their area of responsibility, such as a store, a district, or a region. They are evaluated based on their ability to meet sales quotas and other measures of success like customer retention.
- **Profit center:** Managers are responsible for earning a profit within their area of responsibility through both revenue generation and cost control. They are typically evaluated based on a profitability measure such as segment margin, which includes only those costs that are within the segment manager's direct control.
- **Investment center:** Managers are responsible for both profit and the investment of assets. They are evaluated based on measures that include both profit and investment, such as return on investment, residual income, or economic value added.

Describe the four dimensions of the balanced scorecard and explain how they are used to evaluate managerial performance. p. 429 LO 10-3

- The balanced scorecard is a comprehensive performance measurement system that translates the organization's vision and strategy into a set of operational performance measures.
- The balanced scorecard measures operational performance on four key dimensions: customer perspective, learning and growth perspective, internal business processes perspective, and financial perspective.
- The customer perspective focuses on customers' perception of the company through measures such as customer retention, customer satisfaction, and market share.
- The learning and growth perspective focuses on the organization's ability to change and improve through measures such as the amount of money spent on research and development and employee education and training.
- The internal business processes perspective focuses on the internal processes required to meet customer needs through measures such as on-time-delivery, quality, inventory stockouts, and process efficiency.

- The financial perspective focuses on traditional financial measures of performance, such as return on investment, residual income, and economic value added.

LO 10-4 **Compute and interpret return on investment, investment turnover, and profit margin. p. 433**

- Return on investment (ROI) is the most common measure for evaluating financial performance.
- ROI is computed by dividing net operating income by average invested assets.
- The DuPont formula shows that ROI equals the profit margin multiplied by the investment turnover ratio.
- Profit margin is the amount of profit generated for every dollar of sales revenue.
- Investment turnover is the amount of sales revenue generated for every dollar of invested assets.
- Companies can increase ROI either by increasing the profit margin (reducing costs without reducing sales) or by increasing the asset turnover rate (increasing sales without increasing assets).

LO 10-5 **Compute and interpret residual income. p. 437**

- Residual income equals the difference between an investment center's net operating income and the minimum profit it must make to cover its hurdle rate (that is, the minimum rate of return on its assets).
- Managers can earn residual income by investing in projects that earn more than the required rate of return (or hurdle rate).
- Economic value added is similar to residual income, but focuses on how much economic wealth the company generates over and above its cost of capital.

LO 10-6 **Explain how transfer prices are set in decentralized organizations. p. 440**

- A transfer price is the price charged when one unit or division of a company sells goods or services to another unit or division of the same company.
- The maximum transfer price (*ceiling*) is the external market price, or the amount that would be charged to an unrelated party.
- The minimum transfer price (*floor*) is the variable cost (to the seller) of producing the product.
- The market-price method is based on the price that an unrelated party would pay for the product or service.
- Cost-based transfer prices can be set based on variable cost, full cost, or cost plus some percentage markup.
- Transfer prices can also be set through negotiation between the buying and selling divisions.

KEY TERMS

Balanced Scorecard p. 429
Centralized Organization p. 423
Controllability Principle p. 425
Cost Center p. 425
Decentralized Organization p. 423
DuPont Method p. 435
Economic Value Added p. 439
Goal Incongruence p. 439
Hurdle Rate p. 437
Investment Center p. 425
Investment Turnover p. 435
Profit Center p. 425
Profit Margin p. 435
Related-Party Transactions p. 440
Required Rate of Return p. 437
Residual Income p. 437
Responsibility Accounting p. 425
Responsibility Center p. 425
Return on Investment p. 433
Revenue Center p. 425
Transfer Price p. 440

See complete definitions in the glossary in the back of this text.

PRACTICE MATERIAL

QUESTIONS

1. Explain how centralized and decentralized companies differ. What are the advantages and disadvantages of each?
2. Why does decentralization create the need for responsibility accounting in an organization?
3. What is the controllability principle and why is it crucial to responsibility accounting?
4. Name the four types of responsibility centers and describe the managers' responsibilities and authority in each.
5. Briefly explain the difference between segment margin and net operating income.
6. Why are profit center managers evaluated on segment margin instead of net operating income?
7. How do investment center managers differ from profit center managers?
8. What role do return on investment and residual income play in responsibility accounting?
9. Return on investment may be separated into two components. Name them and describe what each can tell you.
10. Explain how relying on return on investment for performance evaluation of investment center managers could lead to goal incongruence.
11. How is residual income calculated?
12. What benefit does residual income offer in comparison to return on investment when evaluating performance?
13. How does EVA differ from residual income?
14. What are the primary limitations of financial measures of performance?
15. Other than the one(s) mentioned in the text, give an example of an action that management might take to improve financial performance in the short run that could prove detrimental in the long run.
16. Explain the balanced scorecard approach to performance evaluation. What advantages does this approach have over using only financial measurements?
17. What are the four dimensions of a balanced scorecard? What does each dimension represent?
18. Why must a company consider its incentive and reward system when implementing a balanced scorecard approach?
19. Why are incentive systems that emphasize long-term performance more consistent with a balanced scorecard approach?
20. What is a transfer price?
21. Explain why two managers employed by the same company may be diametrically opposed to each other when considering a transfer price.
22. Explain the meaning of minimum and maximum transfer prices and identify who (the buyer or the seller) would determine each.
23. What is the market-price method of transfer pricing?
24. How does excess capacity affect a transfer price?
25. Describe the cost-based method of transfer pricing.
26. What are negotiated transfer prices? Explain two possible disadvantages of allowing managers to negotiate a transfer price.

MULTIPLE CHOICE

1. Sally Thorne is a profit center manager for ABC Company's Phoenix district. Last year, her performance evaluation was based on the operating performance of ABC's entire Southwest region. This is a violation of
   - **a.** The hurdle rate principle.
   - **b.** The controllability principle.
   - **c.** The balanced scorecard approach.
   - **d.** Negotiated transfer pricing rules.
2. Responsibility centers include
   - **a.** Cost centers.
   - **b.** Profit centers.
   - **c.** Investment centers.
   - **d.** All of these.
3. Which of the following statements is true?
   - **a.** A profit center manager is responsible for investing company assets.
   - **b.** A cost center manager should be evaluated based on sales revenue.
   - **c.** A profit center manager should be evaluated based on return on investment.
   - **d.** An investment center manager is responsible for costs, revenue, and the investment of assets.
4. Which of the following is most likely to be classified as a cost center manager?
   - **a.** Accounting manager.
   - **b.** Sales manager.
   - **c.** Regional manager.
   - **d.** All of these are cost center managers.
5. Return on investment and residual income are useful for evaluating
   - **a.** Cost center managers.
   - **b.** Revenue center managers.
   - **c.** Profit center managers.
   - **d.** Investment center managers.

6. EVA is a variation of:
   a. Residual income
   b. Return on investment
   c. The DuPont method
   d. All of the above.
7. Raymond Calvin is an investment center manager for XYZ Corp. and is evaluated solely on the return on investment for his division. Which of the following will improve Raymond's evaluation?
   a. Increasing the amount invested in assets while keeping operating income the same.
   b. Increasing the amount of operating income while keeping invested assets the same.
   c. Decreasing the amount invested in assets while keeping operating income the same.
   d. Either b or c.
8. Which of the following statements is true?
   a. Return on investment considers a company's hurdle rate for investments.
   b. Residual income considers a company's hurdle rate for investments.
   c. Projects may be rejected based on return on investment even though they produce positive residual income.
   d. Both b and c.
9. Which of the following is not a component of the balanced scorecard method of measuring performance?
   a. Customer perspective.
   b. Management perspective.
   c. Learning and growth perspective.
   d. Internal business processes perspective.
10. Transfer price could be based on:
   a. Variable costs.
   b. Full cost.
   c. Market price.
   d. Any of the above.

Answers to Multiple-Choice Questions located in back of the text.

MINI-EXERCISES

connect

LO 10-1, 10-2, 10-3, 10-4, 10-5, 10-6

M10-1 Using Terms to Complete Sentences about Decentralized Performance Evaluation

Use the following terms to complete the sentences that follow; terms may be used once, more than once, or not at all:

Congruence	Increase
Controllability principle	Internal business
Customer	Investment
Decentralization	Learning and growth
Decrease	Profit
Economic value added (EVA)	Residual income (RI)
External market price	Responsibility accounting
Financial	Return on investment (ROI)
Full cost	Sales revenue
Incongruence	Transfer pricing

1. Managers of a(n) _____ center are evaluated based on measures such as ROI and residual income.
2. Suboptimal decisions and duplication of resources are considered disadvantages of _____.
3. A positive _____ results when managers invest in projects that earn more than the hurdle rate.
4. The _____ perspective focuses on processes required to meet customer needs through measures such as on-time delivery and quality.
5. The _____ states that managers should be held responsible only for what they can control.
6. _____ measures the economic wealth that is created when a company's after-tax operating income exceeds its cost of capital.
7. The _____ perspective typically contains leading indicators, which are measures that reflect future performance.
8. A change in the investment turnover ratio from 1.5 to 3.2 will _____ the division's ROI.
9. The maximum transfer price is the _____.
10. Goal _____ results when there is conflict between a manager and the organization as a whole.

M10-2 Describing Difference in Centralized and Decentralized Organizations LO 10-1

Lupe Bornes recently graduated from college and received job offers in management from two different companies. The positions are similar in terms of title, salary, and benefits, but the companies vary in organizational structure. Alpha Company is centralized while Beta Company is decentralized. Explain to Lupe what he can infer about each company and how it is likely to affect his position within each one.

M10-3 Describing Structure of Real-World Organizations Responsibility Centers LO 10-2

Responsibility centers can be created in a variety of ways. Give a real-world example of a company whose responsibility centers would likely be created on the basis of each of the following: functional area, product line, and geographic area.

M10-4 Applying Balanced Scorecard to Real-World Company LO 10-3

Consider the manager of your local Applebee's restaurant. Using a balanced scorecard approach, identify three measures for each of the four dimensions of the balanced scorecard.

M10-5 Applying Balanced Scorecard to Online Company LO 10-3

Choose a company that has an online sales segment; it can be a company that operates entirely online or a brick-and-mortar store with an online site. Assuming a balanced scorecard approach, identify five specific measures that the company could use to measure performance from the customer perspective. For each measure identified, indicate how that information would be obtained.

M10-6 Calculating Return on Investment, Residual Income LO 10-4, 10-5

Violet Company has sales of $520,000, net operating income of $310,000, average invested assets of $940,000, and a hurdle rate of 10 percent. Calculate Violet's return on investment and its residual income.

M10-7 Calculating Return on Investment, Residual Income LO 10-4, 10-5

Myrtle Company has sales of $140,000, cost of goods sold of $70,000, operating expenses of $20,000, average invested assets of $400,000, and a hurdle rate of 6 percent. Calculate Myrtle's return on investment and its residual income.

M10-8 Calculating Return on Investment, Residual Income LO 10-4, 10-5

Augusta Corp's Golf Division has sales of $200,000, cost of goods sold of $105,000, operating expenses of $35,000, average invested assets of $900,000, and a hurdle rate of 12 percent. Calculate the Golf Division's return on investment and its residual income.

M10-9 Impact of New Investment on ROI, Residual Income LO 10-4, 10-5

The Western Division of Claremont Company had net operating income of $135,000 and average invested assets of $560,000. Claremont has a required rate of return of 15 percent. Western has an opportunity to increase operating income by $12,000 with a $108,000 investment in assets. Compute Western Division's return on investment and residual income currently and if it undertakes the project.

M10-10 Describing Transfer Pricing Implications LO 10-2, 10-6

Assume that your cousin Matilda Flores manages a local glass shop that was recently bought by a company that produces custom picture frames. As a result, Matilda will soon be providing glass to the Frame Division. She has heard upper management mention a transfer price but does not understand what this term means or how it might affect her division. Briefly explain transfer pricing to Matilda and how it will impact her division's performance in the future.

M10-11 Identifying Minimum, Maximum Transfer Prices LO 10-6

Peppertree Company has two divisions, East and West. Division East manufactures a component that Division West uses. The variable cost to produce this component is $2.00 per unit; full cost is $2.75. The component sells on the open market for $3.10. Assuming Division East has excess capacity, what is the lowest price Division East will accept for the component? What is the highest price that Division West will pay for it?

M10-12 Calculating Cost-Plus Transfer Price LO 10-6

Medlock Company has two divisions, Wheel and Chassis. The Wheel Dvision manufactures a wheel assembly that the Chassis Division uses. The variable cost to produce this assembly is $4.00 per unit; full cost is $5.00. The component sells on the open market for $9.00. What will the transfer price be if Medlock uses a pricing rule of variable cost plus 60 percent?

LO 10-6 **M10-13 Negotiating Transfer Prices**

Tuckey Company is considering allowing the managers of its two divisions to negotiate a transfer price for the component that Division A manufactures and sells to Division B. Identify the range of possible transfer prices that could result from the negotiation. Briefly describe benefits and possible negative consequences of allowing the managers to negotiate a transfer price.

EXERCISES

connect

LO 10-1, 10-2, 10-3 **E10-1 Explaining Relationships among Decentralization, Responsibility Accounting, Controllability, Balanced Scorecard**

Assume you are the vice president of operations for a local company. Your company is in the process of converting from a small, centralized organization in which its president makes all decisions to a larger, geographically dispersed one with decentralized decision-making authority.

Required:

Write a brief memo to other company managers explaining how decentralization, responsibility accounting, controllability, and the balanced scorecard method of performance evaluation are all related. Include the most obvious changes the managers are likely to see as this transition takes place and how it will impact their performance evaluations in the future.

LO 10-2 **E10-2 Identifying Responsibility Center Types**

Match the most likely type of responsibility center classification to each of the following positions. You may use a classification once, more than once, or not at all.

Employment Positions	Possible Responsibility Center Classification
_____ Sales manager	a. Cost center
_____ Regional manager	b. Revenue center
_____ Company president	c. Profit center
_____ Purchasing manager	d. Investment center
_____ Human resources manager	
_____ Chief financial officer	
_____ Production facility manager	

LO 10-4 **E10-3 Finding Unknowns Using Return on Investment, Profit Margin, Investment Turnover**

Fleetwood Company recently had a computer malfunction and lost a portion of its accounting records. The company has reconstructed some of its financial performance measurements, including components of the return on investment calculations.

Required:

Help Fleetwood rebuild its information database by completing the following table:

Return on Investment	Profit Margin	Investment Turnover
?	5%	1.9
18%	?	2.0
3%	5%	?
23%	?	1.5

LO 10-4 **E10-4 Finding Unknowns Using Return on Investment, Profit Margin, Investment Turnover**

Krall Company recently had a computer malfunction and lost a portion of its accounting records. The company has reconstructed some of its financial performance measurements including components of the return on investment calculations.

Required:

Help Krall rebuild its information database by completing the following table:

Return on Investment	Profit Margin	Investment Turnover	Operating Income	Sales Revenue	Average Invested Assets
?	?	?	$ 70,000	$ 700,000	$1,400,000
?	8%	0.50	100,000	?	2,500,000
?	12%	1.25	?	1,400,000	?
10%	?	2.00	?	600,000	?

E10-5 Calculating Return on Investment, Residual Income, Determining Effect of Changes in Sales, Expenses, Invested Assets, Hurdle Rate on Each LO 10-4, 10-5

Solano Company has sales of $500,000, cost of goods sold of $370,000, other operating expenses of $50,000, average invested assets of $1,600,000, and a hurdle rate of 6 percent.

Required:

1. Determine Solano's return on investment (ROI), investment turnover, profit margin, and residual income.
2. Several possible changes that Solano could face in the upcoming year follow. Determine each scenario's impact on Solano's ROI and residual income. (**Note:** Treat each scenario independently.)
   a. Company sales and cost of goods sold increase by 30 percent.
   b. Operating expenses decrease by $10,000.
   c. Operating expenses increase by 20 percent.
   d. Average invested assets increase by $300,000.
   e. Solano changes its hurdle rate to 12 percent.

E10-6 Calculating Return on Investment, Residual Income, Determining Effect of Changes in Sales, Expenses, Invested Assets, Hurdle Rate on Each LO 10-4, 10-5

Kaler Company has sales of $1,210,000, cost of goods sold of $735,000, other operating expenses of $148,000, average invested assets of $3,400,000, and a hurdle rate of 12 percent.

Required:

1. Determine Kaler's return on investment (ROI), investment turnover, profit margin, and residual income.
2. Several possible changes that Kaler could face in the upcoming year follow. Determine each scenario's impact on Kaler's ROI and residual income. (**Note:** Treat each scenario independently.)
   a. Company sales and cost of goods sold increase by 15 percent.
   b. Operating expenses increase by $73,000.
   c. Operating expenses decrease by 10 percent.
   d. Average invested assets decrease by $285,000.
   e. Kaler changes its hurdle rate to 9 percent.

E10-7 Evaluating Managerial Performance Using Return on Investment, Residual Income LO 10-4, 10-5

Orange Corp. has two divisions: Fruit and Flower. The following information for the past year is available for each division:

	Fruit Division	Flower Division
Sales revenue	$ 600,000	$ 900,000
Cost of goods sold and operating expenses	450,000	600,000
Net operating income	$ 150,000	$ 300,000
Average invested assets	$1,200,000	$1,600,000

Orange has established a hurdle rate of 12 percent.

Required:

1. Compute each division's return on investment (ROI) and residual income for last year. Determine which manager seems to be performing better.
2. Suppose Orange is investing in new technology that will increase each division's operating income by $144,000. The total investment required is $1,600,000, which will be split evenly between the two divisions. Calculate the ROI and return on investment for each division after the investment is made.
3. Determine whether both managers will support the investment. Explain how their support will differ depending on which performance measure (ROI or residual investment) is used.

LO 10-4, 10-5

E10-8 Evaluating Managerial Performance Using Return on Investment, Residual Income

Luke Company has three divisions: Peak, View, and Grand. The company has a hurdle rate of 6 percent. Selected operating data for the three divisions follow:

	Peak	View	Grand
Sales revenue	$ 325,000	$220,000	$ 298,000
Cost of goods sold	216,000	123,000	202,000
Miscellaneous operating expenses	45,000	36,000	39,000
Average invested assets	1,100,000	990,000	1,000,000

Required:

1. Compute the return on investment for each division.
2. Compute the residual income for each division.

LO 10-3

E10-9 Developing Balanced Scorecard

Choose a company with which you regularly do business. Assume you have been hired as a consultant to help overhaul its performance evaluation system.

Required:

1. Briefly outline a balanced scorecard approach that could be used to evaluate the performance of the company's managers.
2. For each of the four perspectives, identify three metrics that could be part of the balanced scorecard.
3. Explain the reasoning behind each metric that you chose.

LO 10-4, 10-5

E10-10 Determining the Impact of Various Transactions on Investment Turnover, ROI, Residual Income, and Profit Margin

LEVEL UP

Poseidon Corporation manufactures a variety of gear for water sports. Poseidon has three divisions: Lake, River, and Ocean. Each division is managed as an investment center. During the current year, the Ocean division experienced the following transactions:

a. A special order was accepted at a selling price significantly less than the ordinary selling price. The sale will not impact other sales because this was a one-time order and Ocean has excess capacity. The selling price was in excess of total variable costs.

b. One of three production managers in the Ocean Division submitted his resignation. The position will not be filled due to current efficiencies experienced in the production department.

c. Due to the popularity of open-ocean swimming during the Olympics, the company experienced a surge in sales during the summer months. Sales returned to their normal level for the remainder of the year.

d. Equipment costing $500,000 was purchased to replace fully depreciated, obsolete equipment.

e. The company's after-tax cost of capital increased from 8 percent to 10 percent, with no effect on the minimum required rate of return.

f. The company's effective tax rate decreased from 35 percent to 30 percent.

Required:

For each transaction listed in this exercise, determine the impact on investment turnover, return on investment, residual income, and economic value added. Use the following table to organize your answers. Use (I) for increase, (D) for decrease, (N) for no effect, or a question mark (?) if you're unable to determine the impact of the transaction. Each transaction should be treated independently.

Transaction	Return on Investment	Residual Income	Economic Value Added
a.			
b.			
c.			
d.			
e.			
f.			

E10-11 Describing Balanced Scorecard Objectives and Perspectives LO 10-3

Your brother-in-law, Fred Miles, has just taken a new position as the plant manager of a local production facility. He has been told that the company uses a balanced scorecard approach to evaluate its managers. Fred is not familiar with this approach because his previous experience as a production manager focused only on whether the plant met the company's budgeted production.

Required:

1. Briefly explain to Fred how performance evaluations at his new company will differ from those at his previous company.
2. Give Fred five possible objectives that the new company will use, in addition to production level, to evaluate his performance. For each objective that you identify, be sure to indicate a plausible metric for measuring it.

E10-12 Understanding Transfer Price Importance LO 10-6

Refer to E10-11. Suppose Fred's plant manufactures a component used by another division of the organization. He has approached you for help in understanding why everyone seems to be making such a big deal about the transfer price that he plans to charge for the component. Fred's comment was, "Transfer prices do not impact the amount of profit earned by the company as a whole, so they don't affect me. I don't care what transfer price is used."

Required:

1. Explain whether Fred is correct or incorrect.
2. Explain how the transfer price could affect Fred or someone he works with.

E10-13 Determining Different Types of Responsibility Centers LO 10-2

The University of Dental Health (UDH) is a state-run university focusing on the education and training of dentists, dental assistants, dental hygienists, and other dental professionals. UDH has just hired a new controller who wants to organize UDH by responsibility centers so that responsibility accounting can be implemented. The controller has asked for your assistance in identifying each of the following UDH functions as either a cost center (C) or a profit center (P).

UDH Center	Cost or Profit
Accounting	
Bookstore	
Cafeterias	
Career services	
Community workshops (providing continuing professional education necessary for state licensure)	
Custodial services	
Financial aid	
Human resources	
Information technology	
Residence halls	
Student parking lots (fee based)	
University newspaper/radio station	

LO 10-6

E10-14 Determining Transfer Price

The Molding Division of Cotwold Company manufactures a plastic casing used by the Assembly Division. This casing is also sold to external customers for $25 per unit. Variable costs for the casing are $12 per unit and fixed cost is $3 per unit. Cotwold executives would like for the Molding Division to transfer 8,000 units to the Assembly Division at a price of $18 per unit.

Required:

1. Assume the Molding Department is operating at full capacity. Explain whether it should accept the transfer price proposed by management.
2. Identify the minimum transfer price that the Molding Division will accept and explain why.

LO 10-6

E10-15 Determining Transfer Price

Refer to the information presented in E10-14. Assume that the Molding Division has enough excess capacity to accommodate the request.

Required:

1. Explain whether the Molding Division should accept the $18 transfer price proposed by management.
2. Calculate the effect on Molding Division's net income if it accepts the $18 transfer price.

LO 10-6

E10-16 Determining Transfer Price

Refer to the information presented in E10-14. Assume that the Molding Department has excess capacity, but the Assembly Department requires the casing to be made from a specific blend of plastics. This would raise the variable cost per unit to $20.

Required:

1. Explain whether the Molding Department should accept the $18 transfer price proposed by management.
2. Determine the minimum transfer price that it will accept.
3. Determine the mutually beneficial transfer price so that the two divisions equally split the profits from the transfer.

LO 10-3

E10-17 Matching Measures of Performance with the Correct Balanced Scorecard Perspective

The following is a list of various metrics used to measure performance. For each metric, identify the correct balanced scorecard perspective with which the metric is associated. For Learning and Growth, use LG; for Customer, use C; for Financial, use F; and for Internal Business use IB. Each perspective may be used once, more than once, or not at all.

Metric	Balanced Scorecard Perspective
Average stock price	
Economic value added	
Employee turnover rates	
Manufacturing cycle time	
Market share	
Number of days from product launch to shelf	
Number of defects	
Number of new patent applications	
Percentage of repeat customers	
Percentage decrease in operating costs	
Percentage of sales generated by new products	
Research and development spending as a percentage of net revenues	

E10-18 Determining Minimum, Maximum, Negotiated Transfer Prices LO 10-6

Shaw is a lumber company that also manufactures custom cabinetry. It is made up of two divisions: Lumber and Cabinetry. The Lumber Division is responsible for harvesting and preparing lumber for use; the Cabinetry Division produces custom-ordered cabinetry. The lumber produced by the Lumber Division has a variable cost of $2.00 per linear foot and full cost of $3.00. Comparable quality wood sells on the open market for $6.00 per linear foot.

Required:

1. Assume you are the manager of the Cabinetry Division. Determine the maximum amount you would pay for lumber.
2. Assume you are the manager of the Lumber Division. Determine the minimum amount you would charge for the lumber if you have excess capacity. Repeat assuming you have no excess capacity.
3. Assume you are the president of Shaw. Determine a mutually beneficial transfer price assuming there is excess capacity.
4. Explain the possible consequences of simply letting the two division managers negotiate a price.

E10-19 Identifying Minimum, Maximum Transfer Prices, Determining Effect on Each Division's Profit LO 10-6

Tulip Company is made up of two divisions: A and B. Division A produces a widget that Division B uses in the production of its product. Variable cost per widget is $0.75; full cost is $1.00. Comparable widgets sell on the open market for $1.50 each. Division A can produce up to 2 million widgets per year but is currently operating at only 50 percent capacity. Division B expects to use 100,000 widgets in the current year.

Required:

1. Determine the minimum and maximum transfer prices.
2. Calculate Tulip Company's total benefit of having the widgets transferred between these divisions.
3. If the transfer price is set at $0.75 per unit, determine how much profit Division A will make on the transfer. Determine how much Division B will save by not purchasing the widgets on the open market.
4. If the transfer price is set at $1.50 per unit, determine how much profit Division A will make on the transfer. Determine how much Division B will save by not purchasing the widgets on the open market.
5. What transfer price would you recommend to split the difference?

E10-20 Identifying Balanced Scorecard Perspectives LO 10-3

Identify which perspective(s) of the balanced scorecard each of the following critical success factors relates to by placing an X in the appropriate cell. Each success factor could relate to more than one category.

	BALANCED SCORECARD PERSPECTIVES			
Critical Success Factor	Financial	Customer	Internal Business	Learning and Growth
Contribution margin by product				
Quality				
Employee empowerment				
Information systems capabilities				
New markets				
Product innovation				
Productivity				

GROUP A PROBLEMS

connect

LO 10-4, 10-5

PA10-1 Calculating Return on Investment, Residual Income, Determining Effect of Changes in Sales, Expenses, Invested Assets, Hurdle Rate on Each

Coolbrook Company has the following information available for the past year:

	River Division	Stream Division
Sales revenue	$1,200,000	$1,800,000
Cost of goods sold and operating expenses	900,000	1,300,000
Net operating income	$ 300,000	$ 500,000
Average invested assets	$1,200,000	$1,800,000

The company's hurdle rate is 6 percent.

Required:

1. Calculate return on investment (ROI) and residual income for each division for last year.
2. Recalculate ROI and residual income for each division for each independent situation that follows:
   a. Operating income increases by 10 percent.
   b. Operating income decreases by 10 percent.
   c. The company invests $250,000 in each division, an amount that generates $100,000 additional income per division.
   d. Coolbrook changes its hurdle rate to 10 percent.

LO 10-4, 10-5

PA10-2 Calculating Unknowns, Predicting Relationship among Return on Investment, Residual Income, Hurdle Rates

The following is partial information for Charleston Company's most recent year of operation. It manufactures lawn mowers and categorizes its operations into two divisions: Bermuda and Midiron.

	Bermuda Division	Midiron Division
Sales revenue	?	$600,000
Average invested assets	$2,500,000	?
Net operating income	$ 160,000	$150,000
Profit margin	20%	?
Investment turnover	?	0.16
Return on investment	?	?
Residual income	$ 40,000	$ (30,000)

Required:

1. Without making any calculations, determine whether each division's return on investment is above or below Charleston's hurdle rate. How can you tell?
2. Determine the missing amounts in the preceding table.
3. What is Charleston's hurdle rate?
4. Suppose Charleston has the opportunity to invest additional assets to help expand the company's market share. The expansion would require an average investment of $2,800,000 and would generate $140,000 in additional income. From Charleston's perspective, is this a viable investment? Why or why not?
5. Suppose the two divisions would equally share the investment and profits from the expansion project. If return on investment is used to evaluate performance, what will each division manager think about the proposed project?
6. In requirement 5, will either manager's preference change if residual income is used to measure division performance? Explain your answer.

PA10-3 Evaluating Managerial Performance, Proposed Project Impact on Return on Investment, Residual Income LO 10-4, 10-5

Wescott Company has three divisions: A, B, and C. The company has a hurdle rate of 8 percent. Selected operating data for the three divisions are as follows:

	Division A	Division B	Division C
Sales revenue	$1,255,000	$ 920,000	$ 898,000
Cost of goods sold	776,000	675,000	652,000
Miscellaneous operating expenses	64,000	52,000	53,100
Interest and taxes	48,000	41,000	41,500
Average invested assets	8,300,000	1,930,000	3,215,000

Wescott is considering an expansion project in the upcoming year that will cost $5 million and return $450,000 per year. The project would be implemented by only one of the three divisions.

Required:

1. Compute the ROI for each division.
2. Compute the residual income for each division.
3. Rank the divisions according to the ROI and residual income of each.
4. Compute the return on the proposed expansion project. Is this an acceptable project?
5. Without any additional calculations, state whether the proposed project would increase or decrease each division's ROI.
6. Compute the new ROI and residual income for each division if the project was implemented within that division.

PA10-4 Identifying Minimum, Maximum, Mutually Beneficial Transfer Prices LO 10-6

Grover Corp. is a manufacturing company that produces golf clubs. Birdie is a division of Grover that manufactures putters. Birdie's putters are used in Grover's golf club sets and are sold to other golf wholesalers. Cost information per putter follows:

Variable cost	$25.00
Full cost	28.00
Market price	42.00

In addition, its capacity data follow:

Capacity per year	40,000 putters
Current production level	30,000 putters

Required:

1. Assuming Grover produces 3,000 putters per year, determine the overall benefit of using putters from Birdie instead of purchasing them externally.
2. Determine the maximum price that the production facility would be willing to pay to purchase the putters from Birdie. How is the overall benefit divided between the two divisions if this transfer price is used?
3. Determine the minimum that Birdie will accept as a transfer price. How is the overall benefit divided between the two divisions if this transfer price is used?
4. Determine the mutually beneficial transfer price for the putters.
5. How would your answer change if Birdie were currently operating at capacity?

PA10-5 Identifying Minimum, Maximum, Mutually Beneficial Transfer Prices LO 10-6

Going Places, Inc., manufactures a variety of luggage for airline passengers. The company has several luggage production divisions, including the Suitable Cases Division, as well as a wholly owned subsidiary, It's Mine, that manufactures small identification tags used on luggage. Each piece of luggage that Suitable Cases produces has two identification tags for which it previously paid the going market price of $2 each. Financial information for Suitable Cases and It's Mine follows:

	Suitable Cases Division	It's Mine
Sales		
4,500 bags × $150.00 each	$675,000	
200,000 tags × $2.00 each		$400,000
Variable expenses		
4,500 bags × $85.00 each	382,500	
200,000 tags × $0.50 each		100,000

It's Mine has a production capacity of 250,000 tags.

Required:

1. Determine how much Going Places will save on each tag if the Suitable Cases Division obtains them from It's Mine instead of an external supplier.
2. Determine the maximum and minimum transfer prices for the tags. Who sets these?
3. Suppose Going Places has set a transfer price policy of variable cost plus 60 percent for all related-party transactions. Determine how much each party will benefit from the internal transfer.
4. Determine the mutually beneficial transfer price.

LO 10-3

PA10-6 Categorizing Sustainability Metrics based on the Triple Bottom Line and the Balanced Scorecard

The following table lists several metrics from the Global Reporting Initiatives' (GRI) sustainability reporting standards and other industry sources.

For each metric, classify it based on its impact on the triple bottom line (People, Profit, or Planet) and indicate which balanced scorecard perspective it is most likely to fall within (Financial, Customer, Internal Business, Learning and Growth, or Society/Community). You can use more than one category when appropriate. The first metric is shown as an example.

Sustainability Metric	Triple bottom line impact: People, Profit, or Planet?	Balanced Scorecard Perspective: Financial, Customer, Internal Business, Learning/ Growth, or Society/Community
Gallons of water consumed	Planet	Internal Business
Hours of R&D devoted to environmentally-friendly products		
Average hours of training per employee by gender		
Number of substantiated complaints related to product health hazards		
Dollars invested in area of high poverty		
Number of formal grievances about environmental impacts		
Tons of nonrenewable materials used in manufacturing		
Total hours of employee training on human rights policies		
Total cost of work-related injuries, diseases, and fatalities		
Total green house gas (GHG) emissions		
Total utilities cost		

GROUP B PROBLEMS

PB10-1 Calculating Return on Investment, Residual Income, Determining Effect of Changes in Sales, Expenses, Invested Assets, Hurdle Rate on Each LO 10-4, 10-5

Escuda Company has the following information available for the past year:

	Fence Division	Brick Division
Segment sales	$2,200,000	$1,300,000
Segment cost of goods sold and operating expenses	1,700,000	1,000,000
Segment income	$ 500,000	$ 300,000
Average invested assets	$4,100,000	$3,000,000

The company's hurdle rate is 12 percent.

1. Determine Escuda's return on investment (ROI) and residual income for each division for last year.
2. Recalculate Escuda's ROI and residual income for both divisions for each independent situation that follows:
   a. Net operating income increases by 10 percent.
   b. Net operating income decreases by 10 percent.
   c. The company invests $400,000 in each division, an amount that generates $80,000 additional income per division.
   d. Escuda changes its hurdle rate to 9 percent.

PB10-2 Calculating Unknowns, Predicting Relationship among Return on Investment, Residual Income, Hurdle Rates LO 10-4, 10-5

The following is partial information for Tonopah Company's most recent year of operation. Tonopah manufactures children's shoes and categorizes its operations into two divisions: Girls and Boys.

	Girls Division	Boys Division
Sales revenue	$2,000,000	?
Average invested assets	?	$1,250,000
Net operating income	$ 500,000	$ 300,000
Profit margin	?	15%
Investment turnover	0.8	?
Return on investment	?	?
Residual income	$ 260,000	$ 180,000

Required:

1. Without making any calculations, determine whether each division's return on investment is above or below Tonopah's hurdle rate. How can you tell?
2. Determine the missing amounts in the preceding table.
3. What is Tonopah's hurdle rate?
4. Suppose Tonopah has the opportunity to invest additional assets to help expand the company's market share. The expansion would require an investment of $6,200,000 and would generate $800,000 in additional income. From Tonopah's perspective, is this a viable investment? Why or why not?
5. Suppose the two divisions would equally share the investment and profits from the expansion project. If return on investment is used to evaluate performance, what will each division think about the proposed project?
6. In requirement 5, will either manager's preference change if residual income is used to measure division performance? Explain your answer.

LO 10-4, 10-5 **PB10-3 Evaluating Managerial Performance, Impact of Proposed Project on Return on Investment, Residual Income**

Yummy Company has three divisions: Chips, Cookies, and Crackers. The company has a hurdle rate of 7 percent. Selected operating data for the three divisions follow:

	Chips Division	Cookies Division	Crackers Division
Sales revenue	$ 458,000	$ 560,000	$ 486,000
Cost of goods sold	316,000	313,925	233,600
Miscellaneous operating expenses	58,000	72,000	42,000
Interest and taxes	29,000	39,000	35,500
Average invested assets	1,600,000	1,450,000	2,630,000

Yummy is considering an expansion project in the upcoming year that will cost $5,250,000 and return $525,000 per year. The project would be implemented by only one of the three divisions.

Required:

1. Compute the ROI for each division.
2. Compute the residual income for each division.
3. Rank the divisions according to the ROI and residual income of each.
4. Compute the return on the proposed expansion project. Is this an acceptable project to Yummy?
5. Without any additional calculations, state whether the proposed project would increase or decrease each division's ROI.
6. Compute the new ROI and residual income for each division if the project was implemented within that division.

LO 10-6 **PB10-4 Identifying Minimum, Maximum, Mutually Beneficial Transfer Prices**

Quail Company produces outdoor gear. Salter is a division of Quail that manufactures unbreakable zippers used in Quail's gear and sold to other manufacturers. Cost information per zipper follows:

Variable cost	$1.60
Full cost	2.20
Market price	5.00

In addition, Salter's capacity data follow:

Capacity per year	2,000,000 zippers
Current production level	1,500,000 zippers

Required:

1. Assuming Quail produces 300,000 sleeping bags per year, what is the overall benefit of using zippers from Salter instead of purchasing them externally?
2. Determine the maximum price that the sleeping bag production facility would be willing to pay to purchase the zippers from Salter. How is the overall benefit divided between the two divisions if this transfer price is used?
3. Determine the minimum that Salter will accept as a transfer price. How is the overall benefit divided between the two divisions if this transfer price is used?
4. Determine the mutually beneficial transfer price for the zippers.
5. How would your answer change if Salter were currently operating at capacity?

LO 10-6 **PB10-5 Identifying Minimum, Maximum, Mutually Beneficial Transfer Prices**

Monona produces bottled water. The company recently purchased Cabot Co., a manufacturer of plastic bottles. In the past, Monona has purchased plastic bottles on the open market at $0.20 each. Financial information for the past year for Monona and Cabot follows:

	Monona	Cabot
Sales		
500,000 units × $2.00 each	$1,000,000	
1,200,000 units × $0.20 each		$240,000
Variable expenses		
500,000 units × $0.25 each	125,000	
1,200,000 units × $0.04 each		48,000

Cabot has a production capacity of 2 million units.

Required:

1. Determine how much Monona will save on each bottle if it obtains them from Cabot instead of an external supplier.
2. Determine the maximum and minimum transfer prices for the plastic bottles. Who sets these?
3. Suppose Monona has determined a transfer price rule of variable cost plus 50 percent for all related-party transactions. Determine how much each party will benefit from the internal transfer.
4. Determine the mutually beneficial transfer price.

PB10-6 Categorizing Sustainability Metrics based on the Triple Bottom Line and the Balanced Scorecard LO 10-3

The following table lists several metrics from the Global Reporting Initiatives' (GRI) sustainability reporting standards and other industry sources.

For each metric, classify it based on its impact on the triple bottom line (People, Profit, or Planet) and indicate which balanced scorecard perspective it is most likely to fall within (Financial, Customer, Internal Business, Learning and Growth, or Society/Community). You can use more than one category when appropriate. The first metric is shown as an example.

Sustainability Metric	Triple bottom line impact: People, Profit, or Planet?	Balanced Scorecard Perspective: Financial, Customer, Internal Business, Learning/Growth, or Society/Community
Total fuel consumption from nonrenewable sources	Planet	Internal Business
Number of new patents for environmentally-friendly technology		
Ratio of salary and other pay (e.g. bonuses) of female to males by employee category		
Total number of grievances about unfair labor practices filed through formal grievance mechanisms		
Revenues generated from environmentally friendly products		
Total employee work hours devoted to volunteer or community service		
Percentage of new suppliers that were screened using human rights criteria		
Total number and cost of hazardous waste spills		
Total number of breaches of customer privacy and loss of customer data		
Percentage of recycled materials used in production		
Total employee wage and benefits expense		

SKILLS DEVELOPMENT CASES

LO 10-3

S10-1 Researching Use of Balanced Scorecard in Business

This chapter discussed the use of the balanced scorecard for evaluating managerial and organizational performance. Many companies have adopted this performance measurement in recent years.

Required:

Research or visit a company that has implemented the balanced scorecard and write a brief report of its experience. You should include information such as when the company implemented the balanced scorecard, what performance measurement approach it had used previously, any difficulties it experienced with the implementation, and the benefits received from the new method.

LO 10-1

S10-2 Explaining Impact of Organizational Structure, Budgetary Processes on Employee Morale

In the last several chapters, you have learned about many aspects of organizational structure, budgeting, and performance evaluation. None of these company characteristics operates in isolation. They all interrelate to form an organization's culture and influence employee morale. The following table has several combinations of organizational structure and budgeting preparation style:

Organizational Structure	Budget Creation Process
Centralized	Top Down
Decentralized	Participative
Centralized	Participative
Decentralized	Top Down

Required:

For each combination in the table, write a brief paragraph summarizing both the potential advantages and disadvantages for a company using the combination. Consider the impact on managers and other employees as well as the potential impact on outside parties such as customers or other organizational stakeholders.

CHAPTER 13

Measuring and Evaluating Financial Performance

YOUR LEARNING OBJECTIVES

- **LO 13-1** Describe the purposes and uses of horizontal, vertical, and ratio analyses.
- **LO 13-2** Use horizontal (trend) analyses to recognize financial changes that unfold over time.
- **LO 13-3** Use vertical (common size) analyses to understand important relationships within financial statements.
- **LO 13-4** Calculate financial ratios to assess profitability, liquidity, and solvency.
- **LO 13-5** Interpret the results of financial analyses.
- **LO 13-6** Describe how analyses depend on key accounting decisions and concepts.

© Kevork Djansezian/Getty Images

FOCUS COMPANY: Lowe's

Measuring and evaluating financial performance is like judging gymnastics or figure skating at the Olympics. You have to know three things: (1) the general categories to evaluate for each event, (2) the particular elements to consider within each category, and (3) how to measure performance for each element. On the financial side, managers and analysts follow the same process. They evaluate general categories such as profitability, liquidity, and solvency, which are separated into particular elements such as gross profit margin and net profit margin. For each of these elements, managers and analysts measure performance by computing various percentages and ratios, which themselves are based on information reported in the financial statements.

In this chapter, we focus on Lowe's, the second largest home improvement retailer in the world. Lowe's is a giant with 1,832 stores and 262,000 employees. Yet the company's continued success still requires innovations to increase sales in existing markets and to successfully enter new markets. At the same time, Lowe's must control costs while maintaining a high level of customer service in its stores. Finally, Lowe's management must anticipate the actions of its larger rival, The Home Depot, and address changes in overall demand for building products over which it has little control.

How do managers, analysts, investors, and creditors assess Lowe's success in meeting these challenges? This is the purpose of financial statement analysis. Our discussion begins with an explanation of how to analyze financial statements to understand the financial results of a company's business activities. We conclude the chapter with a review of the key accounting decisions analysts consider when evaluating financial statements.

ORGANIZATION OF THE CHAPTER

Understand the business	Study the accounting methods	Evaluate the results	Review the chapter
• Horizontal, vertical, and ratio analyses	• Horizontal (trend) computations • Vertical (common size) computations • Ratio computations	• Interpreting horizontal and vertical analyses • Interpreting ratio analyses • Underlying accounting decisions and concepts	• Demonstration case • Chapter summary • Key terms • Homework helper • Practice material

Understand the Business

Learning Objective 13-1
Describe the purposes and uses of horizontal, vertical, and ratio analyses.

As you first learned in Chapter 1, the goal of accounting is to provide information that allows decision makers to understand and evaluate the results of business decisions. Managers analyze financial statements to evaluate past financial performance and make future decisions. Creditors use financial statements to assess compliance with loan covenants. And, of course, analysts use financial statements to generate advice for investors and others. You have learned that no single number fully captures the results of all business activities nor does it predict a company's success or failure. Instead, to understand and evaluate the results of business activities, you need to look at a business from many different angles. An understanding of whether a business is successful will emerge only after you have learned to combine all of your evaluations into a complete picture or story that depicts the company's performance. Our goal for this chapter is to demonstrate how you can do this, relying on horizontal, vertical, and ratio analyses to develop the "story" of how well a company has performed.

HORIZONTAL, VERTICAL, AND RATIO ANALYSES

Most good stories have a plot, which the reader comes to understand as it unfolds over time or as one event relates to another. This is the same way that financial analyses work. **Horizontal (trend) analyses are conducted to help financial statement users recognize important financial changes that unfold over time.** Horizontal analyses compare individual financial statement line items horizontally (from one period to the next), with the general goal of identifying significant sustained changes (trends). These changes are typically described in terms of dollar amounts and year-over-year percentages. For example, trend analyses could be used to determine the dollar amount and percentage by which Cost of Goods Sold increased this year, relative to prior years. **Vertical analyses focus on important relationships between items on the same financial statement.** These items are compared vertically (one account balance versus another) and are typically expressed as percentages to reveal the relative contributions made by each financial statement item. For example, vertical analyses could show that operating expenses consume one quarter of a company's net sales revenue. **Ratio analyses are conducted to understand relationships among various items reported in one or more of the financial statements.** Ratio analyses allow you to evaluate how well a company has performed given the level of other company resources. For example, while vertical analyses can show that Cost of Goods Sold consumes 65 percent of Net Sales and horizontal analyses can show that this percentage has increased over time, ratio analyses can relate these amounts to inventory levels to evaluate inventory management decisions.

Before we show you how to calculate horizontal, vertical, and ratio analyses (in the next section), we must emphasize that **no analysis is complete unless it leads to an interpretation that helps financial statement users understand and evaluate a company's financial results.** Without interpretation, these computations can appear as nothing more than a list of disconnected numbers.

Study the Accounting Methods

HORIZONTAL (TREND) COMPUTATIONS

Learning Objective 13-2
Use horizontal (trend) analyses to recognize financial changes that unfold over time.

Horizontal (trend) analyses help decision makers and stakeholders recognize financial changes that unfold over time. This approach compares individual financial statement items from year to year with the general goal of identifying significant sustained changes or trends. For example, trend analysis can be used to determine the dollar and percentage changes in the cost of goods sold this year relative to prior years. Because this type of analysis compares the results on each line of the financial statements across several years, trend analysis is also known as horizontal analysis. Because it compares results over a series of periods, it is sometimes called **time-series analysis.**

COACH'S TIP
Horizontal (trend) analyses compare results across time, often expressing changes in account balances as a percentage of prior year balances.

Regardless of the name, trend analyses are usually calculated in terms of year-to-year dollar and percentage changes. A year-to-year percentage change expresses the current year's dollar change as a percentage of the prior year's total by using the following calculation:

$$\text{Year-to-Year Change (\%)} = \frac{\text{Change This Year}}{\text{Prior Year's Total}} \times 100 = \frac{(\text{Current Year's Total} - \text{Prior Year's Total})}{\text{Prior Year's Total}} \times 100$$

To demonstrate how to calculate a trend, we analyze Lowe's financial statements. Summaries of Lowe's balance sheets and income statements from two recent years appear in Exhibits 13.1 and 13.2. Dollar and percentage changes from fiscal year 2012 to 2013[1] are shown to the right of the balance sheet and income statement. The dollar changes were calculated by subtracting the fiscal 2012 balances from the fiscal 2013 balances. The percentage changes were calculated by dividing those differences by the fiscal 2012 balances. For example, according to Exhibit 13.1, Cash decreased by \$150 (=\$391 − \$541) in fiscal 2013 relative to fiscal 2012 (all numbers in millions). That dollar amount represented a decrease of 27.7% [=(\$150 ÷ \$541) × 100].

In a later section, we will explain and evaluate the underlying causes of significant changes in account balances. But before we leave this topic, we must note that not all large percentage changes will be significant. For example, the 48.0 percent increase in Short-term Investments is the largest percentage change on the balance sheet (Exhibit 13.1), but the \$60 increase is relatively small when compared to other changes, such as the \$527 increase in Inventory. To avoid focusing on unimportant changes, use the percentage changes to identify potentially significant changes, but then check the dollar change to make sure that it too is significant.

COACH'S TIP
Vertical (common size) analyses express each financial statement amount as a percentage of another amount on the same financial statement.

VERTICAL (COMMON SIZE) COMPUTATIONS

Learning Objective 13-3
Use vertical (common size) analyses to understand important relationships within financial statements.

A second type of analysis, **vertical (common size) analysis**, focuses on important relationships within a financial statement. When a company is growing or shrinking overall, it is difficult to tell from the dollar amounts whether the proportions within each statement category are

[1] Like many retail companies, Lowe's 2013 fiscal year ends on January 31, 2014.

EXHIBIT 13.1 Horizontal (Trend) Analysis of Lowe's Summarized Balance Sheets

LOWE'S
Balance Sheets
(in millions)

	Fiscal 2013	Fiscal 2012	Increase (Decrease) Amount	Increase (Decrease) Percent*
Assets				
Current Assets				
Cash	$ 391	$ 541	$(150)	(27.7)
Short-term Investments	185	125	60	48.0
Accounts Receivable	—	—	—	—
Inventory	9,127	8,600	527	6.1
Other Current Assets	593	518	75	14.5
Total Current Assets	10,296	9,784	512	5.2
Property and Equipment, Net	20,834	21,477	(643)	(3.0)
Other Assets	1,602	1,405	197	14.0
Total Assets	$32,732	$32,666	$ 66	0.2
Liabilities and Stockholders' Equity				
Current Liabilities	$ 8,876	$ 7,708	$1,168	15.2
Long-term Liabilities	12,003	11,101	902	8.1
Total Liabilities	20,879	18,809	2,070	11.0
Stockholders' Equity	11,853	13,857	(2,004)	(14.5)
Total Liabilities and Stockholders' Equity	$32,732	$32,666	$ 66	0.2

*Amount of Increase (Decrease) ÷ Fiscal 2012 × 100

EXHIBIT 13.2 Horizontal (Trend) Analysis of Lowe's Summarized Income Statements

LOWE'S
Income Statements
(in millions)

Year Ended:	Fiscal 2013	Fiscal 2012	Increase (Decrease) Amount	Increase (Decrease) Percent*
Net Sales Revenue	$53,417	$50,521	$2,896	5.7
Cost of Sales	34,941	33,194	1,747	5.3
Gross Profit	18,476	17,327	1,149	6.6
Operating and Other Expenses	14,327	13,767	560	4.1
Interest Expense	476	423	53	12.5
Income Tax Expense	1,387	1,178	209	17.7
Net Income	$ 2,286	$ 1,959	$ 327	16.7
Earnings per Share	$ 2.14	$ 1.69	$ 0.45	26.6

*Amount of Increase (Decrease) ÷ Fiscal 2012 × 100

changing. Common size financial statements provide this information by expressing each financial statement amount as a percentage of another amount on that statement. The usefulness of common size statements is illustrated by the fact that Lowe's actually presents its balance sheet and income statements in the common size format illustrated in Exhibits 13.3 and 13.4.

EXHIBIT 13.3 Vertical (Common Size) Analysis of Lowe's Summarized Balance Sheets

LOWE'S
Balance Sheets
(in millions)

	Fiscal 2013		Fiscal 2012	
	Amount	**Percent**	**Amount**	**Percent**
Assets				
Current Assets				
Cash	$ 391	1.2%	$ 541	1.7%
Short-term Investments	185	0.6	125	0.4
Inventories	9,127	27.9	8,600	26.3
Other Current Assets	593	1.8	518	1.6
Property and Equipment, Net	20,834	63.6	21,477	65.7
Other Assets	1,602	4.9	1,405	4.3
Total Assets	$32,732	100.0	$32,666	100.0
Liabilities and Stockholders' Equity				
Current Liabilities	$ 8,876	27.1%	$ 7,708	23.6%
Long-term Liabilities	12,003	36.7	11,101	34.0
Total Liabilities	20,879	63.8	18,809	57.6
Stockholders' Equity	11,853	36.2	13,857	42.4
Total Liabilities and Stockholders' Equity	$32,732	100.0	$33,666	100.0

EXHIBIT 13.4 Vertical (Common Size) Analysis of Lowe's Summarized Income Statements

LOWE'S
Income Statements
(in millions)

	Fiscal 2013		Fiscal 2012	
	Amount	**Percent**	**Amount**	**Percent**
Net Sales Revenue	$53,417	100.0%	$50,521	100.0%
Cost of Sales	33,941	65.4	33,194	65.7
Gross Profit	18,476	34.6	17,327	34.3
Operating and Other Expenses	14,327	26.8	13,767	27.3
Interest Expense	476	0.9	423	0.8
Income Tax Expense	1,387	2.6	1,178	2.3
Net Income	$ 2,286	4.3	$ 1,959	3.9

In a common size balance sheet, each asset appears as a percent of total assets, and each liability or stockholders' equity item appears as a percent of total liabilities and stockholders' equity. For example, in Exhibit 13.3, which presents Lowe's common size balance sheets, Cash was 1.2 percent of total assets [=($391 ÷ $32,732) × 100] at the end of fiscal 2013.

The common size income statement reports each income statement item as a percentage of sales. For example, in Exhibit 13.4, cost of sales was equal to 65.4 percent of Net Sales Revenue in 2013 [= ($34,941 ÷ $53,417) × 100].

RATIO COMPUTATIONS

Learning Objective 13-4
Calculate financial ratios to assess profitability, liquidity, and solvency.

Ratio analyses help financial statement users to understand relationships among various items reported in the financial statements. These analyses compare the amounts for one or more line items to the amounts for other line items in the same year. Ratio analyses are useful because they consider differences in the size of the amounts being compared, similar to common size statements. In fact, some of the most popular ratios, such as net profit margin and the debt-to-assets ratio, are taken directly from the common size statements. Ratios allow users to evaluate how well a company has performed given the level of its other resources.

Most analysts classify ratios into three categories:

1. **Profitability** ratios, which relate to the company's performance in the current period—in particular, the company's ability to generate income.
2. **Liquidity** ratios, which relate to the company's short-term survival—in particular, the company's ability to use current assets to repay liabilities as they become due.
3. **Solvency** ratios, which relate to the company's long-run survival—in particular, the company's ability to repay lenders when debt matures and to make the required interest payments prior to the date of maturity.

COACH'S TIP

Profitability is the extent to which a company generates income.
Liquidity is the extent to which a company is able to pay its currently maturing obligations.
Solvency is the ability to survive long enough to repay lenders when debt matures.

Exhibit 13.5 organizes the ratios introduced in previous chapters according to these three categories and demonstrates their calculations for fiscal 2013 using data from Exhibits 13.1 and 13.2.

How's it going? Self-Study Practice

For the year ended February 2, 2014, The Home Depot reported net income of $5.4 billion on sales of $78.8 billion. If the company's cost of goods sold that year was $51.4 billion, what was the company's gross profit percentage and net profit margin? If sales were $74.8 billion in the prior year, what was the year-over-year percentage increase in the most recent year?

$$\text{Gross Profit Percentage} = \frac{(\$\_\_\_ - \$\_\_\_)\text{ billion}}{\$78.8\text{ billion}} \times 100 = \_\_\_$$

$$\text{Net Profit Margin} = \frac{\$5.4\text{ billion}}{\_\_\_} \times 100 = \_\_\_$$

$$\text{Sales Increase (Percentage)} = \frac{(\$\_\_\_ - \$\_\_\_)\text{ billion}}{\$\_\_\_\text{ billion}} \times 100 = \_\_\_$$

After you have finished, check your answers against the solution in the margin.

Solution to Self-Study Practice
Gross Profit Percentage = ($78.8 − $51.4) ÷ $78.8 × 100 = 34.8%
Net Profit Margin = $5.4 ÷ $78.8 × 100 = 6.9%
Sales Increase (Percentage) = ($78.8 − $74.8) ÷ $74.8 × 100 = 5.3%

EXHIBIT 13.5 Common Ratios Used in Financial Statement Analysis

Ratio	Fiscal 2013 Calculations
Profitability Ratios	
(1) Net Profit Margin $= \frac{\text{Net Income}}{\text{Revenues}} \times 100$	$\frac{\$2{,}286}{\$53{,}417} \times 100 = 4.3\%$
(2) Gross Profit Percentage $= \frac{\text{Net Sales Revenue} - \text{Cost of Goods Sold}}{\text{Net Sales Revenue}} \times 100$	$\frac{\$53{,}417 - \$34{,}941}{\$53{,}417} \times 100 = 34.6\%$
(3) Fixed Asset Turnover $= \frac{\text{Net Revenue}}{\text{Average Net Fixed Assets}}$	$\frac{\$53{,}417}{(\$20{,}834 + \$21{,}477)/2} = 2.52$
(4) Return On Equity (ROE) $= \frac{\text{Net Income} - \text{Preferred Dividends}}{\text{Average Common Stockholder's Equity}} \times 100$	$\frac{\$2{,}286 - \$16}{(\$13{,}857 + \$11{,}853)/2} \times 100 = 17.7\%$
(5) Earnings per Share (EPS) $= \frac{\text{Net Income} - \text{Preferred Dividends}}{\text{Average Number of Common Shares Outstanding}}$	$\frac{\$2{,}286 - \$16}{1{,}059} = \$2.14$
(6) Price/Earnings Ratio $= \frac{\text{Stock Price*}}{\text{EPS}}$	$\frac{\$50.72}{\$2.14} = 23.7$
Liquidity Ratios	
(7) Receivables Turnover $= \frac{\text{Net Sales Revenue}}{\text{Average Net Receivables}}$	n/a
Days to Collect $= \frac{365}{\text{Receivable Turnover Ratio}}$	n/a
(8) Inventory Turnover $= \frac{\text{Cost of Goods Sold}}{\text{Average Inventory}}$	$\frac{\$34{,}941}{(\$9{,}127 + \$8{,}600)/2} = 3.9$
Days to Sell $= \frac{365}{\text{Inventory Turnover Ratio}}$	$\frac{365}{3.9} = 93.6$
(9) Current Ratio $= \frac{\text{Current Assets}}{\text{Current Liabilities}}$	$\frac{\$10{,}296}{\$8{,}876} = 1.16$
Solvency Ratios	
(10) Debt-to-Assets $= \frac{\text{Total Liabilities}}{\text{Total Assets}}$	$\frac{\$20{,}879}{\$32{,}732} = 0.64$
(11) Times Interest Earned $= \frac{\text{Net Income} + \text{Interest Expense} + \text{Income Tax Expense}}{\text{Interest Expense}}$	$\frac{\$2{,}286 + \$476 + \$1{,}387}{\$476} = 8.7$

*Stock price is the closing price reported for the day on which the company first reports its annual earnings in a press release.

Evaluate the Results

INTERPRETING HORIZONTAL AND VERTICAL ANALYSES

Learning Objective 13-5
Interpret the results of financial analyses.

As noted in the previous section, financial statement analyses are not complete unless they lead to interpretations that help users understand and evaluate a company's financial results. When interpreting analyses, your goals should be to understand what each analysis is telling you and then combine your findings into a coherent "story" that explains the results of the company's business activities. We demonstrate how to do this, beginning with interpretations of each set of analyses shown in Exhibits 13.1 through 13.5 and later concluding with an overall summary of Lowe's results.

Trends Revealed in Horizontal Analyses

Horizontal (trend) analysis of Lowe's balance sheet in Exhibit 13.1 shows that the company grew only a little in fiscal 2013. Overall, total assets increased a mere 0.2 percent. The most significant change indicated by the balance sheet is that the company relied more on debt and less on equity financing. During 2013, Lowe's total liabilities increased by 11.0 percent, which resulted from issuing $1.0 billion in new bonds, as explained in its financial statement notes. Also, stockholders' equity decreased by 14.5 percent, largely the result of Lowe's repurchasing common shares that were immediately retired and returned to authorized and unissued status.

Horizontal analysis of Lowe's income statement in Exhibit 13.2 shows a 5.7 percent increase in Net Sales Revenue and a 5.3 percent increase in Cost of Sales, as a result of more customer transactions. The company explains in the Management's Discussion and Analysis (MD&A) section of its annual report that 2013 saw 24 million more sales transactions than 2012, attributable in part to better inventory selection and to a general improvement in the economy. Because the increase in Net Sales Revenue (5.7 percent) was larger than the increase in Cost of Goods Sold (5.3 percent), Lowe's saw an increase in 2013 Gross Profit. However, its operating expenses also increased 4.1 percent in 2013, in part because of increases in salaries and wages. According to the MD&A, Lowe's began adding 150 hours of labor time per week to each store to better serve customers, with the goal of closing more sales during peak weekday hours. The final changes in Lowe's 2013 expenses related to interest and income tax expenses, which increased as a direct result of carrying more debt and earning more income.

COACH'S TIP

Industry averages are reported in the *Annual Statement Studies*, which are published by the Risk Management Association at statementstudies.org. You can obtain industry averages also from csimarket.com or google.com/finance, which were available free of charge at the time this book was written.

Relationships Noted in Vertical Analyses

Vertical (common size) analysis of Lowe's balance sheet in Exhibit 13.3 highlights key elements of the company. Its most significant assets have always been Inventory and Property and Equipment, with these assets representing 27.9 and 63.6 percent of Lowe's total assets. As noted in the horizontal analysis, the company's financing strategy shifted in 2013. As a result of the bond issuances and stock repurchases, debt became a significantly greater source of financing (63.8 percent) than equity (36.2 percent) at the end of Fiscal 2013.

Vertical analysis of Lowe's income statement in Exhibit 13.4 indicates that Cost of Sales and Operating Expenses are the most important determinants of the company's profitability. Cost of Sales consumed 65.4 percent of Sales in 2013 and Operating Expenses consumed an additional 26.8 percent. Much of the increase in the company's Net Income (from 3.9 percent of Sales in 2012 to 4.3 in 2013) is explained by greater control of these two categories of expenses, as suggested by the horizontal analyses.

These findings from the vertical analyses serve to underscore findings from the horizontal analyses. The emerging story is that Lowe's success depends on its ability to use significant investments in Inventory and Property and Equipment to generate sales. By focusing on greater sell-through of its products and more efficient operating practices, Lowe's was able to improve its net income in a recovering but still challenging economy.

Fiscal 2013

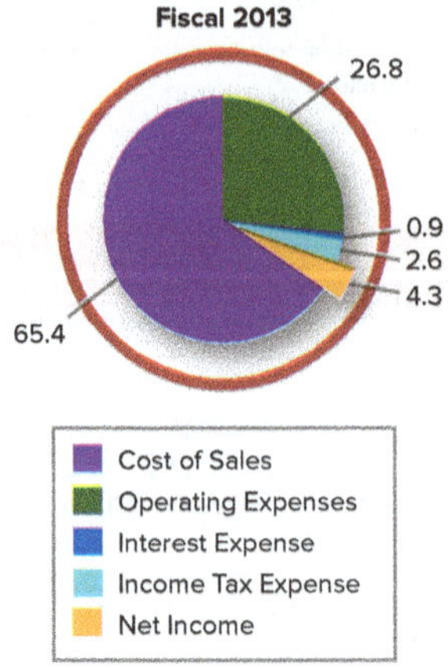

INTERPRETING RATIO ANALYSES

As shown throughout other chapters in this book, benchmarks help when interpreting a company's ratios. These benchmarks can include the company's prior year results, as well as the results of close competitors or the average for the industry. In a competitive economy, companies strive to outperform one another, so comparisons against other companies can provide clues about who is likely to survive and thrive in the long run.

In the following analyses, we compare Lowe's financial ratios to the prior year and in some cases to those for The Home Depot and the home improvement industry as a whole.

Profitability Ratios

The analyses in this section focus on the level of profits the company generated during the period. We will analyze ratios (1) through (6) from Exhibit 13.5. The first two profitability ratios come right from the common size income statement in Exhibit 13.4.

(1) Net Profit Margin Net profit margin represents the percentage of revenue that ultimately makes it into net income, after deducting expenses. Using the equation in Exhibit 13.5, the calculation of Lowe's net profit margin for each of the last two years yields:

Fiscal Year	2013	2012
Net profit margin $= \frac{\text{Net Income}}{\text{Total Revenue}} \times 100$	4.3%	3.9%

As discussed in the previous sections, the slowly improving economy helped boost Lowe's profits in 2013. Lowe's net profit margin increased from 3.9 percent in 2012 to 4.3 percent in 2013. The Home Depot's net profit margin saw a similar increase over this period, rising from 6.1 to 6.8 percent.

(2) Gross Profit Percentage The horizontal analysis indicated that Lowe's gross profit increased from 2012 to 2013 in terms of total dollars, but it did not indicate whether that increase was caused solely by greater total sales or also by more profit per sale. The gross profit percentage addresses these possibilities by indicating how much profit was made, on average, on each dollar of sales after deducting the cost of goods sold. Lowe's gross profit percentage for the last two years was:

Fiscal Year	2013	2012
Gross Profit Percentage $= \frac{\text{Net Sales} - \text{Cost of Goods Sold}}{\text{Net Sales}} \times 100$	34.6%	34.3%

This analysis shows that in 2013, after deducting the cost of merchandise sold, 34.6 cents of each sales dollar were left to cover other costs, such as employee wages, advertising, and utilities and to provide profits to the stockholders. The increase in the gross profit percentage from 2012 to 2013 (34.6% − 34.3%) means that Lowe's made 0.3¢ more gross profit on each dollar of sales in 2013 than in 2012. There are two potential explanations for this increase: (1) Lowe's charged higher selling prices without experiencing a corresponding increase in the cost of merchandise and (2) Lowe's obtained merchandise at a lower unit cost. The MD&A section of Lowe's annual report indicates that the increase in gross profit percentage came from both higher selling prices and a decrease in product costs.

(3) Fixed Asset Turnover The fixed asset turnover ratio indicates how much revenue the company generates for each dollar invested in fixed assets, such as store buildings and the property they sit on. Lowe's fixed asset turnover ratios for the two years were:

	2013	2012
Fixed Asset Turnover $= \frac{\text{Net Revenue}}{\text{Average Net Fixed Assets}}$	2.52	2.33

This analysis shows that Lowe's had $2.52 of sales in 2013 for each dollar invested in fixed assets. By looking at the components of this ratio, we can see that an increase in 2013 sales and a decrease in net fixed assets both contributed to the ratio's increase in 2013. Increased sales resulted from the slight improvement in the economy and decreased net fixed assets resulted from additional depreciation in 2013 coupled with a decision Lowe's made to limit new store openings in 2013.

Although Lowe's fixed asset turnover ratio improved in 2013, it is low compared to that of its main competitor, The Home Depot, whose fixed asset turnover ratio was 3.32 in 2013. In terms of using fixed assets to generate sales revenue, The Home Depot has a competitive advantage over Lowe's. In other words, Lowe's is operating less efficiently than its major competitor.

(4) Return on Equity (ROE) The return on equity ratio compares the amount of net income earned for common stockholders to the average amount of common stockholders' equity. Like the interest rate on your bank account, ROE reports the net amount earned during the period as a percentage of each dollar contributed by common stockholders and retained in the business. Lowe's ROE ratios for the past two years were:

	2013	2012
$\text{Return on Equity (ROE)} = \dfrac{\text{Net Income} \times \text{Preferred Dividends}}{\text{Average Common Stockholders' Equity}} \times 100$	17.7%	12.9%

Lowe's ROE increase from 12.9 to 17.7 percent was inevitable, given our previous analyses. Specifically, horizontal analysis indicated that the company had decreased its common stockholders' equity through a stock repurchase and it had increased its net income in 2013 through more profitable operations. Taken together, these results imply that net income as a percentage of average common stockholders' equity was sure to rise in 2013. Despite this good news, Lowe's 17.7 percent ROE lagged behind The Home Depot's fiscal 2013 ROE of 35.5 percent.

(5) Earnings per Share (EPS) Earnings per share (EPS) indicates the amount of earnings generated for each share of outstanding common stock. Consistent with the increase in ROE, the EPS ratio increased from $1.69 in 2012 to $2.14 in 2013, shown as follows. This represents an increase of $0.45 per share ($2.14 − $1.69).

Fiscal Year	2013	2012
$\text{Earnings per Share (EPS)} = \dfrac{\text{Net Income} \times \text{Preferred Dividends}}{\text{Average Number of Common Shares Outstanding}}$	$2.14	$1.69

(6) Price/Earnings (P/E) Ratio The P/E ratio relates the company's stock price to its EPS, as follows:

Fiscal Year	2013	2012
$\text{Price/Earnings Ratio} = \dfrac{\text{Stock Price}}{\text{EPS}}$	23.7	22.3

Using the stock price immediately after Lowe's announced its 2013 and 2012 earnings during the last week of February 2014 and 2013, the P/E ratio was 23.7 and 22.3, respectively. This means investors were willing to pay 23.7 times earnings to buy a share of Lowe's stock in early 2014 (versus 22.3 times earnings a year earlier). The increase from the prior year suggests investors were more optimistic about the company's future prospects than they were a year earlier. Improvement in the general economy combined with Lowe's strategies for better inventory management contributed to this optimism. The Home Depot's P/E ratio fell slightly from 22.3 to 21.4 during this same period, largely because its most recent monthly sales had declined when Lowe's had increased.

Let's pause to summarize what we've learned so far. Lowe's enjoyed improvement in 2013. Additional customer traffic resulted in increased sales, which contributed to increases in gross profit percentage and net profit margin. Greater sales revenue in 2013 combined with fewer store openings to also boost fixed asset turnover in 2013. These improved results were magnified in the ROE and EPS ratios because Lowe's reduced its stockholders' equity and the number of outstanding common shares in 2013 through stock repurchases. Investors were impressed by these improvements in Lowe's 2013 results, as shown by its higher P/E ratio after the fiscal 2013 results were reported. Although the company trailed The Home Depot on several key ratios, investors could see that Lowe's was narrowing the gap.

Liquidity Ratios

The analyses in this section focus on the company's ability to survive in the short term, by converting assets to cash that can be used to pay current liabilities as they come due. We interpret ratios (7) through (9) from Exhibit 13.5.

(7) Receivables Turnover Most home improvement retailers have low levels of accounts receivable relative to sales revenue because they collect the majority of their sales immediately in cash. Although the formula calls for net **credit** sales in the top of the ratio, companies rarely report their credit sales and cash sales separately. Consequently, financial statement users typically use total net sales revenue in the formula, which results in a receivables turnover ratio that is not terribly meaningful for businesses that make few sales on account. The formula is presented in Exhibit 13.5 simply to remind you of how it's calculated.

(8) Inventory Turnover The inventory turnover ratio indicates how frequently inventory is bought and sold during the year. The measure "days to sell" converts the inventory turnover ratio into the average number of days needed to sell each purchase of inventory.

Fiscal Year	2013	2012
Inventory Turnover = $\frac{\text{Cost of Goods Sold}}{\text{Average Inventory}}$	3.9	3.9
Days to Sell = $\frac{365}{\text{Inventory Turnover Ratio}}$	93.6	93.6

Lowe's inventory turned over at the same rate in 2013 as in 2012. These results were encouraging to Lowe's because the company had decided to carry more diverse lines of inventory in 2013. The goal in carrying more inventory was to better meet customer needs, but this strategy increased the risk that the new lines would not sell as quickly. The stable turnover in 2013 is a positive sign because almost every retailer's success depends on its ability to offer customers the right product when they need it at a price that beats the competition. Lowe's inventory turnover still trails that of The Home Depot (where inventory takes an average of 77 days to sell), but The Home Depot has always had a faster inventory turnover because it carries fewer big-ticket items than Lowe's. According to their 2013 annual reports, the average ticket price was $64.52 at Lowe's and $56.78 at The Home Depot.

Turnover ratios vary significantly from one industry to the next. Companies in the food industry (restaurants and grocery stores) have high inventory turnover ratios because their inventory is subject to spoilage. Companies that sell expensive merchandise (automobiles and high-fashion clothes) have much slower turnover because sales of those items are infrequent, but these companies must carry lots of inventory so that customers have a wide selection to choose from when they do buy.

(9) Current Ratio The current ratio compares current assets to current liabilities, as follows:

Fiscal Year	2013	2012
Current Ratio = $\frac{\text{Current Assets}}{\text{Current Liabilities}}$	1.16	1.27

The current ratio measures the company's ability to pay its current liabilities. Lowe's ratio decreased from 2012 to 2013, ending the year with a ratio of 1.16. In some instances, a decrease in current ratio is a cause for concern. But in this industry, a current ratio greater than 1.0 is deemed acceptable. Plus, Lowe's had a very good reason for its lower current ratio, as explained in the following Spotlight.

SPOTLIGHT ON Decision Making

Lowe's Helps Suppliers Collect on Account

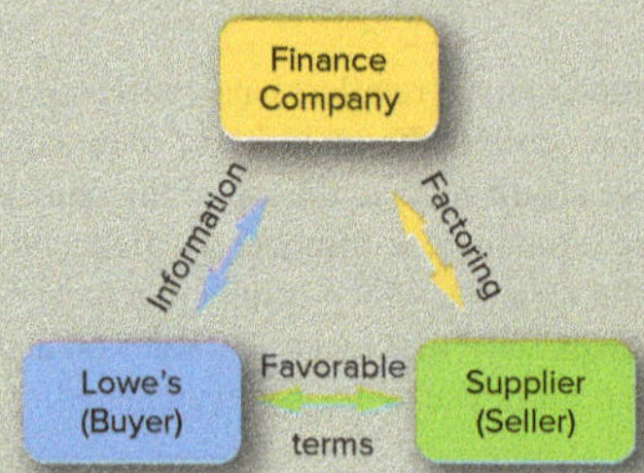

The decrease in Lowe's current ratio in 2013 was caused in part by an increase in its Accounts Payable. That increase in Accounts Payable resulted from suppliers giving Lowe's more favorable payment terms, including a longer period to pay its Accounts Payable. Why would suppliers be willing to allow this? The reason is that Lowe's participates in supply chain financing, or what some call "reverse factoring." The way this works is Lowe's tells a finance company what it owes to particular suppliers. The finance company then contacts the suppliers and offers to take over the collection of Lowe's account balance. Just like a normal factoring arrangement (discussed in Chapter 8), the finance company pays the supplier right away. The finance company charges the supplier a smaller-than-normal factoring fee because it knows Lowe's balance will be easily collected because Lowe's has openly told the finance company how much it owes. The supplier appreciates collecting right away and being charged a smaller factoring fee, so it gives Lowe's more favorable payment terms. Lowe's 2013 annual report indicates it has made this supply chain financing possible for 15 percent of its suppliers.

Solvency Ratios

The analyses in this section focus on Lowe's ability to survive over the long term—that is, its ability to repay debt at maturity and pay interest prior to that time. We interpret ratios (10) and (11) from Exhibit 13.5.

(10) Debt-to-Assets The debt-to-assets ratio indicates the proportion of total assets that creditors finance. Remember that creditors must be paid regardless of how difficult a year the company may have had. The higher this ratio, the riskier is the company's financing strategy. Lowe's ratio for each of the two years was:

	2013	2012
Debt to Assets = $\frac{\text{Total Liabilities}}{\text{Total Assets}}$	0.64	0.58

COACH'S TIP

Instead of the debt-to-assets ratio, analysts might use a debt-to-equity ratio, which gives the same basic information as debt-to-assets. Debt-to-equity typically is calculated as total liabilities ÷ total stockholders' equity. As with debt-to-assets, the higher the debt-to-equity ratio, the more the company relies on debt (rather than equity) financing.

Lowe's ratio of 0.64 in 2013 indicates that creditors contributed 64 percent of the company's financing, implying that it was the company's main source of financing. The debt-to-assets ratio increased from 2012 to 2013 as a result of issuing new bonds and repurchasing common stock. The Home Depot, which had a debt-to-assets ratio of 69 percent in 2013, relies even more on debt financing.

(11) Times Interest Earned The times interest earned ratio indicates how many times the company's interest expense was covered by its operating results. This ratio is calculated using accrual-based interest expense and net income before interest and income taxes, as follows:

	2013	2012
Times Interest Earned = $\frac{\text{Net Income + Interest Expense + Income Tax Expense}}{\text{Interest Expense}}$	8.7	8.4

A times interest earned ratio above 1.0 indicates that net income (before the costs of financing and taxes) is sufficient to cover the company's interest expense. Lowe's ratio of 8.7 indicates the company is generating more than enough profit to cover its interest expense.

COACH'S TIP

If the company reports a net loss, rather than net income, include the loss as a negative number in the formula. A negative ratio indicates that the operating results (before the costs of financing and taxes) are insufficient to cover interest costs.

How's it going? Self-Study Practice

Show the computations for the following two ratios for Lowe's for fiscal 2012. Use the information in Exhibits 13.1 and 13.2.

a. Times interest earned ratio

b. Current ratio

After you have finished, check your answers against the solution in the margin.

Solution to Self-Study Practice

a. ($1,959 + $423 + $1,178) ÷ $423 = 8.4

b. $9,784 ÷ $7,708 = 1.27

UNDERLYING ACCOUNTING DECISIONS AND CONCEPTS

Accounting Decisions

Learning Objective 13-6
Describe how analyses depend on key accounting decisions and concepts.

In the analyses just presented, we compared Lowe's results with those of The Home Depot. When appropriate, we discussed how differences in the two companies' strategies (for example, relying on debt versus equity financing) and business operations (for example, carrying big-ticket versus less expensive items) affected their financial ratios. We should also consider whether differences between the two companies' financial ratios might be caused by differences in their accounting decisions.

The first item to note is that both companies' financial statements have been audited by an independent public accounting firm. The auditors' reports indicate **unqualified opinions** that the companies' financial statements can be relied upon because they are fairly presented. With this overall assurance, we then consider the specific accounting decisions that are summarized in the first note to the financial statements. Exhibit 13.6 shows the policies that three home improvement retailers follow in accounting for inventory and depreciation—two line items that can have a noticeable impact on a retailer's results. Take a moment to study the exhibit.

As you can see, the three companies follow similar but not identical policies. Lowe's and The Home Depot use the FIFO method of accounting for inventory and cost of goods sold; Builder's FirstSource uses the weighted average method. Although these two methods result in different numbers, the overall impact on the companies' financial ratios should be minor because inventory costs did not rise rapidly in 2013.

EXHIBIT 13.6 Comparison of Accounting Methods

	Lowe's	The Home Depot	Builder's FirstSource
Inventory	FIFO	FIFO	Weighted Average Cost
Depreciation	Straight line Buildings: 5–40 yrs Equipment: 3–15 yrs	Straight line Buildings: 5–45 yrs Equipment: 2–20 yrs	Straight line Buildings: 20–40 yrs Equipment: 3–10 yrs

All three companies calculate depreciation using the straight-line method with a similar range of estimated useful lives for buildings and equipment. Because buildings and equipment make up such a large portion of each company's assets, these similarities go a long way toward making their financial results comparable. In conclusion, although the companies' accounting policies differ somewhat, they are unlikely to materially affect our comparisons.

Accounting Concepts

Before wrapping up this chapter, it's worth revisiting the accounting concepts that were introduced in previous chapters. At this stage of the course, you should have developed a fairly good understanding of the rules of accounting and be better able to appreciate why accounting relies on these particular concepts. Exhibit 13.7 summarizes the conceptual framework for financial accounting and reporting that was first introduced in Chapter 1. The concepts that you have already learned about in prior chapters are highlighted in red in Exhibit 13.7.

EXHIBIT 13.7 Conceptual Framework for Financial Accounting and Reporting

Objective of External Financial Reporting
To provide useful financial information to external users for decision making (Ch. 1)
- It must be relevant and a faithful representation of the business
- It is more useful if it is comparable, verifiable, timely, and understandable

Elements to Be Measured and Reported
- Assets, Liabilities, Stockholders' Equity, Revenues, Expenses, Dividends (Ch. 1)

Concepts for Measuring and Reporting Information
- Assumptions: Unit of Measure (Ch. 1), Separate Entity (Ch. 1), Going Concern, Time Period (Ch. 3)
- Principles: Cost (Ch. 2), Revenue and Expense Recognition (Ch. 3), Full Disclosure

As shown in Exhibit 13.7, the primary objective of financial accounting and reporting is to provide useful financial information for people external to a company to use in making decisions about the company. To be useful, this information must be relevant and faithfully represent the underlying business.

As Exhibit 13.7 indicates, only two accounting concepts have not been introduced in previous chapters, so we will explain them here. The **going-concern** (also called *continuity*) **assumption** quietly underlies accounting rules. It is the belief that any business will be capable of continuing its operations long enough to realize the economic benefits

EXHIBIT 13.8 Factors Contributing to Going-Concern Uncertainties

Revealed by Financial Analyses	Revealed by Other Analyses
• Declining sales	• Loss of a key supplier or customer
• Declining gross profit	• Insufficient product innovation/quality
• Significant one-time expenses	• Significant barriers to expansion
• Fluctuating net income	• Loss of key personnel without replacement
• Insufficient current assets	• Unfavorable long-term commitments
• Excessive reliance on debt financing	• Inadequate maintenance of long-lived assets
• Negative operating cash flows	• Loss of a key franchise, license, or patent

of its assets and meet its obligations in the normal course of business. If a company judges it probable that it will be unable to meet its obligations for at least one year after the the financial statements are issued, it must disclose this in the financial statement notes. In severe cases, it may need to adjust the amount and classification of items in its financial statements. Some of the factors that commonly contribute to going-concern uncertainties are listed in Exhibit 13.8. Notice that some of the analyses presented earlier in this chapter are key considerations.

One of the principles of accounting that was not previously explained is full disclosure. Simply put, according to the **full disclosure principle**, financial reports should present all information that is needed to properly interpret the results of the company's business activities. This doesn't mean that every single transaction needs to be explained in detail, but rather that adequate information needs to be presented to allow financial statement users to fairly interpret reports about the company's income, financial position, and cash flows.

Before closing the book on this topic (and possibly this course), take a moment to complete the following Self-Study Practice. It'll give you a good idea of whether you need a detailed review of the concepts introduced in earlier chapters or whether you're ready to move on to review and practice key aspects of this chapter.

How's it going? Self-Study Practice

Match each statement below to the concept to which it most closely relates.

1. Everything comes down to dollars and cents.
2. That's not our issue. It's for somebody else to report.
3. If it relates to this period's earnings, you'd better report it.
4. I've told you everything you could possibly want to know.
5. At that rate, you may not survive past the end of the year.
6. I know it's a long time, but let's break it down into stages.

a. Separate entity
b. Revenue and expense recognition
c. Going concern
d. Unit of measure
e. Time period
f. Full disclosure

After you have finished, check your answers against the solution in the margin.

Solution to Self-Study Practice
1. (d)
2. (a)
3. (b)
4. (f)
5. (c)
6. (e)

REVIEW THE CHAPTER

DEMONSTRATION CASE

The following information was taken from The Home Depot's annual report.

(in millions of dollars)	February 2, 2014 (Fiscal 2013)	
Net Sales Revenue	$78,812	
Cost of Goods Sold	51,422	
Other Expenses	22,005	
Net Income	5,385	
	February 2, 2014 (Fiscal 2013)	**February 3, 2013 (Fiscal 2012)**
Inventory	$11,057	$10,710
Current Assets	15,279	15,372
Property and Equipment, Net	23,348	24,069
Total Assets	40,518	41,084
Current Liabilities	10,749	11,462
Total Liabilities	27,996	23,307
Total Stockholders' Equity	12,522	17,777

Required:

1. Conduct a horizontal analysis of Inventory and a vertical analysis of the income statement items.
2. Compute the following ratios for The Home Depot for the year ended February 2, 2014.

Fixed Asset Turnover	Inventory Turnover	Current Ratio
Return on Equity	Days to Sell	Debt-to-Assets

3. Interpret the meaning of the ratios you calculated in requirement 2.

Suggested Solution

1.

Horizontal Analysis	February 2, 2014	February 3, 2013	Increase	
Inventory	$11,057	$10,710	$347	3.2%

Vertical Analysis		
Net Sales Revenue	$78,812	100.0%
Cost of Goods Sold	51,422	65.2
Other Expenses	22,005	29.0*
Net Income	$5,385	6.8%

*Rounded-up so that total sums to 100%

2. Calculating ratios:
3. Interpreting ratios
   - The fixed asset turnover ratio of 3.32 means that, on average, The Home Depot generated $3.32 of sales for each dollar of fixed assets.
   - The return on equity of 35.5 percent means that The Home Depot's net income for the year was 35.5 percent of the amount investors contributed to and left in the company.
   - The inventory turnover ratio of 4.72 means that The Home Depot turned over (bought and sold) the equivalent of its entire inventory an average of 4.72 times during the year.
   - The days to sell ratio of 77.3 means that, on average, 77.3 days elapsed between the time The Home Depot acquired the inventory and the time the company sold it.

- The current ratio of 1.42 means that at year-end, The Home Depot had $1.42 of current assets for each dollar of current liabilities.
- The debt-to-assets ratio of 0.69 means that The Home Depot relied on current and long-term liabilities to finance 69 percent of its assets, implying that stockholders' equity financed 31 percent (100 − 69) of its total assets.

CHAPTER SUMMARY

Describe the purposes and uses of horizontal, vertical, and ratio analyses. p. 564 **LO 13-1**

- Horizontal analyses (also called trend analyses) compare financial statement items to comparable amounts in prior periods with the goal of identifying sustained changes, or trends.
- Vertical analyses create common size financial statements that express each line of the income statement (or balance sheet) as a percentage of total sales (or total assets).
- Ratio analyses compare one or more financial statement items to an amount for other items for the same year. Ratios take into account differences in the size of amounts to allow for evaluations of performance given existing levels of other company resources.

Use horizontal (trend) analyses to recognize financial changes that unfold over time. p. 565 **LO 13-2**

- Trend analyses involve computing the dollar amount by which each account changes from one period to the next and expressing that change as a percentage of the balance for the prior period.

Use vertical (common size) analyses to understand important relationships within financial statements. p. 565 **LO 13-3**

- Vertical (common size) analyses indicate the proportions within each financial statement category.

Calculate financial ratios to assess profitability, liquidity, and solvency. p. 568 **LO 13-4**

- Financial ratios are commonly classified with relation to profitability, liquidity, or solvency. Exhibit 13.5 lists common ratios in these three categories and shows how to compute them.
- Profitability ratios focus on measuring the adequacy of a company's income by comparing it to other items reported on the financial statements.
- Liquidity ratios measure a company's ability to meet its current debt obligations.
- Solvency ratios measure a company's ability to meet its long-term debt obligations.

Interpret the results of financial analyses. p. 569 **LO 13-5**

- Financial analyses are not complete unless they lead to an interpretation that helps financial statement users understand and evaluate a company's financial results.
- An understanding of whether a business is successful emerges only after you have learned to combine analyses into a complete picture or story that depicts the company's performance.
- To assist in developing this picture or story, most analysts compare to benchmarks such as the company's performance in prior years or to competitors' performance in the current year.

Describe how analyses depend on key accounting decisions and concepts. p. 575 **LO 13-6**

- Before comparing across companies or time periods, users should determine the extent to which differences in accounting decisions (e.g., methods used to account for inventory, depreciation, contingent liabilities, etc.) might reduce comparability or consistency of the financial information being compared.
- Many accounting concepts were presented throughout earlier chapters, all of which aim to make accounting information more useful for creditors and investors. Two new concepts were explained in this chapter:
  - Going-concern (continuity) assumption—a business is assumed to continue to operate into the foreseeable future.
  - Full disclosure principle—a company's financial statements should provide all information that is important to users' decisions.

KEY TERMS

Full Disclosure Principle p. 577
Going-Concern Assumption p. 576
Horizontal (Trend) Analyses p. 565
Liquidity p. 568
Profitability p. 568
Solvency p. 568
Vertical (Common Size) Analyses p. 565

See complete definitions in glossary at back of text.

PRACTICE MATERIAL

QUESTIONS

1. What is the general goal of trend analysis?
2. How is a year-over-year percentage calculated?
3. What is ratio analysis? Why is it useful?
4. What benchmarks are commonly used for interpreting ratios?
5. Into what three categories of performance are most financial ratios reported? To what in particular does each of these categories relate?
6. Why are some analyses called *horizontal* and others called *vertical?*
7. Slow Cellar's current ratio increased from 1.2 to 1.5. What is one favorable interpretation of this change? What is one unfavorable interpretation of this change?
8. From last year to this year, Colossal Company's current ratio increased and its inventory turnover decreased. Does this imply a higher, or lower, risk of obsolete inventory?
9. From last year to this year, Berry Barn reported that its Net Sales increased from $300,000 to $400,000 and its Gross Profit increased from $90,000 to $130,000. Was the Gross Profit increase caused by (*a*) an increase in sales volume only, (*b*) an increase in gross profit per sale only, or (*c*) a combination of both? Explain your answer.
10. Explain whether the following situations, taken independently, would be favorable or unfavorable: (*a*) increase in gross profit percentage, (*b*) decrease in inventory turnover ratio, (*c*) increase in earnings per share, (*d*) decrease in days to collect, and (*e*) increase in net profit margin.

MULTIPLE CHOICE

1. Which of the following ratios is *not* used to analyze profitability?
   a. Net profit margin ratio.
   b. Gross profit percentage.
   c. Current ratio.
   d. Return on equity.
2. Which of the following would *not* directly change the receivables turnover ratio for a company?
   a. Increases in the selling prices of your inventory.
   b. A change in your credit policy.
   c. Increases in the cost you incur to purchase inventory.
   d. All of the above would directly change the receivables turnover ratio.
3. Which of the following ratios is used to analyze liquidity?
   a. Earnings per share.
   b. Debt-to-assets.
   c. Current ratio.
   d. Both *b* and *c*.
4. Analysts use ratios to
   a. Compare different companies in the same industry.
   b. Track a company's performance over time.
   c. Compare a company's performance to industry averages.
   d. All of the above describe ways that analysts use ratios.
5. Which of the following ratios incorporates stock market data?
   a. Inventory turnover.
   b. Earnings per share.
   c. Price/earnings ratio.
   d. All of the above.
6. Given the following ratios for four companies, which company is least likely to experience problems paying its current liabilities promptly?

	Current Ratio	Receivables Turnover Ratio
a.	1.2	7.0
b.	1.2	6.0
c.	1.0	6.0
d.	0.5	7.0

7. A decrease in Selling and Administrative Expenses would directly impact what ratio?
   a. Fixed asset turnover ratio.
   b. Times interest earned.
   c. Current ratio.
   d. Gross profit percentage.
8. A bank is least likely to use which of the following ratios when analyzing the likelihood that a borrower will pay interest and principal on its loans?
   a. Current ratio.
   b. Debt-to-assets ratio.
   c. Times interest earned ratio.
   d. Price/earnings ratio.
9. Which of the following accounting concepts do accountants and auditors assess by using financial analyses?
   a. Time period.
   b. Separate entity.
   c. Full disclosure.
   d. Going-concern assumption.

Answers to Multiple-Choice Questions located in back of the text.

MINI-EXERCISES

connect

M13-1 Calculations for Horizontal Analyses LO 13-2

Using the following income statements, perform the calculations needed for horizontal analyses. Round percentages to one decimal place.

LOCKEY FENCING CORPORATION
Income Statements
For the Years Ended December 31

	Current	Previous
Net Sales	$100,000	$75,000
Cost of Goods Sold	58,000	45,000
Gross Profit	42,000	30,000
Selling, General, and Administrative Expenses	9,000	4,500
Income from Operations	33,000	25,500
Interest Expense	3,000	3,750
Income before Income Tax	30,000	21,750
Income Tax Expense	9,000	6,525
Net Income	$ 21,000	$15,225

M13-2 Calculations for Vertical Analyses LO 13-3

Refer to M13-1. Perform the calculations needed for vertical analyses. Round percentages to one decimal place.

M13-3 Interpreting Horizontal Analyses LO 13-5

Refer to the calculations from M13-1. What are the two most significant year-over-year changes in terms of dollars and in terms of percentages? Give one potential cause of each of these changes.

M13-4 Interpreting Vertical Analyses LO 13-5

Refer to the calculations from M13-2. Which of the ratios from Exhibit 13.5 have been included in these calculations? Have these two ratios improved or deteriorated in the current year compared to the previous year?

M13-5 Inferring Financial Information Using Gross Profit Percentage LO 13-4

Your campus computer store reported Sales Revenue of $168,000. The company's gross profit percentage was 60.0 percent. What amount of Cost of Goods Sold did the company report?

M13-6 Inferring Financial Information Using Gross Profit Percentage and Year-over-Year Comparisons LO 13-2, 13-4

A consumer products company reported a 25 percent increase in sales from last year to this year. Sales last year were $200,000. This year, the company reported Cost of Goods Sold in the amount of $150,000. What was the gross profit percentage this year? Round to one decimal place.

M13-7 Computing the Return on Equity Ratio LO 13-4

Given the following data, compute the return on equity ratio for the current year (expressed as a percentage with one decimal place).

	Current	Previous
Net income	$ 1,850	$ 1,600
Stockholders' equity	10,000	13,125
Total assets	24,000	26,000
Interest expense	400	300

LO 13-4, 13-5 **M13-8 Analyzing the Inventory Turnover Ratio**

A manufacturer reported an inventory turnover ratio of 8.6 last year. During the current year, management introduced a new inventory control system that was expected to reduce average inventory levels by 25 percent without affecting sales volume. Given these circumstances, would you expect the inventory turnover ratio to increase or decrease during the current year? Explain.

LO 13-4 **M13-9 Inferring Financial Information Using the Current Ratio**

Mystic Laboratories reported total assets of $11,200,000 and noncurrent assets of $1,480,000. The company also reported a current ratio of 1.5. What amount of current liabilities did the company report?

LO 13-4 **M13-10 Inferring Financial Information Using the P/E Ratio**

LEVEL UP

Last year, Big W Company reported earnings per share of $2.50 when its stock was selling for $50.00. If its earnings this year increase by 10 percent and the P/E ratio remains constant, what will be the price of its stock? Explain.

LO 13-4, 13-5 **M13-11 Identifying Relevant Ratios**

Identify the ratio that is relevant to answering each of the following questions.

a. How much net income does the company earn from each dollar of sales?
b. Is the company financed primarily by debt or equity?
c. How many dollars of sales were generated for each dollar invested in fixed assets?
d. How many days, on average, does it take the company to collect on credit sales made to customers?
e. How much net income does the company earn for each dollar owners have invested in it?
f. Does the company have sufficient assets to convert into cash for paying liabilities as they come due in the upcoming year?

LO 13-4, 13-5 **M13-12 Interpreting Ratios**

Generally speaking, do the following indicate good news or bad news?

a. Increase in times interest earned ratio.
b. Decrease in days to sell.
c. Increase in gross profit percentage.
d. Decrease in EPS.
e. Increase in fixed asset turnover ratio.

LO 13-6 **M13-13 Analyzing the Impact of Accounting Alternatives**

Nevis Corporation operates in an industry where costs are falling. The company is considering changing its inventory method from FIFO to LIFO and wants to determine the impact that the change would have on selected accounting ratios in future years. In general, what impact would you expect on the following ratios: net profit margin, fixed asset turnover, and current ratio?

LO 13-6 **M13-14 Describing the Effect of Accounting Decisions on Ratios**

For each of the following three accounting choices, indicate the decision that will yield (*a*) a higher net profit margin and (*b*) a lower current ratio. If the decision does not affect the ratio, indicate "no effect."

1. Straight-line versus accelerated depreciation (in the first year of the asset's life).
2. FIFO versus LIFO (in periods of constantly rising costs and rising inventory levels).
3. Straight-line depreciation with a four-year useful life versus a seven-year useful life (no residual value).

EXERCISES

connect

LO 13-2, 13-3, 13-5 **E13-1 Preparing and Interpreting a Schedule for Horizontal and Vertical Analyses**

The average price of a gallon of gas in 2013 dropped $0.12 (3 percent) from $3.61 in 2012 (to $3.49 in 2013). Let's see whether these changes are reflected in the income statement of Chevron Corporation for the year ended December 31, 2013 (amounts in billions).

	2013	2012
Revenues	$220	$231
Costs of Crude Oil and Products	143	149
Other Operating Costs	41	36
Income before Income Tax Expense	36	46
Income Tax Expense	15	20
Net Income	$ 21	$ 26

Required:

1. Conduct a horizontal analysis by calculating the year-over-year changes in each line item, expressed in dollars and in percentages (rounded to one decimal place). How did the change in gas prices compare to the changes in Chevron's total revenues and costs of crude oil and products?
2. Conduct a vertical analysis by expressing each line as a percentage of total revenues (round to one decimal place). Excluding income tax and other operating costs, did Chevron earn more profit per dollar of revenue in 2013 compared to 2012?

E13-2 Computing and Interpreting Profitability Ratios LO 13-4, 13-5

Use the information for Chevron Corporation in E13-1 to complete the following requirements.

Required:

1. Compute the gross profit percentage for each year (rounded to one decimal place). Assuming that the change from 2012 to 2013 is the beginning of a sustained trend, is Chevron likely to earn more or less gross profit from each dollar of sales in 2014?
2. Compute the net profit margin for each year (expressed as a percentage with one decimal place). Given your calculations here and in requirement 1, explain whether Chevron did a better or worse job of controlling expenses other than the costs of crude oil and products in 2013 relative to 2012.
3. Chevron reported average net fixed assets of $150 billion in 2013 and $130 billion in 2012. Compute the fixed asset turnover ratios for both years (round to two decimal places). Did the company better utilize its investment in fixed assets to generate revenues in 2013 or 2012?
4. Chevron reported average stockholders' equity of $140 billion in 2013 and $130 billion in 2012. Compute the return on equity ratios for both years (expressed as a percentage with one decimal place). Did the company generate greater returns for stockholders in 2013 or 2012?

E13-3 Preparing and Interpreting a Schedule for Horizontal and Vertical Analyses LO 13-2, 13-3, 13-5

According to the producer price index database maintained by the Bureau of Labor Statistics, the average cost of computer equipment fell 8.1 percent between 2012 and 2013. Let's see whether these changes are reflected in the income statement of Computer Tycoon Inc. for the year ended December 31, 2013.

	2013	2012
Sales Revenue	$100,000	$120,000
Cost of Goods Sold	60,000	71,500
Gross Profit	40,000	48,500
Selling, General, and Administrative Expenses	36,000	37,000
Interest Expense	500	475
Income before Income Tax Expense	3,500	11,025
Income Tax Expense	1,000	5,000
Net Income	$ 2,500	$ 6,025

Required:

1. Conduct a horizontal analysis by calculating the year-over-year changes in each line item, expressed in dollars and in percentages (rounded to one decimal place). How did the change in computer prices compare to the changes in Computer Tycoon's sales revenues?
2. Conduct a vertical analysis by expressing each line as a percentage of total revenues (round to one decimal place). Excluding income tax, interest, and operating expenses, did Computer Tycoon earn more profit per dollar of sales in 2013 compared to 2012?

LO 13-4, 13-5

E13-4 Computing Profitability Ratios

Use the information in E13-3 to complete the following requirements.

Required:

1. Compute the gross profit percentage for each year (rounded to one decimal place). Assuming that the change from 2012 to 2013 is the beginning of a sustained trend, is Computer Tycoon likely to earn more or less gross profit from each dollar of sales in 2014?
2. Compute the net profit margin for each year (expressed as a percentage with one decimal place). Given your calculations here and in requirement 1, explain whether Computer Tycoon did a better or worse job of controlling operating expenses in 2013 relative to 2012.
3. Computer Tycoon reported average net fixed assets of $54,200 in 2013 and $45,100 in 2012. Compute the fixed asset turnover ratios for both years (round to two decimal places). Did the company better utilize its investment in fixed assets to generate revenues in 2013 or 2012?
4. Computer Tycoon reported average stockholders' equity of $54,000 in 2013 and $40,800 in 2012. Compute the return on equity ratios for both years (expressed as a percentage with one decimal place). Did the company generate greater returns for stockholders in 2013 than in 2012?

LO 13-4, 13-5

E13-5 Computing a Commonly Used Solvency Ratio

Use the information in E13-3 to complete the following requirement.

Required:

Compute the times interest earned ratios for 2013 and 2012. In your opinion, does Computer Tycoon generate sufficient net income (before taxes and interest) to cover the cost of debt financing?

LO 13-4

E13-6 Matching Each Ratio with Its Computational Formula

Match each ratio or percentage with its formula by entering the appropriate letter for each numbered item.

Ratios or Percentages	Formula
____ 1. Current ratio	A. Net income ÷ Total revenue
____ 2. Net profit margin	B. (Net sales revenue − Cost of goods sold) ÷ Net sales revenue
____ 3. Inventory turnover ratio	C. Current assets ÷ Current liabilities
____ 4. Gross profit percentage	D. Cost of goods sold ÷ Average inventory
____ 5. Fixed asset turnover	E. Net credit sales revenue ÷ Average net receivables
____ 6. Return on equity	F. (Net income − Preferred dividends) ÷ Average number of common shares outstanding
____ 7. Times interest earned	G. Total liabilities ÷ Total assets
____ 8. Debt-to-assets ratio	H. (Net income + Interest expense + Income tax expense) ÷ Interest expense
____ 9. Price/earnings ratio	I. Current market price per share ÷ Earnings per share
____ 10. Receivables turnover ratio	J. (Net income − Preferred dividends) ÷ Average common stockholders' equity
____ 11. Earnings per share	K. Total revenue ÷ Average net fixed assets

E13-7 Computing and Interpreting Selected Liquidity Ratios LO 13-4, 13-5

Double West Suppliers (DWS) reported sales for the year of $300,000, all on credit. The average gross profit percentage was 40 percent on sales. Account balances follow:

	Beginning	Ending
Accounts receivable (net)	$45,000	$55,000
Inventory	60,000	40,000

Required:

1. Compute the turnover ratios for accounts receivable and inventory (round to one decimal place).
2. By dividing 365 by your ratios from requirement 1, calculate the average days to collect receivables and the average days to sell inventory (round to one decimal place).
3. Explain what each of these ratios and measures means for DWS.

E13-8 Computing and Interpreting Liquidity Ratios LO 13-4, 13-5

Cintas Corporation is the largest uniform supplier in North America. Selected information from its annual report follows. For the 2013 fiscal year, the company reported sales revenue of $4.3 billion and Cost of Goods Sold of $2.5 billion.

Fiscal Year	2013	2012
Balance Sheet (amounts in millions)		
Cash	$360	$340
Accounts Receivable, net	500	450
Inventory	240	250
Prepaid Rent	525	480
Accounts Payable	120	100
Salaries and Wages Payable	340	340
Income Tax Payable	80	10
Notes Payable (short-term)	10	230

Required:

Assuming that all sales are on credit, compute the current ratio (two decimal places), inventory turnover ratio (one decimal place), and accounts receivable turnover ratio (one decimal place) for 2013. Explain what each ratio means for Cintas.

E13-9 Computing the Accounts Receivable and Inventory Turnover Ratios LO 13-4, 13-5

Procter & Gamble is a multinational corporation that manufactures and markets many products that you use every day. In 2013, sales for the company were $84,000 (all amounts in millions). The annual report did not report the amount of credit sales, so we will assume that all sales were on credit. The average gross profit percentage was 49.6 percent. Account balances for the year follow:

	Beginning	Ending
Accounts receivable (net)	$6,100	$6,500
Inventory	6,700	6,900

Required:

1. Rounded to one decimal place, compute the turnover ratios for accounts receivable and inventory.

2. By dividing 365 by your ratios from requirement 1, calculate the average days to collect receivables and the average days to sell inventory.
3. Interpret what these ratios and measures mean for P&G.

LO 13-4, 13-5

E13-10 Inferring Financial Information from Profitability and Liquidity Ratios

LEVEL UP

Dollar General Corporation operates general merchandise stores that feature quality merchandise at low prices to meet the needs of middle-, low-, and fixed-income families in southern, eastern, and midwestern states. For the year ended January 31, 2014, the company reported average inventories of $2,475 (in millions) and an inventory turnover of 4.89. Average total fixed assets were $2,080 (million) and the fixed asset turnover ratio was 8.14.

Required:

1. Calculate Dollar General's gross profit percentage (expressed as a percentage with one decimal place). What does this imply about the amount of gross profit made from each dollar of sales?
   TIP: Work backward from the fixed asset turnover and inventory turnover ratios to compute the amounts needed for the gross profit percentage.
2. Is this an improvement from the gross profit percentage of 31.7 percent earned during the previous year?

LO 13-4, 13-5

E13-11 Analyzing the Impact of Selected Transactions on the Current Ratio

In its most recent annual report, Appalachian Beverages reported current assets of $54,000 and a current ratio of 1.80. Assume that the following transactions were completed: (1) purchased merchandise for $6,000 on account and (2) purchased a delivery truck for $10,000, paying $1,000 cash and signing a two-year promissory note for the balance.

Required:

Compute the updated current ratio, rounded to two decimal places, after each transaction.

LO 13-4, 13-5

E13-12 Analyzing the Impact of Selected Transactions on the Current Ratio

In its most recent annual report, Sunrise Enterprises reported current assets of $1,090,000 and current liabilities of $602,000.

Required:

Determine for each of the following transactions whether the current ratio, and each of its two components, for Sunrise will increase, decrease, or have no change: (1) sold long-term assets for cash, (2) accrued severance pay for terminated employees, (3) wrote down the carrying value of certain inventory items that were deemed to be obsolete, and (4) acquired new inventory by signing an 18-month promissory note (the supplier was not willing to provide normal credit terms).

LO 13-4, 13-5

E13-13 Analyzing the Impact of Selected Transactions on the Current Ratio

The Sports Authority, Inc., is a private full-line sporting goods retailer. Assume one of the Sports Authority stores reported current assets of $88,000 and its current ratio was 1.75, and then completed the following transactions: (1) paid $6,000 on accounts payable, (2) purchased a delivery truck for $10,000 cash, (3) wrote off a bad account receivable for $2,000, and (4) paid previously declared dividends in the amount of $25,000.

Required:

Compute the updated current ratio, rounded to two decimal places, after each transaction.

LO 13-4, 13-5

E13-14 Analyzing the Impact of Selected Transactions on the Current Ratio

A company has current assets that total $500,000, has a current ratio of 2.00, and uses the perpetual inventory method. Assume that the following transactions are then completed: (1) sold $12,000 in merchandise on short-term credit for $15,000, (2) declared but did not pay dividends of $50,000, (3) paid prepaid rent in the amount of $12,000, (4) paid previously declared dividends in the amount of $50,000, (5) collected an account receivable in the amount of $12,000, and (6) reclassified $40,000 of long-term debt as a current liability.

Required:

Compute the updated current ratio, rounded to two decimal places, after each transaction.

E13-15 Analyzing the Impact of Alternative Inventory Methods on Selected Ratios LO 13-6

Company A uses the FIFO method to cost inventory and Company B uses the LIFO method. The two companies are exactly alike except for the difference in inventory costing methods. Costs of inventory items for both companies have been falling steadily in recent years and each company has increased its inventory each year. Ignore income tax effects.

Required:

Identify which company will report the higher amount for each of the following ratios. If it is not possible to identify which will report the higher amount, explain why.

1. Current ratio.
2. Debt-to-assets ratio.
3. Earnings per share.

GROUP A PROBLEMS

PA13-1 Analyzing Financial Statements Using Horizontal Analyses LO 13-2, 13-5

The comparative financial statements prepared at December 31 for Pinnacle Plus showed the following summarized data:

			Increase (Decrease) in Current (versus Previous)	
	Current	Previous	Amount	Percentage
Income Statement				
Sales Revenue	$110,000	$ 99,000		
Cost of Goods Sold	52,000	48,000		
Gross Profit	58,000	51,000		
Operating Expenses	36,000	33,000		
Interest Expense	4,000	4,000		
Income before Income Tax Expense	18,000	14,000		
Income Tax Expense (30%)	5,400	4,200		
Net Income	$ 12,600	$ 9,800		
Balance Sheet				
Cash	$ 69,500	$ 38,000		
Accounts Receivable, Net	17,000	12,000		
Inventory	25,000	38,000		
Property and Equipment, Net	95,000	105,000		
Total Assets	$206,500	$193,000		
Accounts Payable	$ 42,000	$ 35,000		
Income Tax Payable	1,000	500		
Note Payable, (long-term)	40,000	40,000		
Total Liabilities	83,000	75,500		
Common Stock (par $10)	90,000	90,000		
Retained Earnings†	33,500	27,500		
Total Liabilities and Stockholders' Equity	$206,500	$193,000		

†During the current year, cash dividends amounting to $6,600 were declared and paid.

Required:

1. Complete the two final columns shown beside each item in Pinnacle Plus's comparative financial statements. Round the percentages to one decimal place.

2. Which account increased by the largest dollar amount? Which account increased by the largest percentage?

LO 13-4, 13-5

PA13-2 Analyzing Comparative Financial Statements Using Selected Ratios

Use the data given in PA13-1 for Pinnacle Plus.

Required:

1. Compute the gross profit percentage in the current and previous years. Round the percentages to one decimal place. Are the current year results better, or worse, than those for the previous year?
2. Compute the net profit margin for the current and previous years. Round the percentages to one decimal place. Are the current year results better, or worse, than those for the previous year?
3. Compute the earnings per share for the current and previous years. Are the current year results better, or worse, than those for the previous year?
4. Stockholders' equity totaled $100,000 at the beginning of the previous year. Compute the return on equity (ROE) ratios for the current and previous years. Express the ROE as percentages rounded to one decimal place. Are the current year results better, or worse, than those for the previous year?
5. Net property and equipment totaled $110,000 at the beginning of the previous year. Compute the fixed asset turnover ratios for the current and previous years. Round the ratios to two decimal places. Are the current year results better, or worse, than those for the previous year?
6. Compute the debt-to-assets ratios for the current and previous years. Round the ratios to two decimal places. Is debt providing financing for a larger or smaller proportion of the company's asset growth?
7. Compute the times interest earned ratios for the current and previous years. Round the ratios to one decimal place. Are the current year results better, or worse, than those for the previous year?
8. After Pinnacle Plus released its current year's financial statements, the company's stock was trading at $18. After the release of its previous year's financial statements, the company's stock price was $15 per share. Compute the P/E ratios for both years, rounded to one decimal place. Does it appear that investors have become more (or less) optimistic about Pinnacle's future success?

LO 13-3, 13-5

PA13-3 Vertical Analysis of a Balance Sheet

A condensed balance sheet for Simultech Corporation and a partially completed vertical analysis are presented as follows.

SIMULTECH CORPORATION
Balance Sheet (summarized)
January 31
(in millions of U.S. dollars)

Cash	$ 433	29%	Current Liabilities	$ 409	27%
Accounts Receivable	294	19	Long-term Liabilities	495	33
Inventories	206	14	Total Liabilities	904	*b*
Other Current Assets	109	*a*	Contributed Capital	118	*c*
Property and Equipment	27	2	Retained Earnings	492	32
Other Assets	445	29	Total Stockholders' Equity	610	*d*
Total Assets	$1,514	100%	Total Liabilities & Stockholders' Equity	$1,514	100%

Required:

1. Complete the vertical analysis by computing each line item (*a*) through (*d*) as a percentage of total assets. Round to the nearest whole percentage.

2. What percentages of Simultech's assets relate to inventory versus property and equipment? Which of these two asset groups is more significant to Simultech's business?
3. What percentage of Simultech's assets is financed by total stockholder's equity? By total liabilities?

PA13-4 Vertical Analysis of an Income Statement

LO 13-3, 13-5

A condensed income statement for Simultech Corporation and a partially completed vertical analysis are presented as follows.

SIMULTECH CORPORATION
Income Statement (summarized)
(in millions of U.S. dollars)

	Current Year		Previous Year	
Sales Revenues	$2,062	100%	$2,200	100%
Cost of Goods Sold	1,637	79	1,721	*d*
Selling, General, and Administrative Expenses	333	*a*	346	16
Other Operating Expenses	53	3	12	1
Interest Expense	22	*b*	26	1
Income before Income Tax Expense	17	1	95	*e*
Income Tax Expense	6	0	33	1
Net Income	$ 11	*c*	$ 62	*f*

Required:

1. Complete the vertical analysis by computing each line item (*a*) through (*f*) as a percentage of sales revenues. Round to the nearest whole percentage.
2. Does Simultech's Cost of Goods Sold for the current year, as a percentage of revenues, represent better or worse performance as compared to that for the previous year?
3. Has Simultech's net profit margin increased, or decreased, over the two years?

PA13-5 Interpreting Profitability, Liquidity, Solvency, and P/E Ratios

LO 13-4, 13-5

Coke and Pepsi are well-known international brands. Coca-Cola sells more than $46 billion worth of beverages each year while annual sales of Pepsi products exceed $66 billion. Compare the two companies as a potential investment based on the following ratios:

Ratio	Coca-Cola	PepsiCo
Gross profit percentage	60.7%	53.2%
Net profit margin	18.4%	10.2%
EPS	$1.90	$4.32
Inventory turnover ratio	5.3	8.2
Current ratio	1.13	1.24
Debt-to-assets	0.41	0.38
P/E ratio	20.4	19.3

Required:

1. Which company appears more profitable? Describe the ratio(s) that you used to reach this decision.
2. Which company appears more liquid? Describe the ratio(s) that you used to reach this decision.
3. Which company appears more solvent? Describe the ratio(s) that you used to reach this decision.

4. Are the conclusions from your analyses in requirements 1 to 3 consistent with the value of the two companies, as suggested by their P/E ratios? If not, offer one explanation for any apparent inconsistency.

LO 13-4, 13-5, 13-6

PA13-6 Using Ratios to Compare Loan Requests from Two Companies

The financial statements for Royale and Cavalier companies are summarized here:

	Royale Company	Cavalier Company
Balance Sheet		
Cash	$ 25,000	$ 45,000
Accounts Receivable, Net	55,000	16,000
Inventory	110,000	25,000
Equipment, Net	550,000	160,000
Other Assets	140,000	46,000
Total Assets	$880,000	$292,000
Current Liabilities	$120,000	$ 15,000
Note Payable (long-term)	190,000	55,000
Capital Stock (par $20)	480,000	210,000
Additional Paid-in Capital	50,000	4,000
Retained Earnings	40,000	8,000
Total Liabilities and Stockholders' Equity	$880,000	$292,000
Income Statement		
Sales Revenue	$800,000	$280,000
Cost of Goods Sold	480,000	150,000
Other Expenses	240,000	95,000
Net Income	$ 80,000	$ 35,000
Other Data		
Per share price at end of year	$ 14.00	$ 11.00
Selected Data from Previous Year		
Accounts Receivable, Net	$ 47,000	$ 14,000
Note Payable (long-term)	190,000	55,000
Equipment, Net	550,000	160,000
Inventory	95,000	38,000
Total Stockholders' Equity	570,000	202,000

These two companies are in the same business and state but different cities. Each company has been in operation for about 10 years. Both companies received an unqualified audit opinion on the financial statements. Royale Company wants to borrow $75,000 cash and Cavalier Company is asking for $30,000. The loans will be for a two-year period. Both companies estimate bad debts based on an aging analysis, but Cavalier has estimated slightly higher uncollectible rates than Royale. Neither company issued stock in the current year. Assume the end-of-year total assets and net equipment balances approximate the year's average and all sales are on account.

Required:

1. Calculate the ratios in Exhibit 13.5 for which sufficient information is available. Round all calculations to two decimal places.
2. Assume that you work in the loan department of a local bank. You have been asked to analyze the situation and recommend which loan is preferable. Based on the data given, your analysis prepared in requirement 1, and any other information (e.g., accounting policies and decisions), give your choice and the supporting explanation.

LO 13-5

PA13-7 Analyzing an Investment by Comparing Selected Ratios

You have the opportunity to invest $10,000 in one of two companies from a single industry. The only information you have is shown here. The word *high* refers to the top third of the industry; *average* is the middle third; *low* is the bottom third.

Ratio	Company A	Company B
Current	Low	High
Inventory turnover	High	Low
Debt to assets	Low	Average
Times interest earned	High	Average
Price/earnings	High	Average

Required:

Which company would you select? Write a brief explanation for your recommendation.

GROUP B PROBLEMS

connect

PB13-1 Analyzing Financial Statements Using Horizontal and Ratio Analyses LO 13-2, 13-4, 13-5

The comparative financial statements prepared at December 31 for Tiger Audio showed the following summarized data:

	Current	Previous	Increase (Decrease) in Current (versus Previous) Amount	Percentage
Income Statement				
Sales Revenue	$222,000	$185,000		
Cost of Goods Sold	127,650	111,000		
Gross Profit	94,350	74,000		
Operating Expenses	39,600	33,730		
Interest Expense	4,000	3,270		
Income before Income Tax Expense	50,750	37,000		
Income Tax Expense (30%)	15,225	11,100		
Net Income	$ 35,525	$ 25,900		
Balance Sheet				
Cash	$ 40,000	$ 38,000		
Accounts Receivable, Net	18,500	16,000		
Inventory	25,000	22,000		
Property and Equipment, Net	127,000	119,000		
Total Assets	$210,500	$195,000		
Accounts Payable	$ 27,000	$ 25,000		
Income Tax Payable	3,000	2,800		
Note Payable (long-term)	75,500	92,200		
Total Liabilities	105,500	120,000		
Capital Stock (par $1)	25,000	25,000		
Retained Earnings*	80,000	50,000		
Total Liabilities and Stockholders' Equity	$210,500	$195,000		

*During the current year, cash dividends of $3,000 were declared and paid.

Required:

1. Complete the two final columns shown beside each item in Tiger Audio's comparative financial statements. Round the percentages to one decimal place.
2. Which account increased by the largest dollar amount? Which account increased by the largest percentage?

PB13-2 Analyzing Comparative Financial Statements Using Selected Ratios LO 13-4, 13-5

Use the data given in PB13-1 for Tiger Audio.

Required:

1. Compute the gross profit percentage in the current and previous years. Are the current year results better, or worse, than those for the previous year?
2. Compute the net profit margin for the current and previous years. Are the current year results better, or worse, than those for the previous year?
3. Compute the earnings per share for the current and previous years. Are the current year results better, or worse, than those for the previous year?
4. Stockholders' equity totaled $65,000 at the beginning of the previous year. Compute the return on equity ratios for the current and previous years. Are the current year results better, or worse, than those for the previous year?
5. Net property and equipment totaled $115,000 at the beginning of the previous year. Compute the fixed asset turnover ratios for the current and previous years. Are the current year results better, or worse, than those for the previous year?
6. Compute the debt-to-assets ratios for the current and previous years. Is debt providing financing for a larger or smaller proportion of the company's asset growth?
7. Compute the times interest earned ratios for the current and previous years. Are the current year results better, or worse, than those for the previous year?
8. After Tiger released its current year financial statements, the company's stock was trading at $17. After the release of its previous year financial statements, the company's stock price was $12 per share. Compute the P/E ratios for both years. Round to one decimal place. Does it appear that investors have become more (or less) optimistic about Tiger's future success?

LO 13-3, 13-5

PB13-3 Vertical Analysis of a Balance Sheet

A condensed balance sheet for Southwest Airlines and a partially completed vertical analysis are presented as follows.

SOUTHWEST AIRLINES
Balance Sheet (summarized)
December 31, 2013
(in millions of U.S. dollars)

Cash	$ 1,355	7%	Current Liabilities	$ 5,676	29%
Accounts Receivable	419	2	Long-term Liabilities	6,333	*c*
Inventory of Parts and Supplies	467	*a*	Total Liabilities	12,009	62
Other Current Assets	2,047	11	Common Stock	905	5
Property and Equipment, Net	13,389	*b*	Retained Earnings	6,431	33
Other Assets	1,668	9	Total Stockholders' Equity	7,336	38
Total Assets	$19,345	100	Total Liabilities & Stockholders' Equity	$19,345	100

Required:

1. Complete the vertical analysis by computing each line item (*a*) through (*c*) as a percentage of total assets. Round to the nearest whole percentage.
2. What percentages of Southwest's assets relate to inventory of parts and supplies versus property and equipment? Which of these two asset groups is more significant to Southwest's business?
3. What percentage of Southwest's assets is financed by total stockholders' equity? By total liabilities?

LO 13-3, 13-5

PB13-4 Vertical Analysis of an Income Statement

A condensed income statement for Southwest Airlines and a partially completed vertical analysis follow.

SOUTHWEST AIRLINES
Income Statement (summarized)
For the Year Ended December 31
(in millions of U.S. dollars)

	2013		2012	
Sales Revenues	$17,699	100%	$17,088	100%
Salaries and Wages Expense	5,035	28	4,749	*d*
Fuel, Oil, Repairs, and Maintenance	6,843	*a*	7,252	*e*
Other Operating Expenses	4,543	*b*	4,464	26
Other Expenses (Revenues)	69	—	(62)	—
Income before Income Tax Expense	1,209	7	685	4
Income Tax Expense	455	3	264	2
Net Income	$ 754	*c*	$ 421	*f*

Required:

1. Complete the vertical analysis by computing each line item (*a*) through (*f*) as a percentage of sales revenues. Round to the nearest whole percentage.
2. Does the percentage that you calculated in 1(*a*) suggest that the decline in fuel costs in 2013 contributed to an increase in Southwest's profit in 2013 compared to 2012?
3. Refer to the percentages that you calculated in 1(*c*) and (*f*). Is Southwest's net profit margin improving or declining?

PB13-5 Interpreting Profitability, Liquidity, Solvency, and P/E Ratios LO 13-4, 13-5

Mattel and Hasbro are the two biggest makers of games and toys in the world. Mattel sells over $6 billion of products each year while annual sales of Hasbro products exceed $4 billion. Compare the two companies as a potential investment based on the following ratios:

Ratio	Mattel	Hasbro
Gross profit percentage	53.7%	58.1%
Net profit margin	13.9%	10.0%
Return on equity	28.4%	18.0%
EPS	$ 2.59	$ 2.16
Receivables turnover ratio	5.2	3.8
Inventory turnover ratio	5.8	5.0
Current ratio	3.22	1.82
Debt-to-assets	0.25	0.32
P/E ratio	15.4	25.6

Required:

1. Which company appears more profitable? Describe the ratio(s) that you used to reach this decision.
2. Which company appears more liquid? Describe the ratio(s) that you used to reach this decision.
3. Which company appears more solvent? Describe the ratio(s) that you used to reach this decision.
4. Are the conclusions from your analyses in requirements 1 to 3 consistent with the value of the two companies, as suggested by their P/E ratios? If not, offer one explanation for any apparent inconsistency.

LO 13-4, 13-5, 13-6 **PB13-6 Using Ratios to Compare Loan Requests from Two Companies**

The financial statements for Thor and Gunnar companies are summarized here:

	Thor Company	Gunnar Company
Balance Sheet		
Cash	$ 35,000	$ 32,000
Accounts Receivable, Net	77,000	28,000
Inventory	154,000	30,000
Equipment, Net	770,000	192,000
Other Assets		
Total Assets	$1,232,000	$350,400
Current Liabilities	$ 168,000	$ 18,000
Note Payable (long-term) (12% interest rate)	266,000	66,000
Capital Stock (par $20)	672,000	252,000
Additional Paid-in Capital	70,000	4,800
Retained Earnings		
Total Liabilities and Stockholders' Equity	$1,232,000	$350,400
Income Statement		
Sales Revenue	$1,120,000	$336,000
Cost of Goods Sold	672,000	180,000
Other Expenses		
Net Income	$ 112,000	$ 42,000
Other Data		
Per share price at end of year	$ 13.20	$ 19.60
Selected Data from Previous Year		
Accounts Receivable, Net	$ 65,800	$ 27,200
Inventory	133,000	45,600
Equipment, Net	770,000	192,000
Note Payable (long-term) (12% interest rate)	266,000	66,000
Total Stockholders' Equity	798,000	266,400

These two companies are in the same business and state but different cities. Each company has been in operation for about 10 years. Both companies received an unqualified audit opinion on the financial statements. Thor Company wants to borrow $105,000 and Gunnar Company is asking for $36,000. The loans will be for a two-year period. Neither company issued stock in the current year. Assume the end-of-year total assets and net equipment balances approximate the year's average and all sales are on account.

Required:

1. Calculate the ratios in Exhibit 13.5 for which sufficient information is available. Round all calculations to two decimal places.
2. Assume that you work in the loan department of a local bank. You have been asked to analyze the situation and recommend which loan is preferable. Based on the data given, your analysis prepared in requirement 1, and any other information, give your choice and the supporting explanation.

LO 13-5 **PB13-7 Analyzing an Investment by Comparing Selected Ratios**

You have the opportunity to invest $10,000 in one of two companies from a single industry. The only information you have is shown here. The word *high* refers to the top third of the industry; *average* is the middle third; *low* is the bottom third.

Ratio	Company A	Company B
EPS	High	High
Return on equity	High	Average
Debt to assets	High	Low
Current	Low	Average
Price/earnings	Low	High

Required:

Which company would you select? Write a brief explanation for your recommendation.

SKILLS DEVELOPMENT CASES

connect

S13-1 Computing Ratios

LO 13-4

Access and download the 2013 annual report for The Home Depot or from the Connect library and compute the following ratios for The Home Depot's year ended February 2, 2014: fixed asset turnover, days to sell, and debt-to-assets.

a. 1.95; 50.4; 0.69
b. 1.93; 50.4; 0.69
c. 3.38; 77.3; 0.69
d. 3.32; 77.3; 0.69

S13-2 Evaluating Financial Information

LO 13-5

Lumber Liquidators, Inc., competes with Lowe's in product lines such as hardwood flooring, moldings, and noise-reducing underlay. The two companies reported the following financial results in fiscal 2013:

	Lumber Liquidators	Lowe's
Gross profit percentage	41.1%	34.6%
Net profit margin	7.7%	4.3%
Return on equity	28.5%	17.8%
Earnings per share	$ 2.77	$ 2.18

Required:

1. Calculate the difference in gross profit percentage between Lumber Liquidators and Lowe's.
2. Calculate the difference in net profit margin between Lumber Liquidators and Lowe's.
3. Using your answers to requirements 1 and 2, identify the company that best controls operating expenses other than cost of goods sold.

S13-3 Internet-Based Team Research: Examining an Annual Report

LO 13-1, 13-2, 13-3, 13-4, 13-5, 13-6

As a team, select an industry to analyze. Using your web browser, each team member should access the annual report or 10-K for one publicly traded company in the industry, with each member selecting a different company. (See S1-3 in Chapter 1 for a description of possible resources for these tasks.)

Required:

1. On an individual basis, each team member should write a short report that incorporates horizontal and vertical analyses and as many of the ratios from the chapter as are applicable given the nature of the selected company.
2. Then, as a team, write a short report comparing and contrasting your companies using these attributes. Discuss any patterns across the companies that you as a team observe. Provide potential explanations for any differences discovered. Consider the impact of differences in accounting policies.

S13-4 Ethical Decision Making: A Real-Life Example

LO 13-6

This case is available online in the Connect library. To complete this case, you will consider the negative effects of auditors (*a*) failing to identify going-concern problems that exist and (*b*) reporting going-concern problems that do not exist.

S13-5 Ethical Decision Making: A Mini-Case

LO 13-4, 13-5

Capital Investments Corporation (CIC) requested a sizable loan from First Federal Bank to acquire a large piece of land for future expansion. CIC reported current assets of $1,900,000 (including $430,000 in cash) and current liabilities of $1,075,000. First Federal denied the loan request for a number of reasons, including the fact that the current ratio was below 2:1. When CIC was informed of the loan denial, the controller of the company immediately paid $420,000 that was owed to several trade creditors. The controller then asked First Federal to reconsider the loan application. Based on these abbreviated facts, would you recommend that First Federal approve the loan request? Why? Are the controller's actions ethical?

LO 13-4, 13-5, 13-6

S13-6 Critical Thinking: Analyzing the Impact of Alternative Depreciation Methods on Ratio Analysis

Speedy Company uses the double-declining-balance method to depreciate its property, plant, and equipment and Turtle Company uses the straight-line method. The two companies are exactly alike except for the difference in depreciation methods.

Required:

1. Identify the financial ratios discussed in this chapter that are likely to be affected by the difference in depreciation methods.
2. Which company will report the higher amount for each ratio that you have identified in response to requirement 1? If you cannot be certain, explain why.

LO 13-2, 13-3

S13-7 Using a Spreadsheet to Calculate Financial Statement Ratios

Enter the account names and dollar amounts from the comparative balance sheets in Exhibit 13.1 into a worksheet in a spreadsheet file. Create a second copy of the worksheet in the same spreadsheet file.

Required:

1. To the right of the comparative numbers in the first worksheet, enter the necessary formulas to compute the amount and percent change as shown in Exhibit 13.1.
2. To the right of each column in the second worksheet, enter the necessary formulas to create common size statements similar to those shown in Exhibit 13.3.

Management Accounting, Fifth Edition; Seal, Rohde, Garrison, Noreen; 2014

CHAPTER 14

Performance measurement and reporting on segments

LEARNING OBJECTIVES

After studying Chapter 14, you should be able to:

- LO1 Differentiate between performance measurement in cost centres, profit centres and investment centres
- LO2 Prepare a segmented statement of profit or loss using the contribution format
- LO3 Identify three business practices that hinder proper cost assignment
- LO4 Compute the return on investment (ROI)
- LO5 Show how changes in sales, expenses and assets affect an organization's ROI
- LO6 Compute residual income and understand its strengths and weaknesses
- LO7 Compute economic value added (EVA) and other value management metrics

CONCEPTS IN CONTEXT

Quaker Oats provides an example of how use of a specific performance measure can change the way a company operates. Prior to adopting EVA, 'its businesses had one overriding goal – increasing quarterly earnings. To do it, they guzzled capital. They offered sharp price discounts at the end of each quarter, so plants ran overtime turning out huge shipments of Gatorade, Rice-A-Roni, 100 per cent Natural Cereal, and other products. Managers led the late rush, since their bonuses depended on raising operating profits each quarter . . . Pumping up sales requires many warehouses (capital) to hold vast temporary inventories (more capital). But who cared? Quaker's operating businesses paid no charge for capital in internal accounting, so they barely noticed. It took EVA to spotlight the problem. . . . One plant has trimmed inventories from $15 million to $9 million, even though it is producing much more, and Quaker has closed five of 15 warehouses, saving $6 million a year in salaries and capital costs.'[1]

Once an organization grows beyond a few people, it becomes impossible for the top manager to make decisions about everything. For example, the managing director of the Novotel Hotel chain cannot be expected to decide whether a particular hotel guest at the Novotel in Sheffield should be allowed to check out later than the normal checkout time. To some degree, managers have to delegate decisions to those who are at lower levels in the organization. However, the degree to which decisions are delegated varies from organization to organization.

Decentralization in organizations

A **decentralized organization** is one in which decision making is not confined to a few top executives but rather is spread throughout the organization, with managers at various levels making *key operating decisions* relating to their sphere of responsibility. Decentralization is a matter of degree, since all organizations are decentralized to some extent out of necessity. At one extreme, a strongly decentralized organization is one in which there are few, if any, constraints on the freedom of even the lowest-level managers and employees to make decisions. At the other extreme, in a strongly centralized organization, lower-level managers have little freedom to make a decision. Although most organizations fall somewhere between these two extremes, there is a pronounced trend toward more and more decentralization.

Advantages and disadvantages of decentralization

Decentralization has many benefits, including:

1 Top management is relieved of much day-to-day problem solving and is left free to concentrate on strategy, on higher-level decision making, and on co-ordinating activities.
2 Decentralization provides lower-level managers with vital experience in making decisions. Without such experience, they would be ill-prepared to make decisions when they are promoted.
3 Added responsibility and decision-making authority often result in increased job satisfaction. It makes the job more interesting and provides greater incentives for people to put out their best efforts.
4 Lower-level managers generally have more detailed and up-to-date information about conditions in their own area of responsibility than top managers. Therefore, the decisions of lower-level managers are often based on better information.
5 It is difficult to evaluate a manager's performance if the manager is not given much latitude in what he or she can do.

Decentralization has four major disadvantages:

1 Lower-level managers may make decisions without fully understanding the 'big picture'. While top-level managers typically have less detailed information about operations than the lower-level managers, they usually have more information about the company as a whole and may have a better understanding of the company's strategy. This situation can be avoided to some extent with the use of modern management information systems that can, in principle, give every manager at every level the same information that goes to the managing director and other top-level managers.

2 In a truly decentralized organization, there may be a lack of co-ordination among autonomous managers. This problem can be reduced by clearly defining the company's strategy and communicating it effectively throughout the organization.
3 Lower-level managers may have objectives that are different from the objectives of the entire organization. For example, some managers may be more interested in increasing the size of their department than in increasing the profits of the company.[2] To some degree, this problem can be overcome by designing performance evaluation systems that motivate managers to make decisions that are in the best interests of the company.
4 In a strongly decentralized organization, it may be more difficult effectively to spread innovative ideas. Someone in one part of the organization may have a terrific idea that would benefit other parts of the organization, but without strong central direction the idea may not be shared with and adopted by other parts of the organization.

Decentralization and segment reporting

Effective decentralization requires *segmental reporting*. In addition to the companywide statement of profit or loss, reports are needed for individual segments of the organization. A **segment** is a part or activity of an organization about which managers would like cost, revenue or profit data. Examples of segments include divisions of a company, sales territories, individual stores, service centres, manufacturing plants, marketing departments, individual customers and product lines. As we shall see, a company's operations can be segmented in many ways. For example, a supermarket chain like Tesco or Sainsbury's can segment their businesses by geographic region, by individual store, by the nature of the merchandise (i.e., green groceries, canned goods, paper goods), by brand name, and so on. In this chapter, we learn how to construct statements of profit or loss for such business segments. These segmented statements of profit or loss are useful in analysing the profitability of segments and in measuring the performance of segment managers.

LO1 Cost, profit and investment centres

Decentralized companies typically categorize their business segments into cost centres, profit centres and investment centres – depending on the responsibilities of the managers of the segments.[3]

Cost centre

A **cost centre** is a business segment whose manager has control over costs but not over revenue or investment funds. Service departments such as accounting, finance, general administration, legal, personnel and so on, are usually considered to be cost centres. In addition, manufacturing facilities are often considered to be cost centres. The managers of cost centres are expected to minimize cost while providing the level of services or the amount of products demanded by other parts of the organization. For example, the manager of a production facility would be evaluated at least in part by comparing actual costs to how much the costs should have been for the actual number of units produced during the period. Standard cost variances and flexible budgets variances, such as those discussed in Chapters 12 and 13, are often used to evaluate cost centre performance.

Profit centre

In contrast to a cost centre, a **profit centre** is any business segment whose manager has control over both cost and revenue. Like a cost centre, however, a profit centre generally does not have control over investment funds. For example, the manager in charge of an amusement park would be responsible for both the revenues and costs, and hence the profits, of the amusement park but may not have control over major investments in the park. Profit centre managers are often evaluated by comparing actual profit to targeted or budgeted profit.

Investment centre

An **investment centre** is any segment of an organization whose manager has control over cost, revenue and investments in operating assets. For example, the managing director of the Truck Division at General Motors (one of the companies that pioneered decentralization in the last century)[4] would have a great deal of discretion over investments in the division. The managing director of the Truck Division would be responsible for initiating investment proposals, such as funding research into more fuel-efficient engines for sport utility vehicles. Once the proposal has been approved by the top level of managers at General Motors and the board of directors, the managing director of the Truck Division would then be responsible for making sure that the investment pays off. Investment centre managers are usually evaluated using return on investment or residual income measures as discussed later in the chapter.

LO2

Responsibility centres

A **responsibility centre** is broadly defined as any part of an organization whose manager has control over cost, revenue or investment funds. Cost centres, profit centres and investment centres are all known as responsibility centres.

A partial organization chart for Universal Foods Corporation, a company in the snack food and beverage industry, appears in Exhibit 14.1. This partial organization chart indicates how the various business segments of the company are classified in terms of responsibility. Note that the cost centres are the departments and work centres that do not generate significant revenues by themselves. These are staff departments such as finance, legal and personnel, and operating units such as the bottling plant, warehouse and beverage distribution centre. The profit centres are business segments that generate revenues and include the beverage, salty snacks and confections product segments. The managing director of operations oversees allocation of investment funds across the product segments and is responsible for revenues and costs and so is treated as an investment centre. And finally, corporate headquarters is an investment centre, since it is responsible for all revenues, costs and investments.

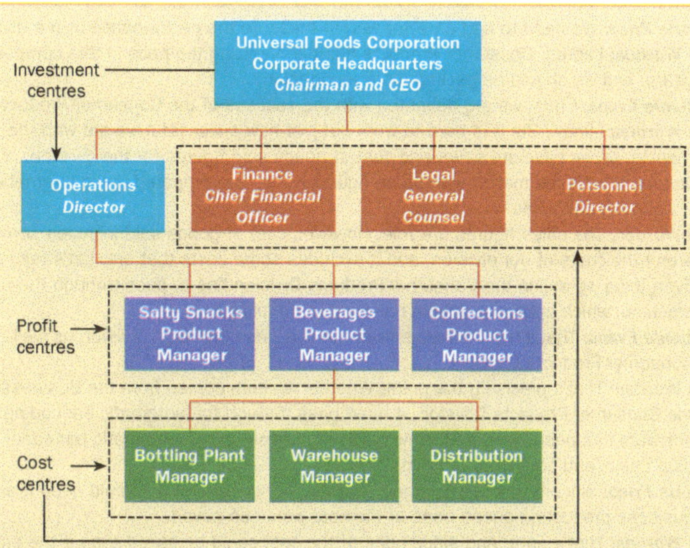

Exhibit 14.1 Business segments classified as cost, profit and investment centres

Segment reporting and profitability analysis

As previously discussed, a different kind of statement of profit or loss is required for evaluating the performance of business segments – a statement of profit or loss that emphasizes segments rather than the performance of the company as a whole. This point is illustrated in the following discussion.

MANAGEMENT ACCOUNTING IN ACTION: THE ISSUE

SoftSolutions Ltd is a rapidly growing computer software company founded by Stephanie Evans, who had previously worked in a large software company, and Marjorie Price, who had previously worked in the hotel industry as a general manager. They formed the company to develop and market user-friendly accounting and operations software designed specifically for hotels. They quit their jobs, pooled their savings, hired several programmers, and got down to work.

The first sale was by far the most difficult. No hotel wanted to be the first to use an untested product from an unknown company. After overcoming this obstacle with persistence, good luck, dedication to customer service and a very low introductory price, the company's sales burgeoned.

The company quickly developed similar business software for other specialized markets and then branched out into clip art and computer games. Within four years of its founding, the organization had grown to the point where Evans and Price were no longer able personally to direct all of the company's activities. Decentralization had become a necessity.

Accordingly, the company was split into two divisions – Business Products and Consumer Products. By mutual consent, Price took the title chief executive officer and Evans took the title managing director of the Business Products Division. Chris Worden, a programmer who had spearheaded the drive into the clip art and computer games markets, was designated managing director of the Consumer Products Division.

Almost immediately, the issue arose of how best to evaluate the performance of the divisions. Price called a meeting to consider this issue and asked Evans, Worden and the chief accountant, Bill Carson, to attend. The following discussion took place at that meeting:

Marjorie Price: We need to find a better way to measure the performance of the divisions.

Chris Worden: I agree. Consumer Products has been setting the pace in this company for the last two years, and we should be getting more recognition.

Stephanie Evans: Chris, we are delighted with the success of the Consumer Products Division.

Chris Worden: I know. But it is hard to work out just how successful we are with the present accounting reports. All we have are sales and cost of goods sold figures for the division.

Bill Carson: What's the matter with those figures? They are prepared using internationally accepted accounting principles.

Chris Worden: The sales figures are fine. However, cost of goods sold includes some costs that really aren't the costs of our division, and it excludes some costs that are. Let's take a simple example. Everything we sell in the Consumer Products Division has to pass through the automatic barcoding machine, which applies a unique bar code to the product.

Stephanie Evans: That's true for items from the Business Products Division as well as for items from the Consumer Products Division.

Chris Worden: That's precisely the point. Whether an item comes from the Business Products Division or the Consumer Products Division, it must pass through the automatic bar-coding machine after the software has been packaged. How much of the cost of the automatic bar coder would be saved if we didn't have any consumer products?

Marjorie Price: Since we have only one automatic bar coder and we would need it anyway to code the business products, I guess none of the cost would be saved.

Chris Worden: That's right. And since none of the cost could be saved even if the entire Consumer Products Division were eliminated, how can we logically say that some of the cost of the automatic bar coder is a cost of the Consumer Products Division?

Stephanie Evans: Just a minute, Chris, are you saying that my Business Products Division should be charged with the entire cost of the automatic bar coder?

Chris Worden: No, that's not what I am saying.

Marjorie Price: But Chris, I don't see how we can have sensible performance reports without making someone responsible for costs like the cost of the automatic bar coder. Bill, as our accounting expert, what do you think?

Bill Carson: I have some ideas for handling issues like the automatic bar coder. The best approach would probably be for me to put together a draft performance report. We can discuss it at the next meeting when everyone has something concrete to look at.

Marjorie Price: Okay, let's see what you come up with.

Bill Carson, the chief accountant of SoftSolutions, realized that segmented statements of profit or loss would be required to evaluate more appropriately the performance of the two divisions. To construct the segmented reports, he would have to segregate carefully costs that are attributable to the two divisions from costs that are not. Since most of the disputes over costs would be about fixed costs such as the automatic bar-coding machine, he knew he would also have to separate fixed from variable costs. Under the conventional absorption costing statement of profit or loss prepared for the entire company, variable and fixed production costs were being commingled in the cost of goods sold.

Largely for these reasons, Bill Carson decided to use the contribution format statement of profit or loss discussed in earlier chapters. Recall that when the contribution format is used: (1) the cost of goods sold consists only of the variable manufacturing costs; (2) the variable and fixed costs are listed in separate sections; and (3) a contribution margin is computed. When such a statement is segmented as in this chapter, fixed costs are broken down further into what are called traceable and common costs as discussed later. This breakdown allows a *segment margin* to be computed for each segment of the company. The segment margin is a valuable tool for assessing the long-run profitability of a segment and is also a much better tool for evaluating performance than the usual absorption costing reports.

Levels of segmented statements

A portion of the segmented report Bill Carson prepared is shown in Exhibit 14.2. The contribution format statement of profit or loss for the entire company appears at the very top of the exhibit under the column labelled Total company. Immediately to the right of this column are two columns – one for each of the two divisions. We can see that the divisional segment margin is £60,000 for the Business Products Division and £40,000 for the Consumer Products Division. This is the portion of the report that was specifically requested by the company's divisional managers. They wanted to know how much each of their divisions was contributing to the company's profits.

However, segmented statements of profit or loss can be prepared for activities at many levels in a company. To provide more information to the company's divisional managers, Bill Carson has further segmented the divisions according to their *major product lines*. In the case of the Consumer Products Division, the product lines are clip art and computer games. Going even further, Bill Carson has segmented each of the product lines according to how they are sold – in retail computer stores or by on-line sales. In Exhibit 14.2, this further segmentation is illustrated for the computer games product line. Notice that as we go from one segmented statement to another, we look at smaller and smaller pieces of the company. While not shown in Exhibit 14.2, Bill Carson also prepared segmented statements of profit or loss for the major product lines in the Business Products Division.

Substantial benefits are received from a series of statements such as those contained in Exhibit 14.2. By carefully examining trends and results in each segment, a manager is able to gain considerable insight into the company's operations viewed from many different angles. And advanced computer-based

Exhibit

Segments defined as divisions

	Total company	Divisions: Business Products Division	Divisions: Consumer Products Division
Sales	£500,000	£300,000	£200,000
Less variable expenses:			
Variable cost of goods sold	180,000	120,000	60,000
Other variable expenses	50,000	30,000	20,000
Total variable expenses	230,000	150,000	80,000
Contribution margin	270,000	150,000	120,000
Less traceable fixed expenses	170,000	90,000	80,000*
Divisional segment margin	100,000	£60,000	£40,000
Less common fixed expenses not traceable to the individual divisions	£85,000		
Operating profit	£15,000		

Segments defined as product lines of the Consumer Products Division

	Consumer Products Division	Product line: Clip art	Product line: Computer games
Sales	£200,000	£75,000	£125,000
Less variable expenses:			
Variable cost of goods sold	60,000	20,000	40,000
Other variable expenses	£20,000	5,000	15,000
Total variable expenses	£80,000	£25,000	£55,000
Contribution margin	120,000	50,000	70,000
Less traceable expenses	£70,000	30,000	£40,000
Product-line segment margin	50,000	£20,000	£30,000
Less common fixed expenses not traceable to the individual product lines	£10,000		
Divisional segment margin	£40,000		

Segments defined as sales channels for one product line, computer games, of the Consumer Products Division

	Computer games	Sales channels: Retail stores	Sales channels: On-line sales
Sales	£125,000	£100,000	£25,000
Less variable expenses:			
Variable cost of goods sold	40,000	32,000	8,000
Other variable expenses	15,000	5,000	10,000
Total variable expenses	55,000	37,000	18,000
Contribution margin	70,000	63,000	7,000
Less traceable expenses	25,000	15,000	10,000
Sales-channel segment margin	45,000	£48,000	£(3,000)
Less common fixed expenses not traceable to the individual sales channels	15,000		
Product-line segment margin	£30,000		

*Notice that this £80,000 in traceable fixed expenses is divided into two parts – £70,000 traceable and £10,000 common – when the Consumer Products Division is broken down into product lines. The reasons for this are discussed later under 'Traceable costs can become common costs'.

Exhibit 14.2 SoftSolutions Ltd – segmented profit statements in the contribution format

information systems are making it easier and easier to construct such statements and to keep them current.

Sales and contribution margin

To prepare a statement of profit or loss for a particular segment, variable expenses are deducted from the sales to yield the contribution margin for the segment. It is important to keep in mind that the contribution margin tells us what happens to profits as volume changes – holding a segment's capacity and fixed costs constant. The contribution margin is especially useful in decisions involving temporary uses of capacity such as special orders. Decisions concerning the most effective uses of existing capacity often involve only variable costs and revenues, which, of course, are the very elements involved in contribution margin. Such decisions were discussed in detail in Chapter 9.

Traceable and common fixed costs

The most puzzling aspect of Exhibit 14.2 is probably the treatment of fixed costs. The report has two kinds of fixed costs – *traceable* and *common*. Only the *traceable fixed costs* are charged to the segments in the segmented statement of profit or loss in the report. If a cost is not traceable to a segment, then it is not assigned to the segment.

A **traceable fixed cost** of a segment is a fixed cost that is incurred because of the existence of the segment – if the segment had never existed, the fixed cost would not have been incurred; and/or if the segment were eliminated, the fixed cost would disappear. Examples of traceable fixed costs include the following:

- The salary of the Fritos product manager at PepsiCo is a *traceable* fixed cost of the Fritos business segment of PepsiCo.
- The maintenance cost for the building in which Boeing 747s are assembled is a *traceable* fixed cost of the 747 business segment of Boeing.
- The liability insurance at Disney World is a *traceable* fixed cost of the Disney World business segment of the Disney Corporation.

A **common fixed cost** is a fixed cost that supports the operations of more than one segment but is not traceable in whole or in part to any one segment. Even if a segment were entirely eliminated, there would be no change in a true common fixed cost. Note the following:

- The salary of the Managing Director of General Motors is a *common* fixed cost of the various divisions of General Motors.
- The cost of the automatic bar-coding machine at SoftSolutions is a *common* fixed cost of the Consumer Products Division and of the Business Products Division.
- The cost of the receptionist's salary at an office shared by a number of doctors is a *common* fixed cost of the doctors. The cost is traceable to the office, but not to any one of the doctors individually.

Identifying traceable fixed costs

The distinction between traceable and common fixed costs is crucial in segment reporting, since traceable fixed costs are charged to the segments, whereas common fixed costs are not. In an actual situation, it is sometimes hard to determine whether a cost should be classified as traceable or common.

The general guideline is to treat as traceable costs *only those costs that would disappear over time if the segment itself disappeared*. For example, if the Consumer Products Division were sold or discontinued, it would no longer be necessary to pay the division manager's salary. Therefore the division manager's salary should be classified as a traceable fixed cost of the division. On the other hand, the managing director of the company undoubtedly would continue to be paid even if the Consumer Products Division were dropped. In fact, he or she might even be paid more if dropping the division was a good idea. Therefore, the managing director's salary is common to both divisions and should not be charged to either division.

Activity-based costing

Some costs are easy to identify as traceable costs. For example, the costs of advertising Crest toothpaste on television are clearly traceable to Crest. A more difficult situation arises when a building, machine, or other resource is shared by two or more segments. For example, assume that a multi-product company leases warehouse space that is used for storing the full range of its products. Would the lease cost of the warehouse be a traceable or a common cost of the products? Managers familiar with activity-based costing might argue that the lease cost is traceable and should be assigned to the products according to how much space the products use in the warehouse. In like manner, these managers would argue that order processing costs, sales support costs and other *selling, general and administrative (SG&A) expenses* should also be charged to segments according to the segments' consumption of SG&A resources.

To illustrate, consider Holt Corporation, a company that manufactures concrete pipe for industrial uses. The company has three products – 9-centimetre pipe, 12-centimetre pipe and 18-centimetre pipe. Space is leased in a large warehouse on a yearly basis as needed. The lease cost of this space is £4 per square metre per year. The 9-centimetre pipe occupies 1,000 square metres of space, 12-centimetre pipe occupies 4,000 square metres, and 18-centimetre pipe occupies 5,000 square metres. The company also has an order processing department that incurred £150,000 in order processing costs last year. Management believes that order processing costs are driven by the number of orders placed by customers in a year. Last year 2,500 orders were placed, of which 1,200 were for 9-centimetre pipe, 800 were for 12-centimetre pipe, and 500 were for 18-centimetre pipe. Given these data, the following costs would be assigned to each product using the activity-based costing approach:

Warehouse space cost:	
9-centimetre pipe: £4 × 1,000 square metres	£4,000
12-centimetre pipe: £4 × 4,000 square metres	16,000
18-centimetre pipe: £4 × 5,000 square metres	20,000
Total cost assigned	£40,000
Order processing costs:	
£150,000/2,500 orders = £60 per order	
9-centimetre pipe: £60 × 1,200 orders	£72,000
12-centimetre pipe: £60 × 800 orders	48,000
18-centimetre pipe: £60 × 500 orders	30,000
Total cost assigned	£150,000

This method of assigning costs combines the strength of activity-based costing with the power of the contribution approach and greatly enhances the manager's ability to measure the profitability and performance of segments. However, managers must still ask themselves if the costs would in fact disappear over time if the segment itself disappeared. In the case of Holt Corporation, it is clear that the £20,000 in warehousing costs for the 18-centimetre pipe would be eliminated if they were no longer being produced. The company would simply rent less warehouse space the following year. However, suppose the company owns the warehouse. Then it is not so clear that £20,000 of the cost of the warehouse would really disappear if the 18-centimetre pipes were discontinued as a product. The company might be able to sublease the space, or use it for other products, but then again the space might simply be empty while the costs of the warehouse continue to be incurred.

In assigning costs to segments, the key point is to resist the temptation to allocate costs (such as depreciation of corporate facilities) that are clearly common in nature and that would continue regardless of whether the segment exists or not. *Any allocation of common costs to segments will reduce the value of the segment margin as a guide to long-run segment profitability and segment performance.* This point will be discussed at length later in the chapter.

Traceable costs can become common costs

Fixed costs that are traceable to one segment may be a common cost of another segment. For example, an airline might want a segmented statement of profit or loss that shows the segment margin for a particular flight from Los Angeles to Paris, further broken down into first-class, business-class and economy-class *segment margins.* The airline must pay a substantial landing fee at Charles DeGaulle airport in Paris. This fixed landing fee is a traceable cost of the flight, but it is a common cost of the first-class, business-class and economy-class segments. Even if the first-class cabin is empty, the entire landing fee must be paid. So the landing fee is not a traceable cost of the first-class cabin. But on the other hand, paying the fee is necessary in order to have any first-class, business-class, or economy-class passengers. So the landing fee is a common cost of these three classes.

The dual nature of some of the fixed costs can be seen from the diagram in Exhibit 14.3. Notice from the diagram that when segments are defined as divisions, the Consumer Products Division has £80,000 in traceable fixed expenses. Only £70,000 of this amount remains traceable, however, when we narrow the definition of a segment from divisions to product lines. Notice that the other £10,000 then becomes a common cost of the two product lines of the Consumer Products Division.

Exhibit

		Segment	
	Total company	Business Products Division	Consumer Products Division
Contribution margin	£270,000	£150,000	£120,000
Less traceable fixed expenses	170,000	90,000	80,000

		Segment	
	Consumer Products Division	Clip art	Computer games
Contribution margin	£120,000	£50,000	£70,000
Less traceable fixed expenses	70,000	30,000	40,000
Product-line segment margin	50,000	£20,000	£30,000
Less common fixed expenses	10,000		
Divisional segment margin	£40,000		

Exhibit 14.3 Reclassification of traceable fixed expenses from Exhibit 14.2

Why would £10,000 of traceable fixed cost become a common cost when the division is divided into product lines? The £10,000 is the monthly salary of the manager of the Consumer Products Division. This salary is a traceable cost of the division as a whole, but it is a common cost of the division's product lines. The manager's salary is a necessary cost of having the two product lines, but even if one of the product lines were discontinued entirely, the manager's salary would probably not be cut. Therefore, none of the manager's salary can be really traced to the individual products.

The £70,000 traceable fixed cost of the product lines consists of the costs of product-specific advertising. A total of £30,000 was spent on advertising clip art and £40,000 was spent on advertising computer games. These costs can clearly be traced to the individual product lines.

Segment margin

Observe from Exhibit 14.2 that the **segment margin** is obtained by deducting the traceable fixed costs of a segment from the segment's contribution margin. It represents the margin available after a segment has covered all of its own costs. *The segment margin is the best gauge of the long-run profitability of a segment,* since it includes only those costs that are caused by the segment. If a segment cannot cover its own costs, then that segment probably should not be retained (unless it has important side effects on other segments). Notice from Exhibit 14.2, for example, that online sales has a negative segment margin. This means that the segment is not covering its own costs; it is generating more costs than it collects in revenue.

From a decision-making point of view, the segment margin is most useful in major decisions that affect capacity such as dropping a segment. By contrast, as we noted earlier, the contribution margin is most useful in decisions relating to short-run changes in volume, such as pricing special orders that involve utilization of existing capacity.

MANAGEMENT ACCOUNTING IN ACTION: THE WRAP-UP

Shortly after Bill Carson, SoftSolutions Ltd's chief accountant, completed the draft segmented statement of profit or loss, he sent copies to the other managers and scheduled a meeting in which the report could be explained. The meeting was held on the Monday following the first meeting; and Marjorie Price, Stephanie Evans and Chris Worden were all in attendance.

Stephanie Evans: I think these segmented statements of profit or loss are fairly self-explanatory. However, there is one thing I wonder about.

Bill Carson: What's that?

Stephanie Evans: What is this common fixed expense of £85,000 listed under the total company? And who is going to be responsible for it if neither Chris nor I have responsibility?

Bill Carson: The £85,000 of common fixed expenses represents expenses like general administrative salaries and the costs of common production equipment such as the automatic bar-coding machine. Marjorie, do you want to respond to the question about responsibility for these expenses?

Marjorie Price: Sure. Since I'm the managing director of the company, I'm responsible for those costs. Some things can be delegated, others cannot. It wouldn't make any sense for either you or Chris to make decisions about the bar coder, since it affects both of you. That's an important part of my job – Segment making decisions about resources that affect all parts of the organization. This report makes it much clearer who is responsible for what. I like it.

Chris Worden: So do I – my division's segment margin is higher than the operating profit for the entire company.

Marjorie Price: Don't get carried away, Chris. Let's not misinterpret what this report means. The segment margins have to be big to cover the common costs of the company. We can't let the big segment margins lull us into a sense of complacency. If we use these reports, we all have to agree that our objective is to increase all of the segment margins over time.

Stephanie Evans: I'm willing to give it a try.

Chris Worden: The reports make sense to me.

Marjorie Price: So be it. Then the first item of business would appear to be a review of on-line sales of computer games, where we appear to be losing money. Chris, could you brief us on this at our next meeting?

Chris Worden: I'd be happy to. I have been suspecting for some time that our sales strategy could be improved.

Marjorie Price: We look forward to hearing your analysis. Meeting's adjourned.

There is more than one way to segment a company

SoftSolutions segmented its sales by division, by product line within each division, and by sales channel. An organization can be segmented in many ways. For example, two different ways of segmenting the sales of the General Electric Company are displayed in Exhibit 14.4. In the first diagram, the company's sales are segmented by geographic region. In the second diagram, they are segmented by products. Note that each of the diagrams could be continued, providing progressively more detailed segment data. For example, the sales in France could be broken down by major product line, then by product. Similar breakdowns could be done of General Electric's costs and segment margins, although that would require substantial additional analytical work to identify the segments to which various costs should be assigned.

Segment breakdowns such as those shown in Exhibit 14.4 give a company's managers the ability to look at the company from many different directions. With the increasing availability of companywide databases and

Exhibit

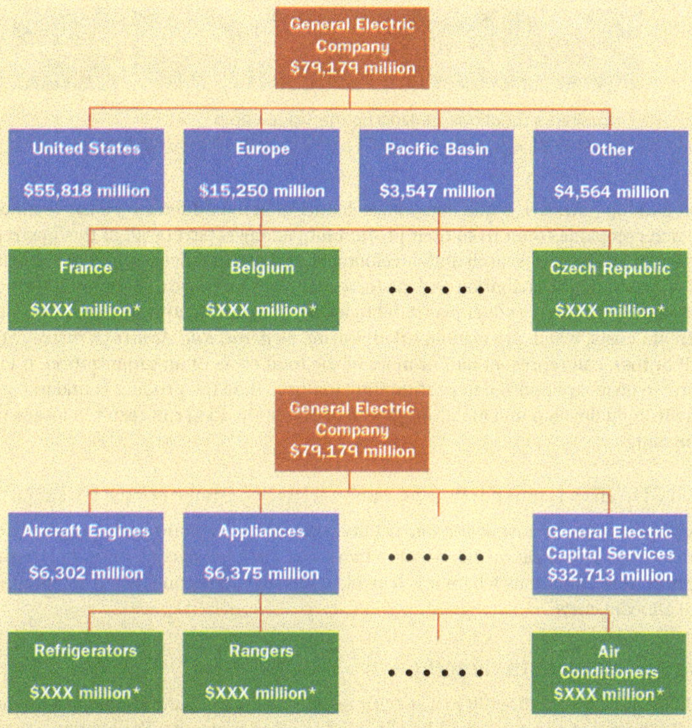

*These sales figures are not publicly disclosed by GE, but they are readily available within the company to managers.

Exhibit 14.4 General Electric Company's revenues segmented by geographic region and products

sophisticated management information system software, detailed segmental reports of revenues, costs and margins are becoming much easier to do.

LO3

Hindrances to proper cost assignment

For segment reporting to accomplish its intended purposes, costs must be properly assigned to segments. If the purpose is to determine the profits being generated by a particular division, then all of the costs attributable to that division – and only those costs – should be assigned to it. Unfortunately, three business practices greatly hinder proper cost assignment: (1) omission of some costs in the assignment process, (2) the use of inappropriate methods for allocating costs among segments of a company, and (3) assignment to segments of costs that are really common costs.

Omission of costs

The costs assigned to a segment should include all costs attributable to that segment from the company's entire *value chain*. The **value chain**, which is illustrated in Exhibit 14.5, consists of the major business functions that add value to a company's products and services. All of these functions, from research and development, through product design, manufacturing, marketing, distribution and customer service, are required to bring a product or service to the customer and generate revenues.

However, as discussed in Chapters 2, 4 and 6, only manufacturing costs are included in product costs for financial reporting purposes. Consequently, when trying to determine product profitability for internal

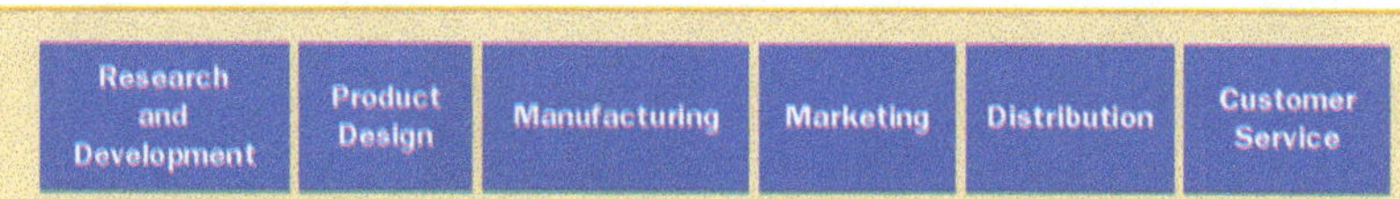

Exhibit 14.5 Business functions making up the value chain

decision-making purposes, some companies deduct only manufacturing costs from product revenues. As a result, such companies omit from their profitability analysis part or all of the 'upstream' costs in the value chain, which consist of research and development and product design, and the 'downstream' costs, which consist of marketing, distribution and customer service. Yet these non-manufacturing costs are just as essential in determining product profitability as are the manufacturing costs. These upstream and downstream costs, which are usually titled *Selling, General, and Administrative (SG&A)* on the statement of profit or loss, can represent half or more of the total costs of an organization. If either the upstream or downstream costs are omitted in profitability analysis, then the product is undercosted and management may unwittingly develop and maintain products that in the long run result in losses rather than profits for the company.

Inappropriate methods for allocating costs among segments

Cross-subsidization, or cost distortion, occurs when costs are improperly assigned among a company's segments. Cross-subsidization can occur in two ways: first, when companies fail to trace costs directly to segments in those situations where it is feasible to do so; and second, when companies use inappropriate bases to allocate costs.

Failure to trace costs directly

Costs that can be traced directly to a specific segment of a company should be charged directly to that responsible segment and should not be allocated to other segments. For example, the rent for a branch office of an insurance company should be charged directly against the branch to which it relates rather than included in a companywide overhead pool and then spread throughout the company.

Inappropriate allocation base

Some companies allocate costs to segments using arbitrary bases such as sales or cost of goods sold. For example, under the sales approach, costs are allocated to the various segments according to the percentage of company sales generated by each segment. Thus, if a segment generates 20% of total company sales, it would be allocated 20% of the company's SG&A expenses as its 'fair share'. This same basic procedure is followed if costs of goods sold or some other measure is used as the allocation base.

Costs should be allocated to segments for internal decision-making purposes only when the allocation base drives the costs being allocated (or is at least very highly correlated with the real cost driver). For example, when sales are used as the allocation base for SG&A expenses, it is implicitly assumed that SG&A expenses change in proportion to changes in total sales. If that is not true, the SG&A expenses allocated to segments will be misleading.

Arbitrarily dividing common costs among segments

The third business practice that leads to distorted segment costs is the practice of assigning non-traceable costs to segments. For example, some companies allocate the costs of the corporate headquarters building to products on segment reports. However, in a multi-product company, no single product is likely to be responsible for any significant amount of this cost. Even if a product were eliminated entirely, there would usually be no significant effect on any of the costs of the corporate headquarters building. In short, there is no cause-and-effect relation between the cost of the corporate headquarters building and the existence of any one product. As a consequence, any allocation of the cost of the corporate headquarters building to the products must be arbitrary.

Common costs like the costs of the corporate headquarters building are necessary, of course, to have a functioning organization. The common practice of arbitrarily allocating these costs to segments is often justified on the grounds that 'someone' has to 'cover the common costs'. While it is undeniably true that the common costs must be covered to earn a profit, arbitrarily allocating common costs to segments does not ensure that this will happen. In fact, adding a share of common costs to the real costs of a segment may make an otherwise profitable segment appear to be unprofitable. If a manager erroneously eliminates the segment, the revenues will be lost, the real costs of the segment will be saved, but the common costs will still be there. The net effect will be to reduce the profits of the company as a whole and make it even more difficult to 'cover the common costs'.

Additionally, common costs are not manageable by the manager to whom they are arbitrarily allocated; they are the responsibility of higher-level managers. When common fixed costs are allocated to managers, they are held responsible for those costs even though they cannot control them.

In sum, the way many companies handle segment reporting results in *cost distortion*. This distortion results from three practices – the failure to trace costs directly to a specific segment when it is feasible to do so, the use of inappropriate bases for allocating costs and the allocation of common costs to segments. These practices are widespread. One study found that 60% of the companies surveyed made no attempt to assign SG&A costs to segments on a cause-and-effect basis.[5]

LO4

Rate of return for measuring managerial performance

When a company is truly decentralized, segment managers are given a great deal of autonomy. So great is this autonomy that the various profit and investment centres are often viewed as being virtually independent businesses, with their managers having about the same control over decisions as if they were in fact running their own independent firms. With this autonomy, fierce competition often develops among managers, with each striving to make his or her segment the 'best' in the company.

Competition between investment centres is particularly keen for investment funds. How do top managers in corporate headquarters go about deciding who gets new investment funds as they become available, and how do these managers decide which investment centres are most profitably using the funds that have already been entrusted to their care? One of the most popular ways of making these judgements is to measure the rate of return that investment centre managers are able to generate on their assets. This rate of return is called *the return on investment (ROI)*.

The return on investment (ROI) formula

The **return on investment (ROI)** is defined as operating profit divided by average operating assets:

$$\text{ROI} = \frac{\text{Operating profit}}{\text{Average operating assets}}$$

Although there are some issues about how to measure operating profit and average operating assets, this formula seems clear enough. The higher the return on investment of a business segment, the greater the *profit generated per pound invested* in the segment's operating assets.

Operating profit and operating assets

Note that *operating profit,* rather than profit, is used in the ROI formula. Recall that **operating profit** is profit before interest and taxes and is sometimes referred to as EBIT (earnings before interest and taxes). The reason for using operating profit in the formula is that the profit figure used should be consistent with the base to which it is applied. Notice that the base (i.e., denominator) consists of *operating assets.* Thus, to be consistent we use operating profit in the numerator.

Operating assets include cash, accounts receivable, inventory, plant and equipment, and all other assets held for operating purposes. Examples of assets that would not be included in the operating assets category (i.e., examples of non-operating assets) would include land held for future use, an investment in another company, or a factory building rented to someone else. These assets are not held for operating purposes and therefore are excluded from operating assets. The operating assets base used in the formula is typically computed as the average of the operating assets between the beginning and the end of the year.

Plant and equipment: net book value or gross cost?

A major issue in ROI computations is the monetary measure of plant and equipment that should be included in the operating assets base. To illustrate the problem involved, assume that a company reports the following amounts for plant and equipment on its balance sheet:

Plant and equipment	£3,000,000
Less accumulated depreciation	900,000
Net book value	£2,100,000

What amount of plant and equipment should the company include with its operating assets in computing ROI? One widely used approach is to include only the plant and equipment's *net book value* – that is, the plant's original cost less accumulated depreciation (£2,100,000 in the example above). A second approach is to ignore depreciation and include the plant's entire *gross cost* in the operating assets base (£3,000,000 in the example above). Both of these approaches are used in actual practice, even though they will obviously yield very different operating asset and ROI figures.

The following arguments can be raised for using *net book value* to measure *operating assets* and for using *gross cost* to measure operating assets in ROI computation.

Arguments for using net book value to measure operating assets in ROI computations:

1 The net book value method is consistent with how plant and equipment are reported on the balance sheet (i.e., cost less accumulated depreciation to date).
2 The net book value method is consistent with the computation of operating profit, which includes depreciation as an operating expense.

Arguments for using gross cost to measure operating assets in ROI computations:

1 The gross cost method eliminates both the age of equipment and the method of depreciation as factors in ROI computations. (Under the net book value method, ROI will tend to increase over time as net book value declines due to depreciation.)
2 The gross cost method does not discourage replacement of old, worn out equipment. (Under the net book value method, replacing fully depreciated equipment with new equipment can have a dramatic, adverse effect on ROI.)

Managers generally view consistency as the most important of the considerations above. As a result, a majority of companies use the net book value approach in ROI computations. In this text, we will also use the net book value approach unless a specific exercise or problem directs otherwise.

LO5 Controlling the rate of return

When we first defined the return on investment, we used the following formula:

$$\text{ROI} = \frac{\text{Operating profit}}{\text{Average operating assets}}$$

We can modify this formula slightly by introducing sales as follows:

$$\text{ROI} = \frac{\text{Operating profit}}{\text{Sales}} \times \frac{\text{Sales}}{\text{Average operating assets}}$$

The first term on the right-hand side of the equation is the *margin*, which is defined as follows:

$$\text{Margin} = \frac{\text{Operating profit}}{\text{Sales}}$$

The **margin** is a measure of management's ability to control operating expenses in relation to sales. The lower the operating expenses per pound of sales, the higher the margin earned.

The second term on the right-hand side of the preceding equation is *turnover* which is defined as follows:

$$\text{Turnover} = \frac{\text{Sales}}{\text{Average operating assets}}$$

Turnover is a measure of the sales that are generated for each pound invested in operating assets.

The following alternative form of the ROI formula, which we will use most frequently, combines margin and turnover:

$$\text{ROI} = \text{Margin} \times \text{Turnover}$$

Which formula for ROI should be used – the original one stated in terms of operating profit and average operating assets or this one stated in terms of margin and turnover? Either can be used – they will always give the same answer. However, the margin and turnover formulation provides some additional insights.

Some managers tend to focus too much on margin and ignore turnover. To some degree at least, the margin can be a valuable indicator of a manager's performance. Standing alone, however, it overlooks one crucial area of a manager's responsibility – the investment in operating assets. Excessive funds tied up in operating assets, which depresses turnover, can be just as much of a drag on profitability as excessive operating expenses, which depresses margin. One of the advantages of ROI as a performance measure is that it forces the manager to control the investment in operating assets as well as to control expenses and the margin.

E.I. du Pont de Nemours and Company (better known as Du Pont) pioneered the ROI concept and recognized the importance of looking at both margin and turnover in assessing the performance of a manager. The ROI formula is now widely used as the key measure of the performance of an investment centre. The ROI formula blends together many aspects of the manager's responsibilities into a single figure that can be compared to the returns of competing investment centres, the returns of other firms in the industry, and to the past returns of the investment centre itself.

Du Pont also developed the diagram that appears in Exhibit 14.6. This exhibit helps managers understand how they can improve ROI. An investment centre manager can increase ROI in basically three ways:

1. Increase sales
2. Reduce expenses
3. Reduce assets.

To illustrate how the rate of return can be improved by each of these three actions, consider how the manager of the Raffles Burger Grill is evaluated. Burger Grill is a small chain of upmarket casual restaurants that has been rapidly adding outlets via franchising. The Raffles franchise is owned by a group of local surgeons who have little time to devote to management and little expertise in business matters. Therefore, they delegate operating decisions – including decisions concerning investment in operating assets such as inventories – to a professional manager they have hired. The manager is evaluated largely based on the ROI the franchise generates.

The following data represent the results of business activity for the most recent month:

Sales	100,000
Operating profit	10,000
Average operating assets	50,000

The rate of return generated by the Raffles Burger Grill investment centre is as follows:

$$\text{ROI} = \text{Margin} \times \text{Turnover}$$

$$\frac{\text{Operating profit}}{\text{Sales}} \times \frac{\text{Sales}}{\text{Average operating assets}}$$

$$\frac{£10{,}000}{£1{,}000{,}000} \times \frac{£100{,}000}{£50{,}000}$$

$$10\% \times 2 = 20\%$$

As we stated above, to improve the ROI figure, the manager can (1) increase sales, (2) reduce expenses, or (3) reduce the operating assets.

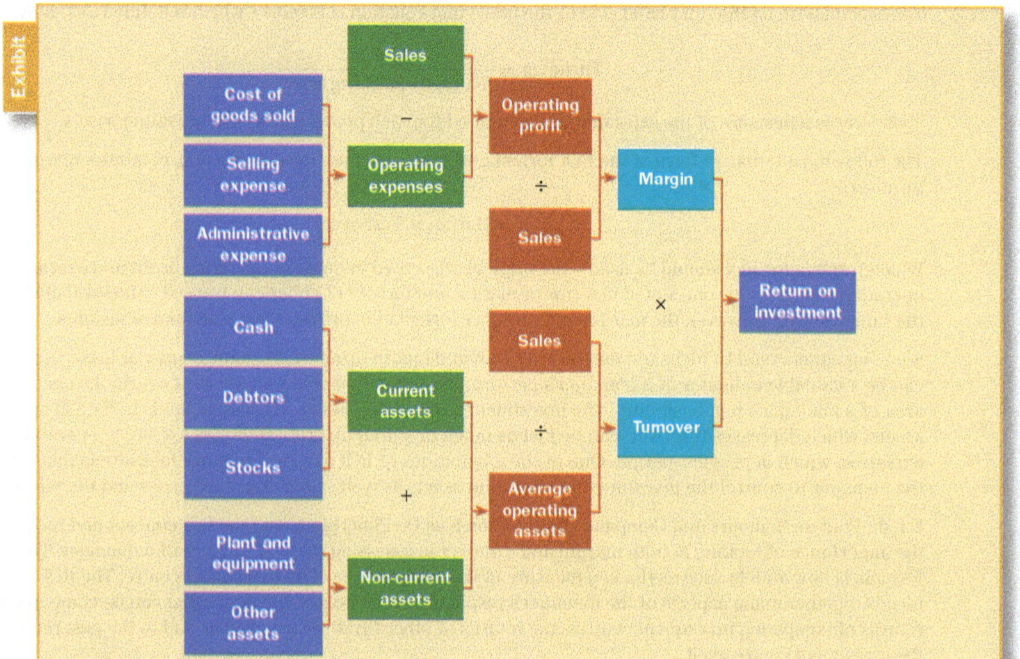

Exhibit 14.6 Elements of return on investment (ROI)

(1) Increase sales

Assume that the manager of the Raffles Burger Grill is able to increase sales from £110,000 to £110,000. Assume further that either because of good cost control or because some costs in the company are fixed, the operating profit increases even more rapidly, going from £10,000 to £12,000 per period. The operating assets remain constant.

$$\text{ROI} = \frac{£12{,}000}{£110{,}000} \times \frac{£110{,}000}{£50{,}000}$$

$$10.91\% \times 2.2 = 24\% \text{ (as compared to 20\% above)}$$

(2) Reduce expenses

Assume that the manager of the Raffles Burger Grill is able to reduce expenses by £1,000 so that operating profit increases from £10,000 to £11,000. Both sales and operating assets remain constant.

$$\text{ROI} = \frac{£11{,}000}{£100{,}000} \times \frac{£100{,}000}{£50{,}000}$$

$$11\% \times 2 = 22\% \text{ (as compared to 20\% above)}$$

(3) Reduce assets

Assume that the manager of the Raffles Burger Grill is able to reduce operating assets from £50,000 to £40,000. Sales and operating profit remain unchanged.

$$\text{ROI} = \frac{£10{,}000}{£100{,}000} \times \frac{£100{,}000}{£40{,}000}$$

$$10\% \times 2.5 = 25\% \text{ (as compared to 20\% above)}$$

A clear understanding of these three approaches to improving the ROI figure is critical to the effective management of an investment centre. We will now look at each approach in more detail.

Increase sales

In first looking at the ROI formula, one is inclined to think that the sales figure is neutral, since it appears as the denominator in the margin computation and as the numerator in the turnover computation. We *could* cancel out the sales figure, but we do not do so for two reasons. First, this would tend to draw attention away from the fact that the rate of return is a function of *two* variables, margin and turnover. And second, it would tend to conceal the fact that a change in sales can affect both the *margin* and the turnover in an organization. To explain, a change in sales can affect the margin if expenses increase or decrease at a different rate than sales. For example, a company may be able to keep a tight control on its costs as its sales go up, with the result that operating profit increases more rapidly than sales and increases the margin. Or a company may have fixed expenses that remain constant as sales go up, resulting in an increase in the operating profit and in the margin. Either (or both) of these factors could have been responsible for the increase in the margin percentage from 10 to 10.91 illustrated in (1) above.

Further, a change in sales can affect the *turnover* if sales either increase or decrease without a proportionate increase or decrease in the operating assets. In the first approach above, for example, sales increased from £100,000 to £110,000, but the operating assets remained unchanged. As a result, the turnover increased from 2 to 2.2 for the period.

Reduce expenses

Often the easiest route to increased profitability and to a stronger ROI figure is simply to cut the 'fat' out of an organization through a concerted effort to control expenses. When margins begin to be squeezed, this is generally the first line of attack by a manager. Discretionary fixed costs usually come under scrutiny first, and various programmes are either curtailed or eliminated in an effort to cut costs. Managers must be careful, however, not to cut out muscle and bone along with the fat. Also, they must remember that frequent cost-cutting binges can destroy morale. Most managers now agree that it is best to stay 'lean and mean' all the time.

Reduce operating assets

Managers have always been sensitive to the need to control sales, operating expenses and operating margins. However, they have not always been equally sensitive to the need to control investment in operating assets. Firms that have adopted the ROI approach to measuring managerial performance report that one of the first reactions of investment centre managers is to trim their investment in operating assets. The reason, of course, is that these managers soon realize that an excessive investment in operating assets reduces turnover and hurts the ROI. As these managers reduce their investment in operating assets, funds are released that can be used elsewhere in the organization.

How can an investment centre manager control the investment in operating assets? One approach is to eliminate unneeded inventory. Just-in-time (JIT) purchasing and JIT manufacturing (see Chapter 18) have been extremely helpful in reducing inventories of all types, with the result that ROI figures have improved dramatically in some companies. Another approach is to devise various methods of speeding up the collection of accounts receivable.

Criticisms of ROI

Although ROI is widely used in evaluating performance, it is not a perfect tool. The method is subject to the following criticisms:

1 Just telling managers to increase ROI may not be enough. Managers may not know how to increase ROI; they may increase ROI in a way that is inconsistent with the company's strategy; or they may take actions that increase ROI in the short run but harm the company in the long run (such as cutting back on research and development). This is why ROI is best used as part of a balanced scorecard, as we will discuss in

Chapter 16. A balanced scorecard can provide concrete guidance to managers, make it more likely that actions taken are consistent with the company's strategy, and reduce the likelihood that short-run performance will be enhanced at the expense of long-term performance.

2 A manager who takes over a business segment typically inherits many committed costs over which the manager has no control. These committed costs may be relevant in assessing the performance of the business segment as an investment but make it difficult fairly to assess the performance of the manager relative to other managers.

3 As discussed in the next section, a manager who is evaluated based on ROI may reject profitable investment opportunities.

LO6 LO7

Residual income[6] – another measure of performance

Another approach to measuring an investment centre's performance focuses on a concept known as *residual income*. **Residual income** is the operating profit that an investment centre earns above the minimum required return on its operating assets. In equation form, residual income is calculated as follows:

Residual = Net operating income − (Average operating assets × Minimum required rate of return)

Economic value added (EVA) is a similar concept that differs in some details from residual income.[7] For example, under the economic value added concept, funds used for research and development are treated as investments rather than as expenses.[8] However, for our purposes, we will not draw any distinction between residual income and economic value added.

When residual income or economic value added is used to measure performance, the purpose is to maximize the total amount of residual income or economic value added, not to maximize overall ROI. For purposes of illustration, consider the following data for an investment centre – the Scottish Division of Alaskan Marine Services Corporation.

Alaskan Marine Services Corporation
Scottish Division
Basic data for performance evaluation

Average operating assets	£100,000
Operating profit	£20,000
Minimum required rate of return	15%

Alaskan Marine Services Corporation has long had a policy of evaluating investment centre managers based on ROI, but it is considering a switch to residual income. The finance director of the company, who is in favour of the change to residual income, has provided the following table that shows how the performance of the division would be evaluated under each of the two methods:

Marine Services Corporation
Scottish Division
Alternative performance measures

	ROI	Residual income
Average operating assets	£100,000 (a)	£100,000
Operating profit	£20,000 (b)	£20,000
ROI, (b) ÷ (a)	20%	
Minimum required return (15% × £100,000)		15,000
Residual income		£5,000

The reasoning underlying the residual income calculation is straightforward. The company is able to earn a rate of return of at least 15% on its investments. Since the company has invested £100,000 in the Scottish Division in the form of operating assets, the company should be able to earn at least £15,000 (15% × £100,000) on this investment. Since the Scottish Division's operating profit is £20,000, the residual income above and beyond the minimum required return is £5,000. If *residual income* is adopted as the performance measure to replace ROI, the manager of the Scottish Division would be evaluated based on the growth from year to year in residual income.

Motivation and residual income

One of the primary reasons why the chief accountant of Marine Services Corporation would like to switch from ROI to residual income has to do with how managers view new investments under the two performance measurement schemes. The residual income approach encourages managers to make investments that are profitable for the entire company but that would be rejected by managers who are evaluated by the ROI formula.

To illustrate this problem, suppose that the manager of the Scottish Division is considering purchasing a computerized diagnostic machine to aid in servicing marine diesel engines. The machine would cost £25,000 and is expected to generate additional operating profit of £4,500 a year. From the standpoint of the company, this would be a good investment since it promises a rate of return of 18% (£4,500/£25,000), which is in excess of the company's minimum required rate of return of 15%.

If the manager of the Scottish Division is evaluated based on residual income, she would be in favour of the investment in the diagnostic machine as shown below:

Marine Services Corporation
Scottish Division
Perfomance evaluated using residual income

	Present	New project	Overall
Average operating assets	£100,000	£25,000	£125,000
Operating profit	£20,000	£4,500	£24,500
Minimum required return	15,000	3,750*	18,750
Residual income	£5,000	£750	£5,750

*£25,000 × 15% = £3,750.

Since the project would increase the residual income of the Scottish Division, the manager would want to invest in the new diagnostic machine.

Now suppose that the manager of the Scottish Division is evaluated based on ROI. The effect of the diagnostic machine on the division's ROI is computed below:

Marine Services Corporation
Scottish Division
Performance evaluated using ROI

	Present	New project	Overall
Average operating assets (a)	£100,000	£25,000	£125,000
Operating profit (b)	£20,000	£4,500†	£24,500
ROI, (b)/(a)	20%	18%	19.6%

†£25,000 × 18% = £4,500.

The new project reduces the division's ROI from 20% to 19.6%. This happens because the 18% rate of return on the new diagnostic machine, while above the company's 15% minimum rate of return, is below the division's present ROI of 20%. Therefore, the new diagnostic machine would drag the division's ROI down even though it would be a good investment from the standpoint of the company as a whole. If the manager of the division is evaluated based on ROI, she will be reluctant even to propose such an investment.

Basically, a manager who is evaluated based on ROI will reject any project whose rate of return is below the division's current ROI even if the rate of return on the project is above the minimum required rate of return for the entire company. In contrast, any project whose rate of return is above the minimum required rate of return for the company will result in an increase in residual income. Since it is in the best interests of the company as a whole to accept any project whose rate of return is above the minimum required rate of return, managers who are evaluated based on residual income will tend to make better decisions concerning investment projects than managers who are evaluated based on ROI.

Divisional comparison and residual income

The residual income approach has one major disadvantage. It cannot be used to compare the performance of divisions of different sizes. You would expect larger divisions to have more residual income than smaller divisions, not necessarily because they are better managed but simply because of the bigger numbers involved.

As an example, consider the following residual income computations for Division X and Division Y:

	Division	
	X	Y
Average operating assets (a)	£1,000,000	£250,000
Operating profit	£120,000	£40,000
Minimum required return: 10% × (a)	100,000	25,000
Residual income	£20,000	£15,000

FOCUS ON PRACTICE

Value-based management at Allianz

At Allianz, the company explains the principles behind its use of EVA®. They calculate EVA® as normalized profit minus capital charges, where capital charges are defined as a measure of the company's capital multiplied by the cost of capital. New investment in each division is based on their risk-return profile and their strategic position. Using this process, the divisions can only ensure that they receive growth capital if they:

- operate in a profitable market or business;
- transform their market position into sustainable creation of value and a leading market position;
- maintain an orientation and competency that fits within the long-term strategy of the Allianz Group; and
- are able to generate distributable earnings in an amount that is at least equal to their cost of capital.

The requirement to meet the cost of capital is just the minimum. Over the medium term, the objective is to generate a return of 15% or more on the capital employed. Therefore, companies must determine what business activities will increase their value and concentrate their efforts and resources on these activities. Further, new value drivers must be created, for example, through new products, more cost-effective processes and optimized distribution channels. Local management must also prevent value being destroyed along the complete value chain. If value diminishes, countermeasures must be implemented immediately. Because EVA® is an important factor in managing the business, senior management compensation is based on this measurement to a significant extent.

Exercise: Consider what issues might be neglected by a company that uses ROI rather than EVA as a key performance metric.

Source: adapted from Allianz website; reproduced with permission.

Observe that Division X has slightly more residual income than Division Y, but that Division X has £1,000,000 in operating assets as compared to only £250,000 in operating assets for Division Y. Thus, Division X's greater residual income is probably more a result of its size than the quality of its management. In fact, it appears that the smaller division is better managed, since it has been able to generate nearly as much residual income with only a quarter as much in operating assets to work with. This problem can be reduced to some degree by focusing on the percentage change in residual income from year to year rather than on the absolute amount of the residual income.

The problem of single period metrics: the bonus bank approach

The problem with ROI, RI and EVA is that they are all single period metrics. Thus, although it can be shown that under certain assumptions the capitalized value of residual income equals the net present value of the company,[9] a one-period measure cannot capture the economic value of a division or investment. From this point of view, investment decisions based on these techniques will not be identical to those based on the 'correct' NPV rule.

Advocates of EVA have tried to respond to this problem by basing executive remuneration on a 'bonus bank' system. The aim of this approach is that bonuses are not just based on a single year's performance but may be accumulated over a number of years. The aim is to discourage managers who may be able to boost EVA in the very short term, take a bonus and then leave the company. In fact, one of the distinguishing features of EVA over RI is the great care that is devoted to designing managerial compensation schemes that are aligned with shareholder wealth objectives.[10]

SUMMARY

- Segment reports can provide information for evaluating the profitability and performance of divisions, product lines, sales territories and other segments of a company. Under the contribution approach to segment reporting, only those costs that are traceable are assigned to a segment. Fixed common costs and other non-traceable costs are not allocated to a segment. A cost is considered to be traceable to a segment only if the cost is caused by the segment and eliminating the segment would result in avoiding the cost.
- Costs that are traceable to a segment are further classified as either variable or fixed. The contribution margin is sales less variable costs. The segment margin is the contribution margin less the traceable fixed costs of the segment.
- For purposes of evaluating the performance of managers, there are at least three kinds of business segments – cost centres, profit centres and investment centres.
- Return on investment (ROI) is widely used to evaluate investment centre performance. However, there is a trend towards using residual income or economic value added instead of ROI.
- The residual income and economic value added approaches encourage profitable investments in many situations where the ROI approach would discourage investment.

KEY TERMS FOR REVIEW

Common fixed cost (p. 611)
Cost centre (p. 606)
Decentralized organization (p. 605)
Economic value added (EVA) (p. 622)
Investment centre (p. 606)
Margin (p. 618)
Operating profit (p. 617)
Operating assets (p. 617)
Profit centre (p. 606)
Residual income (p. 622)
Responsibility centre (p. 607)
Return on investment (ROI) (p. 617)
Segment (p. 606)
Segment margin (p. 613)
Traceable fixed cost (p. 611)
Turnover (p. 619)
Value chain (p. 615)

Review problem 1: segmented statements

The business staff of the legal firm Frampton, Davis & Smythe have constructed the following report which breaks down the firm's overall results for last month in terms of its two main business segments – family law and commercial law:

	Total	Family law	Commercial law
Revenues from clients	£1,000,000	£400,000	£600,000
Less variable expenses	220,000	100,000	120,000
Contribution margin	780,000	300,000	480,000
Less traceable fixed expenses	670,000	280,000	390,000
Segment margin	110,000	20,000	90,000
Less common fixed expenses	60,000	24,000	36,000
Operating profit	£50,000	£(4,000)	£54,000

However, this report is not quite correct. The common fixed expenses such as the managing partner's salary, general administrative expenses, and general firm advertising have been allocated to the two segments based on revenues from clients.

Required

1. Redo the segment report, eliminating the allocation of common fixed expenses. Show both amount and percentage columns for the firm as a whole and for each of the segments. Would the firm be better off financially if the family law segment were dropped? (*Note:* Many of the firm's commercial law clients also use the firm for their family law requirements such as drawing up wills.)
2. The firm's advertising agency has proposed an ad campaign targeted at boosting the revenues of the family law segment. The ad campaign would cost £20,000, and the advertising agency claims that it would increase family law revenues by £100,000. The managing partner of Frampton, Davis & Smythe believes this increase in business could be accommodated without any increase in fixed expenses. What effect would this ad campaign have on the family law segment margin and on overall Operating profit of the firm?

Solution to review problem 1: segmented statements

1. The corrected segmented statement of profit or loss appears below:

	Total		Family law		Commercial law	
	Amount	%	Amount	%	Amount	%
Revenues from clients	£1,000,000	100	£400,000	100	£600,000	100
Less variable expenses	220,000	22	100,000	25	120,000	20
Contribution margin	780,000	78	300,000	75	480,000	80
Less traceable fixed expenses	670,000	67	280,000	70	390,000	65
Segment margin	110,000	11	£20,000	5	£90,000	15
Less common fixed expenses	60,000	6				
Operating profit	£50,000	5				

No, the firm would not be financially better off if the family law practice were dropped. The family law segment is covering all of its own costs and is contributing £20,000 per month to covering the common fixed expenses of the firm. While the segment margin as a percentage of sales is much lower for family law than for commercial law, it is still profitable; and it is likely that family law is a service that the firm must provide to its commercial clients in order to remain competitive.

2 The ad campaign would be expected to add £55,000 to the family law segment as follows:

Increased revenues from clients	£100,000
Family law contribution margin ratio	×75%
Incremental contribution margin	75,000
Less cost of the ad campaign	20,000
Increased segment margin	£55,000

Since there would be no increase in fixed expenses (including common fixed expenses), the increase in overall operating profit should also be £55,000.

Review problem 2: return on investment (ROI) and residual income

The Magnetic Imaging Division of Medical Diagnostics plc has reported the following results for last year's operations:

Sales	£25 million
Operating profit	3 million
Average operating assets	10 million

Required

1 Compute the margin, turnover and ROI for the Magnetic Imaging Division.

2 Top management of Medical Diagnostics plc has set a minimum required rate of return on average operating assets of 25%. What is the Magnetic Imaging Division's residual income for the year?

Solution to review problem 2: return on investment (ROI) and residual income

1 The required calculations appear below:

$$\text{Margin} = \frac{\text{Operating profit, £3,000,000}}{\text{Sales, £25,000,000}}$$

$$= 12\%$$

$$\text{Turnover} = \frac{\text{Sales, £25,000,000}}{\text{Average operating assets, £10,000,000}}$$
$$= 2.5\%$$
$$\text{ROI} = \text{Margin} \times \text{Turnover}$$
$$= 12\% \times 2.5$$
$$= 30\%$$

2 The residual income for the Magnetic Imaging Division is computed as follows:

Average operating assets	£10,000,000
Net operating income	£3,000,000
Minimum required return (25% × £10,000,000)	2,500,000
Residual income	£500,000

Level of difficulty: BASIC INTERMEDIATE ADVANCED

Questions

connect

14-1 What is meant by the term *decentralization?*

14-2 What benefits result from decentralization?

14-3 Distinguish between a cost centre, a profit centre and an investment centre.

14-4 Define a segment of an organization. Give several examples of segments.

14-5 How does the contribution approach assign costs to segments of an organization?

14-6 Distinguish between a traceable cost and a common cost. Give several examples of each.

14-7 Explain how the segment margin differs from the contribution margin.

14-8 Why aren't common costs allocated to segments under the contribution approach?

14-9 How is it possible for a cost that is traceable to a segment to become a common cost if the segment is divided into further segments?

14-10 What is meant by the terms *margin* and *turnover?*

14-11 What are the three basic approaches to improving return on investment (ROI)?

14-12 What is meant by residual income?

14-13 In what way can the use of ROI as a performance measure for investment centres lead to bad decisions? How does the residual income approach overcome this problem?

Applying Excel

The Excel worksheet form that appears below is to be used to recreate the Review Problem 2 in the text on pages 627–628. Download the workbook containing this form from the Online Learning Centre at www.mcgraw-hill.co.uk/textbooks/seal. *On the website you will also receive instructions about how to use this worksheet form.*

	A	B	C	D
1	Chapter 14: Applying Excel			
2				
3	**Data**			
4	Sales	£25,000,000		
5	Net operating profit	£3,000,000		
6	Average operating assets	£10,000,000		
7	Minimum required rate of return	25%		
8				
9	*Enter a formula into each of the cells marked with a ? below*			
10	**Review Problem: Return on Investment (ROI) and Residual Income**			
11				
12	***Compute the ROI***			
13	Margin	?		
14	Turnover	?		
15	ROI	?		
16				
17	***Compute the residual income***			
18	Average operating assets	?		
19	Net operating profit	?		
20	Minimum required return	?		
21	Residual income	?		
22				

Chapter 14 Form / Filled in Chapter 14

You should proceed to the requirements below only after completing your worksheet.

Required

1 Check your worksheet by changing the average operating assets in cell B6 to £8,000,000. The ROI should now be 38% and the residual income should now be £1,000,000. If you do not get these answers, find the errors in your worksheet and correct them.

Explain why the ROI and the residual income both increase when the average operating assets decrease.

2 Revise the data in your worksheet as follows:

Data	
Sales	£1,200
Net operating income	£72
Average operating assets	£500
Minimum required rate of return	15%

(a) What is the ROI?

(b) What is the residual income?

(c) Explain the relationship between the ROI and the residual income.

Exercises

connect

E14-1 Time allowed: 15 minutes

Royal Lawncare Company produces and sells two packaged products, Weedban and Greengrow. Revenue and cost information relating to the products follows:

	Product	
	Weedban	**Greengrow**
Selling price per unit	£6.00	£7.50
Variable expenses per unit	2.40	5.25
Traceable fixed expenses per year	45,000	21,000

Common fixed expenses in the company total £33,000 annually. Last year the company produced and sold 15,000 units of Weedban and 28,000 units of Greengrow.

Required

Prepare a statement of profit or loss segmented by product lines. Show both amount and percentage columns for the company as a whole and for each of the products.

E14-2 Time allowed: 20 minutes

Raner, Harris & Chan is a consulting firm that specializes in information systems for medical and dental clinics. The firm has two offices – one in Chicago and one in Minneapolis. The firm classifies the direct costs of consulting jobs as variable costs. A segmented statement of profit or loss for the company's most recent year follows:

			Segment			
	Total company Amount	**%**	**Chicago Amount**	**%**	**Minneapolis Amount**	**%**
Sales	$450,000	100	$150,000	100	$300,000	100
Less variable expenses	225,000	50	45,000	30	180,000	60
Contribution margin	225,000	50	105,000	70	120,000	40
Less traceable fixed expenses	126,000	28	78,000	52	48,000	16
Office segment margin	99,000	22	$27,000	18	$72,000	24
Less common fixed expenses not traceable to segments	63,000	14				
Operating profit	$36,000	8				

Required

1 By how much would the company's operating profit increase if Minneapolis increased its sales by $75,000 per year? Assume no change in cost behaviour patterns.

2 Refer to the original data. Assume that sales in Chicago increase by $50,000 next year and that sales in Minneapolis remain unchanged. Assume no change in fixed costs.

(a) Prepare a new segmented statement of profit or loss for the company using the format above. Show both amounts and percentages.

(b) Observe from the statement of profit or loss you have prepared that the contribution margin ratio for Chicago has remained unchanged at 70% (the same as in the data above) but that the segment margin ratio has changed. How do you explain the change in the segment margin ratio?

E14-3 Time allowed: 15 minutes

Refer to the data in E14–2. Assume that Minneapolis' sales by major market are:

	Minneapolis Amount	%	Segment: Medical Amount	%	Dental Amount	%
Sales	$300,000	100	$200,000	100	$100,000	100
Less variable expenses	180,000	60	128,000	64	52,000	52
Contribution margin	120,000	40	72,000	36	48,000	48
Less traceable fixed expenses	33,000	11	12,000	6	21,000	21
Product-line segment margin	87,000	29	$60,000	30	$27,000	27
Less common fixed expenses not traceable to segments	15,000	5				
Divisional segment margin	$72,000	24				

The company would like to initiate an intensive advertising campaign in one of the two market segments during the next month. The campaign would cost $5,000. Marketing studies indicate that such a campaign would increase sales in the medical market by $40,000 or increase sales in the dental market by $35,000.

Required

1. In which of the markets would you recommend that the company focus its advertising campaign? Show computations to support your answer.
2. In E14-2, Minneapolis shows $48,000 in traceable fixed expenses. What happened to the $48,000 in this exercise?

E14-4 Time allowed: 20 minutes

Wingate Company, a wholesale distributor of DVDs, has been experiencing losses for some time, as shown by its most recent monthly statement of profit or loss below:

Sales	£1,000,000
Less variable expense	390,000
Contribution margin	610,000
Less fixed expenses	625,000
Operating profit (loss)	£(15,000)

In an effort to isolate the problem, the managing director has asked for a statement of profit or loss segmented by division. Accordingly, the Accounting Department has developed the following information:

	Division: East	Central	West
Sales	£250,000	£400,000	£350,000
Variable expenses as a percentage of sales	52%	30%	40%
Traceable fixed expenses	£160,000	£200,000	£175,000

Required

1 Prepare a statement of profit or loss segmented by divisions, as desired by the managing director. Show both amount and percentage columns for the company as a whole and for each division.

2 As a result of a marketing study, the managing director believes that sales in the West Division could be increased by 20% if advertising in that division was increased by £15,000 each month. Would you recommend the increased advertising? Show computations.

E14-5 Time allowed: 15 minutes

You have a client who operates a large upmarket grocery store that has a full range of departments. The management has encountered difficulty in using accounting data as a basis for decisions as to possible changes in departments operated, products, marketing methods, and so forth. List several overhead costs, or costs not applicable to a particular department, and explain how the existence of such costs (sometimes called *common costs*) complicates and limits the use of accounting data in making decisions in such a store.

(*CPA*, adapted)

E14-6 Time allowed: 15 minutes

Selected operating data for two divisions of Outback Brewing Ltd of Australia are given below:

	Division	
	Queensland	**New South Wales**
Sales	$4,000,000	$7,000,000
Average operating assets	2,000,000	2,000,000
Operating profit	360,000	420,000
Property, plant, and equipment (net)	950,000	800,000

Required

1 Compute the rate of return for each division using the return on investment (ROI) formula stated in terms of margin and turnover.

2 As far as you can tell from the data, which divisional manager seems to be doing the better job? Why?

E14-7 Time allowed: 15 minutes

Provide the missing data in the following tabulation:

	Division		
	Alpha	**Bravo**	**Charlie**
Sales	£?	£11,500,000	£?
Operating profit	?	920,000	210,000
Average operating assets	800,000	?	?
Margin	4%	?	7%
Turnover	5	?	?
Return on investment (ROI)	?	20%	14%

E14-8 Time allowed: 20 minutes

Meiji Isetan Corp. of Japan has two regional divisions with headquarters in Osaka and Yokohama. Selected data on the two divisions follow (in millions of yen, denoted by ¥):

	Division	
	Osaka	Yokohama
Sales	¥3,000,000	¥9,000,000
Operating profit	210,000	720,000
Average operating assets	1,000,000	4,000,000

Required

1 For each division, compute the return on investment (ROI) in terms of margin and turnover. Where necessary, carry computations to two decimal places.

2 Assume that the company evaluates performance by use of residual profit and that the minimum required return for any division is 15%. Compute the residual profit for each division.

3 Is Yokohama's greater amount of residual profit an indication that it is better managed? Explain.

E14-9 Time allowed: 30 minutes

Selected sales and operating data for three divisions of a multinational structural engineering firm are given below:

	Division		
	Asia	Europe	North America
Sales	£12,000,000	£14,000,000	£25,000,000
Average operating assets	3,000,000	7,000,000	5,000,000
Operating profit	600,000	560,000	800,000
Minimum required rate of return	14%	10%	16%

Required

1 Compute the return on investment (ROI) for each division using the formula stated in terms of margin and turnover.

2 Compute the residual income for each division.

3 Assume that each division is presented with an investment opportunity that would yield a 15% rate of return.

(a) If performance is being measured by ROI, which division or divisions will probably accept the opportunity? Reject? Why?

(b) If performance is being measured by residual income, which division or divisions will probably accept the opportunity? Reject? Why?

E14-10 Time allowed: 15 minutes

A family friend has asked your help in analysing the operations of three anonymous companies operating in the same service sector industry. Supply the missing data in the table below:

	Company		
	A	B	C
Sales	£400,000	£750,000	£600,000
Net operating income	?	45,000	?
Average operating assets	160,000	?	150,000
Return on investment (ROI)	20%	18%	?
Minimum required rate of return:			
Percentage	15%	?	12%
amount	?	50,000	?
Residual income	?	?	6,000

Problems

connect

P14-11 **Effects of changes in profits and assets on return on investment**
Time allowed: 30 minutes

FysiQ is a chain of fitness centres in South Africa. The managers of the centres, who have authority to make investments as needed, are evaluated based largely on return on investment (ROI). One of the clubs within FysiQ reported the following results for the past year:

Sales	R8,000,000
Net operating income	160,000
Average operating assets	1,000,000

Required

The following questions are to be considered independently. Carry out all computations to two decimal places.

1 Compute the club's return on investment (ROI).

2 Assume that the manager of the club is able to increase sales by R800,000 and that as a result net operating income increases by R60,000. Further assume that this is possible without any increase in operating assets. What would be the club's return on investment (ROI)?

3 Assume that the manager of the club is able to reduce expenses by R32,000 without any change in sales or operating assets. What would be the club's return on investment (ROI)?

4 Assume that the manager of the club is able to reduce operating assets by R200,000 without any change in sales or net operating income. What would be the centre's return on investment (ROI)?

P14-12 **Segment reporting**
Time allowed: 30 minutes

Vulcan Company's statement of profit or loss for last month is given below:

Vulcan Company Statement of profit or loss for the month ended 30 June	
Sales	£750,000
Less variable expenses	336,000
Contribution margin	414,000
Less fixed expenses	378,000
Operating profit	£36,000

Management is disappointed with the company's performance and is wondering what can be done to improve profits. By examining sales and cost records, you have determined the following:

1. The company is divided into two sales territories – Northern and Southern. The Northern territory recorded £300,000 in sales and £156,000 in variable expenses during June; the remaining sales and variable expenses were recorded in the Southern territory. Fixed expenses of £120,000 and £108,000 are traceable to the Northern and Southern territories, respectively. The rest of the fixed expenses are common to the two territories.
2. The company sells two products – Paks and Tibs. Sales of Paks and Tibs totalled £50,000 and £250,000, respectively, in the Northern territory during June. Variable expenses are 22% of the selling price for Paks and 58% for Tibs. Cost records show that £30,000 of the Northern territory's fixed expenses are traceable to Paks and £40,000 to Tibs, with the remainder common to the two products.

Required

1. Prepare segmented statements of profit or loss first showing the total company broken down between sales territories and then showing the Northern territory broken down by product line. Show both amount and percentage columns for the company in total and for each segment.
2. Look at the statement you have prepared showing the total company segmented by sales territory. Which points revealed by this statement should be brought to the attention of management?
3. Look at the statement you have prepared showing the Northern territory segmented by product lines. Which points revealed by this statement should be brought to the attention of management?

P14-13 **Return on investment (ROI) and residual income**
Time allowed: 20 minutes

Financial data for Joel de Paris plc for last year follow:

Joel de Paris plc Balance sheet		
Assets	**Ending balance**	**Beginning balance**
Cash	£120,000	£140,000
Accounts receivable	530,000	450,000
Inventory	380,000	320,000
Plant and equipment, net	620,000	680,000
Investment in Buisson SA	280,000	250,000
Land (undeveloped)	170,000	180,000
Total assets	£2,100,000	£2,020,000

Liabilities and shareholders' equity		
Accounts payable	£310,000	£360,000
Long-term debt	1,500,000	1,500,000
Shareholders' equity	290,000	160,000
Total liabilities and shareholders' equity	£2,100,000	£2,020,000

Joel de Paris plc Statement of profit or loss		
Sales		£4,050,000
Less operating expenses		3,645,000
Operating profit		405,000
Less interest and taxes:		
Interest expense	£150,000	
Tax expense	110,000	260,000
Operating profit		£145,000

The company paid dividends of £15,000 last year. The 'Investment in Buisson', on the balance sheet represents an investment in the shares of another company.

Required

1 Compute the company's margin, turnover and ROI for last year.

2 The board of directors of Joel de Paris plc has set a minimum required return of 15%. What was the company's residual income last year?

P14-14 Restructuring a segmented statement

Time allowed: 60 minutes

Losses have been incurred in Millard Company for some time. In an effort to isolate the problem and improve the company's performance, management has requested that the monthly statement of profit or loss be segmented by sales region. The company's first effort at preparing a segmented statement is given below. This statement is for May, the most recent month of activity.

Cost of goods sold and shipping expense are both variable; other costs are all fixed.

Millard Company is a wholesale distributor of office products. It purchases office products from manufacturers and distributes them in the three regions given below. The three regions are about the same size, and each has its own manager and sales staff. The products that the company distributes vary widely in profitability.

Required

1 List any disadvantages or weaknesses that you see to the statement format illustrated below.

2 Explain the basis that is apparently being used to allocate the corporate expenses to the regions. Do you agree with these allocations? Explain.

3 Prepare a new segmented statement of profit or loss for May using the contribution approach. Show a Total column as well as data for each region. Include percentages on your statement for all columns.

	Sales region		
	West	**Central**	**East**
Sales	£450,000	£800,000	£750,000
Less regional expenses (traceable):			
Cost of goods sold	162,900	280,000	376,500
Advertising	108,000	200,000	210,000
Salaries	90,000	88,000	135,000
Utilities	13,500	12,000	15,000
Depreciation	27,000	28,000	30,000
Shipping expense	17,100	32,000	28,500
Total regional expenses	418,500	640,000	795,000
Regional profit (loss) before corporate expenses	31,500	160,000	(45,000)
Less corporate expenses:			
Advertising (general)	18,000	32,000	30,000
General administrative expense	50,000	50,000	50,000
Total corporate expenses	68,000	82,000	80,000
Operating profit (loss)	£(36,500)	£78,000	£(125,000)

4 Analyse the statement that you prepared in Requirement 3 above. Which points that might help to improve the company's performance would you be particularly anxious to bring to the attention of management?

P14-15 **Segment reporting; activity-based cost assignment**
Time allowed: 60 minutes

Diversified Products plc has recently acquired a small publishing company that Diversified Products intends to operate as one of its investment centres. The newly acquired company has three books that it offers for sale – a cookbook, a travel guide and a handy speller. Each book sells for £10. The publishing company's most recent monthly statement of profit or loss is given below:

	Total company		Product line		
			Cookbook	Travel guide	Handy speller
Sales	£300,000	100%	£90,000	£150,000	£60,000
Less expenses:					
Printing costs	102,000	34%	27,000	63,000	12,000
Advertising	36,000	12%	13,500	19,500	3,000
General sales	18,000	6%	5,400	9,000	3,600
Salaries	33,000	11%	18,000	9,000	6,000
Equipment depreciation	9,000	3%	3,000	3,000	3,000
Sales commissions	30,000	10%	9,000	15,000	6,000
General administration	42,000	14%	14,000	14,000	14,000
Warehouse rent	12,000	4%	3,600	6,000	2,400
Depreciation – office facilities	3,000	1%	1,000	1,000	1,000
Total expenses	285,000	95%	94,500	139,500	51,000
Operating profit (loss)	£15,000	5%	£(4,500)	£10,500	£9,000

The following additional information is available about the company:

1 Only printing costs and sales commissions are variable; all other costs are fixed. The printing costs (which include materials, labour and variable overhead) are traceable to the three product lines as shown in the statement above. Sales commissions are 10% of sales for any product.

2 The same equipment is used to produce all three books, so the equipment depreciation cost has been allocated equally among the three product lines. An analysis of the company's activities indicates that the equipment is used 30% of the time to produce cookbooks, 50% of the time to produce travel guides, and 20% of the time to produce handy spellers.

3 The warehouse is used to store finished units of product, so the rental cost has been allocated to the product lines on the basis of sales. The warehouse rental cost is £3 per square metre per year. The warehouse contains 48,000 square metres of space, of which 7,200 square metres is used by the cookbook line, 24,000 square metres by the travel guide line, and 16,800 square metres by the handy speller line.

4 The general sales cost above includes the salary of the sales manager and other sales costs not traceable to any specific product line. This cost has been allocated to the product lines on the basis of sales pounds.

5 The general administration cost and depreciation of office facilities both relate to overall administration of the company as a whole. These costs have been allocated equally to the three product lines.

6 All other costs are traceable to the three product lines in the amounts shown on the statement above.

The management of Diversified Products plc is anxious to improve the new investment centre's 5% return on sales.

Required

1 Prepare a new segmented statement of profit or loss for the month using the contribution approach. Show both an amount column and a percentage column for the company as a whole and for each product line. Adjust allocations of equipment depreciation and of warehouse rent as indicated by the additional information provided.

2 After seeing the statement of profit or loss in the main body of the problem, management has decided to eliminate the cookbook, since it is not returning a profit, and to focus all available resources on promoting the travel guide.

(a) Based on the statement you have prepared, do you agree with the decision to eliminate the cookbook? Explain.

(b) Based on the statement you have prepared, do you agree with the decision to focus all available resources on promoting the travel guide? Explain. (You may assume that an ample market is available for all three product lines.)

3 What additional points would you bring to the attention of management that might help to improve profits?

P14-16 Return on investment (ROI); comparison of company performance

Time allowed: 30 minutes

Comparative data on three companies in the same industry are given below:

	Company		
	A	B	C
Sales	£600,000	£500,000	£?
Operating profit	84,000	70,000	?
Average operating assets	300,000	?	1,000,000
Margin	?	?	3.5%
Turnover	?	?	2
ROI	?	7%	?

Required

1 What advantages can you see in breaking down the ROI computation into two separate elements, margin and turnover?

2 Fill in the missing information above, and comment on the relative performance of the three companies in as much detail as the data permit. Make specific recommendations on steps to be taken to improve the return on investment, where needed.

(Adapted from National Association of Accountants, Research Report No. 35, p. 34)

P14-17 Return on investment (ROI) and residual income

Time allowed: 30 minutes

'I know headquarters wants us to add on that new product line,' said Dell Havasi, manager of Billings Company's Office Products Division. 'But I want to see the numbers before I make any move. Our division has led the company for three years, and I don't want any letdown.'

Billings Company is a decentralized organization with five autonomous divisions. The divisions are evaluated on the basis of the return that they are able to generate on invested assets, with year-end bonuses given to the divisional managers who have the highest ROI figures. Operating results for the company's Office Products Division for the most recent year are given below:

Sales	£10,000,000
Less variable expenses	6,000,000
Contribution margin	4,000,000
Less fixed expenses	3,200,000
Operating profit	800,000
Divisional operating assets	£4,000,000

The company had an overall ROI of 15% last year (considering all divisions). The Office Products Division has an opportunity to add a new product line that would require an additional investment in operating assets of £1,000,000. The cost and revenue characteristics of the new product line per year would be:

Sales	£2,000,000
Variable expenses	60% of sales
Fixed expenses	£640,000

Required

1 Compute the Office Products Division's ROI for the most recent year; also compute the ROI as it will appear if the new product line is added.

2 If you were in Dell Havasi's position, would you be inclined to accept or reject the new product line? Explain.

3 Why do you suppose headquarters is anxious for the Office Products Division to add the new product line?

4 Suppose that the company views a return of 12% on invested assets as being the minimum that any division should earn and that performance is evaluated by the residual income approach.

(a) Compute the Office Products Division's residual income for the most recent year; also compute the residual income as it will appear if the new product line is added.

(b) Under these circumstances, if you were in Dell Havasi's position, would you accept or reject the new product line? Explain.

P14-18 **Activity-based segment reporting**
Time allowed: 60 minutes

'That commercial market has been dragging us down for years,' complained Shanna Reynolds, managing director of Morley Products. 'Just look at that anaemic profit figure for the commercial market. That market had three million pounds more in sales than the home market, but only a few thousand pounds more in profits. What a loser it is!'

The statement of profit or loss to which Ms Reynolds was referring follows:

	Total company		Commercial market	Home market	School market
Sales	£20,000,000	100.0%	£8,000,000	£5,000,000	£7,000,000
Less expenses:					
Cost of goods sold	9,500,000	47.5%	3,900,000	2,400,000	3,200,000
Sales support	3,600,000	18.0%	1,440,000	900,000	1,260,000
Order processing	1,720,000	8.6%	688,000	430,000	602,000
Warehousing	940,000	4.7%	376,000	235,000	329,000
Packing and shipping	520,000	2.6%	208,000	130,000	182,000
Advertising	1,690,000	8.5%	676,000	422,500	591,500
General management	1,310,000	6.6%	524,000	327,500	458,500
Total expenses	19,280,000	96.4%	7,812,000	4,845,000	6,623,000
Operating profit	£720,000	3.6%	£188,000	£155,000	£377,000

'I agree,' said Walt Divot, the company's deputy managing director. 'We need to focus more of our attention on the school market, since it's our best segment. Maybe that will bolster profits and get the shareholders off our backs.'

The following additional information is available about the company:

1 Morley Products is a wholesale distributor of various goods; the cost of goods sold figures above are traceable to the markets in the amounts shown.

2 Sales support, order processing, and packing and shipping are considered by management to be variable costs. Warehousing, general management and advertising are fixed costs. These costs have all been allocated to the markets on the basis of sales pounds – a practice that the company has followed for years.

3 You have compiled the following data:

		Amount of activity			
Cost pool and allocation base	Total cost	Total	Commercial market	Home market	School market
Sales support (number of calls)	£3,600,000	24,000	8,000	5,000	11,000
Order processing (number of orders)	1,720,000	8,600	1,750	5,200	1,650
Warehousing (square metres of space)	940,000	117,500	35,000	65,000	17,500
Packing and shipping (kilos shipped)	520,000	104,000	24,000	16,000	64,000

4 You have determined the following breakdown of the company's advertising expense and general management expense:

		Market		
	Total	Commercial	Home	School
Advertising:				
Traceable	£1,460,000	£700,000	£180,000	£580,000
Common	230,000			
General management:				
Traceable – salaries	410,000	150,000	120,000	140,000
Common	900,000			

The company is searching for ways to improve profit, and you have suggested that a segmented statement in which costs are assigned on the basis of activities might provide some useful insights for management.

Required

1 Refer to the data in (3) above. Determine a rate for each cost pool. Then, using this rate, compute the amount of cost assignable to each market.

2 Using the data from Requirement 1 above and other data from the problem, prepare a revised segmented statement for the company. Use the contribution format. Show an amount column and a percentage column for the company as a whole and for each market segment. Carry percentage figures to one decimal place. (Remember to include warehousing among the fixed expenses.)

3 What, if anything, in your segmented statement should be brought to the attention of management? Explain.

P14-19 **Multiple segmented statements of profit or loss**
Time allowed: 60 minutes

Companhia Bradesco SA of Brazil has two divisions. The company's statement of profit or loss segmented by divisions for last year is given below (the currency in Brazil is the real, denoted here by R):

	Total company	Division	
		Plastic	Glass
Sales	R1,500,000	R900,000	R600,000
Less variable expenses	700,000	400,000	300,000
Contribution margin	800,000	500,000	300,000
Less traceable fixed expenses:			
Advertising	300,000	180,000	120,000
Depreciation	140,000	92,000	48,000
Administration	220,000	118,000	102,000
Total	660,000	390,000	270,000
Divisional segment margin	140,000	R 110,000	R 30,000
Less common fixed expenses	100,000		
Operating profit	R 40,000		

Top management does not understand why the Glass Division has such a low segment margin when its sales are only one-third less than sales in the Plastics Division. Accordingly, management has directed that the Glass Division be further segmented into product lines. The following information is available on the product lines in the Glass Division:

	Glass Division product lines		
	Flat glass	Auto glass	Speciality glass
Sales	R200,000	R300,000	R100,000
Traceable fixed expenses:			
Advertising	30,000	42,000	48,000
Depreciation	10,000	24,000	14,000
Administration	14,000	21,000	7,000
Variable expenses as a percentage of sales	65%	40%	50%

Analysis shows that R60,000 of the Glass Division's administration expenses are common to the product lines.

Required

1 Prepare a segmented statement of profit or loss for the Glass Division with segments defined as product lines. Use the contribution approach. Show both an amount column and a percentage column for the division in total and for each product line.

2 Management is surprised by Speciality Glass's poor showing and would like to have the product line segmented by market. The following information is available about the two markets in which speciality glass is sold:

	Speciality glass markets	
	Domestic	Foreign
Sales	R60,000	R40,000
Traceable fixed expenses:		
Advertising	18,000	30,000
Variable expenses as a percentage of sales	50%	50%

All of Speciality Glass's depreciation and administration expenses are common to the markets in which the product is sold. Prepare a segmented statement of profit or loss for Speciality Glass with segments defined as markets. Again use the contribution approach and show both amount and percentage columns.

3 Refer to the statement prepared in Requirement 1 above. The sales manager wants to run a special promotional campaign on one of the products over the next month. A market study indicates that such a campaign would increase sales of Flat Glass by R40,000 or sales of Auto Glass by R30,000. The campaign would cost R8,000. Show computations to determine which product line should be chosen.

P14-20 Return on investment (ROI) analysis

Time allowed: 30 minutes

The statement of profit or loss for Huerra Company for last year is given below:

	Total	Unit
Sales	£4,000,000	£80.00
Less variable expenses	2,800,000	56.00
Contribution margin	1,200,000	24.00
Less fixed expenses	840,000	16.80
Operating profit	360,000	7.20
Less profit taxes (30%)	108,000	2.16
Operating profit	£252,000	£5.04

The company had average operating assets of £2,000,000 during the year.

Required

1 Compute the company's ROI for the period using the ROI formula stated in terms of margin and turnover.

For each of the following questions, indicate whether the margin and turnover will increase, decrease, or remain unchanged as a result of the events described, and then compute the new ROI figure. Consider each question separately, starting in each case from the data used to compute the original ROI in Requirement 1 above.

2 By use of just-in-time (JIT), the company is able to reduce the average level of inventory by £400,000. (The released funds are used to pay off short-term creditors.)

3 The company achieves a cost saving of £32,000 per year by using less costly materials.

4 The company issues bonds and uses the proceeds to purchase £500,000 in machinery and equipment. Interest on the bonds is £60,000 per year. Sales remain unchanged. The new, more efficient equipment reduces production costs by £20,000 per year.

5 As a result of a more intense effort by salespeople, sales are increased by 20%; operating assets remain unchanged.

6 Obsolete items of inventory carried on the records at a cost of £40,000 are scrapped and written off as a loss since they are unsaleable.

7 The company uses £200,000 of cash (received on accounts receivable) to repurchase and retire some of its common inventory.

P14-21 Return on investment (ROI) and residual income

Time allowed: 30 minutes

Raddington Industries produces tool and die machinery for manufacturers. The company expanded vertically several years ago by acquiring Reigis Steel Company, one of its suppliers of alloy steel plates. Raddington decided to maintain Reigis's separate identity and therefore established the Reigis Steel Division as one of its investment centres.

Raddington evaluates its divisions on the basis of ROI. Management bonuses are also based on ROI. All investments in operating assets are expected to earn a minimum rate of return of 11%.

Reigis's ROI has ranged from 14% to 17% since it was acquired by Raddington. During the past year, Reigis had an investment opportunity that would yield an estimated rate of return of 13%. Reigis's management decided against the investment because it believed the investment would decrease the division's overall ROI.

Last year's statement of profit or loss for Reigis Steel Division is given below. The division's operating assets employed were £12,960,000 at the end of the year, which represents an 8% increase over the previous year-end balance.

Reigis Steel Division Divisional statement of profit or loss for the year ended 31 December		
Sales		£31,200,000
Cost of goods sold		16,500,000
Gross margin		14,700,000
Less operating expenses:		
Selling expenses	£5,620,000	
Administrative expenses	7,208,000	12,828,000
Operating profit		£1,872,000

Required

1 Compute the following performance measures for the Reigis Steel Division:

(a) ROI. (Remember, ROI is based on the average operating assets, computed from the beginning-of-year and end-of-year balances.) State ROI in terms of margin and turnover.

(b) Residual profit.

2 Would the management of Reigis Steel Division have been more likely to accept the investment opportunity it had last year if residual profit were used as a performance measure instead of ROI? Explain.

3 The Reigis Steel Division is a separate investment centre within Raddington Industries. Identify the items Reigis must be free to control if it is to be evaluated fairly by either the ROI or residual profit performance measures.

(*CMA*, adapted)

P14-22 **Cost-volume-profit analysis; return on investment (ROI); transfer pricing**
Time allowed: 45 minutes

The Valve Division of Bendix plc produces a small valve that is used by various companies as a component part in their products. Bendix plc operates its divisions as autonomous units, giving its divisional managers great discretion in pricing and other decisions. Each division is expected to generate a rate of return of at least 14% on its operating assets. The Valve Division has average operating assets of £700,000. The valves are sold for £5 each. Variable costs are £3 per valve, and fixed costs total £462,000 per year. The division has a capacity of 300,000 valves each year.

Required

1 How many valves must the Valve Division sell each year to generate the desired rate of return on its assets?

(a) What is the margin earned at this level of sales?

(b) What is the turnover at this level of sales?

2 Assume that the Valve Division's current ROI is just equal to the minimum required 14%. In order to increase the division's ROI, the divisional manager wants to increase the selling price per valve by 4%. Market studies indicate that an increase in the selling price would cause sales to drop by 20,000 units each year.

However, operating assets could be reduced by £50,000 due to decreased needs for accounts receivable and inventory. Compute the margin, turnover and ROI if these changes are made.

3 Refer to the original data. Assume again that the Valve Division's current ROI is just equal to the minimum required 14%. Rather than increase the selling price, the sales manager wants to reduce the selling price per valve by 4%. Market studies indicate that this would fill the plant to capacity. In order to carry the greater level of sales, however, operating assets would increase by £50,000. Compute the margin, turnover and ROI if these changes are made.

4 Refer to the original data. Assume that the normal volume of sales is 280,000 valves each year at a price of £5 per valve. Another division of the company is currently purchasing 20,000 valves each year from an overseas supplier, at a price of £4.25 per valve. The manager of the Valve Division has adamantly refused to meet this price, pointing out that it would result in a loss for his division:

Selling price per valve		£4.25
Cost per valve:		
Variable	£3.00	
Fixed (£462,000 ÷ 300,000 valves)	1.54	4.54
Net loss per valve		£(0.29)

The manager of the Valve Division also points out that the normal £5 selling price barely allows his division the required 14% rate of return. 'If we take on some business at only £4.25 per unit, then our ROI is obviously going to suffer', he reasons, 'and maintaining that ROI figure is the key to my future. Besides, taking on these extra units would require us to increase our operating assets by at least £50,000 due to the larger inventories and receivables we would be carrying.' Would you recommend that the Valve Division sell to the other division at £4.25? Show ROI computations to support your answer.

P14-23 Segmented statements; product-line analysis

Time allowed: 90 minutes

'At last, I can see some light at the end of the tunnel,' said Steve Adams, managing director of Jelco Products. 'Our losses have shrunk from over £75,000 a month at the beginning of the year to only £26,000 for August. If we can just isolate the remaining problems with products A and C, we'll be in the black by the first of next year.'

The company's statement of profit or loss for the latest month (August) is presented below (absorption costing basis):

Jelco Products
Statement of profit or loss for August

		Product		
	Total company	**A**	**B**	**C**
Sales	£1,500,000	£600,000	£400,000	£500,000
Less cost of goods sold	922,000	372,000	220,000	330,000
Gross margins	578,000	228,000	180,000	170,000
Less operating expenses:				
Selling	424,000	162,000	112,000	150,000
Administrative	180,000	72,000	48,000	60,000
Total operating expenses	604,000	234,000	160,000	210,000
Operating profit (loss)	£(26,000)	£(6,000)	£20,000	£(40,000)

'What recommendations did that business consultant make?' asked Mr Adams. 'We paid the guy £100 an hour; surely he found something wrong.' 'He says our problems are concealed by the way we make up our statements,' replied Sally Warren, the deputy managing director. 'He left us some data on what he calls "traceable" and "common" costs that he says we should be isolating in our reports.' The data to which Ms Warren was referring are shown as follows:

	Total company	Product A	Product B	Product C
Variable costs:*				
Production (materials, labour, and variable overhead)	–	18%	32%	20%
Selling	–	10%	8%	10%
Traceable fixed costs:				
Production	£376,000	£180,000	£36,000	£160,000
Selling	282,000	102,000	80,000	100,000
Common fixed costs:				
Production	210,000	–	–	–
Administrative	180,000	–	–	–

*As a percentage of sales.

'I don't see anything wrong with our statements,' said Mr Adams. 'Bill, our chief accountant, says that he has been using this format for over 30 years. He's also very careful to allocate all of our costs to the products.'

'I'll admit that Bill always seems to be on top of things,' replied Ms Warren. 'By the way, Purchasing says that the X7 chips we use in products A and B are on back order and won't be available for several weeks. From the looks of August's statement of profit or loss, we had better concentrate our remaining inventory of X7 chips on product B.' (Two X7 chips are used in both product A and product B.)

The following additional information is available on the company:

1 Work in progress and finished goods inventories are negligible and can be ignored.
2 Products A and B each sell for £250 per unit, and product C sells for £125 per unit. Strong market demand exists for all three products.

Required

1 Prepare a new statement of profit or loss for August, segmented by product and using the contribution approach. Show both amount and percentage columns for the company in total and for each product.
2 Assume that Mr Adams is considering the elimination of product C due to the losses it is incurring. Based on the statement you prepared in Requirement 1 above, what points would you make for or against elimination of product C?
3 Do you agree with the company's decision to concentrate the remaining inventory of X7 chips on product B? Why or why not?
4 Product C is sold in both a vending and a home market with sales and cost data as follows:

	Total	Market: Vending	Market: Home
Sales	£500,000	£50,000	£450,000
Variable costs:*			
Production	–	20%	20%
Selling	–	28%	8%
Traceable fixed costs:			
Selling	£75,000	£45,000	£30,000

*As a percentage of sales.

The remainder of product C's fixed selling costs and all of product C's fixed production costs are common to the markets in which product C is sold.

(a) Prepare a statement of profit or loss showing product C segmented by market. Use the contribution approach and show both amount and percentage columns for the product in total and for each market.

(b) Which points revealed by this statement would you be particularly anxious to bring to the attention of management?

P14-24 Decentralization

Time allowed: 50 minutes

PQR is a company that develops bespoke educational computer software. The company is based in Germany. It has recently acquired two companies: W and Z. W is a well-established company that is also based in Germany. It develops educational computer software and was a direct competitor of PQR. Z, which is based in Malaysia, is a new but rapidly growing company that develops off-the-shelf educational software and also produces CD ROMs. Z was acquired so that it could produce CD ROMs for PQR and W.

The Managing Director of PQR has now realized that the acquisition of these two companies will cause problems for him in terms of planning, control and decision making. He is thinking of implementing a decentralized structure but is unsure of the advantages and disadvantages of such a structure, of how much autonomy to grant the new companies, and also which performance measure to use to appraise their performance. Consequently he has contacted you, the Finance Director of PQR, for help.

Required

Write a report to the Managing Director which:

(a) explains the advantages and disadvantages that would be experienced by PQR in operating a decentralized structure;

(b) explains which types of responsibility centres you would recommend as being most appropriate for W and Z in a decentralized structure;

(c) critically evaluates the possible use of the financial performance measures 'return on capital employed' and 'residual income' for the decentralized structure of PQR;

(d) discusses the issues that need to be considered in relation to setting transfer prices for transfers made from Z to PQR and W.

(*CIMA Management Accounting – Decision Making,* adapted)

P14-25 ROI, RI and NPV

Time allowed: 35 minutes

NCL plc, which has a divisionalized structure, undertakes civil engineering and mining activities. All applications by divisional management teams for funds with which to undertake capital projects require the authorization of the board of directors of NCL plc. Once authorization has been granted to a capital application, divisional management teams are allowed to choose the project for investment.

Under the terms of the management incentive plan, which is currently in operation, the managers of each division are eligible to receive annual bonus payments which are calculated by reference to the return on investment (ROI) earned during each of the first two years by new investments. ROI is calculated using the average capital employed during the year. NCL plc depreciates its investments on a straight-line basis.

One of the most profitable divisions during recent years has been the IOA Division, which is engaged in the mining of precious metals. The management of the IOA Division is currently evaluating three projects relating to the extraction of substance 'xxx' from different areas in its country of operation. The management of the IOA Division has been given approval by the board of directors of NCL plc to spend £24 million on one of the three proposals it is considering (i.e. North, East and South projects).

The following net present value (NPV) calculations have been prepared by the management accountant of the IOA Division.

	North Project		East Project		South Project	
	Net cash inflow/ (outflow) £'000	**Present value at 12% £'000**	**Net cash inflow/ (outflow) £'000**	**Present value at 12% £'000**	**Net cash inflow/ (outflow) £'000**	**Present value at 12% £'000**
Year 0	(24,000.0)	(24,000.0)	(24,000.0)	(24,000.0)	(24,000.0)	(24,000.0)
Year 1	6,000.0	5,358.0	11,500.0	10,269.5	12,000.0	10,716.0
Year 2	8,000.0	6,376.0	11,500.0	9,165.5	10,000.0	7,970.0
Year 3	13,500.0	9,612.0	11,500.0	8,188.0	9,000.0	6,408.0
Year 4	10,500.0	6,678.0	–	–	3,000.0	1,908.0
NPV		4,024.0		3,623.0		3,002.0

The following additional information concerning the three projects is available:

1 Each of the above projects has a nil residual value.

2 The life of the East project is three years. The North and South projects are expected to have a life of four years.

3 The three projects have a similar level of risk.

4 Ignore taxation.

Required

1 Explain (with relevant calculations) why the interests of the management of the IOA Division might conflict with those of the board of directors of NCL plc.

2 Explain how the adoption of residual income (RI) using the annuity method of depreciation might prove to be a superior basis for the management incentive plan operated by NCL plc. (*Note:* No illustrative calculations should be incorporated into your explanation).

3 The IOA Division is also considering whether to undertake an investment in the West of the country (the West Project). An initial cash outlay investment of £12 million will be required and a net cash inflow amounting to £5 million is expected to arise in each of the four years of the life of the project.

The activities involved in the West project will cause the local river to become polluted and discoloured due to the discharge of waste substances from mining operations.

It is estimated that at the end of year four a cash outlay of £2 million would be required to restore the river to its original colour. This would also clear 90% of the pollution caused as a result of the mining activities of the IOA Division.

The remaining 10% of the pollution caused as a result of the mining activities of the IOA Division could be cleared up by a further cash outlay of £2 million.

Evaluate the West project and, stating your reasons, comment on whether the board of directors of NCL plc should spend the further £2 million in order to eliminate the remaining 10% of pollution. (Ignore taxation.)

(*ACCA Performance Management*, adapted)

Cases

C14-26 **Service organization; segment reporting**

Time allowed: 75 minutes

Music Teachers is an educational association for music teachers that has 20,000 members. The association operates from a central headquarters but has local membership chapters throughout the United States. Monthly meetings are held by the local chapters to discuss recent developments on topics of interest to music teachers. The association's journal, *Teachers' Forum,* is issued monthly with features about recent developments in the field. The association publishes books and reports and also sponsors professional courses that qualify for continuing professional education credit. The association's statement of revenues and expenses for the current year is presented below.

Music Teachers **Statement of revenues and expenses for the year ended 30 November**	
Revenues	$3,275,000
Less expenses:	
Salaries	920,000
Personnel costs	230,000
Occupancy costs	280,000
Reimbursement of member costs to local chapters	600,000
Other membership services	500,000
Printing and paper	320,000
Postage and shipping	176,000
Instructors' fees	80,000
General and administrative	38,000
Total expenses	3,144,000
Excess of revenues over expenses	$131,000

The board of directors of Music Teachers has requested that a segmented statement of operations be prepared showing the contribution of each profit centre to the association. The association has four profit centres: Membership Division, Magazine Subscriptions Division, Books and Reports Division, and Continuing Education Division. Mike Doyle has been assigned responsibility for preparing the segmented statement, and he has gathered the following data prior to its preparation.

1 Membership dues are $100 per year, of which $20 is considered to cover a one-year subscription to the association's journal. Other benefits include membership in the association and chapter affiliation. The portion of the dues covering the magazine subscription ($20) should be assigned to the Magazine Subscription Division.

2 One-year subscriptions to *Teachers' Forum* were sold to non-members and libraries at $30 per subscription. A total of 2,500 of these subscriptions were sold last year. In addition to subscriptions, the magazine generated $100,000 in advertising revenues. The costs per magazine subscription were $7 for printing and paper and $4 for postage and shipping.

3 A total of 28,000 technical reports and professional texts were sold by the Books and Reports Division at an average unit selling price of $25. Average costs per publication were $4 for printing and paper and $2 for postage and shipping.

4 The association offers a variety of continuing education courses to both members and non-members. The one-day courses had a tuition cost of $75 each and were attended by 2,400 students. A total of 1,760 students took two-day courses at a tuition cost of $125 for each student. Outside instructors were paid to teach some courses.

5 Salary costs and space occupied by division follow:

	Salaries	Space occupied (square metres)
Membership	210,000	2,000
Magazine Subscriptions	150,000	2,000
Books and Reports	300,000	3,000
Continuing Education	180,000	2,000
Corporate staff	80,000	1,000
Total	$920,000	10,000

Personnel costs are 25% of salaries in the separate divisions as well as for the corporate staff. The $280,000 in occupancy costs includes $50,000 in rental cost for a warehouse used by the Books and Reports Division for storage purposes.

6 Printing and paper costs other than for magazine subscriptions and for books and reports relate to the Continuing Education Division.

7 General and administrative expenses include costs relating to overall administration of the association as a whole. The company's corporate staff does some mailing of materials for general administrative purposes.

The expenses that can be traced or assigned to the corporate staff, as well as any other expenses that are not traceable to the profit centres, will be treated as common costs. It is not necessary to distinguish between variable and fixed costs.

Required

1 Prepare a segmented statement of revenues and expenses for Music Teachers. This statement should show the segment margin for each division as well as results for the association as a whole.

2 Give arguments for and against allocating all costs of the association to the four divisions.

(*CMA*, adapted)

Further reading

For a thorough explanation of the industrial context for the development of return of investment (ROI) and the residual income metrics (RI) see Johnson and Kaplan (1987).

Endnotes

1 Tully (1993).

2 There is a similar problem with top-level managers as well, as we shall see in Chapter 17.

3 Some companies classify business segments that are responsible mainly for generating revenue, such as an insurance sales office, as revenue centres. Other companies would consider this to be just another type of profit centre, since costs of some kind (salaries, rent, utilities) are usually deducted from the revenues in the segment's profit statement.

4 See Johnson and Kaplan (1987).

5 Emore and Ness (1991), p. 39.

6 Since residual income was developed in the United States, the term 'income' rather than 'profit' is used.

7 The basic idea underlying residual income and economic value added has been around for over 100 years. In recent years, economic value added has been popularized and trademarked by the consulting firm Stern, Stewart & Co.

8 Over 100 different adjustments could be made for deferred taxes, LIFO reserves, provisions for future liabilities, mergers and acquisitions, gains or losses due to changes in accounting rules, operating leases, and other accounts, but most companies make only a few. For further details, see Young and O'Byrne (2001).

9 O'Hanlon and Peasnell (1998).

10 See, for example, Young and O'Byrne (2001).

CHAPTER 18

Business process management: towards the lean operation

LEARNING OBJECTIVES

After studying Chapter 18, you should be able to:

- LO1 Appreciate the business process and lean approach to the management of organizations
- LO2 Determine the reorder point using the EOQ model
- LO3 Consider the impact of JIT approaches to inventory management
- LO4 Review the role of management accounting in business models that minimize working capital
- LO5 Evaluate the contribution of ERP models
- LO6 Review the role of management accounting in e-commerce
- LO7 Measure the costs of quality
- LO8 Review the relationship between management accounting and TQM systems
- LO9 Understand the technique of benchmarking
- LO10 Understand the contribution of business process re-engineering
- LO11 Appreciate the contribution of Six Sigma and lean production

CONCEPTS IN CONTEXT

A good example of a business that has used the internet is provided by Cheshire ironmonger, Cooksons. The weakness of their old business was that they only had a single outlet in Stockport which was vulnerable to out-of-town DIY superstores. The strength of the old business was a good reputation with specialist customers and a good supply chain. With the establishment of www.cooksonhardware.com, these advantages could be made available to a wider customer base. 'The business itself holds no inventory; its suppliers meet the online orders.'[1]

LO1 In this chapter, we take a more operations management perspective. From an operations perspective, the organization is visualized as procuring, transforming and delivering a flow of products or services to customers. Thus, in contrast to some earlier chapters (see especially Chapter 14), the focus is on the management of *business processes* rather than organizational structures such as departments or divisions. In Exhibit 18.1, there is a contrast between a business process perspective and a departmental or divisional perspective. The latter is sometimes visualized as tending to produce a 'silo mentality' with some flows up and down the silo but little communication between individual 'silos'. The business process perspective challenges managers to find metrics which monitor the processes *across* the organization which serve customers and thus generate value.

Over the last few years, new technology, especially *enterprise resource planning* (ERP) packages have generated improved operations management information which may enable the integration of 'end-to-end' business processes from procurement through to final delivery and payment. Even more recently, the internet has created whole new business models with cost and revenue streams that are only just beginning to be understood. In some of these businesses such as online retailers, a company's ability to hold huge inventories and offer an immense choice is a source of commercial strength – in this type of business inventory has to be managed but it cannot be eliminated. Thus although we acknowledge the impact of philosophies such as just-in-time (JIT) that aim at the elimination of inventories, we also review some of the more traditional, **optimizing** approaches to inventory management such as the *economic order quantity* (EOQ) model. As we

Exhibit

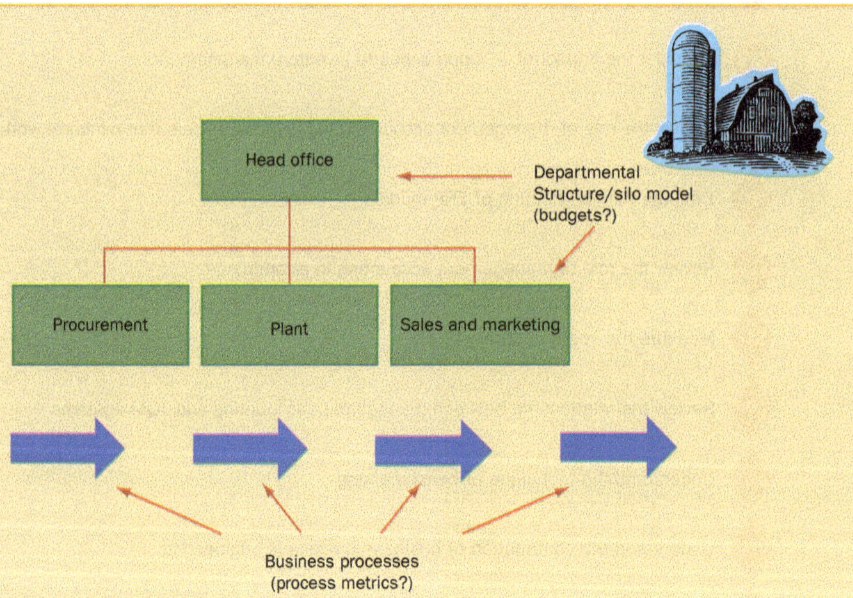

Exhibit 18.1 The process perspective contrasted to the departmental 'silo mentality'

shall see, JIT required an uncompromising attitude to quality as inventories had previously been used to hide the effects of low quality and poor business flow management. Indeed, the JIT approach combined with wider competitive pressures have challenged the traditional, *cost of quality* (COQ) model approach through the practice of *total quality management* (TQM) with its zero defects philosophy. Later on in the chapter we will be looking at techniques that seek to improve business processes, such as *benchmarking* and *business process re-engineering* (BPR), that aim to identify and eliminate non-value adding activities.[2]

Many of these business process improvement techniques are associated with the philosophy of the *lean enterprise* or *lean production*, a strategy that was proposed as an alternative to a market positioning (see Chapter 16). **Lean production** techniques were first introduced in manufacturing (especially by Toyota) but are increasingly being applied in service sectors, including not-for-profit organizations in the public sector.[3] Indeed, there are some similarities between inventories in manufacturing and queues of customers in services particularly since both are the result of failing to match supply and demand. Lean principles also involve other focuses such as the reduction of waste and virtual elimination of defects. Such objectives are now part of management orthodoxy but were seen as revolutionary only a few years ago when the philosophy of *optimization* epitomized by the EOQ model dominated thinking in many business schools.[4]

LO2 Optimizing inventory: the economic order quantity (EOQ) and the reorder point

In the optimization model of inventory management, selecting the 'right' level of inventory involves balancing three groups of costs: *inventory ordering costs, inventory carrying costs,* and the *costs of not carrying sufficient inventory.* These costs are discussed in this section.

Costs associated with inventory

Inventory ordering costs are incurred each time an inventory item is ordered. These costs may include clerical costs associated with ordering inventory, and some handling and transportation costs. They are triggered by the act of ordering inventory and are essentially the same whether 1 unit or 10,000 units are ordered; these costs are driven by the number of orders placed – not by the size of the orders. If inventory ordering costs are large, a manager may want to place small numbers of big orders on an infrequent basis rather than large numbers of small orders.

Inventory carrying costs are incurred to keep units in inventory. These costs include storage costs, handling costs, property taxes, insurance and the interest on the funds invested in inventory. These costs are driven by the amount and value of inventory that is held by the company. In addition to these costs, work in progress creates operating problems. Work in progress may physically get in the way and make it difficult to keep track of operations. Moreover, work in progress tends to hide problems that are not discovered until it is too late to take corrective action. This results in erratic production, inefficient operations, 'lost' orders, high defect rates, and substantial risks of obsolescence. These hidden costs of work in progress inventory are largely responsible for the movement to JIT. If inventory carrying costs are high, managers will want to reduce the overall level of inventory and to place frequent orders in small quantities.

The **costs of not carrying sufficient inventory** result from not having enough inventory to meet customers' needs. These costs include lost sales, customer ill will, and the costs of expediting orders for goods not held in inventory. If these costs are high, managers will want to hold large inventory. Conceptually, the 'right' level of inventory to carry is the level that will minimize the total of these three groups of costs. In the following pages we show how to accomplish this task. The problem is broken down into two dimensions – how much to order (or how much to produce in a single production run or batch) and how often to do it. These two decisions – how much to order and how often to order – determine the average level of inventory and the likelihood of being out of inventory.

Computing the economic order quantity (EOQ)

The question 'How much to order?' is answered by the **economic order quantity (EOQ)**. It is the order size that minimizes the sum of the costs of ordering inventory and the costs of carrying inventory. We will consider two approaches to computing the EOQ – the *tabular approach* and the *formula approach.*

The tabular approach

Suppose that 12,000 units of a particular item are required each year. Managers could order all 12,000 units at once or they could order smaller numbers of units spread over the year – perhaps 1,000 units per month. Placing only one order would minimize the total costs of ordering inventory but would result in high inventory carrying costs, since the average inventory level would be very large. On the other hand, placing many small orders would result in high ordering costs but in low inventory carrying costs, since the average inventory level would be reduced. As stated above, the EOQ is the order size that will optimally balance these two costs – inventory ordering costs and inventory holding costs.

To show how EOQ is computed, assume that a manufacturer uses 3,000 sub-assemblies in the manufacturing process each year. The sub-assemblies are purchased from a supplier at a cost of £20 each. Other cost data are given below:

Inventory carrying costs, per unit, per year	£0.80
Cost of placing a purchase order	10.00

Exhibit 18.2 contains a tabulation of the total costs associated with various order sizes for the sub-assemblies. Most of this table is straightforward, but the average inventory requires some explanation. If 50 units are ordered at a time and the items are ordered only when the inventory gets down to zero, then the size of the inventory will vary from 50 units to 0 units. Thus, on average, there will be 25 units in inventory. Notice that total annual cost is lowest (and is equal) at the 250- and 300-unit order sizes. The EOQ will lie somewhere between these two points. We could locate it precisely by adding more columns to the tabulation, and we would eventually zero in on 274 units as being the exact EOQ.

The cost relationships from this tabulation are shown graphically in Exhibit 18.3. The EOQ is indicated on the graph. Notice that the EOQ minimizes the total annual costs. It also is the point where annual carrying costs and annual ordering costs are equal. At the EOQ, these two costs are exactly balanced.

Exhibit

		Order size in units (O)							
Symbol*		**50**	**100**	**200**	**250**	**300**	**400**	**1,000**	**3,000**
O/2	Average inventory in units	25	50	100	125	150	200	500	1,500
Q/O	Number of orders	60	30	15	12	10	7.5	3	1
C(O/2)	Annual carrying cost at £0.80 per unit	£20	£40	£80	£100	£120	£160	£400	£1,200
P(Q/O)	Annual ordering cost at £10 per order	600	300	150	120	100	75	30	10
T	Total annual cost	£620	£340	£230	£220	£220	£235	£430	£1,210

Minimum total annual cost (arrows pointing to the £220 at 250 and 300 units)

*Symbols:
O = Order size in units (see headings above).
Q = Annual quantity used in units (3,000 in this example).
C = Annual cost of carrying one unit in stock.
P = Cost of placing one order.
T = Total annual cost.

Exhibit 18.2 Tabulation of costs associated with various order sizes

Exhibit

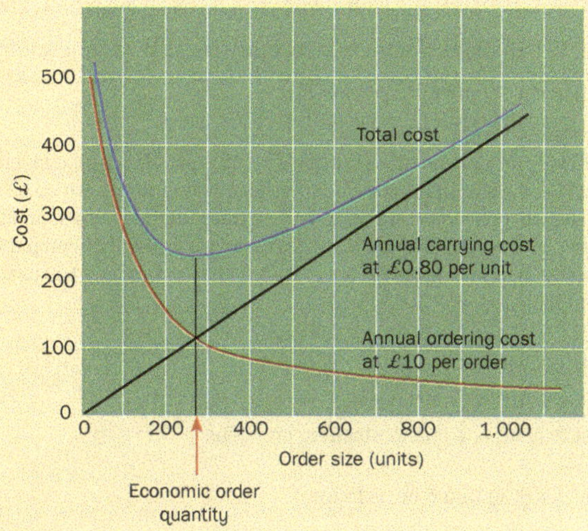

Exhibit 18.3 Graphic solution to economic order quantity (EOQ)

Observe from the graph that total cost shows a tendency to flatten out between 200 and 400 units. Most firms look for this minimum cost range and choose an order size that falls within it, rather than choosing the exact EOQ. The primary reason is that suppliers will often ship goods only in round-lot sizes.

The formula approach

The EOQ can also be found by means of a formula that can be derived using calculus:

$$E = \sqrt{\frac{2QP}{C}}$$

where:

E = economic order quantity (EOQ)
Q = annual quantity used in units
P = cost of placing one order
C = annual cost of carrying one unit in inventory.

Using the data from the preceding example, we can directly compute the EOQ as follows:

Q = 3,000 sub-assemblies used per year
P = £10 cost to place one order
C = £0.80 cost to carry one sub-assembly in stock for one year

$$E = \sqrt{\frac{2QP}{C}} = \sqrt{\frac{2(3{,}000)(£10)}{£0.80}} = \sqrt{\frac{£60{,}000}{£0.80}} = \sqrt{£75{,}000}$$

$E = 274$ units

Just-in-time (JIT) and the economic order quantity (EOQ)

By examining the EOQ formula, you can see that the economic order quantity, E, will decrease if:

1 The cost of placing an order, P, decreases, or
2 The cost of carrying inventory in inventory, C, increases.

As we shall see below, proponents of JIT argue that the cost of carrying inventory is much greater than generally realized because of the waste and inefficiency that inventory create. They also argue that following JIT procedures, such as concentrating all orders on a few high quality suppliers, will dramatically reduce the cost of placing an order. As a consequence, JIT advocates argue that companies should purchase more frequently in smaller amounts. Assume, for example, that a company has used the following data to compute its EOQ:

Q = 4,800 units needed each year
P = £75 cost to place one order
C = £4.50 cost to carry one unit in stock for one year.

Given these data, the EOQ would be as follows:

$$E = \sqrt{\frac{2QP}{C}} = \sqrt{\frac{2(4{,}800)(£75)}{(£4.50)}} = \sqrt{£160{,}000}$$

$$E = 400 \text{ units}$$

Now assume that as a result of JIT purchasing, the company is able to decrease the cost of placing an order to only £3. Also assume that due to the waste and inefficiency caused by inventory, the true cost of carrying a unit in inventory is £8 per year. The revised EOQ would be as follows:

$$E = \sqrt{\frac{2QP}{C}} = \sqrt{\frac{2(4{,}800)(£3)}{(£8)}} = \sqrt{£3{,}600}$$

$$E = 60 \text{ units}$$

Under JIT purchasing, the company would not necessarily order in 60-unit lots, since purchases would be geared to current demand. Nevertheless, this example shows quite dramatically the economics behind reducing order sizes.

Production lot size

The EOQ concept can also be applied to the problem of determining the **economic lot size**. When companies manufacture a variety of products, they must decide how many units of one product should be manufactured before switching over to another product. The number of units in a lot, or production run, is referred to as the *lot size* or *batch size*. For example, Nintendo must decide how many units of a particular game are to be produced in one lot before switching over to production of a different game. This is a problem because switching from one product to another requires changing settings on machines, changing tools, and getting different materials ready for processing. Making these changes requires time and may involve substantial out-of-pocket costs. These **set-up costs** are analogous to the order costs discussed above, and they can be used in the EOQ formula in place of the order costs to determine the optimal lot size.

To illustrate, Chittenden Company has determined that the following costs are associated with one of its products:

Q = 15,000 units produced each year
P = £150 set-up costs to switch production from one product to another
C = £2 to carry one unit in stock for one year.

What is the optimal production lot size for this product? It can be determined by using the EOQ formula:

$$E = \sqrt{\frac{2QP}{C}} = \sqrt{\frac{2(15{,}000)(£150)}{(£2)}} = \sqrt{£2{,}250{,}000}$$

$$E = 1{,}500 \text{ units (economic lot size)}$$

Chittenden Company will minimize its overall costs by producing in lots of 1,500 units each.

In computing the economic lot size, note again the impact of modern manufacturing methods. First, managers now realize that the costs of holding inventory are far higher than previously assumed. Excess work in progress inventory makes it very difficult to operate efficiently and hence generates many unnecessary costs. Second, managers and workers are cutting set-up times from many hours to a few minutes by cleverly applying techniques such as *single-minute-exchange-of-dies* (see page 781). The benefit of reducing *set-up time* is that it makes it economically feasible for the company to produce in smaller lots and to respond much more quickly to the market. Indeed, reducing set-ups to the barest minimum is an essential step in any successful implementation of JIT.

To illustrate how these aspects of modern manufacturing methods affect the economic lot size, consider the Chittenden Company data. Suppose that the company has been able to reduce the cost of a set-up to only £3. Further, suppose that the company realizes, after more careful analysis of all of the costs of holding inventory, that the true cost of carrying a unit in inventory is £36 per year. The new economic lot size would be as follows:

$$E = \sqrt{\frac{2QP}{C}} = \sqrt{\frac{2(15{,}000)(£3)}{(£36)}} = \sqrt{£2{,}500}$$

$$E = 50 \text{ units (economic lot size)}$$

Thus, the company's economic lot size has been reduced from 1,500 units to only 50 units – a reduction of nearly 97%.

Reorder point and safety inventory

We stated that the inventory problem has two dimensions – how much to order and how often to do it. The 'how often to do it' involves what are commonly termed the *reorder point* and the *safety inventory*. The basic idea is to minimize the costs of holding inventory while ensuring that there will be no situations in which there are insufficient inventory to satisfy current production requirements or customer demand. First, we will discuss the reorder point and then we will discuss the safety inventory.

The **reorder point** tells the manager when to place an order or when to initiate production to replenish depleted inventories. It is dependent on three factors – the EOQ (or economic production-run size), the *lead time*, and the rate of usage during the lead time. The **lead time** can be defined as the interval between the time that an order is placed and the time when the order is finally received from the supplier or from the production line.

Constant usage during the lead time

If the rate of usage during the lead time is known with certainty, the reorder point can be determined by the following formula:

$$\text{Reorder point} = \text{Lead time} \times \text{Average daily or weekly usage}$$

To illustrate the formula's use, assume that a company's EOQ is 500 units, that the lead time is three weeks, and that the average weekly usage is 50 units.

$$\text{Reorder point} = 3 \text{ weeks} \times 50 \text{ units per week} = 150 \text{ units}$$

The reorder point would be 150 units. That is, the company will automatically place a new order for 500 units when inventories drop to a level of 150 units, or three weeks' supply, left on hand.

Variable usage during the lead time

The previous example assumed that the 50 units per week usage rate was constant and was known with certainty. Although some firms enjoy the luxury of certainty, the more common situation is to find considerable variation in the rate of usage of inventory items from period to period. If usage varies from period to period, the firm that reorders in the way computed above may soon find itself out of inventory. A sudden spurt in demand, a delay in delivery, or a snag in processing an order may cause inventory levels to be depleted before a new shipment arrives.

Companies that experience problems in demand, delivery, or processing of orders have found that they need some type of buffer to guard against empty inventories. Such a buffer is called a **safety inventory**. A safety inventory serves as a kind of insurance against greater than usual demand and against problems in the ordering and delivery of goods. Its size is determined by deducting *average usage* from the *maximum usage* that can reasonably be expected during a period. For example, if the firm in the preceding example was faced with variable demand for its product, it would compute a safety inventory as follows:

Maximum expected usage per week	65 units
Average usage per week	50 units
Excess	15 units
Lead time	× 3 weeks
Safety inventory	45 units

The reorder point is then determined by *adding the safety inventory to the average usage during the lead time.* In formula form, the reorder point is:

Reorder point = (Lead time × Average daily or weekly usage) + Safety inventory

Computation of the reorder point is shown both numerically and graphically in Exhibit 18.4. As shown in the exhibit, the company will place a new order for 500 units when inventories drop to a level of 195 units left on hand.

Exhibit

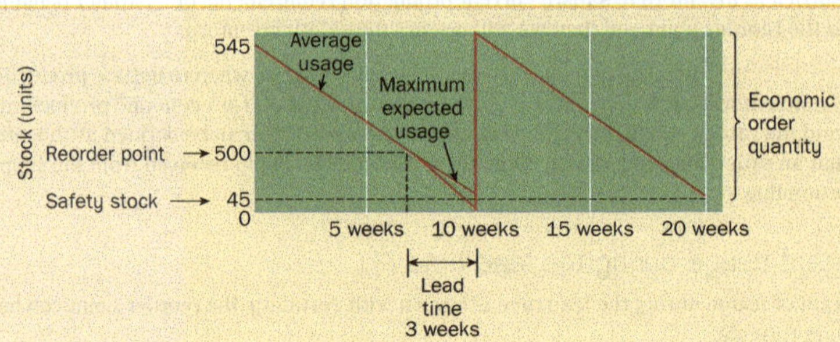

Economic order quantity .... 500 units
Lead time.................... 3 weeks
Average weekly usage .... 50 units
Maximum weekly usage .... 65 units
Safety stock................. 45 units

Reorder point = (3 weeks × 50 units per week) + 45 units = 195 units

Exhibit 18.4 Determining the reorder point – variable usage

LO3 Reducing inventory: just-in-time (JIT)

When companies use the **just-in-time (JIT)** production and inventory control system, they purchase materials and produce units only as needed to meet actual customer demand. In a JIT system, inventories are reduced to the minimum and in some cases to zero. The JIT approach can be used in both merchandising and manufacturing companies. It has the most profound effects, however, on the operations of manufacturing companies, which maintain three classes of inventory – *raw materials, work in progress* and *finished goods.*

Traditionally, manufacturing companies have maintained large amounts of all three kinds of inventory to act as buffers so that operations can proceed smoothly even if there are unanticipated disruptions. Raw materials inventory provides insurance in case suppliers are late with deliveries. Work in progress inventory is maintained in case a workstation is unable to operate due to a breakdown or other reason. Finished goods inventory is maintained to accommodate unanticipated fluctuations in demand.

While these inventories provide buffers against unforeseen events, they have a cost. In addition to the money tied up in the inventory, experts argue that the presence of inventory encourages inefficient and sloppy work, results in too many defects, and dramatically increases the amount of time required to complete a product. None of this is obvious – if it were, companies would have long ago reduced their inventories. Managers at Toyota are credited with the insight that large inventories often create more problems than they solve and Toyota pioneered the JIT approach.

LO4 The JIT concept

Under ideal conditions, a company operating a JIT system would purchase *only* enough materials each day to meet that day's needs. Moreover, the company would have no goods still in progress at the end of the day, and all goods completed during the day would have been shipped immediately to customers. As this sequence suggests, 'just-in-time' means that raw materials are received *just in time* to go into production, manufactured parts are completed *just in time* to be assembled into products, and products are completed *just in time* to be shipped to customers.

Although few companies have been able to reach this ideal, many companies have been able to reduce inventory to only a fraction of their previous levels. The result has been a substantial reduction in ordering and warehousing costs, and much more effective operations.

How does a company avoid a build-up of parts and materials at various workstations and still ensure a smooth flow of goods when JIT is in use? In a JIT environment, the flow of goods is controlled by a *pull approach.* The pull approach can be explained as follows: At the final assembly stage, a signal is sent to the preceding workstation as to the exact amount of parts and materials that will be needed *over the next few hours* to assemble products to fill customer orders, and only that amount of parts and materials is provided. The same signal is sent back through each preceding workstation so that a smooth flow of parts and materials is maintained with no appreciable inventory build-up at any point. Thus, all workstations respond to the pull exerted by the final assembly stage, which in turn responds to customer orders. As one worker explained, 'Under a JIT system you don't produce anything, anywhere, for anybody unless they ask for it somewhere downstream. Inventories are an evil that we're taught to avoid.' The pull approach is illustrated in Exhibit 18.5.

The pull approach described above can be contrasted to the *push approach* used in conventional manufacturing systems. In conventional systems, when a workstation completes its work, the partially completed goods are 'pushed' forward to the next workstation regardless of whether that workstation is ready to receive them. The result is an unintentional inventory piling of partially completed goods that may not be completed for days or even weeks. This ties up funds and also results in operating inefficiencies. For one thing, it becomes very difficult to keep track of where everything is when so much is scattered all over the factory floor.

Another characteristic of conventional manufacturing systems is an emphasis on 'keeping everyone busy' as an end in itself. This inevitably leads to excess inventory – particularly work in progress inventory – for reasons that will be more fully explored in a later section on the theory of constraints. In JIT, the traditional emphasis on keeping everyone busy is abandoned in favour of producing only what customers actually want – even if that means some workers are idle.

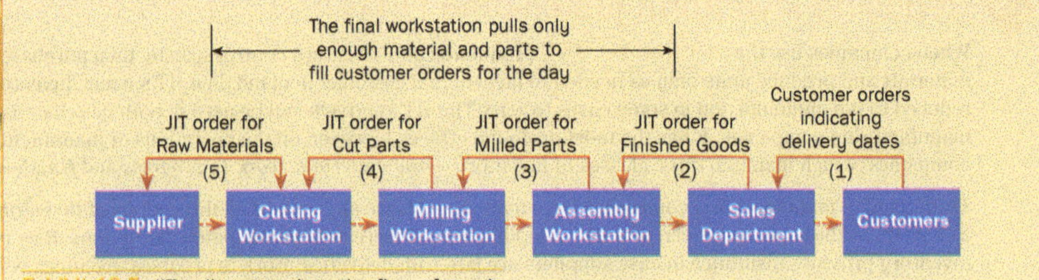

Exhibit 18.5 JIT pull approach to the flow of goods

JIT purchasing

Any organization with inventory – retail, wholesale, distribution, service, or manufacturing – can use *JIT purchasing*. Under JIT purchasing:

1 *A company relies on a few ultra reliable suppliers.* IBM, for example, eliminated 95% of the suppliers from one of its plants, reducing the number from 640 to only 32. Rather than soliciting bids from suppliers each year and going with the low bidder, the dependable suppliers are rewarded with long-term contracts.

2 *Suppliers make frequent deliveries in small lots just before the goods are needed.* Rather than deliver a week's (or a month's) supply of an item at one time, suppliers must be willing to make deliveries as often as several times a day, and in the exact quantities specified by the buyer. Undependable suppliers who do not meet delivery schedules are weeded out. Dependability is essential, since a JIT system is highly vulnerable to any interruption in supply. If a single part is unavailable, the entire assembly operation may have to be shut down. Or, in the case of a merchandising company, if the supplier allows inventory to get down to zero, customers may be turned away unsatisfied.

3 *Suppliers must deliver defect-free goods.* Because of the vulnerability of a JIT system to disruptions, defects cannot be tolerated. Indeed, suppliers must become so reliable that incoming goods do not have to be inspected.

Companies that adopt JIT purchasing often realize substantial savings from streamlined operations. Note that a company does not have to eliminate all inventory to use the JIT approach. Indeed, retail organizations must maintain some inventory or they could not operate. But the amount of time a product spends on a shelf or in a warehouse can be greatly reduced.

Key elements in a JIT system

In addition to JIT purchasing, four key elements are usually required for the successful operation of a JIT manufacturing system. These elements include improving the plant layout, reducing the set-up time needed for production runs, striving for zero defects, and developing a flexible workforce.

Improving plant layout

To implement JIT properly, a company typically must improve the manufacturing *flow lines* in its plant. A flow line is the physical path taken by a product as it moves through the manufacturing process as it is transformed from raw materials to completed goods.

Traditionally, companies have designed their plant floors so that similar machines are grouped together. Such a functional layout results in all drill presses in one place, all lathes in another place, and so forth. This approach to plant layout requires that work in progress be moved from one group of machines to another – frequently across the plant or even to another building. The result is extensive material-handling costs, large work in progress inventory, and unnecessary delays.

In a JIT system, all machines needed to make a particular product are often brought together in one location. This approach to plant layout creates an individual 'mini' factory for each separate product, frequently referred to as a *focused factory* or as a 'factory within a factory'. The flow line for a product can be straight, as shown earlier in Exhibit 18.4, or it can be in a U-shaped configuration. The key point is that all machines in a *product flow line* are tightly grouped together so that partially completed units are not shifted from place to place all over the factory. *Manufacturing cells* are also often part of a JIT product flow line. In a *cell*, a single worker operates several machines.

The *focused factory approach* allows workers to focus all their efforts on a product from start to finish and minimizes handling and moving. After one large manufacturing company rearranged its plant layout and organized its products into individual flow lines, the company determined that the distance travelled by one product had been decreased from 3 miles to just 100 metres. Apart from reductions in handling, this more compact layout makes it much easier to keep track of where a particular job is in the production process.

An improved plant layout can dramatically increase *throughput,* which is the total volume of production through a facility during a period, and it can dramatically reduce **throughput time** (also known as *cycle time*), which is the time required to make a product.

Reduced set-up time

Set-ups involve activities – such as moving materials, changing machine settings, setting up equipment, and running tests – that must be performed whenever production is switched over from making one type of item to another. For example, it may not be a simple matter to switch over from making 1.25 cm brass screws to making 2 cm brass screws on a manually controlled milling machine. Many preparatory steps must be performed, and these steps can take hours. Because of the time and expense involved in such set-ups, many managers believe set-ups should be avoided and therefore items should be produced in large batches. For example, one batch of 400 units requires only one set-up, whereas four batches of 100 units each would require four set-ups. The problem with big batches is that they create large amounts of inventory that must wait for days, weeks, or even months before further processing at the next workstation or before they are sold.

One advantage of a dedicated flow line is that it requires fewer set-ups. If equipment is dedicated to a single product, set-ups are largely eliminated and the product can be produced in any batch size desired. Even when dedicated flow lines are not used, it is often possible to slash set-up time by using techniques such as single-minute-exchange-of-dies. A *die* is a device used for cutting out, forming or stamping material. For example, a die is used to produce the stamped metal door panels on a car. A die must be changed when it wears out or when production is switched to a different product. This changeover can be time consuming. The goal with *single-minute-exchange-of-dies* is to reduce the amount of time required to change a die to a minute or less. This can be done by simple techniques such as doing as much of the changeover work in advance as possible rather than waiting until production is shut down.[5] When such techniques are followed, batch sizes can be very small.

Smaller batches reduce the level of inventory, make it easier to respond quickly to the market, reduce cycle times, and generally make it much easier to spot manufacturing problems before they result in a large number of defective units.

Zero defects and JIT

Defective units create big problems in a JIT environment. If a completed order contains a defective unit, the company must ship the order with less than the promised quantity or it must restart the whole production process to make just one unit. At minimum, this creates a delay in shipping the order and may generate a ripple effect that delays other orders. For this and other reasons, defects cannot be tolerated in a JIT system. Companies that are deeply involved in JIT tend to become zealously committed to a goal of *zero defects.* Even though it may be next to impossible to attain the zero defect goal, companies have found that they can come very close. For example, Motorola, Allied Signal, and many other companies now measure defects in terms of the number of defects per million units of product.

In a traditional company, parts and materials are inspected for defects when they are received from suppliers, and quality inspectors inspect units as they progress along the production line. In a JIT system, the company's suppliers are responsible for the quality of incoming parts and materials. And instead of using quality inspectors, the company's production workers are directly responsible for spotting defective units.

A worker who discovers a defect is supposed to punch an alarm button that stops the production flow line and sets off flashing lights. Supervisors and other workers then descend on the workstation to determine the cause of the defect and correct it before any further defective units are produced. This procedure ensures that problems are quickly identified and corrected, but it does require that defects are rare – otherwise there would be constant disruptions to the production process.

Flexible workforce

Workers on a JIT line must be multiskilled and flexible. Workers are often expected to operate all of the equipment on a JIT product flow line. Moreover, workers are expected to perform minor repairs and do maintenance work when they would otherwise be idle. In contrast, on a conventional assembly line a worker performs a single task all the time every day and all maintenance work is done by a specialized maintenance crew.

Benefits of a JIT system

The main benefits of JIT are the following:

1 Working capital is bolstered by the recovery of funds that were tied up in inventory
2 Areas previously used to store inventory are made available for other more productive uses
3 Throughput time is reduced, resulting in greater potential output and quicker response to customers
4 Defect rates are reduced, resulting in less waste and greater customer satisfaction.

As a result of benefits such as those cited above, more companies are embracing JIT each year. Most companies find, however, that simply reducing inventory is not enough. To remain competitive in an ever-changing and ever more competitive business environment, companies must strive for continuous improvement.

LO5 Inventory control and enterprise resource planning (ERP)

Systems of inventory control such as JIT have been helped by developments in information technology. The most sophisticated example involves the automation of management information systems through the **enterprise resource planning (ERP)** software offered by companies such as Microsoft, Oracle and SAP. Inventory control is only part of an integrated system, which tracks transactions across the company.

The main characteristics, costs and benefits of ERP are:[6]

- Systems are based on integrated client-server technology
- All data are entered only once where the data originate
- The implementation of such a total system is typically costly and time consuming
- But, updating the old heterogeneous system platform (e.g., for euro-currency) is costly as well
- Firms may also aim at business model improvements via the adoption of ERP (e.g., ABC and Balanced Scorecard[7])
- ERP represents a *process-oriented information system* based on *value chain thinking*
- The installation of an ERP may result in a lack of flexibility when a company operates in different countries.[8]

Given the theoretical benefits of a single *IT driven management information system*, it seems strange that for many years companies have been disappointed with the returns from their huge investments in new IT systems.[9] One problem with ERP models is that the benefits of the new systems are not so much in the 'hard returns' of reduced *headcounts* as in 'soft returns' such as revenue or employee gains that are harder to identify.[10] Many of the gains are so-called '*back-door*' gains such as agreeing common data with the same vocabulary and format. Not only are business processes standardized but the implementation process helps to inculcate a more learning, improving culture. Part of the problem with early computer applications was that companies were automating *existing* organizational and production systems. The really significant benefits come when the new technology is used to fundamentally reconfigure business practices.[11] Indeed, some businesses argue that the bulk of benefits come from the organizational changes rather than the new technology.[12]

LO6 E-commerce: new challenges for management accounting

A lot of hype has been generated by the internet. Yet many of the breakthroughs in inter-personal and inter-organizational communication rely on older technologies such as **electronic data interchange (EDI)** and telephones. The power of the telephone has been massively increased because the teleworker can be linked to the company's database via a personal computer. Thus the huge reduction in paper, floor space, queueing and so on, in an operation such as telephone banking or a ticketless airline, does not necessarily require internet technology. But for these operations, the internet is cheaper than both telephone and EDI as well as opening up the possibility of real-time screen communication for both consumers and smaller companies.

FOCUS ON PRACTICE

Performance measurement of internet sites

In the early days, few internet companies could measure their sites' performance or whether their sites were becoming more effective over time. Internet companies attracted visitors to their sites but were less successful at making sales or retaining customers. If anything, the more visitors the sites drew, the more money they lost. As in any business, long-term profitability is based on lifetime customer value: the revenue customers generate over their lives, less the cost of acquiring, converting and retaining them. New site performance indicators are being developed that measure attraction, conversion and retention plus other factors such as the rate at which the number of customers increases, and customer gross margins.[13] Paradoxically, it would be wrong to think that internet companies are the most likely candidates for inventory elimination. For example, part of the success of one of the more established dotcom companies, Amazon.com, is that its inventories of books and CDs are far larger than for local retailers.

More direct relations between customers and producers (disintermediation) means that huge chains of dedicated high street branches are assets of doubtful value. But as companies become more virtual there are new challenges for management accounting. In a virtual company 'assets are not only tangible but also include intangible assets such as brand value, intellectual property, human capital (people), virtual integration, information management, quality of service and customer relations, they need to be factored into performance measurement exercises. Otherwise a company may end up with a distorted picture of its overall economic value, market position and future potential.'[14] Distorted pictures were certainly a feature of the dotcom boom when many internet start-ups attracted both media and investor attention. With inflated inventory market values bearing no relation to traditional indicators of value, there was vague talk of a 'new economic model'.

The hype of the dotcom boom has now passed. Many of the dotcom start-ups have either disappeared or are struggling to make profits. In retrospect, some of these companies may have benefited from more traditional business plans that showed how an internet site could generate profits. The approach to evaluating site performance is becoming more rigorous as the nature of internet commerce is better understood.[15]

Quality and business processes: measurement and management

Earlier we saw how a JIT system is based on defect-free production and inputs. Yet there are more general motives for measuring and managing quality even, or especially, in service companies that do not have inventory. Companies that develop a reputation for low-quality products generally lose market share and face declining profits. It doesn't do much good to have a product with a high-quality design that is made with high-quality materials if the product falls apart on the first use. One very important aspect of quality is the absence of defects. Defective products result in high warranty costs, but more importantly, they result in dissatisfied customers. People who are dissatisfied with a product are unlikely to buy the product again. They are also likely to tell others about their bad experiences. One study found that '[c]ustomers who have bad experiences tell approximately 11 people about it'.[16] This is the worst possible sort of advertising. To prevent such problems, companies have been expending a great deal of effort to reduce defects. The objective is to have high *quality of conformance.*

LO7 The cost of quality model

A product that meets or exceeds its design specifications and is free of defects that mar its appearance or degrade its performance is said to have high quality of conformance. Note that if an economy car is free of defects, it can have a **quality of conformance** that is just as high as a defect-free luxury car. The purchasers of economy cars cannot expect their cars to be as opulently equipped as luxury cars, but they can and do expect them to be free of defects.

Preventing, detecting and dealing with defects cause costs that are called *quality costs* or the *cost of quality*. The use of the term *quality cost* is confusing to some people. It does not refer to costs such as using a higher-grade leather to make a wallet or using 14K gold instead of gold-plating in jewellery. Instead, the term **quality costs** refers to all of the costs that are incurred to prevent defects or that are incurred as a result of defects occurring.

Quality costs can be broken down into four broad groups. Two of these groups – known as *prevention costs* and *appraisal costs* – are incurred in an effort to keep defective products from falling into the hands of customers. The other two groups of costs – known as *internal failure costs* and *external failure costs* – are incurred because defects are produced despite efforts to prevent them. Examples of specific costs involved in each of these four groups are given in Exhibit 18.6.

Several things should be noted about the quality costs shown in the exhibit. First, note that quality costs do not relate to just manufacturing; rather, they relate to all the activities in a company from initial research and

Exhibit

Prevention costs	**Internal failure costs**
Systems development	Net cost of scrap
Quality engineering	Net cost of spoilage
Quality training	Rework labour and overhead
Quality circles	Reinspection of reworked products
Statistical process control activities	Retesting of reworked products
Supervision of prevention activities	Downtime caused by quality problems
Quality data gathering, analysis, and reporting	Disposal of defective products
Quality improvement projects	Analysis of the cause of defects in production
Technical support provided to suppliers	Re-entering data because of keying errors
Audits of the effectiveness of the quality system	Debugging software errors
Appraisal costs	**External failure costs**
Test and inspection of incoming materials	Cost of field servicing and handling complaints
Test and inspection of in-process goods	Warranty repairs and replacements
Final product testing and inspection	Repairs and replacements beyond the warranty period
Supplies used in testing and inspection	Product recalls
Supervision of testing and inspection activities	Liability arising from defective products
Depreciation of test equipment	Returns and allowances arising from quality problems
Maintenance of test equipment	Lost sales arising from a reputation for poor quality
Plant utilities in the inspection area	
Field testing and appraisal at customer site	

Exhibit 18.6 Typical quality costs

development (R&D) through customer service. Second, note that the number of costs associated with quality is very large; therefore, total quality cost can be quite high unless management gives this area special attention. Finally, note how different the costs are in the four groupings. We will now look at each of these groupings more closely.

Prevention costs

The most effective way to minimize quality costs while maintaining high-quality output is to avoid having quality problems arise in the first place. This is the purpose of **prevention costs**; such costs relate to any activity that reduces the number of defects in products or services. Companies have learned that it is much less costly to prevent a problem from ever happening than it is to find and correct the problem after it has occurred.

Note from Exhibit 18.6 that prevention costs include activities relating to quality circles and statistical process control. **Quality circles** consist of small groups of employees that meet on a regular basis to discuss ways to improve the quality of output. Both management and workers are included in these circles. Quality circles are widely used and can be found in manufacturing companies, utilities, health care organizations, banks and many other organizations.

Statistical process control is a technique that is used to detect whether a process is in or out of control. An out-of-control process results in defective units and may be caused by a miscalibrated machine or some other factor. In statistical process control, workers use charts to monitor the quality of units that pass through their workstations. Using these charts, workers can quickly spot processes that are out of control and that are creating defects. Problems can be immediately corrected and further defects prevented rather than waiting for an inspector to catch the defects later.

Note also from the list of prevention costs in Exhibit 18.6 that some companies provide technical support to their suppliers as a way of preventing defects. Particularly in just-in-time (JIT) systems, such support to suppliers is vital. In a JIT system, parts are delivered from suppliers just in time and in just the correct quantity to fill customer orders. There are no stockpiles of parts. If a defective part is received from a supplier, the part cannot be used and the order for the ultimate customer cannot be filled on time. Hence, every part received from a supplier must be free of defects. Consequently, companies that use JIT often require that their suppliers use sophisticated quality control programmes such as statistical process control and that their suppliers certify that they will deliver parts and materials that are free of defects.

Appraisal costs

Any defective parts and products should be caught as early as possible. **Appraisal costs**, which are sometimes called *inspection costs,* are incurred to identify defective products *before* the products are shipped to customers. Unfortunately, performing appraisal activities does not keep defects from happening again, and most managers now realize that maintaining an army of inspectors is a costly (and ineffective) approach to quality control.

Professor John K. Shank of Dartmouth College has aptly stated, 'The old-style approach was to say, "We've got great quality. We have 40 quality control inspectors in the factory." Then somebody realized that if you need 40 inspectors, it must be a lousy factory. So now the trick is to run a factory without any quality control inspectors; each employee is his or her own quality control person.'[17]

Employees in both manufacturing and service functions are increasingly being asked to be responsible for their own quality control. This approach, along with designing products to be easy to manufacture properly, allows quality to be built into products rather than relying on inspection to get the defects out.

Internal failure costs

Failure costs are incurred when a product fails to conform to its design specifications. Failure costs can be either internal or external. **Internal failure costs** result from identification of defects during the appraisal process. Such costs include scrap, rejected products, reworking of defective units, and downtime caused by quality problems. It is crucial that defects be discovered before a product is shipped to customers. Of course, the more effective a company's appraisal activities, the greater the chance of catching defects internally and the greater the level of internal failure costs (as compared to external failure costs). Unfortunately, appraisal activities focus on symptoms rather than on causes and they do nothing to reduce the number of defective items. However, appraisal activities do bring defects to the attention of management, which may lead to efforts to increase prevention activities so that the defects do not happen.

External failure costs

External failure costs result when a defective product is delivered to a customer. As shown in Exhibit 18.6, external failure costs include warranty repairs and replacements, product recalls, liability arising from legal action against a company, and lost sales arising from a reputation for poor quality. Such costs can devastate profits.

In the past, some managers have taken the attitude, 'Let's go ahead and ship everything to customers, and we'll take care of any problems under the warranty.' This attitude generally results in high external failure costs, customer ill will, and declining market share and profits.

Distribution of quality costs

We stated earlier that a company's total quality cost is likely to be very high unless management gives this area special attention. How does a company reduce its total quality cost? The answer lies in how the quality costs are distributed. Refer to the graph in Exhibit 18.7, which shows total quality costs as a function of the quality of conformance.

The graph shows that when the quality of conformance is low, total quality cost is high and that most of this cost consists of costs of internal and external failure. A low quality of conformance means that a high percentage of units are defective and hence the company must incur high failure costs. However, as a company spends more and more on prevention and appraisal, the percentage of defective units drops (the percentage of defect-free units increases). This results in lower costs of internal and external failure. Ordinarily, total quality cost drops rapidly as the quality of conformance increases. Thus, a company can reduce its total quality cost by focusing its efforts on prevention and appraisal. The cost savings from reduced defects usually swamp the costs of the additional prevention and appraisal efforts.

The graph in Exhibit 18.7 has been drawn so that the total quality cost is minimized when the quality of conformance is less than 100%. However, some experts and managers contend that the total quality cost is not minimized until the quality of conformance is 100% and there are no defects. Indeed, many companies have found that the total quality costs seem to keep dropping even when the quality of conformance approaches 100% and defect rates get as low as one in a million units. Others argue that eventually total quality cost increases as the quality of conformance increases. However, in most companies this does not seem to happen until the quality of conformance is very close to 100% and defect rates are very close to zero.

Exhibit

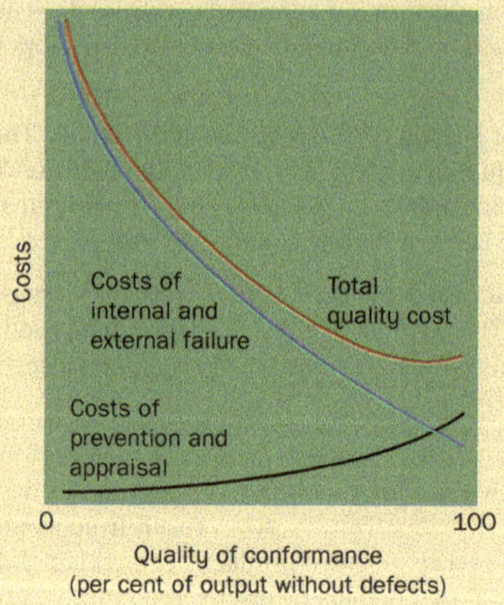

Exhibit 18.7 Effect of quality costs on quality of conformance

As a company's quality programme becomes more refined and as its failure costs begin to fall, prevention activities usually become more effective than appraisal activities. Appraisal can only find defects, whereas prevention can eliminate them. The best way to prevent defects from happening is to design processes that reduce the likelihood of defects and to continually monitor processes using statistical process control methods.

Quality cost reports

As an initial step in quality improvement programmes, companies often construct a *quality cost report* that provides an estimate of the financial consequences of the company's current level of defects. A **quality cost report** details the prevention costs, appraisal costs and costs of internal and external failures that arise from the company's current level of defective products and services. Managers are often shocked by the magnitude of these costs. A typical quality cost report is shown in Exhibit 18.8.

Exhibit

Ventura Company Quality cost report for years 1 and 2

	Year 2		Year 1	
	Amount	**Per cent***	**Amount**	**Per cent***
Prevention costs:				
Systems development	£400,000	0.80%	£270,000	0.54%
Quality training	210,000	0.42%	130,000	0.26%
Supervision of prevention activities	70,000	0.14%	40,000	0.08%
Quality improvement projects	320,000	0.64%	210,000	0.42%
Total	1,000,000	2.00%	650,000	1.30%
Appraisal costs:				
Inspection	600,000	1.20%	560,000	1.12%
Reliability testing	580,000	1.16%	420,000	0.84%
Supervision of testing and inspection	120,000	0.24%	80,000	0.16%
Depreciation of test equipment	200,000	0.40%	140,000	0.28%
Total	1,500,000	3.00%	1,200,000	2.40%
Internal failure costs:				
Net cost of scrap	900,000	1.80%	750,000	1.50%
Rework labour and overhead	1,430,000	2.86%	810,000	1.62%
Downtime due to defects in quality	170,000	0.34%	100,000	0.20%
Disposal of defective products	500,000	1.00%	340,000	0.68%
Total	3,000,000	6.00%	2,000,000	4.00%
External failure costs:				
Warranty repairs	400,000	0.80%	900,000	1.80%
Warranty replacements	870,000	1.74%	2,300,000	4.60%
Allowances	130,000	0.26%	630,000	1.26%
Cost of field servicing	600,000	1.20%	1,320,000	2.64%
Total	2,000,000	4.00%	5,150,000	10.30%
Total quality cost	£7,500,000	15.00%	£9,000,000	18.00%

*As a percentage of total sales. We assume that in each year sales totalled £50,000,000.

Exhibit 18.8 Quality cost report

Several things should be noted from the data in the exhibit. First, note that Ventura Company's quality costs are poorly distributed in both years, with most of the costs being traceable to either internal failure or external failure. The external failure costs are particularly high in Year 1 in comparison to other costs.

Second, note that the company increased its spending on prevention and appraisal activities in Year 2. As a result, internal failure costs go up in that year (from £2 million in Year 1 to £3 million in Year 2), but external failure costs drop sharply (from £5.15 million in Year 1 to only £2 million in Year 2). Because of the increase in appraisal activity in Year 2, more defects are being caught inside the company before they are shipped to customers. This results in more cost for scrap, rework and so forth, but saves huge amounts in warranty repairs, warranty replacements and other external failure costs.

Third, note that as a result of greater emphasis on prevention and appraisal, *total* quality cost has decreased in Year 2. As continued emphasis is placed on prevention and appraisal in future years, total quality cost should continue to decrease. That is, future increases in prevention and appraisal costs should be more than offset by decreases in failure costs. Moreover, appraisal costs should also decrease as more effort is placed into prevention.

Quality cost reports in graphic form

As a supplement to the quality cost report shown in Exhibit 18.8, companies frequently prepare quality cost information in graphic form. Graphic presentations include pie charts, bar graphs, trend lines and so forth. The data for Ventura Company from Exhibit 18.8 are presented in bar graph form in Exhibit 18.9.

The first bar graph in Exhibit 18.9 is scaled in terms of pounds of quality cost, and the second is scaled in terms of quality cost as a percentage of sales. In both graphs, the data are 'stacked' upward. That is, appraisal costs are stacked on top of prevention costs, internal failure costs are stacked on top of the sum of prevention costs plus appraisal costs, and so forth. The percentage figures in the second graph show that total quality cost equals 18% of sales in Year 1 and 15% of sales in Year 2, the same as reported earlier in Exhibit 18.8.

Uses of quality cost information

The information provided by a quality cost report is used by managers in several ways. First, quality cost information helps managers to see the financial significance of defects. Managers usually are not aware of the magnitude of their quality costs because these costs cut across departmental lines and are not normally

Exhibit

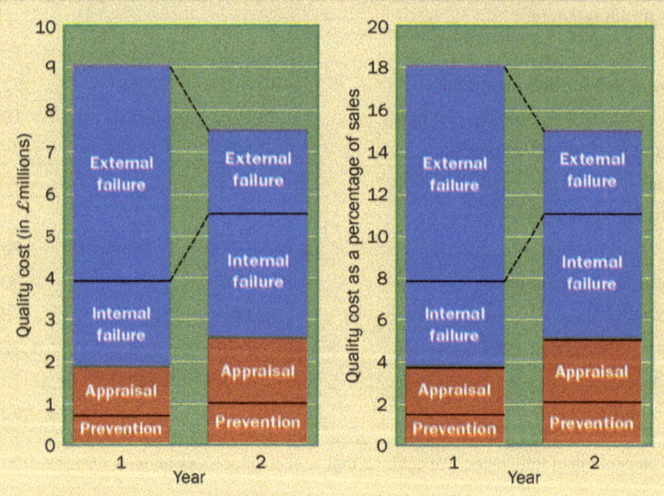

Exhibit 18.9 Quality cost reports in graphic form

tracked and accumulated by the cost system. Thus, when first presented with a quality cost report, managers are often surprised by the amount of cost attributable to poor quality.

Second, quality cost information helps managers to identify the relative importance of the quality problems faced by the firm. For example, the quality cost report may show that scrap is a major quality problem or that the company is incurring huge warranty costs. With this information, managers have a better idea of where to focus efforts.

Third, quality cost information helps managers to see whether their quality costs are poorly distributed. In general, quality costs should be distributed more toward prevention and appraisal activities and less towards failures.

Counterbalancing these uses, three limitations of quality cost information should be recognized. First, simply measuring and reporting quality costs does not solve quality problems. Problems can be solved only by taking action. Second, results usually lag behind quality improvement programmes. Initially, total quality cost may even increase as quality control systems are designed and installed. Decreases in these costs may not begin to occur until the quality programme has been in effect for a year or more. And third, the most important quality cost, lost sales arising from customer ill will, is usually omitted from the quality cost report because it is difficult to estimate.

From modelling the costs of quality to quality management

One way of summarizing and balancing the costs and benefits of quality is to show the trade-offs in a diagram such as that in Exhibit 18.7. The interplay of the various cost functions enables us to identify an optimal level of quality where total costs are minimized. As we saw with the EOQ model and JIT, a cost of quality model can be part of a wider more active management approach that sees quality not as a cost optimizing exercise but as a philosophy that drives the whole organization. Some are more critical of the cost of quality model. For example, Anderson and Sedatole argue that 'accountants' support of quality management is hobbled by a tradition of historical reporting and a focus on one aspect of quality – conformance to design specifications. Conformance quality is a static representation of performance to historical quality standards. A more potent weapon in quality management is the use of performance data to improve new product designs.'[18]

With total quality management the whole organization is called upon to embrace new processes and techniques that strive to make continuous improvements. With continuous improvement, the optimal level of quality as learning-by-doing and further investment push the curves to right over time. Indeed, the dominant ethos of quality management is one of continual improvement rather than static optimization. Typically, during the initial years of a quality improvement programme, the benefits of compiling a quality cost report outweigh the costs and limitations of the reports. As managers gain experience in balancing prevention and appraisal activities, the need for quality cost reports often diminishes.

LO8 Total quality management (TQM)

The most popular approach to continuous improvement is known as **total quality management (TQM)**. There are two major characteristics of TQM: (1) a focus on serving customers and (2) systematic problem solving using teams made up of frontline workers. A variety of specific tools are available to aid teams in their problem solving. One of these tools, **benchmarking**, involves studying organizations that are among the best in the world at performing a particular task. For example, when Xerox wanted to improve its procedures for filling customer orders, it studied how the mail-order company L.L. Bean processes its customer orders.

The plan-do-check-act cycle

Perhaps the most important and pervasive TQM problem-solving tool is the *plan-do-check-act (PDCA)* cycle, which is also referred to as the Deming Wheel.[19] The **plan-do-check-act cycle (PDCA)** is a systematic, fact-based approach to continuous improvement. The basic elements of the PDCA cycle are illustrated in Exhibit 18.10. The PDCA cycle applies the scientific method to problem solving. In the Plan phase, the problem-solving team analyses data to identify possible causes for the problem and then proposes a solution. In the Do phase, an experiment is conducted. In the Check phase, the results of the experiment are analysed. And in the Act phase, if the results of the experiment are favourable, the plan is implemented. If the results of the experiment are not favourable, the team goes back to the original data and starts all over again.

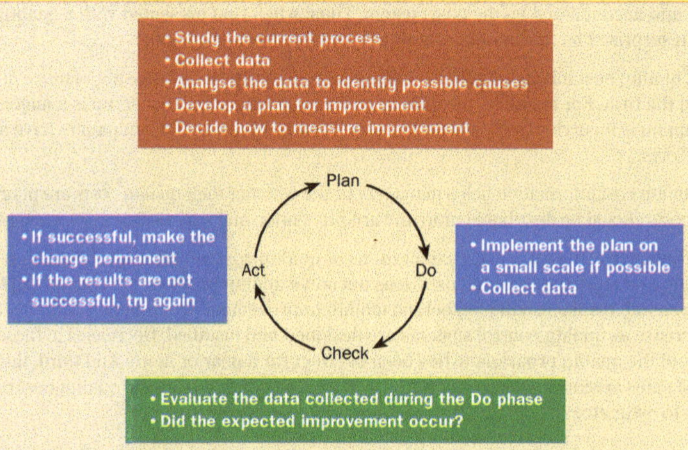

Exhibit 18.10 The plan-do-check-act cycle

An important element of TQM is its focus on the customer. The accounting and consulting firm KPMG periodically surveys its customers' satisfaction with its services. The firm's managing director points out that it costs four times as much to gain a new customer as it does to keep an old customer, and the most satisfied customers are generally the most profitable customers for the firm. 'For each complaint that you hear, there are fifty you don't. If you don't monitor clients' satisfaction, you may find out about their dissatisfaction as they walk out the door.'[20]

In sum, TQM provides tools and techniques for continuous improvement based on facts and analysis; and if properly implemented, it avoids counterproductive organizational infighting.

Some criticisms of TQM

There have been a number of criticisms of TQM. They may not always be justified but managers should be aware of possible pitfalls. TQM has been accused of draining innovation from organizations by standardizing internal processes. It is also accused of making organizations more efficient at what they are doing irrespective of whether they should be doing it. Like other management change initiatives, TQM suffers from the 'Flavour of the month' syndrome. Typically, organizational members have been bombarded with so many fads that they may merely go through the motions of implementation of TQM hoping that senior managers will soon embrace a new 'three letter acronym'.

LO9 Benchmarking

Much of the data gathered through the introduction of quality management may be used as a basis for comparison with other organizations. In particular, it may be useful to identify organizations that are the best at performing specific activities or producing particular products in order to learn how they achieve their relatively high performance. This process is known as *benchmarking*. With *quality management*, the focus may be on *non-financial* measures as much as financial measures such as costs.

In order to achieve the best result from benchmarking a number of principles should be adhered to. Benchmarking may be seen as an exercise that proceeds according to a sequence of steps.

- *Step 1: Internal and competitive analysis.* At this preliminary stage the organization chooses the areas for analysis and undertakes basic comparisons between internal data and external data. External data may be found in marketing reports, consumer surveys and government statistics. It may not be confined to the firm's industry. For example, the particular part of the organization chosen for benchmarking may involve an activity where the best performers are in a completely different industry. For example, a theatre may study the ticketing procedures used in the airline industry. Although there may be a danger of not comparing like with like such as when a tyre retailer sees a formula one team as an appropriate benchmark for tyre-changing, there may still be lessons that can be learned even from such apparently 'unfair' comparisons.

- *Step 2: Building a benchmarking team.* Changes in practice may involve both radical reorganization and long-term commitment. Thus benchmarking teams must ideally have the backing of senior management, the support of the workforce and a long-term orientation. Typically, teams will be from a number of functional areas representing different professional specialisms and change must be supported by dedicated training programmes.
- *Step 3: Choosing benchmarking partners and sharing information.* This step strikes a balance between the need to *'stretch' performance* and not comparing like with like. Furthermore, if partners are really going to learn from each other then detailed information about operational performance has to be shared, implying an atmosphere of co-operation and trust rather than competition. If trust is absent then information may be shared on the basis of quid pro quo or as part of an industry-wide initiative. Alternatively, information may be gathered on a unilateral basis through activities such as reverse engineering. As we saw in Chapter 16, the collection of data on competitors is an important part of strategic management accounting and may be based wholly on competitive rather than co-operative principles. A possible way to overcome competiveness is to gather information of competitor's operational performance by using database benchmarking, that typically is provided by the big consultancy companies. In Chapter 8 we saw an example of how Marketing Resources Group of US WEST benchmarked its accounting department with departments from Fortune top 100 companies and World Class companies using databases from a consultancy company. In addition the internet sometimes provides information that potentially could be relevant for benchmarking studies.
- *Step 4: Taking action to meet benchmark.* It is at this stage that the internal implementation of the external analysis may run into difficulties, especially if best practice threatens job security and/or managerial empires. The issues of organizational change take us beyond the material normally found in management accounting books. However, management accountants and others such as politicians and senior managers should be aware of the technical limitations of benchmarking exercises. Organizational resistance is not always based on vested interests.

Some problems with benchmarking

Using external comparators can lead to criticism on the basis that measures are 'their numbers not ours'. It is therefore important that a consistent set of measures is used with a close match between internal and external indicators. Xerox have overcome this by implementing a structured process based on indicators developed in close collaboration with other people working in industry sectors which have similar operational features. Benchmarking has been described as being a mixed metaphor.[21] On the one hand, we have the language of collaboration with an emphasis on organizational learning. On the other hand, we have descriptions of benchmarking that often convey notions of competition, of being a one-sided attempt by the initiator of the benchmarking exercise to close a perceived performance gap. Even when benchmarking is a public policy initiative, governments often send out a mixed message that both inculcates a 'league table mentality' and tries to nurture a non-blame, learning model.

LO10 Business process re-engineering (BPR)

Process re-engineering is a more radical approach to improvement than either TQM or benchmarking. Instead of tweaking the existing system in a series of incremental improvements, a business process is diagrammed in detail, questioned, and then completely redesigned in order to eliminate unnecessary steps, to reduce opportunities for errors, and to reduce costs. A **business process** is any series of steps that is followed in order to carry out some task in a business. For example, the steps followed to make a large seafood pizza at Pizza Hut are a business process. The steps followed by your bank when you deposit a cheque are a business process. While process re-engineering is similar in some respects to TQM, its proponents view it as a more sweeping approach to change. One difference is that while TQM emphasizes a team approach involving people who work directly in the processes, process re-engineering is more likely to be imposed from above and more likely to use outside consultants.

Process re-engineering focuses on *simplification* and *elimination of wasted effort*. A central idea of process re-engineering is that *all activities that do not add value to a product or service should be eliminated.*[22] Activities that do not add value to a product or service that customers are willing to pay for are known as **non-value-added activities**. For example, moving large batches of work in progress from one workstation to another is a non-value-added activity that can be eliminated by redesigning the factory layout.

The starting point for re-engineering is not 'How do we do something faster or cheaper or better?' but rather 'Why do we do something at all? Is it to meet demands of customers or internal organization?' In short, re-engineering is not piecemeal – it is 'all-or-nothing'.

What does a re-engineered process look like?

The first step in re-engineering is to look at the underlying process and not at the administrative structure set up to perform it. The aim will be to combine several jobs into one – known as *horizontal compression*. If a process is too much for one person then a case-team will be formed. The aim should be that the workers make decisions. Jobs are vertically compressed through the elimination of hierarchy and checking.

Much re-engineering is enabled through new technology, especially the linkage between a telephone-based customer focused personnel with central databases. Shared databases mean that information can appear simultaneously in as many places as it is needed. *Expert systems* mean that the generalist can do the work of the expert. Telecommunications and portable computers mean that field personnel can send and receive information wherever they are. Paradoxically, organizations are both centralized and decentralized by the new technology. Jobs change from simple tasks to multidimensional work which reduces the work that was created by fragmentation such as checking, reconciling, waiting, monitoring and tracking.

The implications of BPR for management accounting are that management accountants have to be more flexible and work in teams with non-accountants. Accounting work is dispersed and may be done by non-accountants. Non-financial performance measures are more important. The emphasis is on eliminating overhead rather than measuring/allocating it. Organizational structures/departments/budgets are less important than *processes*.

Some criticisms of re-engineering

In common with other management panaceas, BPR has suffered from over-hyping and from the evangelical language often associated with the management guru. Action that may be easy to write or talk about may be harder to implement in practice. For example, how easy is it for organizations to distinguish between value adding and non-value adding activity? Mistakes have been made where firms took out 'non-value adding' personnel but then subsequently had to re-hire them as they turned out to have created unanticipated value! BPR is likely to face resistance from managers who have been promoted to manage existing structures not take them out!

A recurrent problem in process re-engineering is employee resistance. The cause of much of this resistance is the fear that people may lose their jobs. Workers reason that if process re-engineering succeeds in eliminating non-value-added activities, there will be less work to do and management may be tempted to reduce the payroll. Process re-engineering, if carried out insensitively and without regard to such fears, can undermine morale and will ultimately fail to improve the bottom line (i.e., profits). As with other improvement projects, employees must be convinced that the end result of the improvement will be more secure, rather than less secure, jobs. Real improvement can have this effect if management uses the improvement to generate more business rather than to cut the workforce. If by improving processes the company is able to produce a better product at lower cost, the company will have the competitive strength to prosper. And a prosperous company is a much more secure employer than a company that is in trouble.

LO11 Six Sigma

Another approach to business improvement is known as *Six Sigma*. It is a strategic, companywide, approach that focuses on quality and reliability. The key aims are to:

- Improve quality as perceived by the customer
- Reduce errors (defects) in the process

- Ensure processes are capable of producing repeatable outputs
- Reduce the variation in these outputs
- Identify the root causes of quality issues and errors
- Prioritize solution options to make the biggest gain
- Monitor and control processes within defined quality criteria.

The term 'Six Sigma' comes from statistics as the approach focuses on *variation reduction* through statistical analysis. The statistical basis of the approach may be illustrated in Exhibit 18.11, in which it is argued that business improvement can come from focusing on *variation from the mean* rather than average times.

The problem: a focus on 'average' isn't sufficient

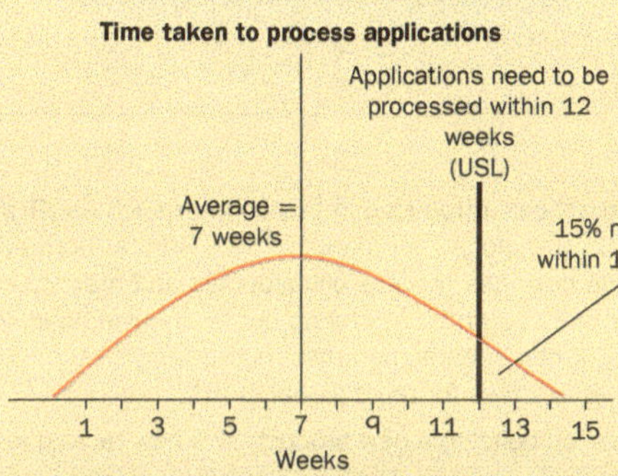

- Processing time **varies significantly** – some can take 1 or 2 weeks, some can take up to 15 weeks
- **Lack of predictability** for business and customer
- How would you ensure customer requirements are satisfied more often?

Six sigma solution: variation provides a more complete understanding of performance – process capability

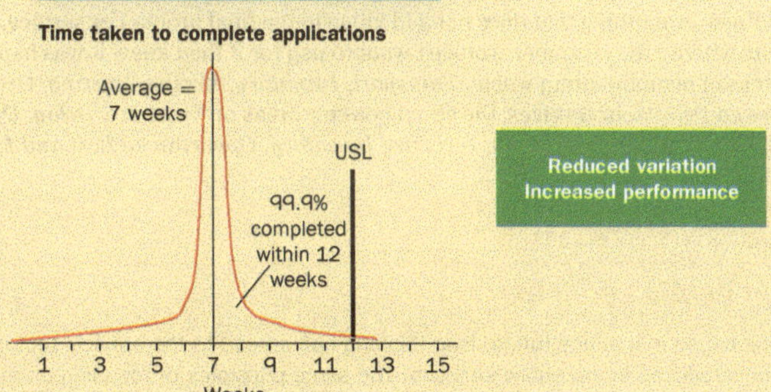

- Processing time has **little variation** (between 6 and 8 weeks)
- Much **higher probability** of meeting **customer specification** – nearly all applications are completed within 12 weeks
- The business could spread its resource, by targeting a longer processing time such as 11 weeks and the majority of applications would still be processed on time.

Exhibit 18.11 Six Sigma approach to problem solving

Lean production

Many of the business process improvement tools can be summarized by a very long-standing and robust philosophy known as lean production.[23] Lean enterprises try to organize work around *business processes* rather than on a departmental basis with a traditional emphasis on specialization and a division of labour.

There are five core principles to represent lean production:

1 Specify the *value desired by the customer*
2 Identify the value stream for each product providing that value and challenge all of the *wasted* steps
3 Make the product *flow continuously*
4 Introduce *pull* between all steps where continuous flow is impossible
5 *Manage toward perfection* so that the number of steps and the amount of time and information needed to serve the customer continually falls.

FOCUS ON PRACTICE

Toyota

Many of the business improvement practices introduced in this chapter such as JIT and lean production are associated with the Japanese (and now global) car manufacturer, Toyota. Some well-publicized recalls of recent models do not mean that the business process philosophies and practices are faulty. According to some, Toyota 'remains the benchmark . . .' and '. . . stands out for innovating in ways that are likely to shape our future' (Fischer, 2010: 12). It has been argued that Toyota 'forgot' some of its principles of quality and knowledge management as it strove for rapid global growth.

In particular, it forgot its 'three nevers' by building a new product, in a new factory with a new workforce.

Exercise: Review the important roles played by learning-by-doing/tacit knowledge and attitude of mind for the successful implementation of business process improvement policies.

Source: Fischer, B. 2010. That was Kaizen; this is now, *Financial Management,* April, p. 12.

An emphasis on eliminating 'waste'

As can be seen, many of the principles of lean may also be found in other approaches to process improvement such as JIT. However, lean production places a great deal of emphasis on the elimination of *waste* where waste is defined as anything that does not add value to the final product or service, in the eyes of the customer; an activity the customer wouldn't want to pay for if they knew it was happening. There are seven possible areas of manufacturing waste: *Transport, Inventory, Motion, Waiting, Overproduction, Over-processing and Defects.* In services, the seven possible areas of waste are: *Delay, Duplication, Unnecessary Movement, Unclear Communication, Incorrect Inventory, Opportunity Lost and Errors.*

FOCUS ON PRACTICE

Lean in public services

Although it began in manufacturing, lean thinking has spread to the service sector. In recent years it has also been introduced in the public services. The same principles of focusing on meeting customer needs, streamlining flows along process lines and reducing waste are very relevant. Lean offers potential not only for cost savings but for improving the service offered to citizens and even improving staff morale. All these issues are becoming increasingly important as governments seek to reduce public spending in the post-credit crunch era.

Exercise: Consider an organization that you are familiar with. How does that organization generate value for its customers? Are there some areas of the organization that do not seem to be part of that value adding process?

Source: In the hot seat: Reducing costs in public sector organizations in an age of austerity, Deloitte Research paper, http://www.deloitte.com/view/en_GB/uk/industries/government-public-sector/, 12 April 2010

Lean accounting

In order to support a lean approach to creating value, accounting measures have to be used selectively and supplemented with non-financial performance measures. The key emphasis should be on measuring flow through the whole process rather than on the more traditional approach of local machine or labour utilization. Such measures include production by the hour, cycle times, and so on. The emphasis is on measuring and minimizing inventory, work in progress and other forms of working capital such as accounts receivables. Managers need to understand the capacity of the process and constantly seek ways that will increase throughput. Financial information should be timely and relevant. In practice that means providing management information in real time or at least so that operations can be supported as they take place rather than 'after the event'. Revenues will be based on actual deliveries to customers rather than production for inventory. In short, lean thinking synthesizes the key insights of JIT, TQM and TOC. Finally, the philosophy of the accounting system should be on continuous improvement with information that is both forward- and outward-looking data.

Obstacles to organizational change and the advantages of a fresh start

As we discussed in connection with TQM and benchmarking, whatever the technical strengths of the techniques or whatever the potential improvements identified, there may be significant implementation problems. For this reason, it may be easier to start up an entirely new organization rather than re-engineer an existing one. As the example of low-cost airlines such as easyJet and Ryanair illustrate, radical changes have been achieved by new entrants to the airline industry. Although they are low cost, these carriers generally meet the quality standards that their customers expect from a no-frills service.

SUMMARY

- This chapter focuses on business processes which may cut across an organization's departments and/or divisions.
- Inventory management is an area that has evolved from the optimizing approach of the EOQ model to the sophistication of the build-to-order company. JIT emphasizes the importance of reducing inventories to the barest minimum possible. This reduces working capital requirements, frees up space, reduces throughput time, reduces defects and eliminates waste.
- New information technology such as ERP and the internet offer new ways to optimize not just on inventory but on other areas of working capital management.
- Quality costs are summarized on a quality cost report. This report shows the type of quality costs being incurred and their significance and trends. The report helps managers to understand the importance of quality costs, spot problem areas, and assess the way in which the quality costs are distributed.
- The measurement of quality costs may be used as part of a more comprehensive approach – TQM – which involves the use of a number of non-financial as well as financial measures. TQM involves focusing on the customer, and it employs systematic problem solving using teams made up of frontline workers. Specific TQM tools include benchmarking and the plan-do-check-act (PDCA) cycle.
- BPR, a related but generally more radical approach to organizational change, aims to push the analysis and optimization of business processes to higher levels. Process re-engineering involves completely redesigning a business process in order to eliminate non-value-added activities and to reduce opportunities for errors.
- Measures may be used to monitor internal processes, supplier and customer perceptions. Organizations may use these measures as a way of comparing or benchmarking themselves against best practice.
- The techniques of work measurement of BPR and ABM can be seen as job- and cost-cutting exercises. Furthermore, there may be technical difficulties in distinguishing between value- and non-value-adding activities.
- Many of the practices in this chapter are associated with the philosophy of lean production.

KEY TERMS FOR REVIEW

Appraisal costs (p. 785)
Benchmarking (p. 789)
Business process (p. 791)
Costs of not carrying sufficient inventory (p. 773)
Economic lot size (p. 776)
Economic order quantity (EOQ) (p. 773)
Electronic data interchange (EDI) (p. 783)
Enterprise resource planning (ERP) (p. 782)
External failure costs (p. 786)
Internal failure costs (p. 785)
Inventory carrying costs (p. 773)
Inventory ordering costs (p. 773)
Just-in-time (JIT) (p. 779)
Lead time (p. 777)
Lean production (p. 773)
Non-value-added activities (p. 792)
Optimizing (p. 772)
Plan-do-check-act (PDCA) cycle (p. 789)
Prevention costs (p. 785)
Process re-engineering (p. 791)
Quality circles (p. 785)
Quality cost report (p. 787)
Quality costs (p. 784)
Quality of conformance (p. 784)
Reorder point (p. 777)
Safety inventory (p. 778)
Set-up costs (p. 776)
Statistical process control (p. 785)
Throughput time (p. 781)
Total quality management (TQM) (p. 789)

Level of difficulty: BASIC INTERMEDIATE ADVANCED

Questions

connect

18-1 What are the three groups of costs associated with the economic order quantity (EOQ) model?

18-2 What is the potential impact of just-in-time (JIT) purchasing on the EOQ?

18-3 What trade-offs in costs are involved in computing the EOQ (economic order quantity)?

18-4 Define lead time and safety inventory.

18-5 In a just-in-time system, what is meant by the pull approach to the flow of goods, as compared to the push approach used in conventional systems?

18-6 How does the plant layout differ in a company using JIT as compared to a company that uses a more conventional approach to manufacturing? What benefits accrue from a JIT layout?

18-7 Identify the benefits that can result from reducing the set-up time for a product.

18-8 How does a workforce in a JIT facility differ from the workforce in a conventional facility?

18-9 What are the major benefits of a JIT system?

18-10 What are three benefits and three costs of installing an ERP system?

18-11 Is there a difference between a virtual company and a dotcom company?

18-12 Costs associated with the quality of conformance can be broken down into four broad groups. What are these four groups and how do they differ?

18-13 In their efforts to reduce the total cost of quality, should companies generally focus on decreasing prevention costs and appraisal costs?

18-14 What is probably the most effective way to reduce a company's total quality costs?

18-15 What are the main uses of quality cost reports?

18-16 Why are managers often unaware of the magnitude of quality costs?

18-17 Explain how the plan-do-check-act cycle applies the scientific method to problem solving.

18-18 Why is process re-engineering a more radical approach to improvement than total quality management?

18-19 How can process re-engineering undermine employee morale?

18-20 Does activity-based costing always precede activity-based management (ABM)?

18-21 What are the problems in the application of ABM to service areas?

Exercises

connect

E18-1 Time allowed: 10 minutes

Listed below are a number of costs that are incurred in connection with a company's quality control system.

(a) Product testing
(b) Product recalls
(c) Rework labour and overhead
(d) Quality circles
(e) Downtime caused by defects
(f) Cost of field servicing
(g) Inspection of goods
(h) Quality engineering
(i) Warranty repairs
(j) Statistical process control
(k) Net cost of scrap
(l) Depreciation of test equipment
(m) Returns and allowances arising from poor quality
(n) Disposal of defective products
(o) Technical support to suppliers
(p) Systems development
(q) Warranty replacements
(r) Field testing at customer site
(s) Product design

Required

1 Classify each of the costs above into one of the following categories: prevention cost, appraisal cost, internal failure cost, or external failure cost.

2 Which of the costs in Requirement 1 above are incurred in an effort to keep poor quality of conformance from occurring? Which of the costs in Requirement 1 above are incurred because poor quality of conformance has occurred?

E18-2 Time allowed: 10 minutes

Listed below are a number of terms relating to quality management:

Appraisal costs	Quality circles
Quality cost report	Prevention costs
Quality of conformance	External failure costs
Internal failure costs	Quality costs

Required

Choose the term or terms that most appropriately complete the following statements. The terms can be used more than once. (A fill-in blank can hold more than one word.)

1 A product that has a high rate of defects is said to have a low _____.

2 All of the costs associated with preventing and dealing with defects once they occur are known as_____.

3 In many companies, small groups of employees, known as _____, meet on a regular basis to discuss ways to improve quality.

4 A company incurs _____ and _____ in an effort to keep defects from occurring.

5 A company incurs _____ and _____ because defects have occurred.

6 Of the four groups of costs associated with quality of conformance, _____ are generally the most damaging to a company.

7 Inspection, testing, and other costs incurred to keep defective products from being shipped to customers are known as _____.

8 _____ are incurred in an effort to eliminate poor product design, defective manufacturing practices, and the providing of substandard service.

9 The costs relating to defects, rejected products, and downtime caused by quality problems are known as _____.

10 When a product that is defective in some way is delivered to a customer, _____ are incurred.

11 Over time a company's total quality costs should decrease if it redistributes its quality costs by placing its greatest emphasis on _____ and _____.

12 One way to ensure that management is aware of the costs associated with quality is to summarize such costs on a _____.

E18-3 Time allowed: 30 minutes

The management at Megafilters Ltd has been discussing the possible implementation of a just-in-time (JIT) production system at its Sheffield plant, where oil and air filters are manufactured. The Metal Stamping Department at the Sheffield plant has already instituted a JIT system for controlling raw materials inventory, but the remainder of the plant is still discussing how to proceed with the implementation of this concept. The Metal Stamping Department implemented JIT with no advance planning, and some of the other department managers have become uneasy about adopting JIT after hearing about the problems that have arisen.

Robert Goertz, manager of the Sheffield plant, is a strong proponent of the JIT approach. He recently made the following statement at a meeting of all departmental managers:

'We will all have to make many changes in the way we think about our employees, our suppliers and our customers if we are going to be successful in using JIT procedures. Rather than dwelling on some of the negative things you have heard from the Metal Stamping Department, I want each of you to prepare a list of things we can do to make a smooth transition to the JIT approach for the rest of the plant.'

Required

1 The JIT approach has several characteristics that distinguish it from conventional production systems. Describe these characteristics.

2 For the JIT approach to be successful, Megafilters Ltd must establish appropriate relationships with its suppliers. Describe these relationships under JIT.

(*CMA*, adapted)

E18-4 Time allowed: 15 minutes

Kaufheim AG of Dresden, Germany, distributes medical supplies throughout Germany. Selected information relating to a quick-developing X-ray film carried by the company is given below:

Economic order quantity (EOQ)	700 units
Maximum weekly usage	60 units
Lead time	4 weeks
Average weekly usage	50 units

Management is trying to determine the proper safety inventory to carry on this item and to determine the proper reorder point.

Required

1 Assume that no safety inventory is to be carried. What is the reorder point?

2 Assume that a full safety inventory is to be carried.

(a) What would be the size of the safety inventory in units?

(b) What would be the reorder point?

E18-5 Time allowed: 20 minutes

Flint Company uses 9,000 units of part AK-4 each year. To get better control over its inventory, the company is anxious to determine the economic order quantity (EOQ) for this part.

Required

1 The company has determined that the cost to place an order for the part is £30, and it has determined that the cost to carry one part in inventory for one year is £1.50. Compute the EOQ for the part.

2 Assume that the cost to place an order increases from £30 to £40 per order. What will be the effect on the EOQ? Show computations.

3 Assume that the cost to carry a part in inventory increases from £1.50 to £2.00 per part. (Ordering costs remain unchanged at £30 per order.) What will be the effect on the EOQ? Show computations.

4 In Requirements 2 and 3 above, why does an increase in cost cause the EOQ to go up in one case and to go down in the other?

Problems

P18-6 **JIT; process re-engineering**

Time allowed: 30 minutes

Snedden Products manufactures athletic equipment, including footballs. The footballs are manufactured in several steps, which are listed below:

1 Leather and other materials are received at a centrally located dock where the materials are checked to be sure they conform to exacting company standards. Rejected materials are returned to the supplier.

2 Acceptable materials are transported to a stores warehouse pending use in production.

3 A materials requisition form is issued, and materials are transferred from the stores warehouse to the Cutting Department where all cutting equipment is located.

4 Since the Cutting Department cuts materials for a variety of products, the leather is placed on large pallets and stationed by the appropriate machines.

5 The leather and other materials are cut to proper shape, with the operator taking care to cut all sections of a football from a single piece of leather. Waste materials are placed in a bin, and at the end of each day the materials are sorted to reclaim the items that can be used in manufacturing other products.

6 Each cut item of material is examined by one of three checkers to ensure uniformity of cut, thickness of the leather, and direction of the grain. Rejected pieces are tossed in the scrap bin.

7 Cut materials are placed on pallets and transferred to the Centralized Sewing Department, where the pallets are placed in a staging area.

8 Materials are taken from the pallets, the company's name and logo are stamped into one section of each set of cut pieces, and the pieces are then sewed together.

9 The sewn pieces are placed in bins, which are then transferred to the staging area of the Assembly Department.

10 An operator in the Assembly Department installs a lining in the football, stitches the ball closed with a stitching machine, and then inflates it.

11 The completed footballs are placed on a conveyor belt that passes by another set of checkers. Each ball is checked for uniformity of shape and for other potential defects.

12 Completed footballs are boxed and transferred to the finished goods warehouse.

Required

Assume that the company adopts JIT inventory practices and establishes individual product flow lines. Explain what changes would have to be made in manufacturing procedures and prepare a sketch of how the football product flow line would be arranged.

P18-7 **EOQ**

Time allowed: 30 minutes

A company uses Material Z (cost £3.50 per kg) in the manufacture of Products A and B. The following forecast information is provided for the year ahead:

	Product A	Product B
Sales (units)	24,600	9,720
Finished goods inventory increase by year end (units)	447	178
Post-production rejection rate (%)	1%	2%
Material Z usage (kg per completed unit, net of wastage)	1.8	3.0
Material Z wastage (%)	5%	11%

Additional information:

- Average purchasing lead time for Material Z is two weeks.
- Usage of Material Z is expected to be even over the year.
- Annual inventory holding costs are 18% of the material cost.
- The cost of placing orders is £30 per order.
- The reorder level for Material Z is set at the average usage in average lead time, plus 1,000 kg of safety (buffer) inventory.

Required

1 State two items that would be regarded as 'inventory holding costs' and explain how they may be controlled effectively.

2 Calculate for the year ahead:

(a) the required production of Products A and B (in units)

(b) the total requirement for Material Z (in kgs)

(c) the economic order quantity for Material Z (in kgs).

3 Calculate the average inventory investment (£) and the annual inventory holding costs (£) for Material Z.

(ACCA Management Information)

P18-8 **Inventory management**

Time allowed: 25 minutes

A traditional view of the environment in which goods are manufactured and sold is where inventories of materials and components are held. Such inventories are then used to manufacture products to agreed standard specifications, aiming at maximizing the use of production capacity. Finished goods are held in inventory to satisfy steady demand for the product range at agreed prices.

Required

1 Discuss aspects of the operation of the management accounting function which are likely to apply in the above system.

2 Describe an alternative sequence from purchasing to the satisfaction of customer demand, which may be more applicable in the current business environment. Your answer should refer to the current 'techniques or philosophies' which are likely to be in use.

3 Name specific ways in which changes suggested in Requirement 2 will affect the operation of the management accounting function.

(*ACCA Information for Control and Decision Making*)

P18-9 **Economic order quantity (EOQ); safety inventory**

Time allowed: 30 minutes

Myron Metal Works uses a small casting in one of its finished products. The castings are purchased from a foundry located in another state. In total, Myron Metal Works purchases 54,000 castings per year at a cost of £8 per casting. The castings are used evenly throughout the year in the production process on a 360-day-per-year basis. The company estimates that it costs £90 to place a single purchase order and about £3 to carry one casting in inventory for a year. The high carrying costs result from the need to keep the castings in carefully controlled temperature and humidity conditions, and from the high cost of insurance. Delivery from the foundry generally takes 6 days, but it can take as much as 10 days. The days of delivery time and the percentage of their occurrence are shown in the following tabulation:

Delivery time (days)	Percentage of occurrence
1–6	75%
7	10%
8	5%
9	5%
10	5%
	100%

Required

1 Compute the economic order quantity (EOQ).

2 Assume that the company is willing to assume a 15% risk of being out of inventory. What would be the safety inventory? The reorder point?

3 Assume that the company is willing to assume only a 5% risk of being out of inventory. What would be the safety inventory? The reorder point?

4 Assume a 5% risk of being out of inventory as stated in (3) above. What would be the total cost of ordering and carrying inventory for one year?

5 Refer to the original data. Assume that using process re-engineering the company reduces its cost of placing a purchase order to only £6. Also, the company estimates that when the waste and

inefficiency caused by inventories are considered, the true cost of carrying a unit in inventory is £7.20 per year.

(a) Compute the new EOQ.

(b) How frequently would the company be placing an order, as compared to the old purchasing policy?

P18-10 Time allowed: 45 minutes

The management team of WZX is about to start preparing the budgets for the year ending 31 December 2010. Relevant information is given below:

Sales

The predicted sales for 2010 are as follows:

	Quarter				
	1	2	3	4	Total
Sales (units)	25,799	24,078	34,763	39,820	124,460

Sales demand is the principal budget factor.

Costs

The production costs have been predicted to be:

Materials	£15 per unit, but if production exceeds 30,000 units in a quarter a discount of 5% will be allowed on all units in the quarter.
Labour	£25 per unit in normal time. However, if production exceeds 30,000 units in a quarter, overtime will have to be worked and costs will rise to £38 per unit for those in excess of 30,000 in the quarter.
Overheads	
Variable	£10 per unit at all levels of activity.
Fixed	£100,000 per quarter for up to 30,000 units produced, but rising by 20% if output exceeds 30,000 units.

Inventories

WZX uses a just-in-time (JIT) system for raw materials.

It is company policy that there should be no inventory of finished goods at the start of any year. Finished goods are valued at the budgeted average annual marginal production cost per unit.

Production schedule

The total annual production requirement will be scheduled to be produced in equal amounts in the four quarters.

Costing system

WZX uses a marginal costing system based on the budgeted average annual cost per unit.

Required

1 Prepare the production cost of sales budget for WZX for 2010 on the basis of its current purchasing, production and inventory holding policies and its use of marginal costing. You should show the costs of each quarter and the total for the year.

2 The management of WZX is thinking of extending its use of a JIT approach to include finished goods and production.

Prepare the production cost of sales budget for 2010 on the basis of this policy change. You should show the costs of each quarter and the total for the year.

3 Explain the reasons for the differences in materials, labour and fixed overhead costs in your answers to parts (a) and (b) above.

4 Sales demand in 2011 is expected to be subject to seasonal fluctuations, as it has been in previous years. These seasonal variations are expected to be as follows:

Quarter	1	2	3	4
% variation	– 10	– 20	+ 10	+ 20

Assume that sales for Quarter 3 of 2010 will be 34,763 units and will continue to show an underlying growth of 5% per quarter. This trend of underlying growth is expected to continue throughout 2011.

Prepare a forecast of the sales volumes expected for each quarter of 2011.

(*CIMA Performance Management*, adapted)

P18-11 Quality cost report

Time allowed: 60 minutes

In response to intensive foreign competition, the management of Florex Company has attempted over the past year to improve the quality of its products. A statistical process control system has been installed and other steps have been taken to decrease the amount of warranty and other field costs, which have been trending upward over the past several years. Costs relating to quality and quality control over the last two years are given below:

	This year	Last year
Inspection	£900,000	£750,000
Quality engineering	570,000	420,000
Depreciation of test equipment	240,000	210,000
Rework labour	1,500,000	1,050,000
Statistical process control	180,000	–
Cost of field servicing	900,000	1,200,000
Supplies used in testing	60,000	30,000
Systems development	750,000	480,000
Warranty repairs	1,050,000	3,600,000
Net cost of scrap	1,125,000	630,000
Product testing	1,200,000	810,000
Product recalls	750,000	2,100,000
Disposal of defective products	975,000	720,000

Sales have been flat over the past few years, at £75,000,000 per year. A great deal of money has been spent in the effort to upgrade quality, and management is anxious to see whether or not the effort has been effective.

Required

1 Prepare a quality cost report that contains data for both this year and last year. Carry percentage computations to two decimal places.

2 Prepare a bar graph showing the distribution of the various quality costs by category.

3 Prepare a written evaluation to accompany the reports you have prepared in Requirements 1 and 2 above. This evaluation should discuss the distribution of quality costs in the company, changes in this distribution that you see taking place, the reasons for changes in costs in the various categories, and any other information that would be of value to management.

P18-12 Quality cost report

Time allowed: 60 minutes

'Maybe the emphasis we've placed on upgrading our quality control system will pay off in the long run, but it doesn't seem to be helping us much right now,' said Renee Penretti, managing director of Halogen Products. 'I thought improved quality would give a real boost to sales, but sales have remained flat at £50,000,000 for the last two years.'

Halogen Products has seen its market share decline in recent years due to increased foreign competition. An intensive effort to strengthen the quality control system was initiated at the beginning of the current year in the hope that better quality would strengthen the company's competitive position and also reduce warranty and servicing costs. Costs relating to quality and quality control over the last two years are given below:

	This year	Last year
Product testing	£800,000	£490,000
Rework labour	1,000,000	700,000
Systems development	530,000	320,000
Warranty repairs	700,000	2,100,000
Net cost of scrap	620,000	430,000
Supplies used in testing	30,000	20,000
Field servicing	600,000	900,000
Quality engineering	400,000	280,000
Warranty replacements	90,000	300,000
Inspection	600,000	380,000
Product recalls	410,000	1,700,000
Statistical process control	370,000	–
Disposal of defective products	380,000	270,000
Depreciation of testing equipment	170,000	110,000

Required

1 Prepare a quality cost report that contains data for both years. Carry percentage computations to two decimal places.

2 Prepare a bar graph showing the distribution of the various quality costs by category.

3 Prepare a written evaluation to accompany the reports you have prepared in Requirements 1 and 2 above. This evaluation should discuss the distribution of quality costs in the company, changes in this distribution that you detect have taken place over the last year, and any other information you believe would be useful to management.

P18-13 Analysing a quality cost report

Time allowed: 45 minutes

Mercury Ltd produces pagers at its plant in Essex. In recent years, the company's market share has been eroded by stiff competition from overseas competitors. Price and product quality are the two key areas in which companies compete in this market.

A year ago, the company's pagers had been ranked low in product quality in a consumer survey. Shocked by this result, Steve Davis, Mercury's managing director, initiated a crash effort to improve product quality. Davis set up a task force to implement a formal quality improvement programme. Included on this task force were representatives from the Engineering, Marketing, Customer Service, Production, and Accounting departments. The broad representation was needed because Davis believed that this was a company-wide programme and that all employees should share the responsibility for its success.

After the first meeting of the task force, Holly Elsoe, manager of the Marketing Department, asked John Tran, production manager, what he thought of the proposed programme. Tran replied, 'I have reservations. Quality is too abstract to be attaching costs to it and then to be holding you and me responsible for cost improvements. I like to work with goals that I can see and count! I'm nervous about having my annual bonus based on a decrease in quality costs; there are too many variables that we have no control over.'

Mercury's quality improvement programme has now been in operation for one year. The company's most recent quality cost report is shown below.

Mercury Ltd Quality cost report (in thousands)

	This year	**Last year**
Prevention costs:		
Machine maintenance	£120	£70
Training suppliers	10	–
Quality circles	20	–
Total	150	70
Appraisal costs:		
Incoming inspection	40	20
Final testing	90	80
Total	130	100
Internal failure costs:		
Rework	130	50
Scrap	70	40
Total	200	90
External failure costs:		
Warranty repairs	30	90
Customer returns	80	320
Total	110	410
Total quality cost	£590	£670
Total production cost	£4,800	£4,200

As they were reviewing the report, Elsoe asked Tran what he now thought of the quality improvement programme. Tran replied. 'I'm relieved that the new quality improvement programme hasn't hurt our bonuses, but the programme has increased the workload in the Production Department. It is true that customer returns are way down, but the pagers that were returned by customers to retail outlets were rarely sent back to us for rework.'

Required

1 Expand the company's quality cost report by showing the costs in both years as percentages of both total production cost and total quality cost. Carry all computations to one decimal place. By analysing the report, determine if Mercury's quality improvement programme has been successful. List specific evidence to support your answer.

2 Do you expect the improvement programme as it progresses to continue to increase the workload in the Production Department?

3 Steve Davis believed that the quality improvement programme was essential and that Mercury could no longer afford to ignore the importance of product quality. Discuss how Mercury could measure the cost of not implementing the quality improvement programme.

(*CMA*, adapted)

P18-14 Process accounting/quality report
Time allowed: 50 minutes

LMN produces a compound T5, which is used to manufacture tyres. The compound, which earns a contribution of £6 per tonne, is produced by mixing two materials, R1 and R2, in a common process. The process causes the production of a by-product Z, which can be sold without further processing for £5 per tonne. The process is inefficient and large losses occur. The losses can currently only be identified at the completion of the process.

Process details

In addition to the costs of materials R1 and R2, variable and fixed processing costs are incurred. The expected inputs and outputs of the process are as follows:

Input:	equal quantities of R1 and R2
Outputs:	T5: 60% of weight of new input
	Z: 10% of weight of new input
Loss:	30% of weight of new input

Data for October

Opening work in progress 200 tonnes of T5 fully complete in respect of materials, but only 30% converted. This inventory was valued at £450.

Inputs:	
Materials:	24,000 tonnes of R1 costing £60,480
	24,000 tonnes of R2 costing £24,000
Conversion costs:	
Variable:	£36,125
Fixed:	£39,015
Outputs	T5: 28,800 tonnes
Z:	4,800 tonnes

Closing work in progress 200 tonnes of T5 fully complete in respect of materials, but only 80% converted.

Note: By-product Z is not considered to be a major source of income and consequently the revenue generated by its sale is credited to the process account.

Required

1 Prepare the process account for LMN for the month of October using a First In, First Out (FIFO) basis of valuation. Show all your workings.

2 The production director of LMN has been investigating alternative production methods to reduce the loss that arises in the process. Two alternatives have been identified:

(a) to change the mix of input materials R1 and R2, such that twice as much R1 is used compared to R2. Conversion costs would not be affected and trials have suggested that this would reduce the expected loss to 15% of the materials input during a period with no effect on the output of the by-product.

(b) to introduce a quality control procedure that would enable any loss to be identified and the units rejected after 60% of the conversion costs had been incurred. It is expected that the quantity of the normal loss will remain at 30% of the input to the process. There would be no capital expenditure costs associated with this quality control procedure, but other costs would comprise £0.20 for every tonne of input materials processed together with a fixed cost of £1,000 per month. The quantity of the by-product produced and its continued saleability would not be affected by this proposed inspection process.

Evaluate each of the separate alternatives (a) and (b) above and recommend which, if either, should be adopted by LMN. Show all your workings.

3 As a management accountant, prepare a report addressed to the Board of Directors of LMN that explains the costs and benefits that would arise following the adoption of a Quality Control Programme. Your answer should refer to the different quality cost classifications that would be used and also to non-financial factors.

(*CIMA Management Accounting – Performance Management*)

Cases

C18-15 Strategy and the internet

Time allowed: 75 minutes

FNJ is a company, which has developed business interests in the very competitive music industry. It produces and sells compact discs (CDs) and traces its history back to when it manufactured vinyl records. It is contracted to produce CDs for many famous recording artists which it is able to distribute through its own worldwide chain of retail music stores.

A new Chief Executive (CJ), who came from an unrelated business, was appointed to run FNJ about 12 months ago. The financial situation for the company has become perilous with falling worldwide sales and difficult trading conditions. The company has issued a number of profit warnings and experienced severe management disputes which have been made public. The result of these factors has been a low share price. CJ implemented cost reductions at FNJ and developed a strategy which focuses the company's attention on the provision of music to customers via the internet, with the eventual aim of replacing CDs with internet sales in the years to come.

WT is a large entertainments group which has growing business interests in producing motion pictures (movies) and retail outlets (trading under its own brand name of WT). The company is well regarded worldwide within its industry. It has augmented the product range with, for example, soft toys (related to its popular movie characters) which are sold through its retail outlets.

The merger

A merger deal has recently been agreed between the directors of FNJ and WT. This has yet to be ratified by both sets of shareholders, but it is expected to be accepted. The new group (FW) aims to achieve a high market share of total worldwide music sales. Following the merger, it is expected that the two companies will shed jobs throughout the world in the interests of improving efficiency. The contracts for some of the recording artists who are not achieving high sales will not be renewed.

Financial summary of the merger

The following details highlight the main points relating to the merger:

1 The merger is worth £10 billion in terms of total asset value.

2 WT has 8 seats while FNJ has 7 seats on the new board of FW.

3 CJ will be the Chief Executive of FW.

4 Shares in FW will be allocated in proportion to the current shareholdings. This will result in each company's shareholders holding 50% of the shares.

5 Directors' share options come to fruition on completion of the merger.

6 The share price of FNJ rose by 11% after the merger was announced.

Selected details relating to FNJ and WT before the proposed merger

	CDs (FNJ)	
	Last year	**2 years ago**
Actual sales	£90 million	£95 million
Budgeted sales	£100 million	£100 million
Average actual price per CD	£20	£20
Average actual cost per CD (⅓ of this is variable cost)	£12	£12
Average budgeted price per CD	£22	£20
Average budgeted cost per CD (⅓ of this is variable cost)	£15	£10.5

The average annual sales of CDs over the last 5 years were £100 million. The trend of changes in sales levels for CDs which has been apparent over the last two years is expected to continue.

	Motion pictures (WT)			
	Last year	**2 years ago**	**3 years ago**	**4 years ago**
Total revenue	£2,000 million	£1,800 million	£1,400 million	£1,000 million
Total costs	£1,900 million	£1,600 million	£1,100 million	£700 million
	Retail music stores (operated by FNJ)			
	Last year	**2 years ago**	**3 years ago**	**4 years ago**
Total revenue	£140 million	£138 million	£136 million	£135 million
Total costs	£136 million	£131 million	£134 million	£135 million

The resale value of FNJ's retail music stores is reducing because of the increasing popularity of alternative methods of shopping.

Strategic development of FW

CJ has forecast that next year sales of music will be available through the internet with digital downloading to the customer's own personal computer. At the moment, most of the FNJ retail music stores' revenue is generated by the sale of FNJ-produced CDs. He believes that by supplying customers through the internet, overall sales revenue (combining internet sales with CDs), will increase by 20%. The average variable costs for internet sales will reduce by 25% on that currently incurred in CD production. This cost reduction is expected as a result of not needing to employ expensive recording studios which are currently required to produce a CD.

The average selling price and average variable cost of a CD are expected to remain at £20 and £4 respectively throughout next year. The average selling price of each internet sale is also expected to be £20.

Independent research has revealed that the market for digitally downloaded music is forecast to grow next year. Customers will have the opportunity to create their own 'do it yourself' compilation albums.

Some of FW's competitors have already made effective use of the internet to distribute CDs and videos, undercutting high street retailers on price. However, digital download through the internet is still experimental.

Required

1 Discuss the dynamic nature of the business environment experienced by FNJ and WT, and explain the rationale for the merger.

2 (a) Analyse the business performance of CDs, motion pictures and FNJ's retail music stores over the period contained in the scenario. Include calculations on the projected change in contribution each year for CD and internet sales if CJ's forecast is accurate.

(b) Calculate and analyse the contribution volume variance relating to CD sales for last year and two years ago.

(c) Recommend ways in which the directors of FW should pursue the strategic development of the CD, motion pictures and FNJ's retail music stores businesses.

(Abbreviated version from *CIMA Management Accounting – Business Strategy*)

C18-16 Inventory management and new technology

Time allowed: 90 minutes

CLB is a profitable manufacturer of clothes with an annual turnover of $650 million. The organization sells by mail order from a paper catalogue sent out to customers and via a website. There are approximately 2.5 million customers on the sales database. Customers spend on average $110 per order.

Clothes are manufactured in 10 different factories, with finished goods being transferred to a central warehouse, where they are placed onto the computerized inventory system for internet and catalogue sales. All customer orders are routed to the central warehouse; the factories do not have any sales facilities.

The clothes produced by CLB are fashionable, with most customers being satisfied by the range available. A recent move to sourcing more supplies from overseas has helped to cut costs, although there is increasing competition from some low-cost imports.

Company aims and mission

The mission of the organization is 'to produce a wide range of reasonably priced clothes that appeal to the majority of the population'. To meet this objective, CLB has three main *critical success factors (CSFs)*:

- Maintain overall gross profit at 40% of sales
- Increase customer satisfaction each year
- Minimize raw material inventory cost.

A 40% gross profit percentage is slightly above the industry standard, but thought to be achievable by the Board of CLB. The organization needs to sell $600 million of clothes each year to break even.

Maintenance of customer satisfaction is essential to selling clothes. However, the directors have had some difficulty in establishing appropriate *performance indicators (PIs)* to measure the CSFs.

Maintaining control over inventory is essential; not only does raw material inventory tie up working capital, but any unused raw materials are difficult to dispose of. Changes in fashion mean that raw material inventory becomes obsolete very quickly. Finished goods inventories are easier to dispose of – completed garments can normally be sold at cost price or slightly above ensuring that some contribution is made.

Trends in sales

For a number of years, the Board of CLB has been concerned that the brand awareness of the company's products has been falling. Sales of new product lines have also been less than budgeted, both in absolute terms and in comparison to similar clothes produced by competitors.

(Information on competitor sales is obtained from their published accounts and for some products from the *Clothing Gazette*, a trade journal.) The fall in brand awareness and sales has provided a *decision trigger* to the directors that some amendments may be required to the information systems in CLB. However, they are unclear regarding the information to be obtained to help them make this decision.

CLB information system

At present, each of the ten factories of CLB maintains its own information system to provide detail on raw material inventories, production and finished goods ready to transfer to the central warehouse. While this means that there is no overall picture of inventories, the benefit of maintaining decentralized control is thought to outweigh this problem. The director of human resources is keen to maintain motivation of individual factory managers by retaining the existing systems.

This strategy has again been queried at board level in the last few months, particularly as manufacturing operations mean that each factory is using similar raw materials. Implementation of a centralized system has been rejected by the HR and IT Directors.

Required

1 (a) Recommend performance indicators (PIs) that can be used to support the *critical success factors (CSFs)* of CLB, discussing why these PIs are appropriate to the company.

(b) Explain the information systems that will be required in order to determine whether the PIs suggested in your answer to Requirement 1(a) have been achieved.

2 With reference to the falling brand awareness, advise the directors on a suitable decision-making process when considering the update of the information systems within CLB. Include relevant examples from the situation in CLB where possible.

3 Describe an information system that can be used to co-ordinate information transfer between the different production factories and between the factories and the central sales warehouse. Explain the business benefits to CLB of such a system and any disadvantages of it.

(CIMA Management Accounting – Information Strategy)

C18-17 Time allowed: 75 minutes

Ochilpark plc has identified and defined a market in which it wishes to operate. This will provide a 'millennium' focus for an existing product range. Ochilpark plc has identified a number of key competitors and intends to focus on close co-operation with its customers in providing products to meet their specific design and quality requirements. Efforts will be made to improve the effectiveness of all aspects of the cycle from product design to after sales service to customers. This will require inputs from a number of departments in the achievement of the specific goals of the 'millennium' product range. Efforts will be made to improve productivity in conjunction with increased flexibility of methods. An analysis of financial and non-financial data relating to the 'millennium' proposal is shown in Schedule 1.1.

Schedule 1.1 'Millennium' proposal – estimated statistics

	2012	2013	2014
Total market size (£m)	120	125	130
Ochilpark plc sales (£m)	15	18	20
Ochilpark plc – total costs (£m)	14.1	12.72	12.55
Ochilpark plc sundry statistics:			
Production achieving design quality standards (%)	95	97	98
Returns from customers as unsuitable (% of deliveries)	3.0	1.5	0.5
Cost of after sales service (£m)	1.5	1.25	1.0
Sales meeting planned delivery dates (%)	90	95	99
Average cycle time (customer enquiry to delivery) (weeks)	6	5.5	5
Components scrapped in production (%)	7.5	5.0	2.5
Idle machine capacity (%)	10	6	2

Required

1 (a) Prepare a table (£m) of the total costs for the 'millennium' proposal for each of years 2012, 2013 and 2014 (as shown in Schedule 1.1), detailing target costs, internal and external failure costs, appraisal costs and prevention costs. The following information should be used in the preparation of the analysis:

	2012	2013	2014
Target costs – variable (as % of sales)	40%	40%	40%
Target costs – fixed (total)	£2m	£2m	£2.5m
Internal failure costs (% of total target cost)	20%	10%	5%
External failure costs (% of total target cost)	25%	12%	5%
Appraisal costs	£0.5m	£0.5m	£0.5m
Prevention costs	£2m	£1m	£0.5m

(b) Explain the meaning of each of the cost classifications in Requirement 1(a) above and comment on their trend and inter-relationship. You should provide examples of each classification.

2 Prepare an analysis (both discursive and quantitative) of the 'millennium' proposal for the period 2012 to 2014. The analysis should use the information provided in the question, together with the data in Schedule 1.1. The analysis should contain the following:

(a) A definition of corporate 'vision or mission' and consideration of how the millennium proposal may be seen as identifying and illustrating a specific sub-set of this 'vision or mission'.

(b) Discussion and quantification of the proposal in both marketing and financial terms.

(c) Discussion of the external effectiveness of the proposal in the context of ways in which *1. Quality* and *2. Delivery* are expected to affect customer satisfaction and hence the marketing of the product.

(d) Discussion of the internal efficiency of the proposal in the context of ways in which the management of 1. Cycle Time and 2. Waste are expected to affect productivity and hence the financial aspects of the proposal.

(e) Discussion of the links between internal and external aspects of the expected trends in performance.

(ACCA Information for Decision Making and Control, adapted)

Further reading

A more comprehensive understanding of lean production can be achieved reading the seminal work by Womack, Jones and Roos (2007).

Endnotes

1 Summers (2002).

2 See Hansen and Mouritsen (2007) for a discussion of the relationship between operations management and management accounting.

3 Radnor, Walley, Stephens and Bucci (2006).

4 See Johnson and Kaplan (1987).

5 Shingo and Robinson (1990).

6 Granlund and Malmi (2001).

7 See, for example, Granlund (2001).

8 Scapens, Jazayeri and Scapens (1998).

9 Currie (2000).

10 Wagle (1998).

11 See, for example, May (2002), Granlund (2001), Scapens, Ezzamel, Burns and Baldvinsdottir (2003).

12 '80% of the benefit that we get from our ERP system comes from changes, such as inventory optimization, which we could have achieved without making the IT investment', Dorien and Wolf (2000), p. 101.

13 Agrawal, Arjona and Lemmens (2001).

14 Currie (2000), p. 117.

15 Barnatt (2004).

16 Hart, Heskett and Sasser (1990).

17 Casey (1990), p. 31.

18 Anderson and Sedatole (1998), p. 214.

19 Dr W. Edwards Deming, a pioneer in TQM, introduced many of the elements of TQM to Japanese industry after the Second World War. TQM was further refined and developed at Japanese companies such as Toyota.

20 Madonna (1992).

21 Cox, Mann and Sampson (1997).

22 Hammer and Champy (1995).

23 See Womack, Jones and Roos (2007).

Contemporary Management, Tenth Edition; Jones, George; 2018

The Environment of Management | part 2

CHAPTER 4

Ethics and Social Responsibility

Learning Objectives

After studying this chapter, you should be able to:

LO4-1 Explain the relationship between ethics and the law.

LO4-2 Differentiate between the claims of the different stakeholder groups that are affected by managers and their companies' actions.

LO4-3 Describe four rules that can help companies and their managers act in ethical ways.

LO4-4 Discuss why it is important for managers to behave ethically.

LO4-5 Identify the four main sources of managerial ethics.

LO4-6 Distinguish among the four main approaches toward social responsibility that a company can take.

© Chris Ryan/age fotostock RF

A MANAGER'S CHALLENGE

TOMS Adds Clean Water and Bullying to Its Social Agenda

Can ethical and socially responsible management be good for the bottom line? One for One—that is the trademark at TOMS. In 2006 the company began selling shoes, and for every pair of shoes purchased, it gave a pair of new shoes to a person in need. In 2011 the company did the same with eyeglasses, donating a pair of glasses for every pair of sunglasses and optical frames purchased. In 2014 TOMS got into the coffee business and now donates one week of water to one person for every bag of coffee purchased. And in 2015 the company added bullying to its social agenda by offering a special selection of Standup backpacks for sale and partnering with the Crisis Text Line and No Bully. For each backpack sold, TOMS gives a donation to its social partners to help provide training for school staff and crisis counselors to help prevent and respond to instances of bullying.[1]

How can TOMS afford to do this? It is estimated that the TOMS shoes cost $9 to manufacture. The "best sellers" in the shoe area on the TOMS website cost $48. Another best seller on the website is a $179 pair of sunglasses. Twelve ounces of TOMS coffee beans cost $12.99, almost the same price as 16 ounces of Starbucks coffee beans. And the new backpack costs $50.[2]

TOMS operates by identifying a global need and creating a product to help address it. It began when Blake Mycoskie, TOMS founder, was traveling in Argentina and found that many children had no shoes. In response, he established a company that donates a pair of shoes for every purchased pair of shoes. Since then more than 60 million pairs of shoes have been purchased, and 60 million pairs have been donated. TOMS are sold at more than 500 stores globally and on the company's website at TOMS.com.

The next global need Mycoskie identified was eyesight. TOMS partnered with the Seva Foundation to provide eyeglasses and surgeries to the millions of people who are visually impaired in the world. Whenever a pair of TOMS sunglasses or an optical frame is purchased, help is given to restore sight and support sustainable community-based eye care

Blake Mycoskie, founder of TOMS, demonstrates his belief in social responsibility via the company's One for One program. He began with shoes, expanded to eyeglasses, and jumped into coffee roasting to help supply clean water. In 2016, TOMS added bullying to its social agenda—making donations when consumers purchased certain TOMS backpacks.
© Nick Ut/AP Images

programs. More than 400,000 people have received eyeglasses or surgery through the One for One program since 2011. TOMS sunglasses, made in Italy, have three hand-painted stripes that symbolize the three elements of One for One: the buyer, the person being helped, and TOMS.[3]

In 2014 the global need identified was clean water. Mycoskie announced that the company would apply its One for One business model to help provide clean drinking water. To do so, TOMS went into the coffee business. For every bag of TOMS beans sold, a person in need will get clean water for a week. TOMS is partnering with Water for People, an international charity based in Denver, to deliver the water to the regions from which the beans are sourced, including Peru, Honduras, Rwanda, Malawi, and Guatemala. To date, TOMS Roasting Company purchases have helped provide more than 335,000 weeks of safe water for people in need.[4]

In 2015 TOMS identified bullying as one of the social needs the company wanted to address. In the United States, nearly one out of every three students between the ages of 12 and 18 reports being bullied—a statistic TOMS and its partners hope to change. One of TOMS's partners, Crisis Text Line (CTL), focuses specifically on how to respond to bullying by providing real-time emotional support to teens in crisis. A person in need of help can text CTL anytime about any crisis. A trained specialist responds quickly to the text and helps the person stay safe with effective crisis counseling and referrals—all done through texting. No Bully is an organization that partners with schools around the country to train staff on how to interrupt bullying and how to bring students together as a "solution team" when bullying or harassment occurs. These teams empower other students to become leaders in their schools, building empathy for bullied students and working together to find ways to treat everyone with more respect and compassion.[5]

TOMS recently celebrated its 10th anniversary, and Mycoskie remains the face of the organization, although people still ask about "Tom." According to him, there is no Tom—the company's name stands for Mycoskie's vision of selling a pair of shoes today, giving away a pair tomorrow. The word *tomorrow* wouldn't fit on the tag that goes in the shoes, so he shortened it to TOMS. Regardless of the name, TOMS has made a significant contribution to the lives and social well-being of people around the world—starting with one pair of shoes at a time.[6]

Overview

As TOMS's "One for One" campaign illustrates, management decision making can have far-reaching implications when it comes to doing business in a socially responsible manner. TOMS's recent antibullying campaign may be targeted to children and teens, but the campaign affects parents, schools, communities, and many other groups. But globally, nations, companies, and managers differ enormously in their commitment to these people, or *stakeholders*—various groups of people who may benefit or be harmed by how managers make decisions that affect them. Managers of some companies make the need to behave ethically toward stakeholders their main priority. Managers of other companies pursue their own self-interest at the expense of their stakeholders and do harm to them—such as the harm done to the millions of people around the world who work in dangerous, unsanitary conditions or who work for a pittance.

In this chapter we examine the obligations and responsibilities of managers and the companies they work for toward the people and society that are affected by their actions. First we examine the nature of ethics and the sources of ethical problems. Next we discuss the major stakeholder groups that are affected by how companies operate. We also look at four rules or guidelines managers can use to decide whether a specific business decision is ethical or unethical. Finally, we consider the sources of managerial ethics and the reasons why it is important for a company to behave in a socially responsible manner. By the end of this chapter you will understand the central role of ethics in shaping the practice of management and the life of a people, society, and nation.

The Nature of Ethics

Suppose you see a person being mugged. Will you act in some way to help even though you risk being hurt? Will you walk away? Perhaps you might not intervene, but will you call the police? Does how you act depend on whether the person being mugged is a fit male, an elderly person, or a homeless person? Does it depend on whether other people are around so you can tell yourself, "Oh, well, someone else will help or call the police. I don't need to"?

Ethical Dilemmas

ethical dilemma The quandary people find themselves in when they have to decide if they should act in a way that might help another person or group even though doing so might go against their own self-interest.

The situation just described is an example of an **ethical dilemma**, the quandary people find themselves in when they have to decide if they should act in a way that might help another person or group and is the right thing to do even though doing so might go against their own self-interest.[7] A dilemma may also arise when a person has to choose between two different courses of action, knowing that whichever course he or she selects will harm one person or group even though it may benefit another. The ethical dilemma here is to decide which course of action is the lesser of two evils.

ethics The inner guiding moral principles, values, and beliefs that people use to analyze or interpret a situation and then decide what is the right or appropriate way to behave.

People often know they are confronting an ethical dilemma when their moral scruples come into play and cause them to hesitate, debate, and reflect upon the rightness or goodness of a course of action. Moral scruples are thoughts and feelings that tell a person what is right or wrong; they are a part of a person's ethics. **Ethics** are the inner guiding moral principles, values, and beliefs that people use to analyze or interpret a situation and then decide what is the right or appropriate way to behave. Ethics also indicate what is inappropriate behavior and how a person should behave to avoid harming another person.

The essential problem in dealing with ethical issues, and thus solving moral dilemmas, is that no absolute or indisputable rules or principles can be developed to decide whether an action is ethical or unethical. Put simply, different people or groups may dispute which actions are ethical or unethical depending on their personal self-interest and specific attitudes, beliefs, and values—concepts we discussed in Chapter 3. How are we and companies and their managers and employees to decide what is ethical and, so, act appropriately toward other people and groups?

LO4-1 Explain the relationship between ethics and the law.

Ethics and the Law

The first answer to this question is that society as a whole, using the political and legal process, can lobby for and pass laws that specify what people can and cannot do. Many different kinds of laws govern business—for example, laws against fraud and deception and laws governing how companies can treat their employees and customers. Laws also specify what sanctions or punishments will follow if those laws are broken. Different groups in society lobby for which laws should be passed based on their own personal interests and beliefs about right and wrong. The group that can summon the most support can pass laws that align with its interests and beliefs. Once a law is passed, a decision about what the appropriate behavior is with regard to a person or situation is taken from the personally determined ethical realm to the societally determined legal realm. If you do not conform to the law, you can be prosecuted; and if you are found guilty of breaking the law, you can be punished. You have little say in the matter; your fate is in the hands of the court and its lawyers.

In studying the relationship between ethics and law, it is important to understand that *neither laws nor ethics are fixed principles* that do not change over time. Ethical beliefs change as time passes; as they do so, laws change to reflect the changing ethical beliefs of a society. It was seen as ethical, and it was legal, for example, to acquire and possess slaves in ancient Rome and Greece and in the United States until the late 19th century. Ethical views regarding whether slavery was morally right or appropriate changed, however. Slavery was made illegal in the United States when those in power decided that slavery degraded the meaning of being human. Slavery makes a statement about the value or worth of human beings and about their right to life, liberty, and the pursuit of happiness. And if we deny these rights to other people, how can we claim to have any natural rights to these things?

Moreover, what is to stop any person or group that becomes powerful enough to take control of the political and legal process from enslaving us and denying us the right to be free and to own property? In denying freedom to others, one risks losing it oneself, just as stealing from others opens the door for them to steal from us in return. "Do unto others as you would have them do unto you" is a common ethical or moral rule that people apply in such situations to decide what is the right thing to do.

Changes in Ethics over Time

There are many types of behavior—such as murder, theft, slavery, rape, and driving while intoxicated—that most people currently believe are unacceptable and unethical and should therefore be illegal. However, the ethics of many other actions and behaviors are open to dispute. Some people might believe a particular behavior—for example, smoking tobacco or possessing guns—is unethical and, so, should be made illegal. Others might argue that it is up to the individual or group to decide if such behaviors are ethical and thus whether a particular behavior should remain legal.

As ethical beliefs change over time, some people may begin to question whether existing laws that make specific behaviors illegal are still appropriate. They might argue that although a specific behavior is deemed illegal, this does not make it unethical and thus the law should be changed. In 25 states, for example, it is illegal to possess or use marijuana (cannabis). To justify this law, it is commonly argued that smoking marijuana leads people to try more dangerous drugs. Once the habit of taking drugs has been acquired, people can get hooked on them. More powerful drugs such as heroin and other narcotics are addictive, and most people cannot stop using them without help. Thus, the use of marijuana, because it might lead to further harm, is an unethical practice.

It has been documented medically, however, that marijuana use can help people with certain illnesses. For example, for cancer sufferers who are undergoing chemotherapy and for those with AIDS who are on potent medications, marijuana offers relief from many treatment side effects, such as nausea and lack of appetite. Yet in the United States it is illegal in some states for doctors to prescribe marijuana for these patients, so their suffering continues. Since 1996, however, 25 states have made it legal to prescribe marijuana for medical purposes; nevertheless, the federal government has sought to stop such state legislation. The U.S. Supreme Court ruled in 2005 that only Congress or the states could decide whether medical marijuana use should be made legal, and people in many states are currently lobbying for a relaxation of state laws against its use for medical purposes.[8] In Canada there has been a widespread movement to decriminalize marijuana. While not making the drug legal, decriminalization removes the threat of prosecution even for uses that are not medically related and allows the drug to be taxed. Initiatives are under way in several states to decriminalize the possession of small amounts of marijuana for personal use as well as to make it more widely available to people legally for medical purposes. A major ethical debate is currently raging over this issue in many states and countries.

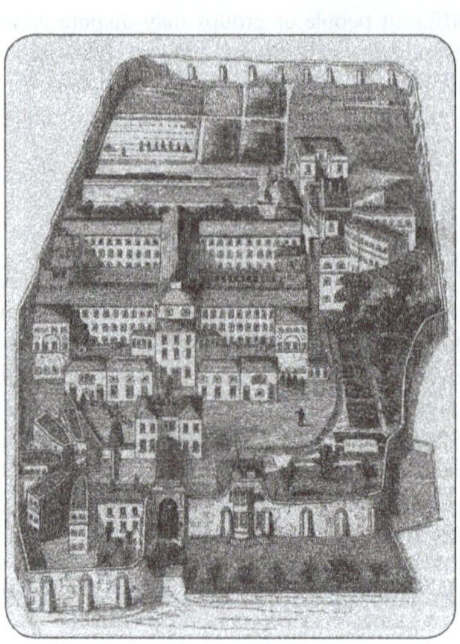

Coldbath Fields Prison, London, circa 1810. The British criminal justice system around this time was severe: A person could be executed for 350 different crimes, including sheep stealing. As ethical beliefs change over time, so do laws.

The important point to note is that while ethical beliefs lead to the development of laws and regulations to prevent certain behaviors or encourage others, laws themselves change or even disappear as ethical beliefs change. In Britain in 1830 a person could be executed for over 350 different crimes, including sheep stealing. Today the death penalty is no longer legal in Britain. Thus, both ethical and legal rules are *relative:* No absolute or unvarying standards exist to determine how we should behave, and people are caught up in moral dilemmas all the time. Because of this, we have to make ethical choices.

The previous discussion highlights an important issue in understanding the relationship among ethics, law, and business. Throughout the 2010s many scandals plagued major companies such as J.P. Morgan Chase, HSBC, Standard Chartered Bank, ING, Barclays, and Capital One. Managers at some of these companies engaged in risky trades, interest rate manipulation, illegal trade facilitation, drug money laundering, and deception of customers.

In other cases no laws were broken, yet outrage was expressed over perceptions of unethical actions. One example of this is the Occupy Wall Street movement, a protest that began on September 17, 2011, in a park close to New York City's Wall Street financial district. The movement was prompted in part by the perceived unethical influence of the financial services sector on the government. On its web page (occupywallstreet.org), the organization says it is "fighting back against the corrosive power of major banks and multinational corporations over the democratic process, and the role of Wall Street in creating an economic collapse that has caused the greatest recession in generations." It also raised issues of social and economic inequality.

Some of the goals of this protest were to reduce the influence of corporations on government and allow a more balanced distribution of income. While the protesters did not allege that what financial institutions were doing was illegal, they asserted that the actions of financial institutions were not congruent with ethical business practices.

In 2011 President Barack Obama commented on Occupy Wall Street's concerns about the way policies are influenced by the financial sector: "It expresses the frustrations that the American people feel that we had the biggest financial crisis since the Great Depression, huge collateral damage all throughout the country, all across Main Street. And yet you're still seeing some of the same folks who acted irresponsibly trying to fight efforts to crack down on abusive practices that got us into this problem in the first place."[9]

Stakeholders and Ethics

Just as people have to work out the right and wrong ways to act, so do companies. When the law does not specify how companies should behave, their managers must decide the right or ethical way to behave toward the people and groups affected by their actions. Who are the people or groups that are affected by a company's business decisions? If a company behaves in an ethical way, how does this benefit people and society? Conversely, how are people harmed by a company's unethical actions?

stakeholders The people and groups that supply a company with its productive resources and, so, have a claim on and a stake in the company.

The people and groups affected by how a company and its managers behave are called its stakeholders. **Stakeholders** supply a company with its productive resources; as a result, they have a claim on and a stake in the company.[10] Because stakeholders can directly benefit or be harmed by its actions, the ethics of a company and its managers are important to them. Who are a company's major stakeholders? What do they contribute to a company, and what do they claim in return? Here we examine the claims of these stakeholders—stockholders; managers; employees; suppliers and distributors; customers; and community, society, and nation-state as Figure 4.1 depicts.

LO4-2 Differentiate between the claims of the different stakeholder groups that are affected by managers and their companies' actions.

Stockholders

Stockholders have a claim on a company because when they buy its stock or shares they become its owners. When the founder of a company decides to publicly incorporate the business to raise capital, shares of the stock of that company are issued. This stock grants its buyers ownership of a certain percentage of the company and the right to receive any future stock dividends. For example, in 2005 Microsoft decided to pay the owners of its 5 billion shares a special dividend payout of $32 billion. Bill Gates received $3.3 billion in dividends based on his stockholding, and he donated this money to the Bill and Melinda Gates Foundation, to which he has reportedly donated over $28 billion to date, with the promise of much more to come; and Warren Buffet committed to donate at least $30 billion to the Gates Foundation over the next decade. The two richest people in the world have decided to give away a large part of their wealth to serve global ethical causes—in particular to address global health concerns such as malnutrition, malaria, tuberculosis, and AIDS. Gates is also donating about $1.8 billion to the Gates Foundation to help eradicate polio as part of the Polio Eradication & Endgame Strategic Plan 2013–2018.[11]

Figure 4.1

Types of Company Stakeholders

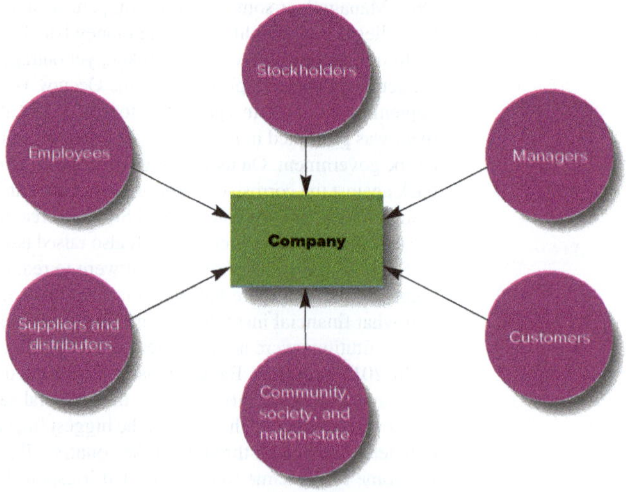

Stockholders are interested in how a company operates because they want to maximize the return on their investment. Thus, they watch the company and its managers closely to ensure that management is working diligently to increase the company's profitability.[12] Stockholders also want to ensure that managers are behaving ethically and not risking investors' capital by engaging in actions that could hurt the company's reputation. No company wants the reputation described by the Occupy Wall Street protesters, who alleged that business organizations value money over people and work in the self-interest of a privileged few. However, experts warn businesses not to ignore the movement. Harvard bloggers say the persistence of Occupy Wall Street is "a signal that there is authentic, deep-seated unhappiness with the failings of the U.S. economic system. It's an indicator that economic inequality is perceived as an important issue—one requiring businesses' immediate attention."[13]

Managers

Managers are a vital stakeholder group because they are responsible for using a company's financial, capital, and human resources to increase its performance and thus its stock price.[14] Managers have a claim on an organization because they bring to it their skills, expertise, and experience. They have the right to expect a good return or reward by investing their human capital to improve a company's performance. Such rewards include good salaries and benefits, the prospect of promotion and a career, and stock options and bonuses tied to company performance.

Managers are the stakeholder group that bears the responsibility to decide which goals an organization should pursue to most benefit stakeholders and how to make the most efficient use of resources to achieve those goals. In making such decisions, managers frequently must juggle the interests of different stakeholders, including themselves.[15] These sometimes difficult decisions challenge managers to uphold ethical values because some decisions that benefit certain stakeholder groups (managers and stockholders) harm other groups (individual workers and local communities). For example, in economic downturns or when a company experiences performance shortfalls, layoffs may help cut costs (thus benefiting shareholders) at the expense of the employees laid off. Many U.S. managers have recently faced this difficult decision. Until the 2009 financial crisis sent unemployment soaring over 10 percent, on average about 1.6 million U.S. employees out of a total labor force of 140 million were affected by mass layoffs each year; and over 3 million jobs from the United States, Europe, and Japan have been outsourced to Asia since 2005. Layoff decisions are always difficult: They not only take a heavy toll on workers, their families, and local communities but also

Layoff decisions are always difficult. Bank of America recently announced plans to reduce the workforce in its consumer-banking unit by thousands, as more and more customers are using mobile technology to do their banking.
© Steve Debenport/E+/Getty Images

mean the loss of the contributions of valued employees to an organization. In 2016, Bank of America announced plans to reduce the workforce in its consumer-banking unit by thousands, explaining that more and more customers are using mobile and online technology instead of local bank branches to do their banking.[16]

As we discussed in Chapter 1, managers must be motivated and given incentives to work hard in the interests of stockholders. Their behavior must also be scrutinized to ensure they do not behave illegally or unethically, pursuing goals that threaten stockholders and the company's interests.[17] Unfortunately, we have seen in the 2010s how easy it is for top managers to find ways to ruthlessly pursue their self-interest at the expense of stockholders and employees because laws and regulations are not strong enough to force them to behave ethically.

In a nutshell, the problem has been that in many companies corrupt managers focus not on building the company's capital and stockholders' wealth but on maximizing their own personal capital and wealth. In an effort to prevent future scandals, the Securities and Exchange Commission (SEC), the government's top business watchdog, has begun to rework the rules governing a company's relationship with its auditor, as well as regulations concerning stock options, and to increase the power of outside directors to scrutinize a CEO. The SEC's goal is to outlaw many actions that were previously classified as merely unethical. For example, companies are now forced to reveal to stockholders the value of the stock options they give their top executives and directors and when they give them these options; this shows how much such payments reduce company profits. Managers and directors can now be prosecuted if they disguise or try to hide these payments. In the 2010s the SEC announced many new rules requiring that companies disclose myriad details of executive compensation packages to investors; already the boards of directors of many companies have stopped giving CEOs perks such as free personal jet travel, membership in exclusive country clubs, and luxury accommodations on "business trips." Also, in 2010 Congress passed new laws preventing the many unethical and illegal actions of managers of banks and other financial institutions that led to the 2009 financial crisis. One of these regulations, the "Volcker Rule," seeks to reduce the chances that banks will put depositors' money at risk.[18]

Indeed, many experts argue that the rewards given to top managers, particularly the CEO and COO, grew out of control in the 2000s. Top managers are today's "aristocrats," and through their ability to influence the board of directors and raise their own pay, they have amassed personal fortunes worth hundreds of millions of dollars. For example, according to a study by the Federal Reserve, U.S. CEOs now get paid about 600 times what the average worker earns, compared to about 40 times in 1980—a staggering increase. In 2016 the median CEO compensation was $10.8 million.[19] We noted in Chapter 1 that besides their salaries, top managers often receive tens of millions in stock bonuses and options—even when their companies perform poorly.

Is it ethical for top managers to receive such vast amounts of money from their companies? Do they earn it? Remember, this money could have gone to shareholders in the form of dividends. It could also have reduced the huge salary gap between those at the top and those at the bottom of the hierarchy. Many people argue that the growing disparity between the rewards given to CEOs and to other employees is unethical and should be regulated. CEO pay has skyrocketed because CEOs are the people who set and control one another's salaries and bonuses; they can do this because they sit on the boards of other companies as outside directors. Others argue that because top managers play an important role in building a company's capital and wealth, they deserve a significant share of its profits. Some recent research has suggested that the companies whose CEO compensation includes a large percentage of stock options tend to experience big share losses more often than big gains, and on average, company performance improves as stock option use declines.[20] The debate over how much money CEOs and other top managers should be paid is still raging, particularly because the financial crisis beginning in 2009 showed how much money the CEOs of troubled financial companies earned even as their companies' performance and stock prices collapsed. For example, Countrywide Mortgage, which pioneered the subprime business, suffered losses of over $1.7 billion in 2007, and its stock fell 80 percent, yet its CEO, Angelo Mozilo, still received $20 million in stock awards and sold stock options worth $121 million before the company's price collapsed.

Ethics and Nonprofit Organizations

The issue of what is fair compensation for top managers is not limited to for-profit companies; it is one of many issues facing nonprofits. The many ethics scandals that have plagued companies in the 2010s might suggest that the issue of ethics is important only for profit-seeking companies, but this is untrue. There are almost 2 million private nonprofit charitable and philanthropic organizations in the United States, and charges that their managers have acted in unethical and even illegal ways have grown in the 2010s. For example, many states and the federal government are investigating the huge salaries that the top executives of charitable institutions earn.

One impetus for this was the revelation that the NYSE, which is classified as a charitable organization, paid its disgraced top executive, Richard A. Grasso, over $187 million in pension benefits. It turns out that over 80 nonprofits pay their top executives more than $1 million a year in salary, bonus, and other benefits, and the boards of trustees or directors of many of these organizations also enjoy lavish perks and compensation for attendance at board meetings. And unlike for-profit companies, which are required by law to provide detailed reports of their operations to their shareholders, nonprofits do not have shareholders, so the laws governing disclosure are far weaker. As a result, the board and its top managers have considerable latitude to decide how they will spend a nonprofit's resources, and little oversight exists.

To remedy this situation, many states and the federal government are considering new laws that would subject nonprofits to strict Sarbanes-Oxley-type regulations that force the disclosure of issues related to managerial compensation and financial integrity. There are also efforts in progress to strengthen the legal power of the IRS to oversee nonprofits' expenditures so that it has more authority to examine how these organizations spend their resources on managerial and director compensation and perks.

Experts hope that the introduction of new rules and regulations to monitor and oversee how nonprofits spend their funds will result in much more value being created from the funds given by donors. After all, every cent that is spent administering a nonprofit is a cent not being used to help the people or cause for which the money was intended. Ethical issues are involved because some badly run charities spend 70 cents of every dollar on administration costs. And charges have been leveled against charities such as the Red Cross for mishandling the hundreds of millions of dollars they received in donations after Hurricane Katrina struck; changes have been made in the Red Cross to address these issues. Clearly, the directors and managers of all organizations need to carefully consider the ethical issues involved in their decision making.

Employees

A company's employees are the hundreds of thousands of people who work in its various departments and functions, such as research, sales, and manufacturing. Employees expect to receive rewards consistent with their performance. One principal way that a company can act ethically toward employees and meet their expectations is by creating an occupational structure that fairly and equitably rewards employees for their contributions. Companies, for example, need to develop recruitment, training, performance appraisal, and reward systems that do not discriminate against employees and that employees believe are fair.

Suppliers and Distributors

No company operates alone. Every company is in a network of relationships with other companies that supply it with the inputs (such as raw materials, components, contract labor, and clients) that it needs to operate. It also depends on intermediaries such as wholesalers and retailers to distribute its products to the final customers. Suppliers expect to be paid fairly and promptly for their inputs; distributors expect to receive quality products at agreed-upon prices. Once again, many ethical issues arise in how companies contract and interact with their suppliers and distributors. Important issues concerning safety specifications are governed by the contracts a company signs with its suppliers and distributors, for example; however, lax oversight can have tragic consequences, as the accompanying "Ethics in Action" feature shows.

ETHICS IN ACTION

Keeping Garment Industry Workers Safe

Why have more than 220 international brands and retailers, including Abercrombie & Fitch, American Eagle Outfitters, Fruit of the Loom, and PVH, signed the Accord on Fire and Building Safety in Bangladesh? The accord is a five-year agreement stating that the signing companies and organizations commit to meet the minimum safety standards for the textile industry in Bangladesh.

Could it be that the buying power of consumers in their mid-twenties—-consumers very concerned about the plight of the global worker—encouraged brands and retailers to sign the agreement? Sébastien Breteau, founder and chief executive officer of AsiaInspection, a quality control service provider of supplier audits, product inspections, and lab testing for consumer goods and food importers, believes young people have raised awareness of social accountability in global supply chain management. "This generation cares a lot about transparency," he said. "They want to know that what they are buying doesn't kill the planet."[21] This means that organizations that do not monitor their suppliers carefully risk paying a steep price with young consumers.

Several industrial accidents in 2013 catalyzed social accountability in global supply chain management, according to Breteau's firm. Probably the most tragic of the tipping points was the collapse of the Rana Plaza in Dhaka, Bangladesh. The collapse of the eight-story commercial building killed 1,132 workers and injured more than 2,500 on April 24, 2013. The day before the collapse, building inspectors had found cracks in the structure and warned business owners to evacuate. A few shops and a bank heeded the warning, but owners of garment factories in the building ordered employees to come to work. The collapse was the deadliest disaster in the history of the garment industry worldwide.

There are parallels between the collapse of Rana Plaza and a tragedy in the history of American garment factories. In 1911 a fire destroyed the Triangle Shirtwaist Factory and killed 146 garment workers. The factory was on the top floors of a building in Greenwich Village, New York City. When the fire broke out, workers found the exit doors locked from the outside, a common practice at the time to stop theft and unauthorized breaks. Many workers died by jumping out the windows to escape the flames. The outrage that followed the Triangle fire was a catalyst for change in factory conditions, much like the outrage that followed the Rana Plaza collapse. In the aftermath of the fire, the Factory Investigating Commission was formed and, much like the Accord on Fire and Building Safety in Bangladesh, began factory inspections. Many factories in New York City were found to have the same conditions that caused the Triangle fire, such as flammable materials, locked exit doors, and inadequate fire alarms and fire suppression systems. Between 1911 and 1913, 60 new laws were passed to improve factory conditions.

In March 2014 engineering teams organized through the accord issued inspection reports on 10 Bangladesh factories. The reports indicated many factories did not have adequate fire alarm and sprinkler systems and that some fire exits were locked.[22] Also, many factories had dangerously high weight loads on floors, which is believed to be a cause of the Rana Plaza collapse.

Following the Rana Plaza collapse, clients of Breteau's inspection firm have become less reluctant to commit to the creation and enforcement of programs to audit factory working conditions. "Suddenly, we saw a switch in our clients' attitude to social accountability," according to Breteau. "They became very serious about running audit programs through their supply chains."[23] The company's audit programs include quality management standards according to the ISO 9001 or U.S. C-TPAT standards, social compliance according to SA 8000 standards, and ethical trading according to Sedex Ethical Trade Audits.

Will this change in attitudes toward social accountability in global supply chains have a lasting impact? *Forbes* blogger Robert Bowman, managing editor of SupplyChainBrain, a website and magazine covering global supply chains, names several reasons that retailers have failed to take aggressive action to stop unsafe working conditions in the past. From the retailers' point of view, it can be difficult to keep track of complex supply chains. Multiple layers of suppliers and subcontractors in some supply chains make it complicated to know exactly how and where goods are being produced, Bowman says. From the consumer's point of view, shocking revelations of poor labor practices cause temporary indignation. After headlines and media stories about sweatshops and safety violations, shoppers quickly return to being indifferent about how clothing is produced, Bowman says. However, the shocking collapse of Rana Plaza and the resulting signatures on the Accord on Fire and Building Safety in Bangladesh bode well for change in global supply chain ethics.

Many other issues depend on business ethics. For example, numerous products sold in U.S. stores have been outsourced to countries that do not have U.S.-style regulations and laws to protect the workers who make these products. All companies must take an ethical position on the way they obtain and make the products they sell. Commonly, this stance is published on a company's website. Table 4.1 presents part of the Gap's statement about its approach to global ethics (www.gapinc.com).

Customers

Customers are often regarded as the most critical stakeholder group because if a company cannot attract them to buy its products, it cannot stay in business. Thus, managers and employees must work to increase efficiency and effectiveness in order to create loyal customers and attract new ones. They do so by selling customers quality products at a fair price and providing good after-sales service. They can also strive to improve their products over time and provide guarantees to customers about the integrity of their products, like the Soap Dispensary, profiled in the accompanying "Ethics in Action" feature.

Community, Society, and Nation

The effects of the decisions made by companies and their managers permeate all aspects of the communities, societies, and nations in which they operate. *Community* refers to physical locations like towns or cities or to social milieus like ethnic neighborhoods in which companies are located. A community provides a company with the physical and social infrastructure that allows it to operate; its utilities and labor force; the homes in which its managers and employees live; the schools, colleges, and hospitals that serve their needs; and so on.

Through the salaries, wages, and taxes it pays, a company contributes to the economy of its town or region and often determines whether the community prospers or declines. Similarly, a company affects the prosperity of a society and a nation and, to the degree that a company is involved in global trade, all the countries it operates in and thus the prosperity of the global economy. We have already discussed the many issues surrounding global outsourcing and the loss of jobs in the United States, for example.

Table 4.1

Some Principles from the Gap's Code of Vendor Conduct

As a condition of doing business with Gap Inc., each and every factory must comply with this Code of Vendor Conduct. Gap Inc. will continue to develop monitoring systems to assess and ensure compliance. If Gap Inc. determines that any factory has violated this Code, Gap Inc. may either terminate its business relationship or require the factory to implement a corrective action plan. If corrective action is advised but not taken, Gap Inc. will suspend placement of future orders and may terminate current production.

I. General Principles

Factories that produce goods for Gap Inc. shall operate in full compliance with the laws of their respective countries and with all other applicable laws, rules, and regulations.

II. Environment

Factories must comply with all applicable environmental laws and regulations. Where such requirements are less stringent than Gap Inc.'s own, factories are encouraged to meet the standards outlined in Gap Inc.'s statement of environmental principles.

III. Discrimination

Factories shall employ workers on the basis of their ability to do the job, without regard to race, color, gender, nationality, religion, age, maternity, or marital status.

IV. Forced Labor

Factories shall not use any prison, indentured, or forced labor.

V. Child Labor

Factories shall employ only workers who meet the applicable minimum legal age requirement or are at least 15 years of age, whichever is greater. Factories must also comply with all other applicable child labor laws. Factories are encouraged to develop lawful workplace apprenticeship programs for the educational benefit of their workers, provided that all participants meet both Gap Inc.'s minimum age standard of 15 and the minimum legal age requirement.

VI. Wages & Hours

Factories shall set working hours, wages, and overtime premiums in compliance with all applicable laws. Workers shall be paid at least the minimum legal wage or a wage that meets local industry standards, whichever is greater. While it is understood that overtime is often required in garment production, factories shall carry out operations in ways that limit overtime to a level that ensures humane and productive working conditions.

ETHICS IN ACTION

Helping to Keep the Soap Market Green

Soap consumption is not as clean a business as you might think. First, soap is often packaged in plastic, and that's beyond the bar: dishwashing detergent, clothing detergent, shampoos, body washes, liquid hand soaps—they're all in plastic containers. With over 33 million tons of plastic being discarded yearly by Americans, only about 14 percent is recycled or sent to waste-to-energy facilities. The rest goes to landfills, where it may leak pollutants into the soil and water, or into the ocean, where an estimated 100 million tons of plastic debris already threatens the health of marine life.[24]

Second, many soaps have chemicals that contain suspected or known carcinogens (cancer-causing agents). One study of 25 household products found that many of their fragrances emitted hazardous chemicals.[25] One such chemical is triclosan, which is commonly found in soap products. Triclosan is toxic to aquatic plants and animals. When it reacts with chlorine in water, it can cause cancer, nerve disorders, and immune system disorders. It also contributes to antibiotic resistance in bacteria that cause infection in humans.

At the Soap Dispensary in Vancouver, owner Linh Truong sells biodegradable household and personal products free from fillers, dyes, and perfumes. Customers bring their own containers to refill over and over again, and Linh tracks the savings to the environment with each bottle refilled.

To combat the dirty residue of soap consumption, stores like the Soap Dispensary in Vancouver, Canada, are popping up. The Soap Dispensary is a refill store specializing in soaps, household cleaners, and personal care products that are not harmful to humans or the environment. Instead of harsh chemicals, the Soap Dispensary's products are selected to be as free as possible from fillers, dyes, and synthetic perfumes. The products are also biodegradable and animal cruelty–free, and some are vegan certified.

Customers take their own containers back to the store again and again to refill instead of throwing them away, or they can pay a small deposit fee to obtain a reusable container from the store. The store also sells ingredients customers can use to make their own soaps (as well as other products) and conducts classes to teach customers how to make them at home. Classes range from simple soap making to aromatherapy. Besides soap, the store sells nonplastic cleaning supplies, reusable razors, natural beeswax candles, repurposed fabric, and other environmentally friendly items.

Linh Truong and Stewart Lampe, owners of the Soap Dispensary, estimate that in the first two years of the store's existence, it kept more than 12,000 plastic containers from being thrown away.

The store also has provided a venue where customers can purchase locally made products. Among the local brands sold at the Soap Dispensary are Curiosities Tallow Soap and Sadie's Soap. Curiosities Tallow Soap's ingredients include beef fat collected from local butcher shops, and Sadie's Soap's ingredients include hops from locally crafted beer.[26] These locally made soaps and their locally acquired ingredients make a short supply chain that is easier on the environment than a national or international one. When locally owned businesses provide supplies for other locally owned businesses, less fuel and other energy is spent on transportation, creating less pollution in the environment.[27]

The Soap Dispensary tracks the savings to the environment of each bottle refilled, which Truong uses to inspire her customers to keep conserving. Refill stores like the Soap Dispensary make a difference by focusing on one feasible aspect of sustainability. Truong also achieves her mission of reducing waste by encouraging her suppliers to switch to more sustainable packaging and by washing out some delivery containers to return to suppliers for reuse.

"Refilling soap is just one way to do it," she said. "It's just the art of shifting consumers' mentality. Once you start that shift, it can be applied to lots of other things in their lives, and also to how a business is run."[28]

Although the individual effects of the way each McDonald's restaurant operates might be small, for instance, the combined effects of how all McDonald's and other fast-food companies do business are enormous. In the United States alone, more than 3 million people work in the fast-food industry, and many thousands of suppliers, like farmers, paper cup manufacturers, and builders, depend on it for their livelihood. Small wonder, then, that the ethics of the fast-food business are scrutinized closely. This industry was the major lobbyer against attempts to raise the national minimum wage (which was raised to $7.25 an hour in 2009, where it remains in 2016, up from $5.15—a figure that had not changed since 1997), for example, because a higher minimum wage would substantially increase its operating costs. However, responding to protests about chickens raised in cages where they cannot move, McDonald's—the largest egg buyer in the United States—issued new ethical guidelines concerning cage size and related matters that its egg suppliers must abide by if they are to retain its business. What ethical rules does McDonald's use to decide its stance toward minimum pay or minimum cage size?

Business ethics are also important because the failure of a company can have catastrophic effects on a community; a general decline in business activity affects a whole nation.

The decision of a large company to pull out of a community, for example, can threaten the community's future. Some companies may attempt to improve their profits by engaging in actions that, although not illegal, can hurt communities and nations. One of these actions is pollution. For example, many U.S. companies reduce costs by trucking their waste to Mexico, where it is legal to dump waste in the Rio Grande. The dumping pollutes the river from the Mexican side, but the U.S. side of the river is increasingly experiencing pollution's negative effects.

LO4-3 Describe four rules that can help companies and their managers act in ethical ways.

Rules for Ethical Decision Making

When a stakeholder perspective is taken, questions on company ethics abound.[29] What is the appropriate way to manage the claims of all stakeholders? Company decisions that favor one group of stakeholders, for example, are likely to harm the interests of others.[30] High prices charged to customers may bring high returns to shareholders and high salaries to managers in the short run. If in the long run customers turn to companies that offer lower-cost products, however, the result may be declining sales, laid-off employees, and the decline of the communities that support the high-priced company's business activity.

When companies act ethically, their stakeholders support them. For example, banks are willing to supply them with new capital, they attract highly qualified job applicants, and new customers are drawn to their products. Thus, ethical companies grow and expand over time, and all their stakeholders benefit. The results of unethical behavior are loss of reputation and resources, shareholders selling their shares, skilled managers and employees leaving the company, and customers turning to the products of more reputable companies.

When making business decisions, managers must consider the claims of all stakeholders.[31] To help themselves and employees make ethical decisions and behave in ways that benefit their stakeholders, managers can use four ethical rules or principles to analyze the effects of their business decisions on stakeholders: the *utilitarian, moral rights, justice,* and *practical* rules (Figure 4.2).[32] These rules are useful guidelines that help managers decide on the appropriate way to behave in situations where it is necessary to balance a company's self-interest

Figure 4.2
Four Ethical Rules

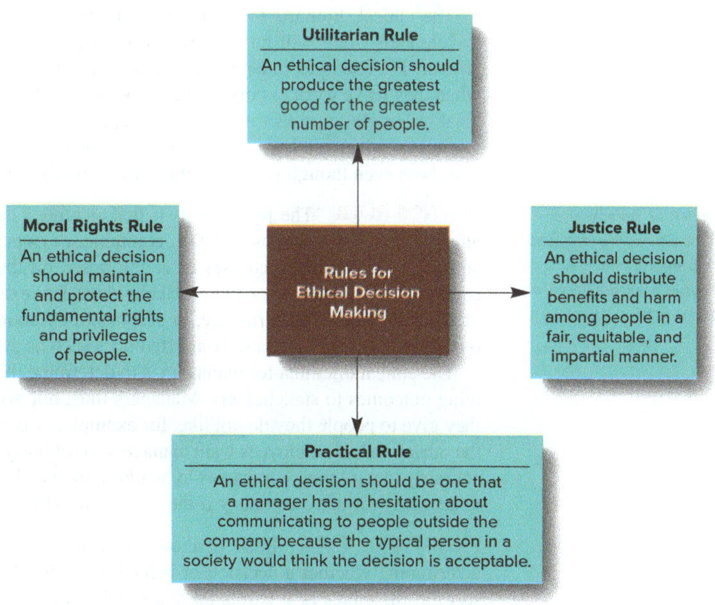

and the interests of its stakeholders. Remember, the right choices will lead resources to be used where they can create the most value. If all companies make the right choices, all stakeholders will benefit in the long run.[33]

utilitarian rule An ethical decision is a decision that produces the greatest good for the greatest number of people.

UTILITARIAN RULE The **utilitarian rule** is that an ethical decision is a decision that produces the greatest good for the greatest number of people. To decide which is the most ethical course of business action, managers should first consider how different possible courses of business action would benefit or harm different stakeholders. They should then choose the course of action that provides the most benefits, or, conversely, the one that does the least harm, to stakeholders.[34]

The ethical dilemma for managers is this: How do you measure the benefit and harm that will be done to each stakeholder group? Moreover, how do you evaluate the rights of different stakeholder groups, and the relative importance of each group, in coming to a decision? Because stockholders own the company, shouldn't their claims be held above those of employees? For example, managers might face a choice of using global outsourcing to reduce costs and lower prices or continuing with high-cost production at home. A decision to use global outsourcing benefits shareholders and customers but will result in major layoffs that will harm employees and the communities in which they live. Typically, in a capitalist society such as the United States, the interests of shareholders are put above those of employees, so production will move abroad. This is commonly regarded as being an ethical choice because in the long run the alternative, home production, might cause the business to collapse and go bankrupt, in which case greater harm will be done to all stakeholders.

moral rights rule An ethical decision is one that best maintains and protects the fundamental or inalienable rights and privileges of the people affected by it.

MORAL RIGHTS RULE Under the **moral rights rule**, an ethical decision is one that best maintains and protects the fundamental or inalienable rights and privileges of the people affected by it. For example, ethical decisions protect people's rights to freedom, life and safety, property, privacy, free speech, and freedom of conscience. The adage "Do unto others as you would have them do unto you" is a moral rights principle that managers should use to decide which rights to uphold. Customers must also consider the rights of the companies and people who create the products they wish to consume.

From a moral rights perspective, managers should compare and contrast different courses of business action on the basis of how each course will affect the rights of the company's different stakeholders. Managers should then choose the course of action that best protects and upholds the rights of *all* stakeholders. For example, decisions that might significantly harm the safety or health of employees or customers would clearly be unethical choices.

The ethical dilemma for managers is that decisions that will protect the rights of some stakeholders often will hurt the rights of others. How should they choose which group to protect? For example, in deciding whether it is ethical to snoop on employees, or search them when they leave work to prevent theft, does an employee's right to privacy outweigh an organization's right to protect its property? Suppose a coworker is having personal problems and is coming in late and leaving early, forcing you to pick up the person's workload. Do you tell your boss even though you know this will probably get that person fired?

justice rule An ethical decision distributes benefits and harms among people and groups in a fair, equitable, or impartial way.

JUSTICE RULE The **justice rule** is that an ethical decision distributes benefits and harms among people and groups in a fair, equitable, or impartial way. Managers should compare and contrast alternative courses of action based on the degree to which they will fairly or equitably distribute outcomes to stakeholders. For example, employees who are similar in their level of skill, performance, or responsibility should receive similar pay; allocation of outcomes should not be based on differences such as gender, race, or religion.

The ethical dilemma for managers is to determine the fair rules and procedures for distributing outcomes to stakeholders. Managers must not give people they like bigger raises than they give to people they do not like, for example, or bend the rules to help their favorites. On the other hand, if employees want managers to act fairly toward them, then employees need to act fairly toward their companies by working hard and being loyal. Similarly, customers need to act fairly toward a company if they expect it to be fair to them.

PRACTICAL RULE Each of these rules offers a different and complementary way of determining whether a decision or behavior is ethical, and all three rules should be used to sort out the ethics of a particular course of action. Ethical issues, as we just discussed, are seldom clear-cut, however, because the rights, interests, goals, and incentives of different stakeholders often conflict. For this reason many experts on ethics add a fourth rule to determine whether a business decision is ethical: The **practical rule** is that an ethical decision is one that a manager has no hesitation or reluctance about communicating to people outside the company because the typical person in a society would think it is acceptable. A business decision is probably acceptable on ethical grounds if a manager can answer yes to each of these questions:

practical rule An ethical decision is one that a manager has no reluctance about communicating to people outside the company because the typical person in a society would think it is acceptable.

1. Does my decision fall within the accepted values or standards that typically apply in business activity today?
2. Am I willing to see the decision communicated to all people and groups affected by it—for example, by having it reported on TV or via social media?
3. Would the people with whom I have a significant personal relationship, such as family members, friends, or even managers in other organizations, approve of the decision?

Applying the practical rule to analyze a business decision ensures that managers are taking into account the interests of all stakeholders.[35] After applying this rule, managers can judge if they have chosen to act in an ethical or unethical way, and they must abide by the consequences.

Why Should Managers Behave Ethically?

LO4-4 Discuss why it is important for managers to behave ethically.

Why is it so important that managers, and people in general, act ethically and temper their pursuit of self-interest by considering the effects of their actions on others? The answer is that the relentless pursuit of self-interest can lead to a collective disaster when one or more people start to profit from being unethical because this encourages other people to act in the same way.[36] More and more people jump onto the bandwagon, and soon everybody is trying to manipulate the situation to serve their personal ends with no regard for the effects of their action on others. This is called the "tragedy of the commons."

Suppose that in an agricultural community there is common land that everybody has an equal right to use. Pursuing self-interest, each farmer acts to make the maximum use of the free resource by grazing his or her own cattle and sheep. Collectively, all the farmers overgraze the land, which quickly becomes worn out. Then a strong wind blows away the exposed topsoil, so the common land is destroyed. The pursuit of individual self-interest with no consideration of societal interests leads to disaster for each individual and for the whole society because scarce resources are destroyed.[37] Consider digital piracy: The tragedy that would result if all people were to steal digital media would be the disappearance of music, movie, and book companies as creative people decided there was no point in working hard to produce original songs, stories, and so on.

We can look at the effects of unethical behavior on business activity in another way. Suppose companies and their managers operate in an unethical society, meaning one in which stakeholders routinely try to cheat and defraud one another. If stakeholders expect each other to cheat, how long will it take them to negotiate the purchase and shipment of products? When they do not trust each other, stakeholders will probably spend hours bargaining over fair prices, and this is a largely unproductive activity that reduces efficiency and effectiveness.[38] The time and effort that could be spent improving product quality or customer service are lost to negotiating and bargaining. Thus, unethical behavior ruins business commerce, and society has a lower standard of living because fewer goods and services are produced, as Figure 4.3 illustrates.

On the other hand, suppose companies and their managers operate in an ethical society, meaning stakeholders believe they are dealing with others who are basically moral and honest. In this society stakeholders have a greater reason to trust others. **Trust** is the willingness of one person or group to have faith or confidence in the goodwill of another person, even though this puts them at risk (because the other might act in a deceitful way). When trust exists, stakeholders are likely to signal their good intentions by cooperating and providing information that makes it easier to exchange and price goods and services. When one person acts in a trustworthy way, this encourages others to act in the same way. Over time, as greater trust between stakeholders develops, they can work together more efficiently and effectively,

trust The willingness of one person or group to have faith or confidence in the goodwill of another person, even though this puts them at risk.

Figure 4.3
Some Effects of Ethical and Unethical Behavior

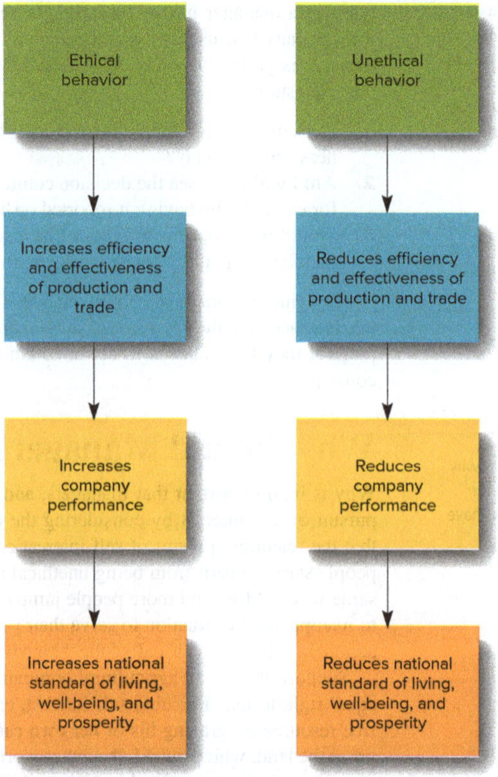

which raises company performance (see Figure 4.3). As people see the positive results of acting in an honest way, ethical behavior becomes a valued social norm, and society in general becomes increasingly ethical.

As noted in Chapter 1, a major responsibility of managers is to protect and nurture the resources under their control. Any organizational stakeholders—managers, workers, stockholders, suppliers—who advance their own interests by behaving unethically toward other stakeholders, either by taking resources or by denying resources to others, waste collective resources. If other individuals or groups copy the behavior of the unethical stakeholder, the rate at which collective resources are misused increases, and eventually few resources are available to produce goods and services. Unethical behavior that goes unpunished creates incentives for people to put their unbridled self-interests above the rights of others.[39] When this happens, the benefits that people reap from joining together in organizations disappear quickly.

An important safeguard against unethical behavior is the potential for loss of reputation.[40] **Reputation**, the esteem or high repute that people or organizations gain when they behave ethically, is an important asset. Stakeholders have valuable reputations, which they must protect because their ability to earn a living and obtain resources in the long run depends on how they behave.

reputation The esteem or high repute that individuals or organizations gain when they behave ethically.

If a manager misuses resources and other parties regard that behavior as being at odds with acceptable standards, the manager's reputation will suffer. Behaving unethically in the short run can have serious long-term consequences. A manager who has a poor reputation will have difficulty finding employment with other companies. Stockholders who see managers behaving unethically may refuse to invest in their companies, and this will decrease the stock price, undermine the companies' reputations, and ultimately put the managers' jobs at risk.[41]

All stakeholders have reputations to lose. Suppliers who provide shoddy inputs find that organizations learn over time not to deal with them, and eventually they go out of business. Powerful customers who demand ridiculously low prices find that their suppliers become less willing to deal with them, and resources ultimately become harder for them to obtain. Workers who shirk responsibilities on the job find it hard to get new jobs when they are fired. In general, if a manager or company is known for being unethical, other stakeholders are likely to view that individual or organization with suspicion and hostility, creating a poor reputation. But a manager or company known for ethical business practices will develop a good reputation.[42]

In summary, in a complex, diverse society, stakeholders, and people in general, need to recognize they are part of a larger social group. How they make decisions and act not only affects them personally but also affects the lives of many other people. Unfortunately, for some people, the daily struggle to survive and succeed or their total disregard for others' rights can lead them to lose that bigger connection to other people. We can see our relationships to our families and friends, school, church, and so on. But we must go further and keep in mind the effects of our actions on other people—people who will be judging our actions and whom we might harm by acting unethically. Our moral scruples are like those "other people" but are inside our heads.

Ethics and Social Responsibility

Some companies, like UPS, PepsiCo, Kellogg, Marriott International, and Aflac, are know for their ethical business practices.[43] Other companies such as Enron, which is out of business, or WorldCom, Tyco, and Siemens, which have been totally restructured, repeatedly engaged in unethical and illegal business activities. What explains such differences between the ethics of these companies and their managers?

There are four main determinants of differences in ethics among people, employees, companies, and countries: *societal* ethics, *occupational* ethics, *individual* ethics, and *organizational* ethics—especially the ethics of a company's top managers.[44] (See Figure 4.4.)

Figure 4.4

Sources of Ethics

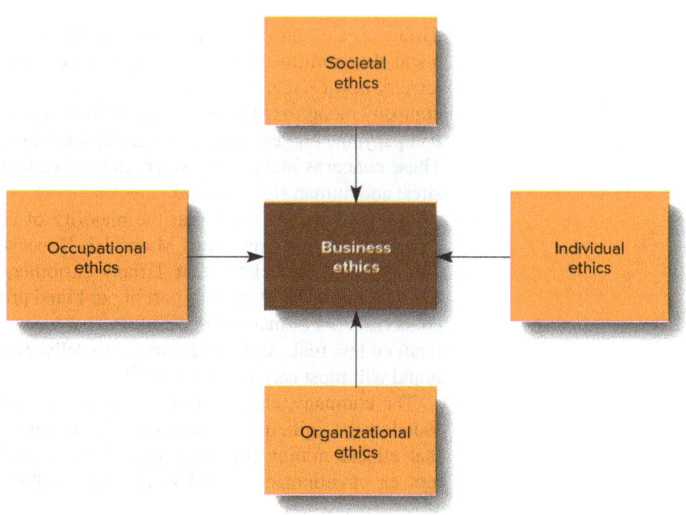

LO4-5 Identify the four main sources of managerial ethics.

Societal Ethics

societal ethics Standards that govern how members of a society should deal with one another in matters involving issues such as fairness, justice, poverty, and the rights of the individual.

Societal ethics are standards that govern how members of a society should deal with one another in matters involving issues such as fairness, justice, poverty, and the rights of the individual. Societal ethics emanate from a society's laws, customs, and practices and from the unwritten values and norms that influence how people interact with each other. People in a particular country may automatically behave ethically because they have *internalized* (made a part of their morals) certain values, beliefs, and norms that specify how they should behave when confronted with an ethical dilemma.

Societal ethics vary among societies. Countries like Germany, Japan, Sweden, and Switzerland are known as being some of the most ethical countries in the world, with strong values about social order and the need to create a society that protects the welfare of all their citizens. In other countries the situation is different. In many economically poor countries, bribery is standard practice to get things done—such as getting a telephone installed or a contract awarded. In the United States and other economically advanced countries, bribery is considered unethical and has been made illegal.

German engineering firm Siemens reported its involvement in a price-fixing cartel in Brazil so that it could build the Sao Paolo Metro.[45] Brazil ranks 76 out of 168 countries in the corruption perceptions index compiled by Transparency International.[46] However, that perception could soon change. In 2014 Brazil began imposing harsh penalties on any organization operating in Brazil that engages in corruption through its Law to Combat Corruption. The 2016 Olympic Games took place in Brazil, and companies working on the Games were subject to abiding by the new anti-corruption laws.[47]

Countries also differ widely in their beliefs about appropriate treatment for their employees. In general, the poorer a country is, the more likely employees are to be treated with little regard. One issue of concern is how an organization uses the resources of another country. The accompanying "Ethics in Action" feature discusses how the jewelry company Tiffany works to be ethical in its sourcing.

ETHICS IN ACTION

Finding Diamonds in a Rough Ethical Landscape

Tiffany & Co., an American multinational luxury jewelry and specialty retailer, has a stated commitment to "obtaining precious metals and gemstones and crafting our jewelry in ways that are socially and environmentally responsible." On its website the company recognizes the challenges of living up to that commitment. According to the company, the biggest concern is the impact of large, industrial-scale mining activities. These concerns include air, water, and soil contamination; the destruction of cultural sites; and human rights abuses.

"I would like to think that the majority of consumers are genuinely concerned about ethical sourcing," says Michael J. Kowalski, then chairman of the board and CEO. ". . . I do believe that Tiffany customers trust, either explicitly or through assumption, that Tiffany—as part of our brand promise—has in fact attended to those concerns. . . . For many of our customers those promises may be implicit, but it makes them no less real. And should we fail to deliver on those promises, the damage to our brand will most certainly be real."[48]

The company, along with the Jewelers of America and other organizations, has founded the Initiative for Responsible Mining Assurance (IRMA) to help ensure that ethical mining practices are followed. IRMA is creating a certification system for environmentally and socially responsible mining, which took effect in 2015.

The vision statement of IRMA calls for practices that "respect human rights and aspirations of affected communities, provide safe, healthy and respectful workplaces, avoid or minimize harm to the environment and leave positive legacies."[49] IRMA believes that most negative social and environmental impacts can be avoided if responsible mining practices are followed. These practices include careful choice of mine location to preserve ecologically and culturally significant areas, reduction of environmental impact from habitat loss and pollution, informed consent of indigenous peoples for mining, health and safety provisions, and transparency in revenue and corporate governance.[50]

In other ethical sourcing efforts, Tiffany & Co. purchases diamonds only from countries that use the Kimberley Process Certification Scheme (KPCS). This process was established by a United Nations General Assembly Resolution to stop the smuggling of "conflict diamonds" or diamonds that are sold to support violence, war efforts, or other malevolent activities. While the company believes the Kimberley Process has made a difference, it would like to see the definition of "conflict diamonds" expanded to include diamond-related human rights abuses.[51]

"While we certainly have a deep moral commitment to act responsibly—a commitment which emanates not just from myself or the senior management group but from all our Tiffany colleagues around the world—we also believe we have a business imperative to act responsibly," Kowalski said. "We have always prided ourselves on managing Tiffany & Co. for the long term. Witness our storied 177-year history. And over the long term, we have no doubt whatsoever that consumers will increasingly demand responsible behavior, and that effectively meeting that demand will be a source of brand differentiation and ultimately lead to the creation of long-term shareholder value."[52]

Occupational Ethics

occupational ethics
Standards that govern how members of a profession, trade, or craft should conduct themselves when performing work-related activities.

Occupational ethics are standards that govern how members of a profession, trade, or craft should conduct themselves when performing work-related activities.[53] For example, medical ethics govern how doctors and nurses should treat their patients. Doctors are expected to perform only necessary medical procedures and to act in the patient's interest, not their own self-interest. The ethics of scientific research require that scientists conduct their experiments and present their findings in ways that ensure the validity of their conclusions. Like society at large, most professional groups can impose punishments for violations of ethical standards.[54] Doctors and lawyers can be prevented from practicing their professions if they disregard professional ethics and put their own interests first.

Within an organization, occupational rules and norms often govern how employees such as lawyers, researchers, and accountants should make decisions to further stakeholder interests. Employees internalize the rules and norms of their occupational group (just as they do those of society) and often follow them automatically when deciding how to behave. Because most people tend to follow established rules of behavior, people frequently take ethics for granted. However, when occupational ethics are violated, such as when scientists fabricate data to disguise the harmful effects of products, ethical issues come to the forefront. For example, in 2014 Toyota said it had deceived "U.S. consumers by concealing and making deceptive statements about two safety issues involving its vehicles."[55] Millions of Toyota and Lexus vehicles had problems with unintended acceleration. As part of the $1.2 billion settlement with the Justice Department, Toyota's procedures and practices will be assessed by an independent monitor. As of 2016, this is still the largest criminal penalty ever levied against a U.S. automobile company—surpassing GM's $900 million fine for a defective ignition switch in 2015.[56] Table 4.2 lists some failures or lapses in professional ethics according to type of functional manager.

Table 4.2
Some Failures in Professional Ethics

For manufacturing and materials management managers:
- Releasing products that are not of a consistent quality because of defective inputs
- Producing product batches that may be dangerous or defective and harm customers
- Compromising workplace health and safety to reduce costs (for example, to maximize output, employees are not given adequate training to maintain and service machinery and equipment)

For sales and marketing managers:
- Knowingly making unsubstantiated product claims
- Engaging in sales campaigns that use covert persuasive or subliminal advertising to create customer need for the product
- Marketing to target groups such as the elderly, minorities, or children to build demand for a product
- Having ongoing campaigns of unsolicited junk mail, spam, door-to-door, or telephone selling

For accounting and finance managers:
- Engaging in misleading financial analysis involving creative accounting or "cooking the books" to hide salient facts
- Authorizing excessive expenses and perks to managers, customers, and suppliers
- Hiding the level and amount of top management and director compensation

For human resource managers:
- Failing to act fairly, objectively, and in a uniform way toward different employees or kinds of employees because of personal factors such as personality and beliefs
- Excessively encroaching on employee privacy through non-job-related surveillance or personality, ability, and drug testing
- Failing to respond to employee observations and concerns surrounding health and safety violations, hostile workplace issues, or inappropriate or even illegal behavior by managers or employees

Individual Ethics

Individual ethics Personal standards and values that determine how people view their responsibilities to others and how they should act in situations when their own self-interests are at stake.

Individual ethics are personal standards and values that determine how people view their responsibilities to other people and groups and, thus, how they should act in situations when their own self-interests are at stake.[57] Sources of individual ethics include the influence of one's family, peers, and upbringing in general. The experiences gained over a lifetime—through membership in social institutions such as schools and religions, for example—also contribute to the development of the personal standards and values that a person uses to evaluate a situation and decide what is the morally right or wrong way to behave. However, suppose you are the son or daughter of a mobster, and your upbringing and education take place in an organized crime context; this affects how you evaluate a situation. You may come to believe that it is ethical to do anything and perform any act, up to and including murder, if it benefits your family or friends. These are your ethics. They are obviously not the ethics of the wider society and, so, are subject to sanction. In a similar way, managers and employees in an organization may come to believe that actions they take to promote or protect their organization are more important than any harm these actions may cause other stakeholders. So they behave unethically or illegally, and when this is discovered, they also are sanctioned—as happened to New York's cab drivers.

In 2009 the New York City taxi commission, which regulates cab fares, began an investigation after it found that one cab driver from Brooklyn, Wasim Khalid Cheema, overcharged 574 passengers in just one month. The taxi drivers' scheme, the commission said, involved 1.8 million rides and cost passengers an average of $4 to $5 extra per trip. The drivers pressed a button on the taxi's payment meter that categorized the fare as a Code No. 4, which is charged for trips outside the city to Nassau or Westchester and is twice the rate of

Code No. 1, which is charged for rides within New York City limits. Passengers can see which rate is being charged by looking at the meter, but few bother to do so; they rely on the cab driver's honesty.

After the commission discovered the fraud, it used GPS data, collected in every cab, to review millions of trips within New York City and found that in 36,000 cabs the higher rates were improperly activated at least once; in each of about 3,000 cabs it was done more than 100 times; and 35,558 of the city's roughly 48,000 drivers had applied the higher rate. This scheme cost New York City riders more than $8 million plus all the higher tips they paid as a result of the higher charges. The fraud ranks as one of the biggest in the taxi industry's history, and New York City Mayor Michael R. Bloomberg said criminal charges could be brought against cab drivers.

As a result of the scandal, a notification system in taxicabs now alerts passengers if the higher rate is activated. The message is displayed on a television screen in the back seat of the cab and encourages riders to call the city to report any suspected abuse. Also, officials said taxi companies would eventually be forced to use meters based on a GPS system that would automatically set the charge based on the location of the cab, and drivers would no longer be able to manually activate the higher rate—and cheat their customers. In 2011, 630 taxi drivers had their licenses revoked.

In general, many decisions or behaviors that one person finds unethical, such as using animals for cosmetics testing, may be acceptable to another person. If decisions or behaviors are not illegal, individuals may agree to disagree about their ethical beliefs, or they may try to impose their own beliefs on other people and make those ethical beliefs the law. In all cases, however, people should develop and follow the ethical criteria described earlier to balance their self-interests against those of others when determining how they should behave in a particular situation.

Organizational Ethics

organizational ethics The guiding practices and beliefs through which a particular company and its managers view their responsibility toward their stakeholders.

Organizational ethics are the guiding practices and beliefs through which a particular company and its managers view their responsibility toward their stakeholders. The individual ethics of a company's founders and top managers are especially important in shaping the organization's code of ethics. Organizations whose founders had a vital role in creating a highly ethical code of organizational behavior include UPS, Procter & Gamble, Johnson & Johnson, and the Prudential Insurance Company. Johnson & Johnson's code of ethics—its credo—reflects a well-developed concern for its stakeholders (see Figure 4.5). Company credos, such as that of Johnson & Johnson, are meant to deter self-interested, unethical behavior; to demonstrate to managers and employees that a company will not tolerate people who, because of their own poor ethics, put their personal interests above the interests of other organizational stakeholders and ignore the harm they are inflicting on others; and to demonstrate that those who act unethically will be punished.

Managers or workers may behave unethically if they feel pressured to do so by the situation they are in and by unethical top managers. People typically confront ethical issues when weighing their personal interests against the effects of their actions on others. Suppose a manager knows that promotion to vice president is likely if she can secure a $100 million contract, but getting the contract requires bribing the contract giver with $1 million. The manager reasons that performing this act will ensure her career and future, and what harm would it do, anyway? Bribery is common and she knows that, even if she decides not to pay the bribe, someone else surely will. So what to do? Research seems to suggest that people who realize they have the most at stake in a career sense or a monetary sense are the ones most likely to act unethically. And it is exactly in this situation that a strong code of organizational ethics can help people behave in the right or appropriate way. *The New York Times* detailed code of ethics, for example, was crafted by its editors to ensure the integrity and honesty of its journalists as they report sensitive information.

If a company's top managers consistently endorse the ethical principles in its corporate credo, they can prevent employees from going astray. Employees are much more likely to act unethically when a credo does not exist or is disregarded. Arthur Andersen, for example, did not follow its credo at all; its unscrupulous partners ordered middle managers to shred records

Figure 4.5
Johnson & Johnson's Credo

Our Credo

We believe our first responsibility is to the doctors, nurses and patients, to mothers and fathers and all others who use our products and services. In meeting their needs everything we do must be of high quality. We must constantly strive to reduce our costs in order to maintain reasonable prices. Customers' orders must be serviced promptly and accurately. Our suppliers and distributors must have an opportunity to make a fair profit.

We are responsible to our employees, the men and women who work with us throughout the world. Everyone must be considered as an individual. We must respect their dignity and recognize their merit. They must have a sense of security in their jobs. Compensation must be fair and adequate, and working conditions clean, orderly and safe. We must be mindful of ways to help our employees fulfill their family responsibilities. Employees must feel free to make suggestions and complaints. There must be equal opportunity for employment, development and advancement for those qualified. We must provide competent management, and their actions must be just and ethical.

We are responsible to the communities in which we live and work and to the world community as well. We must be good citizens — support good works and charities and bear our fair share of taxes. We must encourage civic improvements and better health and education. We must maintain in good order the property we are privileged to use, protecting the environment and natural resources.

Our final responsibility is to our stockholders. Business must make a sound profit. We must experiment with new ideas. Research must be carried on, innovative programs developed and mistakes paid for. New equipment must be purchased, new facilities provided and new products launched. Reserves must be created to provide for adverse times. When we operate according to these principles, the stockholders should realize a fair return.

Johnson & Johnson

Source: © Johnson & Johnson. Used with permission.

that showed evidence of their wrongdoing. Although the middle managers knew this was wrong, they followed the orders because they responded to the personal power and status of the partners and not the company's code of ethics. They were afraid they would lose their jobs if they did not behave unethically, but their actions cost them their jobs anyway.

Top managers play a crucial role in determining a company's ethics. It is clearly important, then, that when making appointment decisions, the board of directors should scrutinize the reputations and ethical records of top managers. It is the responsibility of the board to decide whether a prospective CEO has the maturity, experience, and integrity needed to head a company and be entrusted with the capital and wealth of the organization, on which the fate of all its stakeholders depends. Clearly, a track record of success is not enough to decide whether a top manager is capable of moral decision making; a manager might have achieved this success through unethical or illegal means. It is important to investigate prospective top managers and examine their credentials. Although the best predictor of future behavior is often past behavior, the board of directors needs to be on guard against unprincipled executives who use unethical means to rise to the top of the organizational hierarchy. For this reason it is necessary that a company's directors continuously monitor the behavior of top executives. In the 2000s this increased scrutiny led to the dismissal of many top executives for breaking ethical rules concerning issues such as excessive personal loans, stock options, inflated expense accounts, and even sexual misconduct. As illustrated in the accompanying "Ethics in Action" feature, the tone set by the founder and leader of an organization can set its ethical tone and business model.

ETHICS IN ACTION

Michelle Obama Leads Challenge to Get Kids Moving

Childhood obesity is an ongoing concern in the United States. According to the U.S. government, more than 33 percent of children are overweight or obese. To help combat the problem, First Lady Michelle Obama started the Let's Move! campaign to end childhood obesity in a generation's time.[58]

There are several causes for the rising numbers of overweight children. Children used to play outside, where they would run around and burn calories. However, with television and video games providing enticing entertainment, children now do their playing mostly indoors on a mobile device. Sugars and fats are much more prevalent in foods, and what we eat today is more processed than ever before, robbing our kids of vital nutrients. Being overweight is unhealthy, especially in children. It may lead to serious health problems such as type 2 diabetes or heart disease. In addition to health risks, being overweight or obese can make children the targets of social discrimination. And the chances that a child will "grow out of it" are small—obese children are likely to become obese adults.[59]

To bring awareness and activism to the problem, Mrs. Obama's campaign targets not just parents and caregivers but the community at large, too. Let's Move! has five pillars: (1) Create a healthy start for children; (2) empower parents and caregivers; (3) provide healthful food in schools; (4) improve access to healthful, affordable foods; and (5) increase physical activity. Mrs. Obama says the movement will continue even after her husband leaves office and she is no longer First Lady.

First Lady Michelle Obama tends the White House garden with a group of children as part of the *Let's Move!* campaign to end childhood obesity.
© Evan Vucci/AP Images

Some accomplishments of the movement so far include the MyPlate and MiPlato icon, which makes it easy to understand healthful food choices; the closing of city streets to create areas where children can be active without worrying about traffic; and higher standards for nutrition and fitness in schools.[60]

Let's Move! collaborates with the Partnership for a Healthier America (PHA), which works with government agencies on industry-specific solutions to fight obesity. Partnership for a Healthier America aims to bring together leaders from all sectors to reduce childhood obesity.

Many food companies also have joined the Let's Move! campaign. For example, Darden, which owns popular restaurant chains such as Olive Garden, has pledged to offer a fruit or vegetable and low-fat milk with every kid's meal and to reduce the amount of calories and sodium in its menu items by 20 percent over the next 10 years. Walmart committed to lowering the cost of fruits, vegetables, and other healthful options and to work with manufacturers to reduce the amount of sugar and sodium in products throughout the store.

In 2010 the Healthy Weight Commitment Foundation agreed with Let's Move! and PHA to cut 1.5 trillion calories in food products over the next five years. The companies developed lower-calorie options, reduced calories in existing products, and made portion sizes smaller. An independent evaluator announced that by 2014 the foundation had exceeded its goal and removed 6.4 trillion calories from food products.

Being socially responsible can also help the bottom line. As the demand for healthier food items continues to rise, studies are being conducted to see how companies are faring. According to the Hudson Institute, "better-for-you" foods made up about 40 percent of sales for the companies studied but created 70 percent or more in sales growth over a four-year span. The report concludes that "sound strategic planning with a commitment to growing sales of better-for-you foods is good business."[61]

Approaches to Social Responsibility

LO4-6 Distinguish among the four main approaches toward social responsibility that a company can take.

A company's ethics are the result of differences in societal, organizational, occupational, and individual ethics. In turn, a company's ethics determine its stance on social responsibility. A company's stance on **social responsibility** is the way its managers and employees view their duty or obligation to make decisions that protect, enhance, and promote the welfare and well-being of stakeholders and society as a whole. As we noted earlier, when no laws specify how a company should act toward stakeholders, managers must decide the right, ethical, and socially responsible thing to do. Differences in business ethics can lead companies to diverse positions or views on their responsibility toward stakeholders.

social responsibility The way a company's managers and employees view their duty or obligation to make decisions that protect, enhance, and promote the welfare and well-being of stakeholders and society as a whole.

Many kinds of decisions signal a company's beliefs about its obligations to make socially responsible business decisions (see Table 4.3). The decision to spend money on training and educating employees—investing in them—is one such decision; so is the decision to minimize or avoid layoffs whenever possible. The decision to act promptly and warn customers when a batch of defective merchandise has been accidentally sold is another one. Companies that try to hide such problems show little regard for social responsibility. In the past both GM and Ford tried to hide the fact that several of their vehicles had defects that made them dangerous to drive; the companies were penalized with hundreds of millions of dollars in damages for their unethical behavior, and today they move more quickly to recall vehicles to fix problems. In 2014 General Motors CEO Mary Barra admitted that the automaker did not react fast enough when fault was found with an ignition switch that triggered the recall of eventually more than 10 million cars worldwide.[62] On the other side, also in 2014, Fitbit voluntarily recalled its activity tracking wrist band, the Fitbit Force, due to skin rash issues. The company offered to send consumers a return kit and promised a reimbursement check or exchange within two to six weeks of receipt.[63] The way a company announces business problems or admits its mistakes provides strong clues about its stance on social responsibility.

Four Different Approaches

obstructionist approach Companies and their managers choose *not* to behave in a socially responsible way and instead behave unethically and illegally.

The strength of companies' commitment to social responsibility can range from low to high (see Figure 4.6). At the low end of the range is an **obstructionist approach**, in which companies and their managers choose *not* to behave in a socially responsible way. Instead they behave unethically and often illegally and do all they can to prevent knowledge of their behavior from reaching other organizational stakeholders and society at large. Managers at the Manville Corporation adopted this approach when they sought to hide evidence that asbestos causes lung damage; so, too, did tobacco companies when they sought to hide evidence that cigarette smoking causes lung cancer. In 2010 it was revealed that the managers of Lehman Brothers, whose bankruptcy helped propel the 2008–2009 financial crisis, used

Table 4.3

Forms of Socially Responsible Behavior

Managers are being socially responsible and showing their support for their stakeholders when they

- Provide severance payments to help laid-off workers make ends meet until they can find another job.
- Give workers opportunities to enhance their skills and acquire additional education so they can remain productive and do not become obsolete because of changes in technology.
- Allow employees to take time off when they need to and provide health care and pension benefits for employees.
- Contribute to charities or support various civic-minded activities in the cities or towns in which they are located (Target and Levi Strauss both contribute 5 percent of their profits to support schools, charities, the arts, and other good works).
- Decide to keep open a factory whose closure would devastate the local community.
- Decide to keep a company's operations in the United States to protect the jobs of American workers rather than move abroad.
- Decide to spend money to improve a new factory so it will not pollute the environment.
- Decline to invest in countries that have poor human rights records.
- Choose to help poor countries develop an economic base to improve living standards.

loopholes in U.K. law to hide billions of dollars of worthless assets on its balance sheet to disguise its poor financial condition. The fall of Lehman Brothers has been recorded in several films, including the 2009 British television film *The Last Days of Lehman Brothers,* the 2011 American independent film *Margin Call,* and the 2011 HBO movie *Too Big to Fail.* It is also referenced in the 2010 animated film *Despicable Me.* In that film the criminal mastermind Gru goes into a building called the "Bank of Evil," which displays a small banner with the words "Formerly Lehman Brothers."

Top managers at Enron also acted in an obstructionist way when they prevented employees from selling Enron shares in their pension funds while they sold hundreds of millions of dollars' worth of their own Enron stock. Most employees lost all their retirement savings. Senior partners at Arthur Andersen who instructed their subordinates to shred files chose an obstructionist approach that caused not only a loss of reputation but devastation for the organization and for all stakeholders involved. These companies are no longer in business.

defensive approach Companies and their managers behave ethically to the degree that they stay within the law and strictly abide by legal requirements.

A **defensive approach** indicates at least some commitment to ethical behavior.[64] Defensive companies and managers stay within the law and abide strictly by legal requirements but make no attempt to exercise social responsibility beyond what the law dictates; thus, they can and often do act unethically. These are the kinds of companies, like Computer Associates, WorldCom, and Merrill Lynch, that gave their managers large stock options and bonuses even as company performance was declining rapidly. The managers are the kind who sell their stock in advance of other stockholders because they know their company's performance is about to fall. Although acting on inside information is illegal, it is often hard to prove because top managers have wide latitude regarding when they sell their shares. The founders of most dot-com companies took advantage of this legal loophole to sell billions of dollars of their dot-com shares before their stock prices collapsed. When making ethical decisions, such managers put their own interests first and commonly harm other stakeholders.

accommodative approach Companies and their managers behave legally and ethically and try to balance the interests of different stakeholders as the need arises.

An **accommodative approach** acknowledges the need to support social responsibility. Accommodative companies and managers agree that organizational members ought to behave legally and ethically, and they try to balance the interests of different stakeholders so the claims of stockholders are seen in relation to the claims of other stakeholders. Managers adopting this approach want to make choices that are reasonable in the eyes of society and want to do the right thing.

This approach is the one taken by the typical large U.S. company, which has the most to lose from unethical or illegal behavior. Generally, the older and more reputable a company, the more likely its managers are to curb attempts by their subordinates to act unethically.

Figure 4.6

Four Approaches to Social Responsibility

Large companies, like GM, Intel, DuPont, and Dell, seek every way to build their companies' competitive advantage. Nevertheless, they rein in attempts by their managers to behave unethically or illegally, knowing the grave consequences such behavior can have on future profitability. Sometimes they fail, however, such as in 2013 when SAC Capital Advisors (among others) agreed to pay $1.8 billion and plead guilty to criminal insider trading charges. To date, this is the biggest insider trading settlement in history.[65]

proactive approach Companies and their managers actively embrace socially responsible behavior, going out of their way to learn about the needs of different stakeholder groups and using organizational resources to promote the interests of all stakeholders.

Companies and managers taking a **proactive approach** actively embrace the need to behave in socially responsible ways. They go out of their way to learn about the needs of different stakeholder groups and are willing to use organizational resources to promote the interests not only of stockholders but also of the other stakeholders such as their employees and communities. U.S. steelmaker Nucor is one such company. In 1977 its visionary CEO Ken Iverson announced that throughout its history Nucor had never laid off one employee, and even though a major recession was raging, it did not plan to start now. In 2009 Nucor CEO Daniel R. DiMicco announced that Nucor again would not start layoffs despite the fact its steel mills were operating at only 50 percent of capacity (compared to 95 percent just months earlier) because customers had slashed orders due to the recession. While rivals laid off thousands of employees, Nucor remained loyal to its employees. However, even though there were no layoffs, both managers and employees took major cuts in pay and bonuses to weather the storm together, as they always had, and they searched for ways to reduce operating costs so they would all benefit when the economy recovered, and by 2012 their sacrifice had paid off: Nucor was doing well again. By 2014, it had reported above-expected earnings per share. In 2015 Nucor paid out an increased cash dividend for the 43rd year in a row.[66]

Proactive companies are often at the forefront of campaigns for causes such as a pollution-free environment; recycling and conservation of resources; the minimization or elimination of the use of animals in drug and cosmetics testing; and the reduction of crime, illiteracy, and poverty. For example, companies such as McDonald's, Google, REI, Whole Foods, and Target all have reputations for being proactive in the support of stakeholders such as their suppliers or the communities in which they operate.

Why Be Socially Responsible?

Several advantages result when companies and their managers behave in a socially responsible manner. First, demonstrating its social responsibility helps a company build a good reputation. Reputation is the trust, goodwill, and confidence others have in a company that lead them to want to do business with it. The rewards for a good company reputation are increased business and improved ability to obtain resources from stakeholders.[67] Reputation thus can enhance profitability and build stockholder wealth, and behaving responsibly socially is the economically right thing to do because companies that do so benefit from increasing business and rising profits.

A second major reason for companies to act responsibly toward employees, customers, and society is that, in a capitalist system, companies as well as the government, have to bear the costs of protecting their stakeholders, providing health care and income, paying taxes, and so on. So if all companies in a society act responsibly, the quality of life as a whole increases.

Moreover, how companies behave toward their employees determines many of a society's values and norms and the ethics of its citizens, as already noted. It has been suggested that if all organizations adopted a caring approach and agreed that their responsibility is to promote the interests of their employees, a climate of caring would pervade the wider society. Experts point to Japan, Sweden, Germany, the Netherlands, and Switzerland as countries where organizations are highly socially responsible and where, as a result, crime, poverty, and unemployment rates are relatively low, literacy rates are relatively high, and sociocultural values promote harmony between different groups of people. Business activity affects all aspects of people's lives, so how business behaves toward stakeholders affects how stakeholders behave toward business. You "reap what you sow," as the adage goes.

The Role of Organizational Culture

Although an organization's code of ethics guides decision making when ethical questions arise, managers can go one step further by ensuring that important ethical values and norms are key features of an organization's culture. For example, Herb Kelleher and Coleen Barrett created Southwest Airlines's culture in which promoting employee well-being is a main company priority; this translates into organizational values and norms dictating that layoffs should be avoided and employees should share in the profits the company makes.[68] Google, UPS, and Toyota are among the many companies that espouse similar values. When ethical values and norms such as these are part of an organization's culture, they help organizational members resist self-interested action because they recognize that they are part of something bigger than themselves.[69]

Managers' roles in developing ethical values and standards in other employees are important. Employees naturally look to those in authority to provide leadership, just as a country's citizens look to its political leaders, and managers become ethical role models whose behavior is scrutinized by subordinates. If top managers are perceived as being self-interested and not ethical, their subordinates are not likely to behave in an ethical manner. Employees may think that if it's all right for a top manager to engage in dubious behavior, it's all right for them, too, and for employees this might mean slacking off, reducing customer support, and not taking supportive actions to help their company. The actions of top managers such as CEOs and the president of the United States are scrutinized so closely for ethical improprieties because their actions represent the values of their organizations and, in the case of the president, the values of the nation.

ethics ombudsperson A manager responsible for communicating and teaching ethical standards to all employees and monitoring their conformity to those standards.

Managers can also provide a visible means of support to develop an ethical culture. Increasingly, organizations are creating the role of ethics officer, or **ethics ombudsperson**, to monitor their ethical practices and procedures. The ethics ombudsperson is responsible for communicating ethical standards to all employees, designing systems to monitor employees' conformity to those standards, and teaching managers and employees at all levels of the organization how to respond to ethical dilemmas appropriately.[70] Because the ethics ombudsperson has organizationwide authority, organizational members in any department can communicate instances of unethical behavior by their managers or coworkers without fear of retribution. This arrangement makes it easier for everyone to behave ethically. In addition, ethics ombudspeople can provide guidance when organizational members are uncertain about whether an action is ethical. Some organizations have an organizationwide ethics committee to provide guidance on ethical issues and help write and update the company code of ethics.

Ethical organizational cultures encourage organizational members to behave in a socially responsible manner. As mentioned earlier in this chapter, one company epitomizing an ethical, socially responsible firm is Johnson & Johnson (J&J). The ethical values and norms in Johnson & Johnson's culture, along with its credo, have guided its managers to make the right decision in difficult situations for decades.

Summary and Review

THE NATURE OF ETHICS Ethical issues are central to how companies and their managers make decisions, and they affect not only the efficiency and effectiveness of company operations but also the prosperity of the nation. The result of ethical behavior is a general increase in company performance and in a nation's standard of living, well-

LO4-1 being, and wealth. An ethical dilemma is the quandary people find themselves in when they have to decide if they should act in a way that might help another person or group and is the right thing to do, even though it might go against their own self-interest. Ethics are the inner guiding moral principles, values, and beliefs that people use to analyze or interpret a situation and then decide what is the right or appropriate way to behave.

Ethical beliefs alter and change as time passes, and as they do so, laws change to reflect the changing ethical beliefs of a society.

LO4-2, 4-4 **STAKEHOLDERS AND ETHICS** Stakeholders are people and groups who have a claim on and a stake in a company. The main stakeholder groups are stockholders, managers, employees, suppliers and distributors, customers, and the community, society, and nation. Companies and their managers need to make ethical business decisions that promote the well-being of their stakeholders and avoid doing them harm.

LO4-3, 4-5 **ETHICS AND DECISION MAKING** To determine whether a business decision is ethical, managers can use four ethical rules to analyze it: the utilitarian, moral rights, justice, and practical rules. Managers should behave ethically because this avoids the tragedy of the commons and results in a general increase in efficiency, effectiveness, and company performance. The main determinants of differences in a manager's, company's, and country's business ethics are societal, occupational, individual, and organizational.

LO4-6 **ETHICS AND SOCIAL RESPONSIBILITY** A company's stance on social responsibility is the way its managers and employees view their duty or obligation to make decisions that protect, enhance, and promote the welfare and well-being of stakeholders and society as a whole.

LO4-6 **ETHICS AND SOCIAL RESPONSIBILITY** There are four main approaches to social responsibility: obstructionist, defensive, accommodative, and proactive. The rewards from behaving in a socially responsible way are a good reputation, the support of all organizational stakeholders, and thus superior company performance.

Management in Action

Topics for Discussion and Action

Discussion

1. What is the relationship between ethics and the law? [LO4-1]
2. Why do the claims and interests of stakeholders sometimes conflict? [LO4-2]
3. Why should managers use ethical criteria to guide their decision making? [LO4-3]
4. As an employee of a company, what are some of the most unethical business practices that you have encountered in its dealings with stakeholders? [LO4-4]
5. What are the main determinants of business ethics? [LO4-5]

Action

6. Find a manager and ask about the most important ethical rules he or she uses to make the right decisions. [LO4-3]
7. Find an example of (a) a company that has an obstructionist approach to social responsibility and (b) one that has an accommodative approach. [LO4-6]

Building Management Skills

Dealing with Ethical Dilemmas [LO4-1, 4-4]

Use the chapter material to decide how you, as a manager, should respond to each of the following ethical dilemmas:

1. You are planning to leave your job to go work for a competitor; your boss invites you to an important meeting where you will learn about new products your company will be bringing out next year. Do you go to the meeting?
2. You're the manager of sales in an expensive sports car dealership. A young executive who has just received a promotion comes in and wants to buy a car that you know is out of her price range. Do you encourage the executive to buy it so you can receive a big commission on the sale?
3. You sign a contract to manage a young rock band, and that group agrees to let you produce their next five records, for which they will receive royalties of 5 percent. Their first record is a smash hit and sells millions. Do you increase their royalty rate on future records?

Managing Ethically [LO4-3, 4-5]

Apple Juice or Sugar Water?

In the early 1980s Beech-Nut, a maker of baby foods, was in grave financial trouble as it tried to compete with Gerber Products, the market leader. Threatened with bankruptcy if it could not lower its operating costs, Beech-Nut entered an agreement with a low-cost supplier of apple juice concentrate. The agreement would save the company over $250,000 annually when every dollar counted. Soon one of Beech-Nut's food scientists became concerned about the quality of the concentrate. He believed it was not made from apples alone but contained large quantities of corn syrup and cane sugar. He brought this information to the attention of top managers at Beech-Nut, but they were obsessed with the need to keep costs down and chose to ignore his concerns. The company continued to produce and sell its product as pure apple juice.[71]

Eventually, investigators from the U.S. Food and Drug Administration (FDA) confronted Beech-Nut with evidence that the concentrate was adulterated. The top managers issued denials and quickly shipped the remaining stock of apple juice to the market before their inventory could be seized. The scientist who had questioned the purity of the apple juice had resigned from Beech-Nut, but he decided to blow the whistle on the company. He told the FDA that Beech-Nut's top management had known of the problem with the concentrate and had acted to maximize company profits rather than to inform customers about the additives in the apple juice. In 1987 the company pleaded guilty to charges that it had deliberately sold adulterated juice and was fined over $2 million. Its top managers were also found guilty and were sentenced to prison terms. The company's reputation was ruined, and it was eventually sold to Ralston Purina, now owned by Nestlé, which installed a new management team and a new ethical code of values to guide future business decisions.

Questions

1. Why is it that an organization's values and norms can become too strong and lead to unethical behavior?
2. What steps can a company take to prevent this problem—to stop its values and norms from becoming so inwardly focused that managers and employees lose sight of their responsibility to their stakeholders?

Small Group Breakout Exercise

Is Chewing Gum the "Right" Thing to Do? [LO4-1, 4-3]

Form groups of three or four people, and appoint one member as the spokesperson who will communicate your findings to the class when called on by the instructor. Then discuss the following scenario:

In the United States, the right to chew gum is taken for granted. Although it is often against the rules to chew gum in a classroom, church, and so on, it is legal to do so on the street. If you possess or chew gum on a street in Singapore, you can be arrested. Chewing gum has been made illegal in Singapore because those in power believe it creates a mess on pavements and feel that people cannot be trusted to dispose of their gum properly and, thus, should have no right to use it.

1. What makes chewing gum acceptable in the United States but unacceptable in Singapore?
2. Why can you chew gum on the street but not in a church?
3. How can you use ethical principles to decide when gum chewing is ethical or unethical and if and when it should be made illegal?

Exploring the World Wide Web [LO4-2, 4-5]

Check out *Fortune*'s list of the World's Most Admired Companies (http://fortune.com/worlds-most-admired-companies/). *Fortune* puts this list together each year based on ratings from executives, directors, and analysts.

1. Select a company on the list and go to that company's web page. How would you describe the company's organizational ethics?
2. What do you believe are the occupational ethics of the people who work at the company?

Be the Manager [LO4-3]

Creating an Ethical Code

You are an entrepreneur who has decided to go into business and open a steak and chicken restaurant. Your business plan requires that you hire at least 20 people as chefs, waiters, and so on. As the owner, you are drawing up a list of ethical principles that each of these people will receive and must agree to when he or she accepts a job offer. These principles outline your view of what is right or acceptable behavior and what will be expected both from you and from your employees.

Create a list of the five main ethical rules or principles you will use to govern how your business operates. Be sure to spell out how these principles relate to your stakeholders; for example, state the rules you intend to follow in dealing with your employees and customers.

Bloomberg Case in the News

Can a Bunch of Doctors Keep an $8 Billion Secret? Not on Twitter [LO4-1, 4-3, 4-6]

In New Orleans Monday, a major medical organization attempted a feat perhaps as hard as treating the disease doctors were there to discuss. They asked a packed convention hall of attendees not to tweet the confidential, market-moving data they had flown in to see.

It didn't work.

In an unusual arrangement, the American Diabetes Association let hundreds, if not thousands, of in-person attendees see new data on Novo Nordisk A/S's blockbuster diabetes treatment Victoza more than an hour before its official release to the public and the markets. That's atypical for such sensitive data, which are usually shared only with journalists and researchers who have agreed to abide by strict terms, under threat of losing future access.

As the Monday afternoon presentation neared, attendees posted on Twitter pictures of the packed hall, of the crowds waiting to get in, and of the projection screens touting the trial's name: "LEADER."

After warning attendees not to share the information they were about to post, presenters in the hall put up slides showing that Bagsvaerd, Denmark-based Novo's drug, cut heart attacks and strokes by 13 percent and improved survival, while also lowering blood sugar rates and a host of other complications. While good news for diabetics, it was less than investors had hoped.

Tweets

Within minutes, some Twitter accounts were posting pictures of the charts, including key slides that showed the drug's success in reducing deaths. And as fast as the posts went up, the medical society's communications team issued online pleas for them to stop.

"#2016ADA slides include unpublished data and are the intellectual property of the presenters," the association tweeted at accounts who posted the data. "Please delete immediately."

"Wow—that was fast. Just got slammed for posting embargoed data from the session. Better stop :-(" was posted by the account @LoenborgMadsen, which put up several pictures containing slides [of] the presentation. Attempts to get a person associated with the account to comment were unsuccessful.

It was too little, too late. Some of the tweets had already been retweeted by others, making it impossible to scrub the information from the web. One account, @AndyBiotech, whose online description claims he's an investor, retweeted the images to his more than 18,000 followers. An attempt to reach the person behind the account wasn't immediately successful.

Shares Drop

On Tuesday, Novo's shares fell 5.6 percent to 343 kroner, for their biggest one-day drop since February—confirmation of how important the information was to the market. The decline represented about a 52 billion kroner ($7.77 billion) decline in market value.

Officials from the ADA and Novo Nordisk didn't respond to requests for comment on the way the events of the day unfolded. Earlier Monday, a Novo spokeswoman said a detailed press release after the embargo lifted was sufficient, since the company had previously communicated the general results of the study.

The meeting organizers appeared aware of the potential for a leak. The moderator at the session, Matthew Riddle, an endocrinologist from Oregon Health & Science University in Portland, announced the embargo date and time at the start of the session, and the restrictions on sharing the data were noted on multiple slides.

Not the First Time

It's not the first time medical meeting organizers have tried to restrict the distribution of information from the event they are running, said Ivan Oransky, global editorial director of MedPage Today. Oransky runs the Embargo Watch website, which tracks leaks of confidential medical and scientific data. While the ADA in particular has improved in recent years, Monday's events were a backslide, he said in a telephone interview.

"You can't embargo something that is being discussed publicly," Oransky said. "Why are they trying to control the flow of information, especially in this case where the results could influence public health and the markets? Hopefully other organizations won't take this as a signal they can do the same thing."

Source: Cortez, Michelle, "Can a Bunch of Doctors Keep an $8 Billion Secret? Not on Twitter," *Bloomberg*, June 14, 2016. Used with permission of Bloomberg.

Questions for Discussion

1. Do you think it was unethical that the attendees tweeted out information about the new drug and results of the study? Why or why not?
2. How have social media platforms such as Twitter and Facebook changed the discussion about confidentiality and social responsibility? Explain.
3. Suppose you were the marketing director at a pharmaceutical company that had just received promising results about a new drug still in the development stage. What ethical responsibilities do you have to keep the information confidential?

Notes

1. "Preventing Bullying in Schools with No Bully" and "Responding to Bullying with Crisis Text Line," www.toms.com, accessed June 15, 2016.
2. "Best Sellers: Backpacks," www.toms.com, accessed June 15, 2016.
3. "Giving Sight," www.toms.com, accessed June 15, 2016; "TOMS Introduces TOMS Eyewear, the Next One for One Product," *PR Newswire,* www.prnewswire.com, June 7, 2011.
4. "Giving Water," www.toms.com, accessed June 15, 2016.
5. A. Morris, "How Crisis Text Line Founder Nancy Lublin Is Saving Lives, Text by Text," *Glamour,* www.glamour.com, June 19, 2015 "Preventing Bullying in Schools with No Bully."
6. M. Isaza, "Founder of Shoe Giveaway Company TOMS Looks Back on 10 Years," Associated Press, http://bigstory.ap.org, May 6, 2016.
7. www.apple.com, press release, 2012.
8. E. G. Brosious, "At Least 20 States Could Vote on Marijuana Legalization in 2016," *Sun Times Network,* http://national.suntimes.com, February 19, 2016.
9. "About Occupy Wall Street," http://occupywallst.org, accessed June 15, 2016; M. Bruce, "Obama Says Wall St. Protests Voice Widespread Frustrations," *ABC News,* http://abcnews.go, October 6, 2011.
10. R.E. Freeman, *Strategic Management: A Stakeholder Approach* (Marshfield, MA: Pitman, 1984).
11. "Foundation Fact Sheet: Who We Are," www.gatesfoundation.org, accessed June 15, 2016; S. Bianchi, "Bill Gates Seeks $1.5 Billion More to Eradicate Polio by 2018," *Bloomberg,* www.bloomberg.com, April 25, 2012.
12. J.A. Pearce, "The Company Mission as a Strategic Tool," *Sloan Management Review,* Spring 1982, 15–24.
13. H. Bapuji and S. Riaz, "Occupy Wall Street: What Businesses Need to Know," *Harvard Business Review,* blogs.hbr.org/2011/10/occupy-wall-street-what-business/, October 14, 2011.
14. C.I. Barnard, *The Functions of the Executive* (Cambridge, MA: Harvard University Press, 1948).
15. Freeman, *Strategic Management.*
16. R. Rothacker, "Bank of America Plans to Reduce Consumer Workforce by Thousands More," *The Charlotte Observer,* www.charlotteobserver.com, June 15, 2016.
17. P.S. Adler, "Corporate Scandals: It's Time for Reflection in Business Schools," *Academy of Management Executive* 16 (August 2002), 148–50.
18. K. To, "The Volcker Rule: More Work to Be Done," Global Association of Risk Professionals, www.garp.org, November 6, 2015; C. Main, "Volcker Rule, EU Bank Deadlock, Deutsche Bank Risk: Compliance," *Bloomberg,* www.bloomberg.com, December 10, 2013.
19. Equilar, "Equilar/Associated Press S&P 500 CEO Pay Study 2016," www.equilar.com, May 25, 2016.
20. W.G. Sanders and D.C. Hambrick, "Swinging for the Fences: The Effects of CEO Stock Options on Company Risk Taking and Performance," *Academy of Management Journal* 53, no. 5 (2007), 1055–78.
21. K. Smith, "Who Has Signed the Bangladesh Safety Accord—Update," *Just-Style,* www.just-style.com, February 8, 2016; R. Bowman, Is This the Year When Supply Chains Become Socially Responsible?" *Forbes,* www.forbes.com, March 14, 2011.
22. S. Greenhouse, "Bangladesh Inspections Find Gaps in Safety," *The New York Times,* www.nytimes.com, March 11, 2014.
23. Ibid.
24. R. Cho, "What Happens to All That Plastic?" blogs.ei.columbia.edu/2012/01/31/what-happens-to-all-that-plastic/, January 31, 2012.
25. A.C. Steinemann, I.C. MacGregor, S.M. Gordon, L.G. Gallagher, A.L. Davis, D.S. Ribeiro, et al., "Fragranced Consumer Products: Chemicals Emitted, Ingredients Unlisted," *Environ Impact Review* 31 (2011), 328–33.
26. The Soap Dispensary, www.facebook.com/pages/The-Soap-Dispensary/266253066720178, March 5, 2014.
27. N. Yeh, "Rethink, Re-Use," *Pacific Rim Magazine,* http://langaraprm.com, May 2, 2016.
28. N. Burg, "How One Business Diverted 8,000 Plastic Bottles from Landfills," *Forbes,* www.forbes.com, March 16, 2014.
29. T.L. Beauchamp and N.E. Bowie, eds., *Ethical Theory and Business* (Englewood Cliffs, NJ: Prentice-Hall, 1929); A. MacIntyre, *After Virtue* (South Bend, IN: University of Notre Dame Press, 1981).
30. R.E. Goodin, "How to Determine Who Should Get What," *Ethics,* July 1975, 310–21.
31. E.P. Kelly, "A Better Way to Think about Business" (book review), *Academy of Management Executive* 14 (May 2000), 127–29.
32. T.M. Jones, "Ethical Decision Making by Individuals in Organization: An Issue Contingent Model," *Academy of Management Journal* 16 (1991), 366–95; G.F. Cavanaugh, D.J. Moberg, and M. Velasquez, "The Ethics of Organizational Politics," *Academy of Management Review* 6 (1981), 363–74.
33. L.K. Trevino, "Ethical Decision Making in Organizations: A Person-Situation Interactionist Model," *Academy of Management Review* 11 (1986), 601–17; W.H. Shaw and V. Barry, *Moral Issues in Business,* 6th ed. (Belmont, CA: Wadsworth, 1995).
34. T.M. Jones, "Instrumental Stakeholder Theory: A Synthesis of Ethics and Economics," *Academy of Management Review* 20 (1995), 404–37.
35. B. Victor and J.B. Cullen, "The Organizational Bases of Ethical Work Climates," *Administrative Science Quarterly* 33 (1988), 101–25.
36. D. Collins, "Organizational Harm, Legal Consequences and Stakeholder Retaliation," *Journal of Business Ethics* 8 (1988), 1–13.
37. R.C. Solomon, *Ethics and Excellence* (New York: Oxford University Press, 1992).
38. T.E. Becker, "Integrity in Organizations: Beyond Honesty and Conscientiousness," *Academy of Management Review* 23 (January 1998), 154–62.
39. S.W. Gellerman, "Why Good Managers Make Bad Decisions," in K.R. Andrews, ed., *Ethics in Practice: Managing the Moral Corporation* (Boston: Harvard Business School Press, 1989).
40. J. Dobson, "Corporate Reputation: A Free Market Solution to Unethical Behavior," *Business and Society* 28 (1989), 1–5.
41. M.S. Baucus and J.P. Near, "Can Illegal Corporate Behavior Be Predicted? An Event History Analysis," *Academy of Management Journal* 34 (1991), 9–36.
42. Trevino, "Ethical Decision Making in Organizations."
43. "The World's Most Ethical Companies 2016 Honorees," Ethisphere Institute, http://worldsmostethicalcompanies.ethisphere.com, accessed June 15, 2016.
44. A.S. Waterman, "On the Uses of Psychological Theory and Research in the Process of Ethical Inquiry," *Psychological Bulletin* 103, no. 3 (1988), 283–98.
45. A. Knobloch, "Siemens Bribery Case Spreads to Brazilian Politics," *DW,* www.dw.de/siemens-bribery-case-spreads-to-brazilian-politics/a-17268276, March 12, 2012.

46. "2015 Corruption by Country/Territory: Brazil," Transparency International, https://www.transparency.org, accessed June 15, 2016.
47. I. Watson and V. Cotovio, "Rio Mayor Welcomes Federal Olympic Investigation," *CNN*, www.cnn.com, May 26, 2016.
48. R. Kanani, "CEO of Tiffany & Co. on Ethical Sourcing, Responsible Mining, and Leadership," *Forbes*, www.forbes.com/sites/rahimkanani/2014/01/19/ceo-of-tiffany-co-on-ethical-sourcing-responsible-mining-and-leadership/, January 19, 2014.
49. "About IRMA," www.responsiblemining.net, accessed June 15, 2016.
50. Ibid.
51. "About KP Basics," https://www.kimberleyprocess.com, accessed June 15, 2016.
52. "CEO of Tiffany & Co. on Ethical Sourcing, Responsible Mining, and Leadership."
53. M.S. Frankel, "Professional Codes: Why, How, and with What Impact?" *Ethics* 8 (1989), 109–15.
54. J. Van Maanen and S.R. Barley, "Occupational Communities: Culture and Control in Organizations," in B. Staw and L. Cummings, eds., *Research in Organizational Behavior*, vol. 6 (Greenwich, CT: JAI Press, 1984), 287–365.
55. M. Maynard, "The Steep Cost of Toyota's Settlement with the U.S. Government," *Forbes*, www.forbes.com/sites/michelinemaynard/2014/03/19/the-steep-cost-of-toyotas-settlement-with-the-u-s-government/, March 19, 2014.
56. B. Snyder, "GM's $900 Million Settlement Isn't the Biggest in History," *Fortune*, http://fortune.com, September 17, 2015.
57. Jones, "Ethical Decision Making."
58. "About Let's Move," www.letsmove.gov, accessed June 15, 2016.
59. Ibid.
60. K. Thompson and T. Carman, "A Healthful Legacy: Michelle Obama Looks to the Future of 'Let's Move,'" *The Washington Post*, https://www.washingtonpost.com, May 3, 2015.
61. H. Cardello, "Better-for-You Foods: It's Just Good Business,"www.hudson.org, October 13, 2011.
62. "GM: Steps to a Recall Nightmare," *CNN Money*, http://money.cnn.com, accessed June 15, 2016.
63. "Fitbit Force Skin Irritation FAQs," *fitbithelp*, February 26, 2014, https://help.fitbit.com/customer/portal/articles/1425569.
64. M. Friedman, "A Friedman Doctrine: The Social Responsibility of Business Is to Increase Its Profits," *The New York Times Magazine*, September 13, 1970, 33.
65. P. Hurtado and M. Keller, "How the Feds Pulled Off the Biggest Insider-Trading Investigation in U.S. History," *Bloomberg*, www.bloomberg.com, June 9, 2016.
66. "2015 Annual Report," www.nucor.com, accessed June 15, 2016.
67. P. Engardio and M. Arndt, "What Price Reputation?" July 9, 2007, www.businessweek.com.
68. "2015 Southwest Airlines One Report," www.southwest.com, accessed June 15, 2016.
69. G.R. Jones, *Organizational Theory: Text and Cases* (Englewood Cliffs, NJ: Prentice-Hall, 2008).
70. P.E. Murphy, "Creating Ethical Corporate Structure," *Sloan Management Review*, Winter 1989, 81–87.
71. R. Johnson, "Ralston to Buy Beechnut, Gambling It Can Overcome Apple Juice Scandal," *The Wall Street Journal*, September 18, 1989, B11.

CHAPTER 6

Managing in the Global Environment

Learning Objectives

After studying this chapter, you should be able to:

LO6-1 Explain why the ability to perceive, interpret, and respond appropriately to the global environment is crucial for managerial success.

LO6-2 Differentiate between the global task and global general environments.

LO6-3 Identify the main forces in the global task and general environments, and describe the challenges that each force presents to managers.

LO6-4 Explain why the global environment is becoming more open and competitive, and identify the forces behind the process of globalization that increase the opportunities, complexities, challenges, and threats managers face.

LO6-5 Discuss why national cultures differ and why it is important that managers be sensitive to the effects of falling trade barriers and regional trade associations on the political and social systems of nations around the world.

A MANAGER'S CHALLENGE

Turning Off the Water in Global Manufacturing

As part of globalization, how should managers think about sustainability when it comes to water usage? The textile industry has a huge water footprint. Annually it uses about 6 trillion liters of fresh water in various manufacturing processes, as well as to grow cotton, the material that accounts for 90 percent of the industry's use of natural fibers. One estimate suggests that nearly 700 gallons of water are needed to produce each cotton T-shirt made around the world. The farming of cotton accounts for 2.6 percent of annual global water usage and is the largest water consumption factor in the supply chain of the textile industry. And it's not just quantity. Cotton production has a direct impact on water quality through the use of pesticides, herbicides, and fertilizers.[1]

Problems continue beyond the growing of raw materials. The textile industry uses and pollutes water while dyeing fabrics. It can take more than 6 gallons of water to dye one T-shirt. The polyester apparel industry alone uses 2.4 trillion gallons of water a year. Fabric treatment, rinsing, and dyeing account for about 20 percent of the world's industrial water pollution. Dye houses in China and India have been accused of overusing local water supplies as well as dumping toxic wastewater into local water supplies.[2] In response to concerns about the use and pollution of water to make fabric and garments, several manufacturers have sought no-water and reduced-water ways of working in their supply chains.

In 2016 Levi Strauss & Co., in collaboration with textile technology start-up Evrnu, created the world's first pair of jeans using discarded cotton T-shirts to make new fiber. The new method not only converts consumer waste (like old T-shirts) into renewable fiber but also uses 98 percent less water than other virgin cotton products. Although some virgin cotton was used in the manufacturing process, this method represents a major breakthrough in recycling technology and holds great promise for reducing water usage.[3]

Nike and Adidas also are cutting back on water use in their supply chains by using a

Global companies, in collaboration with the textile industry, are working to reduce the amount of water needed to dye cotton and other fabrics in the manufacturing process for T-shirts and other apparel.
© PhotoLink/Getty Images RF

process that dyes polyester without using water or chemicals. The process, developed by DyeCoo Textile Systems of the Netherlands, dyes fabric by turning carbon dioxide into a liquid by putting it under extreme pressure. As the carbon dioxide cools, it turns back into a gas that can be recycled and used again. Nike began selling products manufactured using the process in 2014 under the name Nike ColorDry, manufactured in the company's water-free dyeing facility in Taiwan.[4] Adidas also started waterless dyeing in 2012, producing a limited collection of 50,000 T-shirts with the Yeh Group, which owns a textile mill in Thailand. More than five years later, Adidas has rolled out the technology across various product categories and has realized major water savings using this innovative process.[5]

Nike COO Eric Sprunk believes that as more companies recognize the need to reduce their dependence on limited resources such as water, manufacturing innovation can play a key role in developing sustainable business practices around the world.[6]

Overview

Top managers of a global company like Nike operate in an environment where they compete with other companies for scarce and valuable resources. Managers of companies large and small have found that to survive and prosper in the 21st century, most organizations must become **global organizations** that operate and compete not only domestically, at home, but also globally, in countries around the world. Operating in the global environment is uncertain and unpredictable because it is complex and changes constantly.

global organization An organization that operates and competes in more than one country.

LO6-1 Explain why the ability to perceive, interpret, and respond appropriately to the global environment is crucial for managerial success.

If organizations are to adapt successfully to this changing environment, their managers must learn to understand the forces that operate in it and how these forces give rise to opportunities and threats. In this chapter we examine why the environment, both domestically and globally, has become more open, vibrant, and competitive. We examine how forces in the task and general environments affect global organizations and their managers. By the end of this chapter, you will appreciate the changes that are taking place in the environment and understand why it is important for managers to develop a global perspective as they strive to increase organizational efficiency and effectiveness.

What Is the Global Environment?

The **global environment** is a set of forces and conditions in the world outside an organization's boundary that affects how it operates and shapes its behavior.[7] These forces change over time and thus present managers with *opportunities* and *threats*. Some changes in the global environment, such as the development of efficient new production technology, the availability of lower-cost components, or the opening of new global markets, create opportunities for managers to make and sell more products, obtain more resources and capital, and thereby strengthen their organization. In contrast, the rise of new global competitors, a global economic recession, or an oil shortage poses threats that can devastate an organization if managers are unable to sell its products. The quality of managers' understanding of forces in the global environment and their ability to respond appropriately to those forces, such as Samsung's managers' ability to make and sell the electronic products that customers around the world want to buy, are critical factors affecting organizational performance.

LO6-2 Differentiate between the global task and global general environments.

global environment The set of global forces and conditions that operates beyond an organization's boundaries but affects a manager's ability to acquire and utilize resources.

In this chapter we explore the nature of these forces and consider how managers can respond to them. To identify opportunities and threats caused by forces in the environment, it is helpful for managers to distinguish between the *task environment* and the more encompassing *general environment* (see Figure 6.1).

Figure 6.1
Forces in the Global Environment

task environment The set of forces and conditions that originates with suppliers, distributors, customers, and competitors and affects an organization's ability to obtain inputs and dispose of its outputs. These forces and conditions influence managers daily.

general environment The wide-ranging global, economic, technological, sociocultural, demographic, political, and legal forces that affect an organization and its task environment.

The **task environment** is the set of forces and conditions that originates with global suppliers, distributors, customers, and competitors; these forces and conditions affect an organization's ability to obtain inputs and dispose of its outputs. The task environment contains the forces that have the most *immediate* and *direct* effect on managers because they pressure and influence managers daily. When managers turn on the radio or television, arrive at their offices in the morning, open their mail, or look at their computer screens, they are likely to learn about problems facing them because of changing conditions in their organization's task environment.

The **general environment** includes the wide-ranging global, economic, technological, sociocultural, demographic, political, and legal forces that affect the organization and its task environment. For the individual manager, opportunities and threats resulting from changes in the general environment are often more difficult to identify and respond to than are events in the task environment. However, changes in these forces can have major impacts on managers and their organizations.

The Task Environment

Forces in the task environment result from the actions of suppliers, distributors, customers, and competitors both at home and abroad (see Figure 6.1). These four groups affect a manager's ability to obtain resources and dispose of outputs daily, weekly, and monthly and thus have a significant impact on short-term decision making.

suppliers Individuals and organizations that provide an organization with the input resources it needs to produce goods and services.

Suppliers

Suppliers are the individuals and companies that provide an organization with the input resources (such as raw materials, component parts, or employees) it needs to produce goods

LO6-3 Identify the main forces in the global task and general environments, and describe the challenges that each force presents to managers.

and services. In return, the suppliers receive payment for those goods and services. An important aspect of a manager's job is to ensure a reliable supply of input resources.

Consider, for example, Dell, a leading PC company. Dell has many suppliers of component parts for its laptops and tablets, such as microprocessors (Intel) and graphics cards (Nvidia and Intel). It also has suppliers of pre-installed software, including the operating system and specific applications software (Microsoft, Google Chrome, and Adobe). Dell's providers of capital, such as banks and other financial institutions, are also important suppliers.

Dell has several suppliers of labor. One source is the educational institutions that train future Dell employees and therefore provide the company with skilled workers. Another is trade unions, organizations that represent employee interests and can control the supply of labor by exercising the right of unionized workers to strike. Unions also can influence the terms and conditions under which labor is employed. Dell's workers are not unionized; when layoffs became necessary because of the financial crisis and recession in 2009, Dell had few problems in laying off workers to reduce costs. In organizations and industries where unions are strong, however, such as the transportation industry, an important part of a manager's job is negotiating and administering agreements with unions and their representatives.

Changes in the nature, number, or type of suppliers produce opportunities and threats to which managers must respond if their organizations are to prosper. For example, a major supplier-related threat that confronts managers arises when suppliers' bargaining positions are so strong that they can raise the prices of the inputs they supply to the organization. A supplier's bargaining position is especially strong when (1) the supplier is the sole source of an input and (2) the input is vital to the organization.[8] For example, for 17 years G. D. Searle was the sole supplier of NutraSweet, the artificial sweetener used in most diet soft drinks. Not only was NutraSweet an important ingredient in diet soft drinks, but it also was one for which there was no acceptable substitute (saccharin and other artificial sweeteners raised health concerns). Searle earned its privileged position because it invented and held the patent for NutraSweet, and patents prohibit other organizations from introducing competing products for 17 years. As a result, Searle was able to demand a high price for NutraSweet, charging twice the price of an equivalent amount of sugar; and paying that price raised the costs of soft drink manufacturers such as Coca-Cola and PepsiCo. When Searle's patent expired, many other companies introduced products similar to NutraSweet, and prices fell.[9] In the 2000s Splenda, which was made by McNeil Nutritionals, owned by Tate & Lyle, a British company, replaced NutraSweet as the artificial sweetener of choice, and NutraSweet's price fell further; Splenda began to command a high price from soft drink companies.[10]

However, a new sweetener introduced less than a decade ago has gained market share on Splenda. The noncaloric, natural sweetener Truvia moved to the number 2 position in the sweetener market recently. The market for stevia-based sweeteners such as Truvia is expected to grow to $275 million—more than double the market size of less than five years ago.[11]

In contrast, when an organization has many suppliers for a particular input, it is in a relatively strong bargaining position with those suppliers and can demand low-cost, high-quality inputs from them. Often an organization can use its power with suppliers to force them to reduce their prices, as Dell frequently does. Dell, for example, is constantly searching for low-cost suppliers abroad to keep its prices competitive. At a global level, organizations can buy products from suppliers overseas or become their own suppliers by manufacturing their products abroad.

It is important that managers recognize the opportunities and threats associated with managing the global supply chain. On one hand, gaining access to low-cost products made abroad represents an opportunity for U.S. companies to lower their input costs. On the other hand, managers who fail to use low-cost overseas suppliers create a threat and put their organizations at a competitive disadvantage.[12] Levi Strauss, for example, was slow to realize that it could not compete with the low-priced jeans sold by Walmart and other retailers, and it was eventually forced to close all its U.S. jean factories and outsource manufacturing to low-cost overseas suppliers to cut the price of its jeans to a competitive level. Now it sells its low-priced jeans in Walmart. The downside to global outsourcing is, of course, the loss of millions of U.S. jobs, an issue we have discussed in previous chapters.

A common problem facing managers of large, global companies such as Ford, Sony, and Dell is managing the development of a global supplier network that will allow their companies to keep costs down and quality high. For example, Boeing's 777 jet was originally built using many components from over 500 global suppliers; eight Japanese suppliers made parts for the 777 fuselage, doors, and wings.[13] Boeing chose these suppliers because they were the best in the world at performing their particular activities, and Boeing's goal was to produce a high-quality final product.[14] Pleased with the outcome, Boeing decided to outsource a greater percentage of components to global suppliers when it designed the new Boeing 787 Dreamliner; however, many serious problems delayed the introduction of the new aircraft for several years.

The purchasing activities of global companies have become increasingly complicated as a result of the development of a whole range of skills and competencies in different countries around the world. It is clearly in companies' interests to search out the lowest-cost, best-quality suppliers. IT and the Internet are continually making it easier for companies to coordinate complicated long-distance exchanges involving the purchasing of inputs and the disposal of outputs—something many global companies have taken advantage of as they consolidate the number of suppliers to reduce costs.

global outsourcing The purchase or production of inputs or final products from overseas suppliers to lower costs and improve product quality or design.

Global outsourcing occurs when a company contracts with suppliers in other countries to make the various inputs or components that go into its products or to assemble the final products to reduce costs. For example, Apple contracts with companies in Taiwan and China to make inputs such as the chips, batteries, and LCD displays that power its digital devices; then it contracts with outsourcers such as Foxconn to assemble its final products—such as iPhones and iPads. Apple also outsources the distribution of its products around the world by contracting with companies such as FedEx or UPS.

Global outsourcing has grown enormously to take advantage of national differences in the cost and quality of resources such as labor or raw materials that can significantly reduce manufacturing costs or increase product quality or reliability. Today such global exchanges are becoming so complex that some companies specialize in managing other companies' global supply chains. Global companies use the services of overseas intermediaries or brokers, which are located close to potential suppliers, to find the suppliers that can best meet the needs of a particular company. They can design the most efficient supply chain for a company to outsource the component and assembly operations required to produce its final products. Because these suppliers are located in thousands of cities in many countries, finding them is difficult. Li & Fung, based in Hong Kong, is one broker that has helped hundreds of major U.S. companies to outsource their component or assembly operations to suitable overseas suppliers, especially suppliers in mainland China.[15]

Although outsourcing to take advantage of low labor costs has helped many companies perform better, in the 2010s its risks have also become apparent, especially when issues such as reliability, quality, and speed are important. In 2012 General Electric moved the production of its hybrid water heater from China to Kentucky due to rising wages in China and increasing transportation costs. Moving production back to the United States also gave the company more control over the product quality. When all the savings were taken into account, the Kentucky plant was able to produce a better product at a lower price than the plant in China. In 2016 GE sold its appliance business to China's Haier Group, which will maintain the GE brand headquarters in Louisville, Kentucky, along with more than 6,000 employees.[16] Apple also brought the manufacture of its next generation of personal computers to the United States. The new Mac Pro is manufactured in Austin, Texas.[17] On the other hand, some companies do not outsource manufacturing; they prefer to establish their own assembly operations and factories in countries around the world to protect their proprietary technology. For example, most global automakers own their production operations in China to retain control over their global decision making and keep their operations secret. Regardless of outsourcing strategies, companies that conduct business via the Internet must ensure that their websites accommodate various cultures and customs around the world. See the accompanying "Managing Globally" feature for more details.

The purchasing activities of global companies have become increasingly complicated. Hundreds of suppliers around the world produce parts for Boeing's 787 Dreamliner.
© John van Hasselt/Corbis via Getty Images

MANAGING GLOBALLY

Going Global on the World Wide Web

Being a global organization is one thing; having a global presence on the Internet is another. Many organizations do not have a truly global website. For companies selling goods or services on the Internet, the checkout process alone is full of challenges. Users who want to buy something will typically be directed to an online checkout form to fill out with shipping and billing information. These forms alone present challenges. For example, when asking customers for information, a U.S. company's website form might ask for the person's "last name." In other cultures, the last name is called the "family name" or "surname." Also, in many cultures, last names are much longer than many Western names and require more spaces in the website's form.[18]

Then there's the name of the checkout area on the website. What do you call the place where a customer can store the names of goods until they are purchased? In the United States, Amazon uses the term *shopping cart* in its checkout process. In the United Kingdom, it uses *shopping basket*.[19]

There are other concerns to be addressed in the checkout process, including having users select their country or region versus using geolocation, offering support via phone, providing billing and shipping information that is country or region specific, and specifying acceptable payment platforms such as Paypal or Visa.[20]

The 2016 Web Globalization Report Card from Byte Level Research provides input into the challenges of globalizing a website.[21] The 280-page report describes the best and worst practices in website globalization and ranks the best and worst sites. It praises companies at the top of the list, including Google, Facebook, and Hotels.com for their efforts at localization. These efforts include using local images instead of stock photos, having culture-specific content, and using language that is not only translated but also culturally nuanced. The 25 companies whose websites ranked at the top of the 2016 list support an average of 52 languages. Use of a global design template also helped company web pages score near the top of the list. While localization is important, the report stresses the importance of a consistent look across countries.[22]

At the other end of the list are those that received poor scores. Their shortcomings, according to the report card, were often the opposite of what the best companies did right. Not every website with a low score did all of these things wrong, but they did some combination of poor practices that put them toward the bottom of the list. Many fell short on localization, especially on language translation. Many did not have "global gateways" to local websites, or they were inconsistent. Another big problem was the lack of a global design template.[23]

To compete successfully in the global marketplace, companies must create websites that can be used by consumers in all parts of the world.
© NetPhotos3/Alamy

"Lack of global consistency is an issue with many websites," John Yunker, author of the Web Globalization Report Card, said in a blog post about the report. "That is, each country web team appears to have gone off on its own and created a website from scratch instead of working across company to share common design templates and resources."[24]

Globalization is a key factor for any business trying to extend its reach across the world. Websites that do not address local customs and cultures stand to lose out when it comes to e-commerce and other web-based business. According to recent data from the 2016 Checkout Conversion Index, ineffective websites for U.S. merchants could cost these companies more than $162 billion in potential sales because their websites are too slow or too complicated for consumers to navigate.[25]

Distributors

distributors Organizations that help other organizations sell their goods or services to customers.

Distributors are organizations that help other organizations sell their goods or services to customers. The decisions managers make about how to distribute products to customers can have important effects on organizational performance. For example, package delivery companies such as Federal Express, UPS, and the U.S. Postal Service have become vital distributors for the millions of items bought online and shipped to customers by Internet companies, both at home and abroad.

The changing nature of distributors and distribution methods can bring opportunities and threats for managers. If distributors become so large and powerful that they can control customers' access to a particular organization's goods and services, they can threaten the organization by demanding that it reduce the prices of its goods and services.[26] For example, the huge retail distributor Walmart controls its suppliers' access to millions of customers and, thus, can demand that its suppliers reduce their prices to keep its business. If an organization such as Procter & Gamble refuses to reduce its prices, Walmart might respond by buying products only from Procter & Gamble's competitors—companies such as Unilever and Colgate. Walmart used its power as a distributor recently to demand additional fees from U.S. suppliers for using Walmart distribution centers and warehouses. The retail giant has also changed the frequency of payments to some vendors—tying payment to how quickly a supplier's inventory moves off the shelves at Walmart stores.[27]

In 2014 the Bridgestone Corporation joined more than two dozen Japanese automotive suppliers who had already pled guilty to conspiring to fix the prices of parts sold to automakers. The Tokyo-based company was accused of conspiring to allocate sales, prearrange bids, and fix prices of parts sold.[28] It paid a $425 million criminal fine, higher than the fines given the other suppliers due to a previous price-fixing conviction. The multiyear investigation was the largest criminal investigation by the Justice Department's Antitrust Division.

Customers

customers Individuals and groups that buy the goods and services an organization produces.

Customers are the individuals and groups that buy the goods and services an organization produces. For example, Dell's customers can be segmented into several distinct groups: (1) individuals who purchase PCs for home use, (2) small companies, (3) large companies, and (4) government agencies and educational institutions. Changes in the number and types of customers or in customers' tastes and needs create opportunities and threats. An organization's success depends on its responsiveness to customers—whether it can satisfy their needs. In the PC industry, customers are demanding smaller computers, longer battery life, new apps, and lower prices—and PC makers must respond to the changing types and needs of customers, such as by introducing smarter systems that recognize voice commands instead of requiring bulky keyboards.[29] A school, too, must adapt to the changing needs of its customers. For example, if more Spanish-speaking students enroll, additional classes in English as a second language may need to be scheduled. A manager's ability to identify an organization's main customer groups, and make the products that best satisfy their particular needs, is a crucial factor affecting organizational and managerial success.

The most obvious opportunity associated with expanding into the global environment is the prospect of selling goods and services to millions or billions of new customers, as Amazon.com's CEO, Jeff Bezos, discovered when he expanded his company's operations in many countries.[30] Similarly, Accenture and Cap Gemini, two large consulting companies, established regional operating centers around the globe, and they recruit and train thousands of overseas consultants to serve the needs of customers in their respective world regions.

Today many products have gained global customer acceptance. This consolidation is occurring both for consumer goods and for business products and has created enormous opportunities for managers. The worldwide acceptance of Coca-Cola, Apple iPads, McDonald's hamburgers, and Samsung smartphones is a sign that the tastes and preferences of customers in different countries may not be so different after all.[31] Likewise, large, global markets exist for business products such as telecommunications equipment, electronic components, and computer and financial services. Thus, Cisco and Siemens sell their telecommunications equipment; Intel, its microprocessors; and Oracle and SAP, their business systems management software, to customers all over the world.

Competitors

competitors Organizations that produce goods and services that are similar to a particular organization's goods and services.

One of the most important forces an organization confronts in its task environment is competitors. **Competitors** are organizations that produce goods and services similar and comparable to a particular organization's goods and services. In other words, competitors are organizations trying to attract the same customers. Dell's competitors include other domestic PC makers (such as Apple and HP) as well as overseas competitors (such as Sony and Toshiba in Japan, Lenovo in China, and Acer in Taiwan). Similarly, online stockbroker E*Trade has other competitors such as Ameritrade, Scottrade, and Charles Schwab.

Rivalry between competitors is potentially the most threatening force managers must deal with. A high level of rivalry typically results in price competition, and falling prices reduce customer revenues and profits. In the early 2000s competition in the PC industry became intense because Dell was aggressively cutting costs and prices to increase its global market share.[32] IBM had to exit the PC business after it lost billions in its battle against low-cost rivals, and HP also suffered losses while Dell's profits soared. By 2006, however, HP's fortunes had recovered because it had found ways to lower its costs and offer stylish new PCs, and Apple was growing rapidly, so Dell's profit margins continued to shrink. In 2009 HP overtook Dell to become the largest global PC maker. However, it did not hold on to the lead. At the end of 2013 Lenovo overtook HP for the top spot, pushing Dell to number 3. Lenovo continues to hold the title of the world's largest PC maker, while Dell has become a privately held company focusing its business strategies on becoming more of an an all-around technology company and less of a PC maker.[33]

potential competitors Organizations that presently are not in a task environment but can enter if they so choose.

Although extensive rivalry between existing competitors is a major threat to profitability, so is the potential for new competitors to enter the task environment. **Potential competitors** are organizations that are not presently in a task environment but have the resources to enter if they so choose. In 2010 Amazon.com, for example, was not in the furniture or large appliance business, but it could enter these businesses if its managers decided it could profitably sell such products online—and by 2012, the e-commerce giant had begun to sell furniture and appliances. When new competitors enter an industry, competition increases and prices and profits decrease—as furniture and electronics stores such as Best Buy have discovered as they battle Amazon.com.

barriers to entry Factors that make it difficult and costly for an organization to enter a particular task environment or industry.

BARRIERS TO ENTRY In general, the potential for new competitors to enter a task environment (and thus increase competition) is a function of barriers to entry.[34] **Barriers to entry** are factors that make it difficult and costly for a company to enter a particular task environment or industry.[35] In other words, the more difficult and costly it is to enter the task environment, the higher are the barriers to entry. The higher the barriers to entry, the fewer the competitors in an organization's task environment and, thus, the lower the threat of competition. With fewer competitors, it is easier to obtain customers and keep prices high.

economies of scale Cost advantages associated with large operations.

Barriers to entry result from three main sources: economies of scale, brand loyalty, and government regulations that impede entry (see Figure 6.2). **Economies of scale** are the cost advantages associated with large operations. Economies of scale result from factors such as manufacturing products in very large quantities, buying inputs in bulk, or making more effective use of organizational resources than do competitors by fully utilizing employees' skills and knowledge. If organizations already in the task environment are large and enjoy significant economies of scale, their costs are lower than the costs that potential entrants will face, and newcomers will find it expensive to enter the industry. Amazon.com, for example, enjoys significant economies of scale relative to most other Internet companies because of its highly efficient distribution system.[36]

brand loyalty Customers' preference for the products of organizations currently existing in the task environment.

Brand loyalty is customers' preference for the products of organizations currently in the task environment. If established organizations enjoy significant brand loyalty, a new entrant will find it difficult and costly to obtain a share of the market. Newcomers must bear huge marketing costs to build customer awareness of the goods or services they intend to provide.[37]

Figure 6.2

Barriers to Entry and Competition

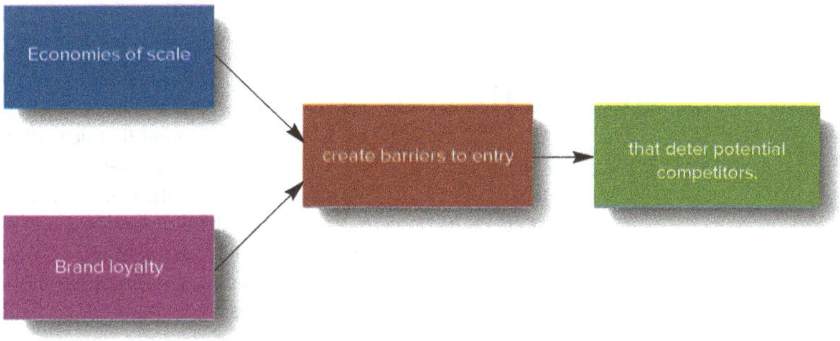

Today Apple, Google, Samsung, and Amazon enjoy a high level of brand loyalty and have some of the highest website hit rates, which allows them to increase their marketing revenues.

In some cases, *government regulations* function as a barrier to entry at both the industry and the country levels. Many industries that were deregulated, such as air transport, trucking, utilities, and telecommunications, experienced a high level of new entry after deregulation; this forced existing companies in those industries to operate more efficiently or risk being put out of business. At the national and global levels, administrative barriers are government policies that create barriers to entry and limit imports of goods by overseas companies. Japan is well known for the many ways in which it attempts to restrict the entry of overseas competitors or lessen their impact on Japanese firms. Japan has come under intense pressure to relax and abolish regulations such as those governing the import of rice, for example.

The Japanese rice market, like many other Japanese markets, was closed to overseas competitors until 1993 to protect Japan's thousands of high-cost, low-output rice farmers. Rice cultivation is expensive in Japan because of the country's mountainous terrain, and Japanese consumers have always paid high prices for rice. Under overseas pressure, the Japanese government opened the market, but overseas competitors are allowed to export to Japan only 8 percent of its annual rice consumption, to protect its farmers.

In the 2000s, however, an alliance between organic rice grower Lundberg Family Farms of California and the Nippon Restaurant Enterprise Co. found a new way to break into the Japanese rice market. Because there is no tariff on rice used in processed foods, Nippon converts the U.S. organic rice into "O-bento," an organic hot boxed lunch packed with rice, vegetables, chicken, beef, and salmon, all imported from the United States. The lunches, which cost about $4 compared to a Japanese rice bento that costs about $9, are sold at railway stations and other outlets throughout Japan and have become very popular. A storm of protest from Japanese rice farmers arose because the entry of U.S. rice growers forced them to leave their rice fields idle or grow less profitable crops. Other overseas companies are increasingly forming alliances with Japanese companies to find new ways to break into the high-priced Japanese market, and little by little, Japan's restrictive trade practices are being whittled away. In addition, as younger Japanese consumers eat less rice than their older relatives, there is some speculation that the government subsidies to protect Japanese farmers may be reduced or eliminated. In 2015 Japanese-grown rice became cheaper to buy than its California-grown equivalent for the first time in more than 60 years.[38]

An O-bento lunch. Now that Japan can import rice from the United States, Japanese rice farmers, who cannot compete against lower-priced imports, have been forced to leave fields idle or grow less profitable crops.

In summary, intense rivalry among competitors creates a task environment that is highly threatening and makes it increasingly difficult for managers to gain access to the resources an organization needs to make goods and services. Conversely, low rivalry results in a task environment where competitive pressures are more moderate and managers have greater opportunities to acquire the resources they need to make their organizations effective.

The General Environment

Economic, technological, sociocultural, demographic, political, and legal forces in the general environment often have important effects on forces in the task environment that determine an organization's ability to obtain resources—effects that managers may not be aware of. For example, the sudden, dramatic upheavals in the mortgage and banking industry that started in 2007 were brought about by a combination of the development of complex new financial lending instruments called derivatives; a speculative boom in commodities and housing prices; and lax government regulation that allowed unethical bankers and financial managers to exploit the derivatives to make immense short-term profits. These events triggered the economic crisis that peaked in 2008 but continued to ripple through the world economy for years, causing stock markets around the world to plummet, devastating the retirement savings of hundreds of millions of ordinary people, and causing layoffs of millions of employees as companies slashed their workforces because customers reduced their spending.

The implication is clear: Managers must continuously analyze forces in the general environment because these forces affect ongoing decision making and planning. How well managers can perform this task determines how quickly an organization can respond to the changes taking place. Next we discuss the major forces in the general environment and examine their impact on an organization's task environment.

Economic Forces

economic forces Interest rates, inflation, unemployment, economic growth, and other factors that affect the general health and well-being of a nation or the regional economy of an organization.

Economic forces affect the general health and well-being of a country or world region. They include interest rates, inflation, unemployment, and economic growth. Economic forces produce many opportunities and threats for managers. Low levels of unemployment and falling interest rates give people more money to spend, and as a result organizations can sell more goods and services. Good economic times affect the supply of resources that become easier or more inexpensive to acquire, and organizations have an opportunity to flourish. High-tech companies enjoyed this throughout the 1990s when computer and electronics companies, like Sony, made record profits as the global economy boomed because of advances in IT and growing global trade.

In contrast, worsening macroeconomic conditions, like those in the 2010s, pose a major threat because they reduce managers' ability to gain access to the resources their organizations need to survive and prosper. Profit-seeking organizations such as hotels and retail stores have fewer customers during economic downturns; hotel rates dropped by 14 percent in 2009 compared to 2008, for example, just as retail sales plunged. Nonprofits such as charities and colleges also saw donations decline by more than 20 percent because of the economic downturn.

Poor economic conditions make the environment more complex and managers' jobs more difficult and demanding. Companies often need to reduce the number of their managers and employees, streamline their operations, and identify ways to acquire and use resources more efficiently and effectively. Successful managers realize the important effects that economic forces have on their organizations, and they pay close attention to what is occurring in the economy at the national and regional levels to respond appropriately.

technology The combination of skills and equipment that managers use in designing, producing, and distributing goods and services.

technological forces Outcomes of changes in the technology managers use to design, produce, or distribute goods and services.

Technological Forces

Technology is the combination of tools, machines, computers, skills, information, and knowledge that managers use to design, produce, and distribute goods and services; **technological forces** are outcomes of changes in that technology. The overall pace of technological change has accelerated greatly in the last decades because technological advances in microprocessors and computer hardware and software have spurred technological advances in most businesses and industries. The effects of changing technological forces are still increasing in magnitude.[39]

Technological forces can have profound implications for managers and organizations. Technological change can make established products obsolete—for example, cathode-ray tube (CRT) computer monitors and televisions (such as Sony's Trinitron), bound sets of encyclopedias, and newspapers and magazines—forcing managers to find new ways to satisfy customer needs. Although technological change can threaten an organization, it also can create a host of new opportunities for designing, making, or distributing new and better kinds of goods and services. In 2014 AMD launched processors with powerful graphics capabilities for games and high-performance apps. The chips use Heterogeneous System Architecture (HSA) to speed up PCs. Innovations like these continue the IT revolution that has spurred demand for all kinds of new digital computing devices and services and that has affected the competitive position of all high-tech companies.[40]

Changes in IT are altering the nature of work itself within organizations, including that of the manager's job. Today telecommuting, videoconferencing, and text messaging are everyday activities that let managers supervise and coordinate geographically dispersed employees. Salespeople in many companies work from home offices and commute electronically to work. They communicate with other employees through companywide electronic communication networks using smartphones and other mobile devices to orchestrate "face-to-face" meetings with coworkers across the country or globe.

Sociocultural Forces

sociocultural forces Pressures emanating from the social structure of a country or society or from the national culture.

social structure The traditional system of relationships established between people and groups in a society.

Sociocultural forces are pressures emanating from the social structure of a country or society or from the national culture, such as the concern for diversity, discussed in the previous chapter. Pressures from both sources can either constrain or facilitate the way organizations operate and managers behave. **Social structure** is the traditional system of relationships established between people and groups in a society. Societies differ substantially in social structure. In societies that have a high degree of social stratification, there are many distinctions among individuals and groups. Caste systems in India and Tibet and the recognition of numerous social classes in Great Britain and France produce a multilayered social structure in each of those countries. In contrast, social stratification is lower in relatively egalitarian New Zealand and in the United States, where the social structure reveals few distinctions among people. Most top managers in France come from the upper classes of French society, but top managers in the United States come from all strata of American society.

Societies also differ in the extent to which they emphasize the individual over the group. Such differences may dictate how managers need to motivate and lead employees.

national culture The set of values that a society considers important and the norms of behavior that are approved or sanctioned in that society.

National culture is the set of values that a society considers important and the norms of behavior that are approved or sanctioned in that society. Societies differ substantially in the values and norms they emphasize. For example, in the United States, individualism is highly valued, but in Korea and Japan individuals are expected to conform to group expectations.[41] National culture, discussed at length later in this chapter, also affects how managers motivate and coordinate employees and how organizations do business. Ethics, an important aspect of national culture, were discussed in detail in Chapter 4.

Social structure and national culture not only differ across societies but also change within societies over time. In the United States, attitudes toward the roles of women, sex, marriage, and gays and lesbians changed in each past decade. Many people in Asian countries such as Hong Kong, Singapore, Korea, and even China think the younger generation is far more individualistic and "American-like" than previous generations. Currently, throughout much of Eastern Europe, new values that emphasize individualism and entrepreneurship are replacing communist values based on collectivism and obedience to the state. The pace of change is accelerating.

Individual managers and organizations must be responsive to changes in, and differences among, the social structures and national cultures of all the countries in which they operate. In today's increasingly integrated global economy, managers are likely to interact with people from several countries, and many managers live and work abroad. Effective managers are sensitive to differences between societies and adjust their behavior accordingly.

Managers and organizations also must respond to social changes within a society. In the last decades, for example, Americans have become increasingly interested in their personal health and fitness. Managers who recognized this trend early and took advantage of the opportunities that resulted from it were able to reap significant gains for their organizations, such as organic food delivery services. The organic produce industry has been growing for the past decade, even during the recession, due to people's interest in chemical-free food.[42] Many organizations have begun to offer weekly home delivery to customers.[43] PepsiCo used the opportunity presented by the fitness trend and took market share from archrival Coca-Cola by being the first to introduce diet colas and fruit-based soft drinks. Then Quaker Oats made Gatorade the most popular energy drink, and now others, like Red Bull, Monster, and Rockstar, are increasing in popularity. The health trend, however, did not offer opportunities to all companies; to some it posed a threat. Tobacco companies came under intense pressure due to consumers' greater awareness of negative health impacts from smoking. The rage for "low-carb" foods in the 2000s increased demand for meat and protein, and bread and doughnut companies such as Kraft and Krispy Kreme suffered—until the ongoing recession boosted the sale of inexpensive products such as macaroni and cheese and dry dinner mixes.

Demographic Forces

demographic forces Outcomes of changes in, or changing attitudes toward, the characteristics of a population, such as age, gender, ethnic origin, race, sexual orientation, and social class.

Demographic forces are outcomes of changes in, or changing attitudes toward, the characteristics of a population, such as age, gender, ethnic origin, race, sexual orientation, and social class. Like the other forces in the general environment, demographic forces present managers with opportunities and threats and can have major implications for organizations. We examined the nature of these challenges in depth in our discussion of diversity in Chapter 5.

Today most industrialized nations are experiencing the aging of their populations as a consequence of falling birth and death rates and the aging of the baby boom generation. Consequently, the absolute number of older people has increased substantially, which has generated opportunities for organizations that cater to older people, such as the home health care, recreation, and medical industries, which have seen an upswing in demand for their services. The aging of the population also has several implications for the workplace. Most significant are a relative decline in the number of young people joining the workforce and an increase in the number of active employees who are postponing retirement beyond the traditional age of 65. Indeed, the continuing financial crisis in the 2010s has made it impossible for millions of older people to retire because their savings have been destroyed. These changes suggest that organizations need to find ways to motivate older employees and use their skills and knowledge—an issue that many Western societies have yet to tackle.

Political and Legal Forces

political and legal forces Outcomes of changes in laws and regulations, such as deregulation of industries, privatization of organizations, and increased emphasis on environmental protection.

Political and legal forces are outcomes of changes in laws and regulations. They result from political and legal developments that take place within a nation, within a world region, or across the world and significantly affect managers and organizations everywhere. Political processes shape a nation's laws and the international laws that govern the relationships between nations. Laws constrain the operations of organizations and managers and thus create both opportunities and threats.[44] For example, throughout much of the industrialized world there has been a strong trend toward deregulation of industries previously controlled by the state and privatization of organizations once owned by the state such as airlines, railways, and utility companies. However, deregulation came under fire following the subprime mortgage crisis of 2007 and the resulting recession. Nobel Prize–winning economist Paul Krugman blamed global financial deregulation for, among other things, unstable economies in India, Brazil, Indonesia, South Africa, and Turkey in 2013.[45]

Another important political and legal force affecting managers and organizations is the political integration of countries that has been taking place during the last decades.[46] Increasingly, nations are forming political unions that allow free exchange of resources and capital. The growth of the European Union (EU) is one example: Common laws govern trade and commerce between EU member countries, and the European Court has the right to examine the business of any global organization and to approve any proposed mergers between overseas companies that operate inside the EU. For example, Microsoft's anticompetitive business practices came under scrutiny, and it was fined hundreds of millions for its uncompetitive practice of bundling its Internet Explorer web browser with its software. As part of its agreement with the European Court, Microsoft agreed that, beginning in 2010, it would ship its Windows 7 software with a choice of 10 web browsers (such as Chrome, Safari, and Mozilla). Also, in 2012, after months of delay, the court allowed the merger between Motorola and Google to proceed, although the court was also investigating Google for possible anticompetitive online advertising practices. In 2016 there are ongoing negotiations between the United States and the European Union concerning the Transatlantic Trade and Investment Partnership (TTIP). The agreement would lower trade barriers to make it easier for organizations in the European Union and the United States to buy and sell each other's goods and services.[47]

Indeed, international agreements to abolish laws and regulations that restrict and reduce trade between countries have been having profound effects on global organizations. The falling legal trade barriers create enormous opportunities for companies to sell goods and services internationally. But by allowing overseas companies to compete in a nation's domestic market for customers, falling trade barriers also pose a serious threat because they increase competition in the task environment. For example, the United States, along with 11 other countries, recently signed the Trans Pacific Partnership, a free-trade agreement that has far-reaching implications. The other nations include Malaysia, Mexico, Australia, Brunei, Canada, Chile, Japan, Peru, Singapore, Vietnam, and New Zealand. However, political and business opposition to the agreement may prevent it from being implemented in the United States. For example, car companies, sugar producers, and textile makers have expressed concern about foreign competition if the agreement goes forward.[48] Some consumer advocacy groups, including Public Citizen, believe the Trans Pacific Partnership will provide companies with incentives to offshore their facilities, which will harm manufacturing in the United States.[49]

LO6-4 Explain why the global environment is becoming more open and competitive, and identify the forces behind the process of globalization that increase the opportunities, complexities, challenges, and threats managers face.

Deregulation, privatization, and the removal of legal barriers to trade are just a few of the many ways in which changing political and legal forces can challenge organizations and managers. Others include increased emphasis on environmental protection and the preservation of endangered species, increased emphasis on workplace safety, and legal constraints against discrimination on the basis of race, gender, or age. Managers face major challenges when they seek to take advantage of the opportunities created by changing political, legal, and economic forces.

The Changing Global Environment

The 21st century has banished the idea that the world is composed of distinct national countries and markets that are separated physically, economically, and culturally. Managers need to recognize that companies compete in a truly global marketplace, which is the source of the opportunities and threats they must respond to. Managers continually confront the challenges of global competition such as establishing operations in a country abroad, obtaining inputs from suppliers abroad, or managing in a different national culture.[50]

In essence, as a result of falling trade barriers, managers view the global environment as open—that is, as an environment in which companies are free to buy goods and services from, and sell goods and services to, whichever companies and countries they choose. They also are free to compete against each other to attract customers around the world. All large companies must establish an international network of operations and subsidiaries to build global competitive advantage. Coca-Cola and PepsiCo, for example, have competed aggressively for decades to develop the strongest global beverage empire, just

Despite recent economic headwinds due to lower commodity prices and other factors, Africa's overall economy is still strong. According to analysts at African Development Bank, Africa is the second fastest-growing continent in the world in 2016 just behind Asia. African countries face economic, political, and environmental challenges as the process of globalization accelerates changes to business and everyday life in cities such as Lagos, Nigeria, pictured here.
© Pius Utomi Ekpei/AFP/Getty Images

as Toyota and Honda have built hundreds of car plants around the world to provide the vehicles that global customers like.

In this section we first explain how this open global environment is the result of globalization and the flow of capital around the world. Next we examine how specific economic, political, and legal changes, such as the lowering of barriers to trade and investment, have increased globalization and led to greater interaction and exchanges between organizations and countries. Then we discuss how declining barriers of distance and culture have also increased the pace of globalization, and we consider the specific implications of these changes for managers and organizations. Finally, we note that nations still differ widely from each other because they have distinct cultural values and norms and that managers must appreciate these differences to compete successfully across countries.

The Process of Globalization

globalization The set of specific and general forces that work together to integrate and connect economic, political, and social systems *across* countries, cultures, or geographic regions so that nations become increasingly interdependent and similar.

Perhaps the most important reason the global environment has become more open and competitive is the increase in globalization. **Globalization** is the set of specific and general forces that work together to integrate and connect economic, political, and social systems across countries, cultures, or geographic regions. The result of globalization is that nations and peoples become increasingly interdependent because the same forces affect them in similar ways. The fates of peoples in different countries become interlinked as the world's markets and businesses become increasingly interconnected. And as nations become more interdependent, they become more similar to one another in the sense that people develop a similar liking for products as diverse as cell phones, iPads, blue jeans, soft drinks, sports teams, hybrid cars, and foods such as curry, green tea, and Colombian coffee. One outcome of globalization is that more women are joining the ranks of leadership. To help women transition to leadership positions, EY, a multinational organization, has begun a special global program, as the accompanying "Managing Globally" feature describes.

MANAGING GLOBALLY

Recruiting Female Athletes for Business Careers

The 2012 London Olympics were a watershed moment for female athletes. For the first time ever, every country sending athletes to the games had women on the team, and women were able to participate in all sports.

"Coming out of London there was so much momentum around women. . . . It reinforced to us that women are an emerging market. The leadership potential that exists in these elite athletes is so consistent with our beliefs in somehow trying to unlock the potential to foster more women's economic empowerment and leadership," said Beth Brooke-Marciniak, global vice chair, public policy at EY (formerly Ernst & Young).[51]

Between the 2012 London Olympics and the 2016 Rio Olympics, EY is working to create a network of retired elite female athletes, former Olympians, and top female

Beth Brooke-Marciniak, global vice chair of policy at EY, leads a drive to recruit female athletes for business careers because their confidence, discipline, high standards, and team experience may help them become successful leaders.
© Buda Mendes/Getty Images For Laureus

leaders and to encourage female athletes to pursue powerful careers after retiring from sports. EY is an official supporter of the Rio games.[52]

The background of this global network involved a study by EY in May 2013 that confirmed a connection between sports and leadership. The study included a survey of 821 female senior managers and executives at companies around the world with annual revenues in excess of $250 million. Results found that almost all female leaders played sports at some point in their lives. More specifically, 96 percent of the women surveyed with board-level jobs played sports at the primary, secondary, postsecondary, or college level. The women in the study agreed that experience in playing sports leads to positive behaviors in the workplace, especially teamwork. Of the study respondents, 72 percent said that there seemed to be a correlation between playing, or having played, sports and teamwork. Also, 76 percent said that behaviors and techniques from sports can be adopted to improve team performance in the workplace. While the study does not conclude that every athlete will become a strong organizational leader, it does conclude that sports can help women develop leadership skills that will serve organizations well.[53]

EY's survey confirms the findings of a 2002 survey of more than 400 senior women executives commissioned by Mass-Mutual Financial Group and Oppenheimer, which found 80 percent or more of those surveyed had participated in an organized sport growing up and that the majority of those surveyed believed sports helped them to become more disciplined and built their leadership skills. Beyond the results of these two surveys, there's anecdotal evidence. For example, former Brazilian President Dilma Rousseff played volleyball. Basketball players who became high-level leaders include Mondolēz International CEO Irene Rosenfeld, former U.S. secretary of state (and 2016 presidential candidate) Hillary Clinton, and former DuPont CEO Ellen Kullman. And Christine Lagarde, head of the International Monetary Fund, was a member of France's national synchronized swimming team.[54]

These women found success after their sports careers ended, but that is not always the case. EY contends that many female athletes encounter difficulties in moving their success from the playing field to the corporate office.[55] The Women Athletes Global Leadership Network has three steps designed to make that transition easier and increase the impact of female leadership:[56]

1. Bringing together former elite athletes, former Olympians, and successful women in EY's business network to form mentoring relationships and provide opportunities.
2. Using multimedia platforms to tell inspirational stories of women who found participation in sports to be important to their success.
3. Conducting research about the relationship between women's participation in sports and their leadership skills, as well as their effect on global education, health, and development.

"Ernst & Young [EY] has seen the power of diversity and inclusion, and we want to build a better working world by expanding opportunities for women leaders. With their inherent confidence, high standards, discipline, and experience in working as a team, female athletes have tremendous value for businesses like ours, governments, and NGOs around the world," said Brooke-Marciniak, a Title IX scholarship recipient herself. "We have a long history of convening networks, helping female entrepreneurs scale their companies, and driving the global dialogue around the advancement of women. The impact of women at the London games was historic, and we want to continue this momentum by helping transform elite female athletes into exceptional leaders."[57]

But what drives or spurs globalization? What makes companies like IKEA, Toyota, or Microsoft want to venture into an uncertain global environment? The answer is that the path of globalization is shaped by the ebb and flow of *capital*—valuable wealth-generating assets or resources that people move through companies, countries, and world regions to seek their greatest returns or profits. Managers, employees, and companies like IKEA and Samsung are motivated to try to profit or benefit by using their skills to make products customers around the world want to buy. The four principal forms of capital that flow between countries are these:

- *Human capital:* the flow of people around the world through immigration, migration, and emigration
- *Financial capital:* the flow of money capital across world markets through overseas investment, credit, lending, and aid
- *Resource capital:* the flow of natural resources, parts, and components between companies and countries, such as metals, minerals, lumber, energy, food products, microprocessors, and auto parts
- *Political capital:* the flow of power and influence around the world using diplomacy, persuasion, aggression, and force of arms to protect the right or access of a country, world region, or political bloc to the other forms of capital

Most of the economic advances associated with globalization are the result of these four capital flows and the interactions between them, as nations compete on the world stage to protect and increase their standards of living and to further the political goals and social causes that are espoused by their societies' cultures. The next sections look at the factors that have increased the rate at which capital flows between companies and countries. In a positive sense, the faster the flow, the more capital is being utilized where it can create the most value, such as people moving to where their skills earn more money, or investors switching to the stocks or bonds that give higher dividends or interest, or companies finding lower-cost sources of inputs. In a negative sense, however, a fast flow of capital also means that individual countries or world regions can find themselves in trouble when companies and investors move their capital to invest it in more productive ways in other countries or world regions—often those with lower labor costs or rapidly expanding markets. When capital leaves a country, the results are higher unemployment, recession, and a lower standard of living for its people.

Declining Barriers to Trade and Investment

tariff A tax that a government imposes on imported or, occasionally, exported goods.

One of the main factors that has speeded globalization by freeing the movement of capital has been the decline in barriers to trade and investment, discussed earlier. During the 1920s and 1930s many countries erected formidable barriers to international trade and investment in the belief that this was the best way to promote their economic well-being. Many of these barriers were high tariffs on imports of manufactured goods. A **tariff** is a tax that a government imposes on goods imported into one country from another. The aim of import tariffs is to protect domestic industries and jobs, such as those in the auto or steel industry, from overseas competition by raising the price of these products from abroad. In 2009, for example, the U.S. government increased the tariffs on vehicle tires imported from China to protect U.S. tire makers from unfair competition. The elevated tariffs expired in 2012, and in 2013 the passenger tire imports from China increased by 55.8 percent to 46 million units, an all-time high. In 2016 the U.S. Commerce Department initiated an investigation of truck and bus tires from China being dumped on the U.S. market, which would cause prices to drop. The petitioners for this investigation included several worker unions that alleged the cheap tires were being subsidized by the Chinese government.[58]

The reason for removing tariffs is that, very often, when one country imposes an import tariff, others follow suit and the result is a series of retaliatory moves as countries progressively raise tariff barriers against each other. In the 1920s this behavior depressed world demand and helped usher in the Great Depression of the 1930s and massive unemployment. Beginning with the 2009 economic crisis, the governments of most countries have worked hard in the 2010s not to fall into the trap of raising tariffs to protect jobs and industries in the short run because they know the long-term consequences of this would be the loss of even more jobs. Governments of countries that resort to raising tariff barriers ultimately reduce employment and undermine the economic growth of their countries because capital and resources will always move to their most highly valued use—wherever that is in the world.[59]

GATT AND THE RISE OF FREE TRADE After World War II, advanced Western industrial countries, having learned from the Great Depression, committed themselves to the goal of removing barriers to the free flow of resources and capital between countries. This commitment was reinforced by acceptance of the principle that free trade, rather than tariff barriers, was the best way to foster a healthy domestic economy and low unemployment.[60]

free-trade doctrine The idea that if each country specializes in the production of the goods and services that it can produce most efficiently, this will make the best use of global resources.

The **free-trade doctrine** predicts that if each country agrees to specialize in the production of the goods and services that it can produce most efficiently, this will make the best use of global capital resources and will result in lower prices.[61] For example, if Indian companies are highly efficient in the production of textiles and U.S. companies are highly efficient in the production of computer software, then, under a free-trade agreement, capital would move to India and be invested there to produce textiles, while capital from around the world would flow to the United States and be invested in its innovative software companies. Consequently, prices of both textiles and software should fall because each product is being produced where it can be made at the lowest cost, benefiting consumers and making the best use of scarce capital. This doctrine is also responsible for the increase in global outsourcing and the loss of millions of U.S. jobs in textiles and manufacturing as capital has been invested in factories in Asian countries such as China and Malaysia. However, millions of U.S. jobs have also been created because of new capital investments in the high-tech, IT, and service sectors, which in theory should offset manufacturing job losses in the long run.

Historically, countries that accepted this free-trade doctrine set as their goal the removal of barriers to the free flow of goods, services, and capital between countries. They attempted to achieve this through an international treaty known as the General Agreement on Tariffs and Trade (GATT). In the years since World War II, there have been eight rounds of GATT negotiations aimed at lowering tariff barriers. The last round, the Uruguay Round, involved 117 countries and succeeded in lowering tariffs by over 30 percent from the previous level. It also led to the dissolving of GATT and its replacement by the World Trade Organization (WTO), which continues the struggle to reduce tariffs and has more power to sanction countries that break global agreements.[62] On average, the tariff barriers among the governments of developed countries declined from over 40 percent in 1948 to about 3 percent today,[63] causing a dramatic increase in world trade.[64]

Declining Barriers of Distance and Culture

Historically, barriers of distance and culture also closed the global environment and kept managers focused on their domestic market. The management problems Unilever, the huge, British-based soap and detergent maker, experienced at the turn of the 20th century illustrate the effect of these barriers.

Founded in London during the 1880s by William Lever, a Quaker, Unilever had a worldwide reach by the early 1900s and operated subsidiaries in most major countries of the British Empire, including India, Canada, and Australia. Lever had a very hands-on, autocratic management style and found his far-flung business empire difficult to control. The reason for Lever's control problems was that communication over great distances was difficult. It took six weeks to reach India by ship from England, and international telephone and telegraph services were unreliable.

Another problem Unilever encountered was the difficulty of doing business in societies that were separated from Britain by barriers of language and culture. Different countries have different sets of national beliefs, values, and norms, and Lever found that a management approach that worked in Britain did not necessarily work in India or Persia (now Iran). As a result, management practices had to be tailored to suit each unique national culture. After

Lever's death in 1925, top management at Unilever lowered or *decentralized* (see Chapter 10) decision-making authority to the managers of the various national subsidiaries so they could develop a management approach that suited the country in which they were operating. One result of this strategy was that the subsidiaries grew distant and remote from one another, which reduced Unilever's performance.[65]

Since the end of World War II, a continuing stream of advances in communications and transportation technology has worked to reduce the barriers of distance and culture that affected Unilever and all global organizations. Over the last decades, global communication has been revolutionized by developments in satellites, digital technology, the Internet and global computer networks, and video teleconferencing that allow transmission of vast amounts of information and make reliable, secure, and instantaneous communication possible between people and companies anywhere in the world.[66] This revolution has made it possible for a global organization—a tiny garment factory in Li & Fung's network or a huge company such as IKEA or Unilever—to do business anywhere, anytime and to search for customers and suppliers around the world.

One of the most important innovations in transportation technology that has opened the global environment has been the growth of commercial jet travel. New York is now closer in travel time to Tokyo than it was to Philadelphia in the days of the 13 colonies—a fact that makes control of far-flung international businesses much easier today than in William Lever's era. In addition to speeding travel, modern communications and transportation technologies have also helped reduce the cultural distance between countries. The Internet and its millions of websites facilitate the development of global communications networks and media that are helping to create a worldwide culture that, in some cases, has diluted unique national cultures. Moreover, television networks such as CNN, MTV, ESPN, BBC, and HBO can now be received in many countries, and Hollywood films are shown throughout the world.

Effects of Free Trade on Managers

The lowering of barriers to trade and investment and the decline of distance and culture barriers have created enormous opportunities for companies to expand the market for their goods and services through exports and investments in overseas countries. The shift toward a more open global economy has created not only more opportunities to sell goods and services in markets abroad but also the opportunity to buy more from other countries. For example, apparel maker Ralph Lauren was heavily criticized when it was discovered that the uniforms it made for the 2012 U.S. Olympics team were made in China. Americans were not ready for their team uniforms to be bought from another country. For the 2016 Olympics, the Ralph Lauren uniform for the U.S. team was made in the United States. A manager's job is more challenging in a dynamic global environment because of the increased intensity of competition that goes hand in hand with the lowering of barriers to trade and investment.

REGIONAL TRADE AGREEMENTS The growth of regional trade agreements, such as the North American Free Trade Agreement (NAFTA), and more recently the Central American Free Trade Agreement (CAFTA), also presents opportunities and threats for managers and their organizations. In North America, NAFTA, which became effective in 1994, had the aim of abolishing the tariffs on 99 percent of the goods traded between Mexico, Canada, and the United States by 2004. Although it did not achieve this lofty goal, NAFTA has removed most barriers on the cross-border flow of resources, giving, for example, financial institutions and retail businesses in Canada and the United States unrestricted access to the Mexican marketplace. After NAFTA was signed, there was a flood of investment into Mexico from the United States, as well as many other countries such as Japan. Walmart, Costco, Ford, and many major U.S. retail chains expanded their operations in Mexico; Walmart, for example, is stocking many more products from Mexico in its U.S. stores, and its Mexican store chain is also expanding rapidly.

The establishment of free-trade areas creates an opportunity for manufacturing organizations because it lets them reduce their costs. They can do this either by shifting production to the lowest-cost location within the free-trade area (for example, U.S. auto and textile companies shifting production to Mexico) or by serving the whole region from one location rather than establishing separate operations in each country. Some managers, however, view regional free-trade agreements as a threat because they expose a company based in one member country to increased competition from companies based in the other member countries. NAFTA has had this effect; today Mexican managers in some industries face the threat of head-to-head competition against efficient U.S. and Canadian companies. But the opposite is true as well: U.S. and Canadian managers are experiencing threats in labor-intensive industries, such as the flooring tile, roofing, and textile industries, where Mexican businesses have a cost advantage.

There are many regional trade agreements around the world. For example, the African Union was founded in 1999. Its purpose is both political and economic. Its goals include removing any remnants of colonization and apartheid, as well as creating cooperation for development.[67] Complementing the role of the African Union is the Southern African Development Community, an economic community whose members include Angola, South Africa, Botswana, Zambia, Democratic Republic of Congo, Seychelles, Lesotho, Madagascar, Mauritius, Malawi, Namibia, Mozambique, Swaziland, United Republic of Tanzania, and Zimbabwe. This intergovernmental organization's goals include socioeconomic development and poverty eradication.[68] Another trade agreement is the Cooperation Council for the Arab States of the Gulf. This agreement was made among several countries, including Qatar, Oman, Bahrain, the United Arab Emirates, Kuwait, and Saudi Arabia. As a part of the agreement, countries cooperate on several issues, including regional cooperation and economic relations with others.[69] All these trade agreements are designed to allow managers to take advantage of opportunities that other members of the agreements can provide.

The Role of National Culture

Despite evidence that countries are becoming more similar because of globalization and that the world may become "a global village," the cultures of different countries still vary widely because of vital differences in their values, norms, and attitudes. As noted earlier, national culture includes the values, norms, knowledge, beliefs, moral principles, laws, customs, and other practices that unite the citizens of a country.[70] National culture shapes individual behavior by specifying appropriate and inappropriate behavior and interaction with others. People learn national culture in their everyday lives by interacting with those around them. This learning starts at an early age and continues throughout their lives.

Cultural Values and Norms

values Ideas about what a society believes to be good, right, desirable, or beautiful.

The basic building blocks of national culture are values and norms. **Values** are beliefs about what a society considers to be good, right, desirable, or beautiful—or their opposites. They provide the basic underpinnings for notions of individual freedom, democracy, truth, justice, honesty, loyalty, social obligation, collective responsibility, the appropriate roles for men and women, love, sex, marriage, and so on. Values are more than merely abstract concepts; they are invested with considerable emotional significance. People argue, fight, and even die over values such as freedom or dignity.

For example, antigovernment demonstrations broke out in the Ukraine after President Viktor Yanukovych chose a $15 billion bailout from Russia to help the country get back on its feet instead of a European trade and political offer. After months of bloody demonstrations, the Parliament voted Yanukovych out of power in February 2014.[71] Part of the problem is that some Ukrainian citizens consider themselves Russians, while other feel closer to their European roots. Likewise, events in Egypt that led to President Hosni Mubarak stepping down in 2011 reflected a desire in the country to draft a new constitution and hold elections.[72]

norms Unwritten, informal codes of conduct that prescribe how people should act in particular situations and are considered important by most members of a group or organization.

mores Norms that are considered to be central to the functioning of society and to social life.

Norms are unwritten, informal codes of conduct that prescribe appropriate behavior in particular situations and are considered important by most members of a group or organization. They shape the behavior of people toward one another. Two types of norms play a major role in national culture: mores and folkways. **Mores** are norms that are considered to be of central importance to the functioning of society and to social life. Accordingly, the violation of mores brings serious retribution. Mores include proscriptions against murder, theft, adultery, and incest. In many societies mores have been enacted into law. Thus, all advanced societies have laws against murder and theft. However, there are many differences in mores from one society to another.[73] In the United States, for example, drinking alcohol is widely accepted, but in Saudi Arabia consumption of alcohol is viewed as a serious violation of social mores and is punishable by imprisonment.

folkways The routine social conventions of everyday life.

Folkways are the routine social conventions of everyday life. They concern customs and practices such as dressing appropriately for particular situations, having good social manners, eating with the correct utensils, and engaging in neighborly behavior. Although folkways define how people are expected to behave, violation of folkways is not a serious or moral matter. People who violate folkways are often thought to be eccentric or ill-mannered, but they are not usually considered immoral or wicked. In many countries, strangers are usually excused for violating folkways because they are unaccustomed to local behavior, but if they repeat the violation, they are censured because they are expected to learn appropriate behavior—hence the importance of managers working in countries abroad to gain wide experience.

LO6-5 Discuss why national cultures differ and why it is important that managers be sensitive to the effects of falling trade barriers and regional trade associations on the political and social systems of nations around the world.

Hofstede's Model of National Culture

Researchers have spent considerable time and effort identifying similarities and differences in the values and norms of different countries. One model of national culture was developed by Geert Hofstede.[74] As a psychologist for IBM, Hofstede collected data on employee values and norms from more than 100,000 IBM employees in 64 countries. Based on his research, Hofstede developed five dimensions along which national cultures can be placed.[75]

individualism A worldview that values individual freedom and self-expression and adherence to the principle that people should be judged by their individual achievements rather than by their social background.

collectivism A worldview that values subordination of the individual to the goals of the group and adherence to the principle that people should be judged by their contribution to the group.

INDIVIDUALISM VERSUS COLLECTIVISM The first dimension, which Hofstede labeled "individualism versus collectivism," has a long history in human thought. **Individualism** is a worldview that values individual freedom and self-expression and adherence to the principle that people should be judged by their individual achievements rather than by their social background. In Western countries, individualism usually includes admiration for personal success, a strong belief in individual rights, and high regard for individual entrepreneurs.[76]

In contrast, **collectivism** is a worldview that values subordination of the individual to the goals of the group and adherence to the principle that people should be judged by their contribution to the group. Collectivism was widespread in communist countries but has become less prevalent since the collapse of communism in most of those countries. Japan is a noncommunist country where collectivism is highly valued.

Collectivism in Japan traces its roots to the fusion of Confucian, Buddhist, and Shinto thought that occurred during the Tokugawa period in Japanese history (1600–1870s).[77] A central value that emerged during this period was strong attachment to the group—whether a village, a work group, or a company. Strong identification with the group is said to create pressures for collective action in Japan, as well as strong pressure for conformity to group norms and a relative lack of individualism.[78]

Managers must realize that organizations and organizational members reflect their national culture's emphasis on individualism or collectivism. Indeed, one of the major reasons Japanese and American management practices differ is that Japanese culture values collectivism and U.S. culture values individualism.[79]

power distance The degree to which societies accept the idea that inequalities in the power and well-being of their citizens are due to differences in individuals' physical and intellectual capabilities and heritage.

POWER DISTANCE By **power distance**, Hofstede meant the degree to which societies accept the idea that inequalities in the power and well-being of their citizens are due to differences in individuals' physical and intellectual capabilities and heritage. This concept also encompasses the degree to which societies accept the economic and social differences in wealth, status, and well-being that result from differences in individual capabilities.

Societies in which inequalities are allowed to persist or grow over time have *high power distance.* In high-power-distance societies, workers who are professionally successful amass wealth and pass it on to their children, and, as a result, inequalities may grow over time. In such societies, the gap between rich and poor, with all the attendant political and social consequences, grows very large. In contrast, in societies with *low power distance,* large inequalities between citizens are not allowed to develop. In low-power-distance countries, the government uses taxation and social welfare programs to reduce inequality and improve the welfare of the least fortunate. These societies are more attuned to preventing a large gap between rich and poor and minimizing discord between different classes of citizens.

Advanced Western countries such as the United States, Germany, the Netherlands, and the United Kingdom have relatively low power distance and high individualism. Economically poor Latin American countries such as Guatemala and Panama, and Asian countries such as Malaysia and the Philippines, have high power distance and low individualism.[80] These findings suggest that the cultural values of richer countries emphasize protecting the rights of individuals and, at the same time, provide a fair chance of success to every member of society.

achievement orientation A worldview that values assertiveness, performance, success, and competition.

nurturing orientation A worldview that values the quality of life, warm personal friendships, and services and care for the weak.

uncertainty avoidance The degree to which societies are willing to tolerate uncertainty and risk.

long-term orientation A worldview that values thrift and persistence in achieving goals.

short-term orientation A worldview that values personal stability or happiness and living for the present.

ACHIEVEMENT VERSUS NURTURING ORIENTATION Societies that have an **achievement orientation** value assertiveness, performance, success, competition, and results. Societies that have a **nurturing orientation** value the quality of life, warm personal relationships, and services and care for the weak. Japan and the United States tend to be achievement-oriented; the Netherlands, Sweden, and Denmark are more nurturing-oriented.

UNCERTAINTY AVOIDANCE Societies as well as individuals differ in their tolerance for uncertainty and risk. Societies low on **uncertainty avoidance** (such as the United States and Hong Kong) are easygoing, value diversity, and tolerate differences in personal beliefs and actions. Societies high on uncertainty avoidance (such as Japan and France) are more rigid and skeptical about people whose behaviors or beliefs differ from the norm. In these societies, conformity to the values of the social and work groups to which a person belongs is the norm, and structured situations are preferred because they provide a sense of security.

LONG-TERM VERSUS SHORT-TERM ORIENTATION The last dimension that Hofstede described is orientation toward life and work.[81] A national culture with a **long-term orientation** rests on values such as thrift (saving) and persistence in achieving goals. A national culture with a **short-term orientation** is concerned with maintaining personal stability or happiness and living for the present. Societies with a long-term orientation include Taiwan and Hong Kong, well known for their high rate of per capita savings. The United States and France have a short-term orientation, and their citizens tend to spend more and save less.

National Culture and Global Management

Differences among national cultures have important implications for managers. First, because of cultural differences, management practices that are effective in one country might be troublesome in another. General Electric's managers learned this while trying to manage Tungsram, a Hungarian lighting products company GE acquired for $150 million. GE was attracted to Tungsram, widely regarded as one of Hungary's best companies, because of Hungary's low wage rates and the possibility of using the company as a base from which to export lighting products to Western Europe. GE transferred some of its best managers to Tungsram and hoped it would soon become a leader in Europe. Unfortunately, many problems arose.

One problem resulted from major misunderstandings between the American managers and the Hungarian workers. The Americans complained that the Hungarians were lazy; the Hungarians thought the Americans were pushy. The Americans wanted strong sales and marketing functions that would pamper customers. In the prior command economy, sales and marketing activities were unnecessary. In addition, Hungarians expected GE to deliver Western-style wages, but GE went to Hungary to take advantage of the country's low wage structure.[82] As Tungsram's losses mounted, GE managers had to admit that because of differences in basic attitudes between countries, they had underestimated the difficulties they would face in turning Tungsram around. Nevertheless, by 2001 these problems had been solved, and the increased efficiency of GE's Hungarian operations made General Electric a major player in the European lighting market, causing it to invest another $1 billion.[83]

Often management practices must be tailored to suit the cultural contexts within which an organization operates. An approach effective in the United States might not work in Japan, Hungary, or Mexico because of differences in national culture. For example, U.S.-style pay-for-performance systems that emphasize the performance of individuals might not work well in Japan, where individual performance in pursuit of group goals is the value that receives emphasis.

Managers doing business with individuals from another country must be sensitive to the value systems and norms of that country and behave accordingly. For example, Friday is the Islamic Sabbath. Thus, it would be impolite and inappropriate for a U.S. manager to schedule a busy day of activities for Saudi Arabian managers on a Friday.

A culturally diverse management team can be a source of strength for an organization participating in the global marketplace. Compared to organizations with culturally homogeneous management teams, organizations that employ managers from a variety of cultures have a better appreciation of how national cultures differ, and they tailor their management systems and behaviors to the differences.[84] Indeed, one advantage that many Western companies have over their Japanese competitors is greater willingness to create global teams composed of employees from different countries around the world who can draw on and share their different cultural experiences and knowledge to provide service that is customized to the needs of companies in different countries. For example, because IT services account for more than half of IBM's $90 billion annual revenues, it has been searching for ways to better use its talented workforce to both lower costs and offer customers unique, specialized kinds of services that its competitors cannot. IBM has developed several kinds of techniques to accomplish this.[85]

In the 2000s, IBM created "competency centers" around the world, staffed by employees who share the same specific IT skill. Most of IBM's employees are concentrated in competency centers located in the countries in which IBM has the most clients and does the most business. These employees have a wide variety of skills, developed from their previous work experience, and the challenge facing IBM is to use these experts efficiently. To accomplish this, IBM used its own IT expertise to develop sophisticated software that allows it to create self-managed teams composed of IBM experts who have the optimum mix of skills to solve a client's particular problems. First, IBM programmers analyze the skills and experience of its 80,000 global employees and enter the results into the software program. Then they analyze and code the nature of a client's specific problem and input that information. IBM's program matches each specific client problem to the skills of IBM's experts and identifies a list of "best fit" employees. One of IBM's senior managers narrows this list and decides on the actual composition of the self-managed team.

Computer technicians at work in a server room. IBM's competency centers customize teams of workers who have just the right mix of skills to address a specific client's business needs.
© Comstock/Getty Images RF

Once selected, team members, from wherever they happen to be in the world, assemble as quickly as possible and go to work analyzing the client's problem. Together, team members use their authority. This new IT lets IBM create an ever-changing set of global self-managed teams that form to develop the software and service packages necessary to solve the problems of IBM's global clients. At the same time, IBM's IT also optimizes the use of its whole talented workforce because each employee is placed in his or her "most highly valued use"—that is, in the team where the employee's skills can best increase efficiency and effectiveness. A lot of factors are involved in working for a global organization. The accompanying "Management Insight" feature describes how managers might educate themselves about some of the issues.

MANAGEMENT INSIGHT

Challenges Expats Face in Moving Abroad

Where in the world would you like to be an expatriate? The annual Expat Explorer Survey by HSBC Bank International could help you decide. The survey ranks the best places in the world to be an expatriate worker. The results are available on the company's website (https://expatexplorer.hsbc.com) and can help people understand what it would be like to be an expatriate in different countries.[86]

The HSBC site also allows users to submit tips based on their expatriate experiences. For example, an expatriate named Curtis provides a list of five tips on "How to 'Succeed' as an Expat":

- Learn the local language, even if you're moving to a place where the locals might speak English.
- Learn the local equivalent of your hobbies and other interests.
- Eat like a local—learning about regional delicacies and trying new foods will help you make the transition to your new location.
- Make friends with locals—this will help you integrate into everyday life.
- Don't pay attention to the exchange rate—converting prices to U.S. currency for local purchases will drive you crazy. Remember, exchange rates are for exchanging money—not for fretting over while trying to acclimate to a new culture and work situation.[87]

Tips provided by an expatriate named Farrah on child health care in the Netherlands begin with "You no longer have a pediatrician. Accept that."[88]

Other information on the site is more general. For example, Singapore, New Zealand, Sweden, and Germany are rated highly for raising children. Sweden, Germany, Taiwan, and Australia get high marks for health care quality and access. When it comes to earning disposable income, New Zealand, Singapore, and Spain top the list.

The HSBC survey ranks countries based on experience, economics, and family. The economics factor includes income, disposable income, and host economic satisfaction. The experience factor includes a long list of issues from entertainment and work–life balance to local culture and making local friends to local weather and learning the local language. The family factor also includes a long list of issues from closeness with partner to quality of child care and schools.

While the factors in the survey can be chosen to tailor a list of the best countries for an individual expatriate, the survey does rank the countries from best to worst. Among the "best" countries on the three factors are Singapore, New Zealand, Sweden, Bahrain, and Germany. The "worst" countries on the three factors include Qatar, Saudi Arabia, Brazil, Egypt, and Kuwait. The United States ranked 16 out of 39 countries overall due to poor scores on experience and family.

There are several tips from foreign workers on how to adapt to life in the United States, including

- Plan on living in a place with a good public school system.
- Make sure you have a good health insurance plan.
- Have a fair amount of savings on hand just in case things take longer than expected (e.g., immigration papers, finding a place to live).
- Travel across country—there is much to see and do.
- Understand U.S. culture, sports, and public holidays as well as important facts Americans treasure about the history of their country.[89]

The website contains a disclaimer that content on the site is the opinion of users and not verified by HSBC. Nevertheless, the information is invaluable to expats and their families as they undertake employment opportunities in countries across the globe.

Summary and Review

LO6-1

WHAT IS THE GLOBAL ENVIRONMENT? The global environment is the set of forces and conditions that operates beyond an organization's boundaries but affects a manager's ability to acquire and use resources. The global environment has two components: the task environment and the general environment.

LO6-2, 6-3 **THE TASK ENVIRONMENT** The task environment is the set of forces and conditions that originates with global suppliers, distributors, customers, and competitors and influences managers daily. The opportunities and threats associated with forces in the task environment become more complex as a company expands globally.

LO6-2, 6-3 **THE GENERAL ENVIRONMENT** The general environment comprises wide-ranging global economic, technological, sociocultural, demographic, political, and legal forces that affect an organization and its task environment.

LO6-4, 6-5 **THE CHANGING GLOBAL ENVIRONMENT** In recent years there has been a marked shift toward a more open global environment in which capital flows more freely as people and companies search for new opportunities to create profit and wealth. This has hastened the process of globalization. Globalization is the set of specific and general forces that work together to integrate and connect economic, political, and social systems across countries, cultures, or geographic regions so that nations become increasingly interdependent and similar. The process of globalization has been furthered by declining barriers to international trade and investment and declining barriers of distance and culture.

Management in Action

Topics for Discussion and Action

Discussion

1. Why is it important for managers to understand the forces in the global environment that are acting on them and their organizations? [LO6-1]
2. Which organization is likely to face the most complex task environment—a biotechnology company trying to develop a cure for cancer or a large retailer such as The Gap or Macy's? Why? [LO6-2, 6-3]
3. The population is aging because of declining birth rates, declining death rates, and the aging of the baby boom generation. What might some of the implications of this demographic trend be for (a) a pharmaceutical company and (b) the home construction industry? [LO6-1, 6-2, 6-3]
4. How do political, legal, and economic forces shape national culture? What characteristics of national culture do you think have the most important effect on how successful a country is in doing business abroad? [LO6-3, 6-5]
5. After the passage of NAFTA, many U.S. companies shifted production operations to Mexico to take advantage of lower labor costs and lower standards for environmental and worker protection. As a result, they cut their costs and were better able to survive in an increasingly competitive global environment. Was their behavior ethical—that is, did the ends justify the means? [LO6-4]

Action

6. Choose an organization, and ask a manager in that organization to list the number and strengths of forces in the organization's task environment. Ask the manager to pay particular attention to identifying opportunities and threats that result from pressures and changes in customers, competitors, and suppliers. [LO6-1, 6-2, 6-3]

Building Management Skills

Analyzing an Organization's Environment [LO6-1, 6-2, 6-3]

Pick an organization with which you are familiar. It can be an organization in which you have worked or currently work or one that you interact with regularly as a customer (such as the college you are attending). For this organization, do the following:

1. Describe the main forces in the global task environment that are affecting the organization.
2. Describe the main forces in the global general environment that are affecting the organization.
3. Explain how environmental forces affect the job of an individual manager within this organization. How do they determine the opportunities and threats that its managers must confront?

Managing Ethically [LO6-4, 6-5]

Home Depot Inc. misjudged the market in China. The world's largest home improvement chain entered the market in China in 2006 and decided to leave six years later. It was not able to sell its do-it-yourself brand to the -Chinese. "China is a do-it-for-me market, not a do-it-yourself market, so we have to adjust," a Home Depot spokeswoman said.[90] Cheap labor in China means many people can hire someone else to do home improvement work for them. Also, apartment-based living in China meant there was not much demand for products such as lumber.[91]

Questions

1. What could Home Depot have done to avoid its mistake?
2. In what cultures might Home Depot find better success?

Small Group Breakout Exercise

How to Enter the Copying Business [LO6-1, 6-2]

Form groups of three to five people, and appoint one group member as the spokesperson who will communicate your findings to the whole class when called on by the instructor. Then discuss the following scenario:

You and your partners have decided to open a small printing and copying business in a college town of 100,000 people. Your business will compete with companies like FedEx Office. You know that over 50 percent of small businesses fail in their first year, so to increase your chances of success, you have decided to perform a detailed analysis of the task environment of the copying business to discover what opportunities and threats you will encounter.

1. Decide what you must know about (a) your future customers, (b) your future competitors, and (c) other critical forces in the task environment if you are to be successful.
2. Evaluate the main barriers to entry into the copying business.
3. Based on this analysis, list some steps you would take to help your new copying business succeed.

Exploring the World Wide Web [LO6-2, 6-3, 6-4]

Go to www.greatplacetowork.com and click on "World's Best Multinationals" under the "Recognition Program" tab. Take a look at the list for this year.

1. Find a company on the list that is based in a country other than your home country. How has that company had to adapt to become a global organization?
2. What are the forces in the global task environment and in the global general environment that affect the organization?
3. What criteria are used to select the great places to work? Do you agree that these criteria are what make an organization a great place to work?

Be the Manager [LO6-1, 6-2]

The Changing Environment of Retailing

You are the new manager of a major clothing store that is facing a crisis. This clothing store has been the leader in its market for the last 15 years. In the last 3 years, however, two other major clothing store chains have opened, and they have steadily been attracting customers away from your store—your sales are down 30 percent. To find out why, your store surveyed former customers and learned that they perceive your store as not keeping up with changing fashion trends and new forms of customer service. In examining how the store operates, you found out that the 10 purchasing managers who buy the clothing and accessories for the store have been buying from the same clothing suppliers and have become reluctant to try new ones. Moreover, salespeople rarely, if ever, make suggestions for changing how the store operates, and they don't respond to customer requests; the culture of the store has become conservative and risk-averse.

Questions

1. Analyze the major forces in the task environment of a retail clothing store.
2. Devise a program that will help other managers and employees to better understand and respond to their store's task environment.

Bloomberg Businessweek Case in the News [LO6-1, 6-4, 6-5]

Life in the People's Republic of WeChat

I've had WeChat on my phone since a vacation to Beijing last year, when friends there essentially ordered me to download it. More than 760 million people use it regularly worldwide; it's basically how people in China communicate now. It's actually a lot of trouble not to use WeChat when you're there, and socially weird, like refusing to wear shoes.

In China, 90 percent of Internet users connect online through a mobile device, and those people on average spend more than a third of their Internet time in WeChat. It's fundamentally a messaging app, but it also serves many of the functions of PayPal, Yelp, Facebook, Uber, Amazon, Expedia, Slack, Spotify, Tinder, and more. People use WeChat to pay rent, locate parking, invest, make a doctor's appointment, find a one-night stand, donate to charity. The police in Shenzhen pay rewards through WeChat to people who rat out traffic violators—through WeChat.

It's nothing special to look at, as far as smartphone apps go. The first screen that opens is the chat stream; a menu at the bottom gets you to other areas, like a WeChat wallet and a "moments" stream for Facebook-like posts. Companies, media outlets, celebrities, and brands also open "official accounts" that you can follow to get news and promotions. The design stands out only for its relative simplicity and calm; the online mainstream in China is overpopulated with weird click-bait and manic GIFs.

Zhang Xiaolong, WeChat's creator and something of a cult figure in China, has called WeChat a lifestyle. I rolled my eyes when I first heard that. Then I went back to Beijing in April.

My colleague Lulu Chen, who covers WeChat's parent, Tencent, has sent me the phone numbers of some potential contacts—but why call when WeChat is so much easier? I use the chat function to set up meetings during my visit. One of my contacts mentions a WeChat convention the day after I arrive, and so, on a Sunday afternoon, I show up at the Design Service Center, an industrial-chic space in the historic city center. The crowd is mostly young, a mix of Chinese and expatriates, and the mood is festive. Free wine stands three bottles deep on the bar.

I drift by company displays and find myself at the table for Yoli, a business that offers a sort of speed dating for English learners: 15-minute on-demand tutoring sessions with native speakers through WeChat. Two sheets of paper taped to the table each bear a pixelated QR code: Scan one to become a teacher, scan the other to become a student.

The Chinese term for this ritual, *sao yi sao,* quickly becomes familiar. Everyone and almost everything on WeChat has a QR code, and sao yi sao-ing with your phone is both constant and strangely satisfying. James, a tanned American with unruly blond hair who mans the Yoli table, is here to host a workshop called "How We Built a WeChat App & Recovered Our Development Costs Within 24hrs." He scans my code, which gives him my WeChat profile and also generates the equivalent of a friend request; I accept, and we agree to meet during the week, skipping right over the old-fashioned niceties of last names and business cards.

The presentations are about to start, and jet lag is kicking in. I hurry to the coffee counter for an iced Americano. There's a QR code in a plastic photo frame. The woman ahead of me is scanning it. I try it, and . . . WeChat fail. I've entered a credit card into WeChat, but it won't work, and my WeChat wallet is empty. I feel distinctly self-conscious fumbling around for yuan. I've been in WeChat-era China one day, and already cash money feels embarrassing.

On Monday, I take the subway to meet Zhu Xiaoxiao, who's built a WeChat-based fitness business. On the train, I notice a woman moving methodically down the car, stopping to talk to the other passengers. Is she begging? Testifying? Only when she stops before the woman next to me do I get it: She's asking for QR scans, trying to get followers for a WeChat official account.

Zhu is an open-faced, bulked-up 25-year-old in a gray T-shirt, blue shorts, and red sneakers. He left China for school in England a skinny kid and returned in 2012 a fitness buff with the germ of a business plan—to make and sell protein powder. He and a friend developed a formula, set up manufacturing and a website, and began marketing online. In late 2013, Zhu started looking for investors, and the next February he got 2 million yuan—roughly $300,000—from a seed fund in Beijing. At the urging of his investors, he stopped selling the protein powder and refocused on building a following of health enthusiasts, opening a WeChat official account that pushed articles on exercise and diet and lots of pictures of six-pack abs. The company, FitTime, quickly racked up 400,000 followers and an additional 9.8 million yuan in funding, and launched a standalone app.

As WeChat boomed, Zhu developed a fitness camp on WeChat, an alternative to expensive personal training in a physical gym for people already on WeChat all the time. Sign up, and you get grouped into a chat with 15 people of similar height and weight and a personal trainer who's there to motivate you (by message and emoji) to stick to the diet and video workout plans. FitTime charges

1,000 yuan for 28 days [roughly $150 USD], and more than 5,000 people have signed up for at least one month.

Stories of sudden success on WeChat abound these days, and Xi Jiutian's is another. She's wearing oversize nerd-cool glasses and bright-red lipstick when we meet for lunch on Tuesday at Cafe Groove. The place looks like something out of my Brooklyn neighborhood, the mismatched chairs, the random shelves of books, even the prices—$10-plus for an avocado salad. This is all familiar—until I go to pay with WeChat, and my credit card is rejected again. I'm definitely losing some face here.

Xi was an interaction designer at Microsoft in Beijing before getting laid off. She tried designing a smartwatch, then consulting for startups. She also began writing on Zhihu, a site similar to Quora, about makeup and skin care. In early 2015 she opened Hibetterme—as in, "Hi, better me"—a WeChat account devoted to the same topics. After a couple of months, her WeChat fans began urging her to sell beauty products. Setting up a shop on WeChat's platform took her a couple of days. Xi, like Zhu, had an easy time finding funding when she began looking last fall. She'd been at it about a week when a friend of a friend put her in touch through WeChat with Eric Tong of Pros & Partners Capital in Shanghai. After they'd messaged on WeChat for about 15 minutes (a lot of their discussion was about tattoos), Tong told her to stop her search and committed 4 million yuan.

Xi introduces us on WeChat, and Tong responds instantly. But when I try to set up a phone call, he ignores me. People seem to talk on the phone less than they used to—though they're happy to leave each other WeChat audio messages. I ask, by chat, how Hibetterme fits with what he looks for in an investment. In a flurry of abbreviations, he says he's looking for professionally generated content across platforms like WeChat. It's an investment theme that's very, very hot, thanks to the Papi impact. Papi is Papi Jiang, known for her speed-talking comedic video monologues. In April, she auctioned off the first advertising spot to appear in one of her videos for 22 million yuan. Um, bubble? Tong's fund stands at about 200 million yuan [about $30.5 million USD] now. He expects to have 600 million by the end of the year.

Even those who aren't directly selling things or running official accounts on WeChat use it constantly for work. A friend who runs restaurants in Beijing operates his entire operation, almost everything except eating and drinking, on WeChat. He trades dish ideas and discusses kitchen operations with the chefs in one group, while his accountant keeps him informed of payments on another. There's even a group devoted to flower care at one of the restaurants. (WeChat introduced a formal enterprise version in April.) Yoli, the tutoring company, takes the all-WeChat model to extremes. James, the American I met on Sunday—his last name, I finally find out, is LaLonde; he's from Texas—moved to Beijing to found a gaming company in 2011. He decided last August to combine his interest in language learning with an experiment in creating a business run entirely on WeChat. It made sense; he rarely left the app as it was. He's met Luke Priddy, one of his two co-founders, only twice in person. Priddy lives in New York and coordinates the growing cadre of teachers. The average wait time for a tutoring session is 20 seconds. The tag line for teachers is "teach on the beach"; Priddy once conducted a tutoring session while floating in a pool.

On Wednesday, I need to get to Shanghai for a day of meetings and can't decide whether to fly or take the train. Buying train tickets with an app may not sound revolutionary, but in China, I promise you, it is. The intricacies of buying tickets used to occupy whole sections of guidebooks and require feverish strategizing before holidays. Opening WeChat, I check the train schedules and get to the point of booking an overnight train—but then decide to fly. I can't quite shake my fear of the Chinese train system.

WeChat has made Beijing a very different place from the city I lived in from 2006 to 2009. There's so much less standing in line and waiting, particularly at the bank. Cash used to be king. I paid my rent in cash, my bills, every restaurant and shop. Now people shoot money around on their phones (not all on WeChat, of course, but a lot of it).

There's also a lot less getting lost. Taking a taxi in China used to require getting the driver to call your destination to verify exactly where you were going. On this trip, everyone I visit drops a map into a message, with the location pinned, and I show that to the driver. The one time I get turned around, walking to an interview, I open real-time location in the WeChat conversation I'm having with my host. She finds me on the map and guides me.

Nobody's too cool to use WeChat, or too uncool. It's how entire families keep in touch. A tech executive told me his mother, at 80-plus, uses it for everything; a marketing entrepreneur said his computer-illiterate parents and his daughters, ages 3 and 5, use it.

By Thursday morning, I've decided something important: I don't like my QR code. The code WeChat randomly generated for me looks like a piece of candy in a blue wrapper. When I click on "Change Style" in my profile, it goes from bad to worse—a piece of toast? A cat? A pink car? Finally, some algorithm spits out a green, leaf-shaped design. I'll take it.

I've also given up on using my credit card. It's "accepted" by WeChat, and I've set up a PIN and all that, but I guess WeChat can't change the fact that few local businesses take international cards. WeChat has given life in China a smoothness, a quality of efficiency I never could have imagined. But for a foreigner like me, at least, it's still a work in progress.

I message a Chinese friend who's in the U.S. on a fellowship and ask for a loan. Within minutes, he's sent me two hong bao, or red envelopes—a play on the red envelopes traditionally used to give gifts of money. They arrive as chat messages that say, "Good fortune and good luck! You've received a red envelope." Once I click on them, I have 200 yuan in my WeChat wallet.

Typically, you hand out red envelopes of cash to younger relatives and friends during the Lunar New Year—to couples getting married, for children's birthdays. Now hong bao are used . . . I don't want to say willy-nilly, but sometimes just for fun.

It's hard to tell what's great strategy and what's luck in WeChat's success, but this hong bao system is genius. The company wasn't first with electronic hong bao; that would be Alipay, the payment platform from Alibaba. But when WeChat introduced its own system just before the Chinese New Year in 2014, it added a gaming element. When you send money to a group of people, one lucky winner within the group gets a bigger windfall than the rest, while a few get nothing at all. People love the element of chance, apparently, because users of WeChat's wallet jumped by 100 million in a month. The figure is now 300 million. For Chinese New Year 2016, 516 million people delivered 32 billion red envelopes.

Midmorning, I go to the Global Mobile Internet Conference in the China National Convention Center. Hundreds of speakers, 20 summits, and a music festival—it's China's South by Southwest, or trying to be. I'm exhausted from running from floor to floor to catch sessions. I stop at a cafe on the second floor to get coffee, my new WeChat riches teed up.

They don't take WeChat. At a tech conference.

The next day, I return to the conference to talk to E Hao, co-CEO of the group that organizes it. I'm accosted in the elevator by a young woman who sees that I'm foreign, explains that her company organizes exchanges with foreign companies, and demands to scan my WeChat QR code. "Nice to meet you!" she sings, striding off without ever telling me her name or asking for mine.

E Hao is hoarse after a late night at the event's opening gala at the Olympic Bird's Nest stadium. His heavy metal band, CXO, newly formed with various fellow executives, performed for the first time. He shows me his WeChat message stream: 3,015 unread messages. He says he's been relying on hong bao to thank and motivate his overworked employees through the long days running up to the event, sending out 1,000 yuan at a time. He sends me 100 yuan to demonstrate. I'm not sure about the etiquette. Is this for demonstration only? Should I send it back? I do, eventually.

When I get back to New York, I join a FitTime WeChat boot camp. The rest of my group seems to be Chinese students studying in the U.S., including the trainer, who's in Iowa. First, there's the horror of taking a selfie in spandex and sending it to a stranger, then the awkwardness of photographing every meal, with one hand held in a fist beside the plate for perspective on serving size. If I'm lucky, the trainer sends me a thumbs-up emoji in response. She frequently has to remind me of the rules, though: No kimchi, for example—too much salt, leads to bloating. The whole thing is vaguely humiliating. On the other hand, I've lost a few pounds, and I now know the characters for chia seeds in Chinese. And I'm on WeChat all day long.

Source: Lawrence, Dune, "Life in the People's Republic of WeChat," *Bloomberg Businessweek*, June 9, 2016. Used with permission of Bloomberg.

Questions for Discussion

1. Do you think WeChat would be as successful in other cultures as it is in China?
2. If you were a manager for a U.S. company in China, would you allow your local employees to use the app as part of their daily business activities?
3. Do you see Facebook or Twitter becoming the dominant social platform in the United States the way WeChat has taken over the Chinese way of life?

Notes

1. "The Impact of a Cotton T-Shirt," www.wwf.org, accessed June 22, 2016; L. Heida, "Can Waterless Dyeing Processes Clean Up the Clothing Industry?" *Environment 360*, http://e60.yale.edu, June 12, 2014; P. Ravasio, "How Can We Stop Water from Becoming a Fashion Victim?" *The Guardian*, www.theguardian.com, March 7, 2012.
2. L. Kaye, "Clothing to Dye For: The Textile Sector Must Confront Water Risks," *The Guardian*, www.theguardian.com, August 12, 2013; D. Ferris, "Nike, Adidas Want to Dye Your Shirt with No Water," *Forbes*, www.forbes.com, August 30, 2012.
3. D. Samaniego, "Levi Strauss & Co. + Evrnu Create First Pair of Jeans from Post-Consumer Cotton Waste," www.levistrauss.com/unzipped-blog, accessed June 22, 2016.
4. S. Hepburn, "Nike and Adidas Show Cautious Support for Eco-Friendly Dye Technology," *The Guardian*, www.theguardian.com, April 24, 2015; A. Brettman, "6 Questions about Nike's Water-Less Fabric Dyeing Technology," *The Oregonian*, www.oregonlive.com, December 3, 2013.
5. P. Meister, "One Million Yards of Water-Saving DryDye Fabric—and Counting!" Adidas Group blog, http://blog.adidas-group.com, June 3, 2013.
6. "Nike, Inc., Unveils ColorDry Technology and High-Tech Facility to Eliminate Water and Chemicals in Dyeing," http://news.nike.com, December 2, 2013.

7. L.J. Bourgeois, "Strategy and Environment: A Conceptual Integration," *Academy of Management Review* 5 (1985), 25–39.
8. M.E. Porter, *Competitive Strategy* (New York: Free Press, 1980).
9. "Coca-Cola versus Pepsi-Cola and the Soft Drink Industry," Harvard Business School Case 9-391–179.
10. www.splenda.com, 2016.
11. C. Birkner, "Will This New Sugar Substitute Help Truvia Win the Sweetener Wars?" *Adweek*, www.adweek.com, May 20, 2016; D. Engber, "The Quest for a Natural Sugar Substitute," *The New York Times*, www.nytimes.com, January 1, 2014.
12. A.K. Gupta and V. Govindarajan, "Cultivating a Global Mind-Set," *Academy of Management Executive* 16 (February 2002), 116–27.
13. "Boeing's Worldwide Supplier Network," *Seattle Post-Intelligencer*, April 9, 1994, 13.
14. I. Metthee, "Playing a Large Part," *Seattle Post-Intelligencer*, April 9, 1994, 13.
15. S. Li, "Li & Fung Sells Its Asia Consumer and Healthcare Distribution Business to DCH for US$350 Million," *South China Morning Post*, www.scmp.com, May 3, 2016.
16. J. Downs and S. S. Shafer, "GE Appliances Sold to Haier," *Courier-Journal*, www.courier-journal.com, June 6, 2016; S. Denning, "Why Apple and GE Are Bringing Back Manufacturing," *Forbes*, www.forbes.com, December 7, 2012.
17. Z. Hall, "Tim Cook Visits Mac Pro Assembly Plant & AppleCare in Austin, Texas," *9to5Mac*, http://9to5mac.com, June 6, 2014.
18. J. Yunker, "How to Improve Online Checkout for Global Markets," *Pitney Bowes* blog, http://blogs.pb.com, accessed June 23, 2016.
19. Ibid.
20. Ibid.
21. "The 2016 Web Globalization Report Card," http://bytelevel.com, accessed June 23, 2016.
22. J. Yunker, "Is Your Website Losing the Language Race?" *Global by Design*, www.globalbydesign, February 18, 2016.
23. J. Yunker, "The Worst Global Websites of the 2014 Web Globalization Report Card, *Global by Design*, www.globalbydesign, March 10, 2014.
24. Ibid.
25. "Checkout Conversion Index—Q2 2016," www.pymnts.com, accessed June 23, 2016; Study Shows Bigger Isn't Always Better When Converting Online Shoppers to Buyers at Checkout," *Business Wire*, www.businesswire.com, June 16, 2016.
26. M.E. Porter, *Competitive Advantage* (New York: Free Press, 1985).
27. S. Pettypiece and M. Townsend, "Wal-Mart's Suppliers Are Finally Fighting Back," *Bloomberg*, www.bloomberg .com, September 10, 2015.
28. J. Trop, "Bridgestone Admits Guilt in U.S. Price-Fixing Case," *The New York Times*, www.nytimes.com/2014/02/14/ business/bridgestone-admits-guilt-in-us-price-fixing-case.html?_r=0, February 13, 2014.
29. "The Future of Computers: What Can We Expect?" *UniBlue*, www.uniblue.com/ news/future-computers-what-can-we-expect/, August 21, 2013.
30. S. Soper, "Amazon Building Global Delivery Business to Take On Alibaba," *Bloomberg Technology*, www.bloomberg .com, February 9, 2016.
31. T. Levitt, "The Globalization of Markets," *Harvard Business Review*, May–June 1983, 92–102.
32. "Dell CEO Would Like 40 Percent PC Market Share," www.dailynews.yahoo .com, June 20, 2001.
33. J. Nylander, "How Lenovo Became the Largest PC Maker in the World," *Forbes*, www.forbes.com, March 2, 2016; C. Nguyen, "Michael Dell Discusses EMC Acquisition, Dell's Vision for Future-Proofing," *Tech Radar*, www. techradar.com, October 21, 2015.
34. For views on barriers to entry from an economics perspective, see Porter, *Competitive Strategy*. For the sociological perspective, see J. Pfeffer and G. R. Salancik, *The External Control of Organization: A Resource Dependence Perspective* (New York: Harper & Row, 1978).
35. Porter, *Competitive Strategy;* J.E. Bain, *Barriers to New Competition* (Cambridge, MA: Harvard University Press, 1956); R.J. Gilbert, "Mobility Barriers and the Value of Incumbency," in R. Schmalensee and R.D. Willig, eds., *Handbook of Industrial Organization*, vol. 1 (Amsterdam: North Holland, 1989).
36. Soper, "Amazon Building Global Delivery Business to Take On Alibaba."
37. C.W.L. Hill, "The Computer Industry: The New Industry of Industries," in Hill and Jones, *Strategic Management: An Integrated Approach* (Boston: Houghton Mifflin, 2010).
38. L. Lewis, "Japan: End of the Rice Age," *Financial Times*, www.ft.com, September 21, 2015.
39. J. Schumpeter, *Capitalism, Socialism and Democracy* (London: Macmillan, 1950), 68. Also see R.R. Winter and S.G. Winter, *An Evolutionary Theory of Economic Change* (Cambridge, MA: Harvard University Press, 1982).
40. "AMD and HSA," www.amd.com, accessed June 23, 2016.
41. N. Goodman, *An Introduction to Sociology* (New York: HarperCollins, 1991); C. Nakane, *Japanese Society* (Berkeley: University of California Press, 1970).
42. Monica Watrous, "Four Trends Driving Growth in Organic," *Food Business News*, www.foodbusinessnews.net, March 14, 2016.
43. Ibid.
44. For a detailed discussion of the importance of the structure of law as a factor explaining economic change and growth, see D.C. North, *Institutions, Institutional Change, and Economic Performance* (Cambridge: Cambridge University Press, 1990).
45. P. Krugman, "This Age of Bubbles," *The New York Times*, August 22, 2013, www.nytimes.com/2013/08/23/opinion/ krug-man-this-age-of-bubbles.html? partner=rssnyt&emc=rss&_r=0.
46. R.B. Reich, *The Work of Nations* (New York: Knopf, 1991).
47. H. Von Der Burchard, "TTIP Leaks Show EU-US Struggles over Cars and Food," *Politico*, www.politico.eu, May 2, 2016.
48. D. Lee, "Signing of Trans-Pacific Partnership Trade Deal Opens Up Tough Battle in U.S.," *Los Angeles Times*, www. latimes.com, February 4, 2016.
49. "Trans-Pacific Partnership (TPP): More Job Offshoring, Lower Wages, Unsafe Food Imports," www.citizen.org, accessed June 23, 2016.
50. M.A. Carpenter and J.W. Fredrickson, "Top Management Teams, Global Strategic Posture, and the Moderating Role of Uncertainty," *Academy of Management Journal* 44 (June 2001), 533–46.
51. A. Glass, "Ernst & Young Launches Women Athletes Global Leadership Network," *Forbes*, www.forbes.com/ sites/alanaglass/2013/03/12/ernst-young-launches-women-athletes-global-leader-ship-network/, March 12, 2013.
52. "Sponsors," https://www.rio2016.com, accessed June 23, 2016; "Ernest & Young to Launch Leadership Network for Elite Female Athletes to address Unmet Global Need," PRWeb, www.prweb.com/ releases/2013/3/prweb10505195.htm, March 8, 2013.
53. "Women Athletes Business Network: Perspectives on Sport and Teams," *EY*, www. ey.com/BR/pt/About-us/Our-sponsorships-and-programs/Women-Athletes-Global-Leadership-Network—perspectives-on-sport-and-teams, May 2013.
54. K. Whiteside, "Survey Ties Female Athletes to Executive Roles," *USA Today*, www.usatoday.com, July 3, 2013.
55. "EY Women Athletes Global Leadership Network," EY, www.leadersmag.com/

issues/2013.4_Oct/EY%20Women%20 Athletes/LEADERS-Beth-Brooke-EY-Donna-de-Varona-DAMAR-Productions .html, n.d.

56. A. Glass, "Ernst & Young Launches Women Athletes Global Leadership Network," *Forbes,* March 12, 2013, www.forbes.com/sites/alanaglass/2013/03/12/ernst-young-launches-women-athletes-global-leadership-network/.
57. "Ernest & Young to Launch Leadership Network for Elite Female Athletes to address Unmet Global Need," PRWeb, www.prweb.com/releases/2013/3/prweb10505195.htm, March 8, 2013.
58. K. Hays, "Commerce Lowers Anti-Dumping Duties for Chinese Tires," *Law360,* www.law360.com, April 19, 2016; B. Davis, "Chinese Car Tire Imports to U.S. at an All-Time High," *tirebusiness.com,* www.tirebusiness.com, March 18, 2014.
59. J. Bhagwati, *Protectionism* (Cambridge, MA: MIT Press, 1988).
60. For a summary of these theories, see P. Krugman and M. Obstfeld, *International Economics: Theory and Policy* (New York: HarperCollins, 1991). Also see C.W.L. Hill, *International Business* (New York: McGraw-Hill, 1997), chap. 4.
61. A.M. Rugman, "The Quest for Global Dominance," *Academy of Management Executive* 16 (August 2002), 157–60.
62. www.wto.org.com, 2016.
63. "Tariff Cuts," *World Trade Organization,* www.wto.org/english/thewto_e/whatis_e/tif_e/agrm2_e.htm, n.d.
64. www.wto.org.com, 2016.
65. C.A. Bartlett and S. Ghoshal, *Managing across Borders* (Boston: Harvard Business School Press, 1989).
66. C. Arnst and G. Edmondson, "The Global Free-for-All," *BusinessWeek,* September 26, 1994, 118–26.
67. "AU in a Nutshell," www.au.int, accessed June 23, 2016.
68. "Member States," www.sadc.int, accessed June 23, 2016.
69. "Member States," www.gcc-sg.org, accessed June 23, 2016.
70. E.B. Tylor, *Primitive Culture* (London: Murray, 1971).
71. "A Quick Guide: What's Happening in Ukraine," *The Wall Street Journal,* online .wsj.com/news/articles/SB1000142405 2702303775504579393324230970300, January 28, 2014.
72. "Timeline: What's Happened Since Egypt's Revolution," *Frontline,* www.pbs.org/wgbh/pages/frontline/foreign-affairs-defense/egypt-in-crisis/timeline-whats-happened-since-egypts-revolution/, September 17, 2013.
73. For details on the forces that shape culture, see Hill, *International Business,* chap. 2. G. Hofstede, B. Neuijen, D.D. Ohayv, and G. Sanders, "Measuring Organizational Cultures: A Qualitative and Quantitative Study across Twenty Cases," *Administrative Science Quarterly* 35 (1990), 286–316.
74. Hofstede et al., "Measuring Organizational Cultures."
75. M.H. Hoppe, "Introduction: Geert Hofstedes Culture's Consequences: International Difference in Work-Related Values," *Academy of Management Executive* 19 (February 2004), 73–75.
76. R. Bellah, *Habits of the Heart: Individualism and Commitment in American Life* (Berkeley: University of California Press, 1985).
77. R. Bellah, *The Tokugawa Religion* (New York: Free Press, 1957).
78. C. Nakane, *Japanese Society* (Berkeley: University of California Press, 1970).
79. Ibid.
80. G. Hofstede, "The Cultural Relativity of Organizational Practices and Theories," *Journal of International Business Studies,* (Fall 1983), 75–89.
81. Hofstede et al., "Measuring Organizational Cultures."
82. J. Perlez, "GE Finds Tough Going in Hungary," *The New York Times,* July 25, 1994, C1, C3.
83. "GE in Hungary," www.ge.com, accessed June 23, 2016.
84. J.P. Fernandez and M. Barr, *The Diversity Advantage* (New York: Lexington Books, 1994).
85. www.ibm.com, 2016.
86. "2015 Expat Explorer Survey," https://expatexplorer.hsbc.com, accessed June 23, 2016.
87. Curtis, "Top 5: How to 'Succeed' as an Expat," Expat Hints & Tips, https://expatexplorer.hsbc.com, accessed June 23, 2016.
88. Farrah@thethreeunder, "Top 5: Tips for Child Healthcare in The Netherlands," Expat Hints & Tips, https://expatexplorer .hsbc.com, accessed June 23, 2016.
89. "Tips about Living in the United States," *2015 Expat Explorer Study,* https://expatexplorer.hsbc.com, accessed June 23, 2016.
90. D. Skariachan and S. Cavale, "Home Depot's Do-It-Yourself Model Fails in China's Do-It-for-Me Market," *The Huffington Post,* www.huffingtonpost.com/2012/09/13/home-depots-china_n_1882779.html, September 13, 2012.
91. L. Burkitt, "Home Depot Learns Chinese Prefer 'Do-It-for-Me,'" *The Wall Street Journal,* online.wsj.com/news/articles/SB10000872396390444433504577651072911154602, September 14, 2012.

